D1466879

# Social Experimentation

A Method for Planning and
Evaluating Social Intervention

# QUANTITATIVE STUDIES IN SOCIAL RELATIONS

*Consulting Editor: Peter H. Rossi*

UNIVERSITY OF MASSACHUSETTS
AMHERST, MASSACHUSETTS

# Social Experimentation
## A Method for Planning and Evaluating Social Intervention

EDITED BY

Henry W. Riecken

Robert F. Boruch

WRITTEN BY
A COMMITTEE OF
THE SOCIAL SCIENCE RESEARCH COUNCIL:

Henry W. Riecken, Chairman
Robert F. Boruch
Donald T. Campbell
Nathan Caplan
Thomas K. Glennan, Jr.
John W. Pratt
Albert Rees
Walter Williams

ACADEMIC PRESS New York San Francisco London
A Subsidiary of Harcourt Brace Jovanovich, Publishers

H
61
R493
1974

COPYRIGHT © 1974, BY ACADEMIC PRESS, INC.
ALL RIGHTS RESERVED.
NO PART OF THIS PUBLICATION MAY BE REPRODUCED OR
TRANSMITTED IN ANY FORM OR BY ANY MEANS, ELECTRONIC
OR MECHANICAL, INCLUDING PHOTOCOPY, RECORDING, OR ANY
INFORMATION STORAGE AND RETRIEVAL SYSTEM, WITHOUT
PERMISSION IN WRITING FROM THE PUBLISHER.

ACADEMIC PRESS, INC.
111 Fifth Avenue, New York, New York 10003

DISCARDED
WIDENER UNIVERSITY
WIDENER COLLEGE
WOLFGRAM
LIBRARY
CHESTER, PA.
133366

*United Kingdom Edition published by*
ACADEMIC PRESS, INC. (LONDON) LTD.
24/28 Oval Road, London NW1


Library of Congress Cataloging in Publication Data

Riecken, Henry W
        Social experimentation: a method for planning and
evaluating social intervention.

        (Quantitative studies in social relations series)
        Bibliography: p.
        1.    Social sciences–Methodology.        2.    Social
sciences–Field work.        3.    Evaluation research (Social
action programs)        I.    Boruch, Robert F., joint author.
II.    Title.
H61.R493            300'.1'8            74-1638
ISBN 0-12-588150-9

PRINTED IN THE UNITED STATES OF AMERICA

# Contents

# Appendix

# Foreword

This book is the product of a committee appointed by the Social Science Research Council in 1971 to summarize the available knowledge about how randomized experiments might be used in planning and evaluating ameliorative social programs. The members of this committee were selected because they were well acquainted with the various aspects of social experimentation—design, measurement, execution, sponsorship, and utilization of results. In pursuing its task, furthermore, the committee expanded the horizon of its experience by involving a number of government officers, social scientists from private organizations and universities, and other people who had been actively concerned in social experimentation. These expert consultants met individually in a series of workshop sessions with the assembled committee to discuss their own work and to amplify the committee's acquaintance with the area.

The result is a comprehensive statement of the promise and the problem of social experimentation. In a straightforward fashion, the committee has examined the whys and the hows, the dilemmas and the difficulties of design and implementation, the political and moral considerations involved in experimenting for public policy development. The issues are not academic; the authors have confronted them on a day-to-day basis. Their experiences and their resultant wisdom produced the ensuing pages.

The book focuses attention on one method for obtaining a firm knowledge base for use in planning and evaluating social programs— namely, social experimentation. The stance taken is that "experimental trials of proposed social programs (interventions into normal social processes) have certain important advantages over other ways to learn what programs (or program elements) are effective under what circumstances and at what cost." As such, the problems of random assignment and the attribution or causal explanation of observed change are fully explicated. The authors strongly endorse experimentation as a superior means for obtaining this requisite knowledge but do not advocate its exclusive use.

Experimentation is viewed as "a cycle that begins with problem analysis; proceeds through the planning of an intervention, its development, experimental trial, and evaluation; and ends in either program implementation or in replanning the intervention." The volume provides a general introduction to experimental design for administrators and managers of social programs, shedding light and guidance on each stage in the cycle.

Some readers may be interested in how the project came into being. The original impetus for the formation of the committee was an interest on the part of some directors of the Social Science Research Council in the problems of analysis of causality in social behavior. Following a successful conference that dealt with causal analysis of nonexperimental data a decision was made to explore the complementary approach to causality through social experimentation. In the course of that exploration, another director of the Council became actively involved in the project. Albert Rees, who had participated in the design of the New Jersey Negative Income Tax experiment, had become convinced of the need for systematic attention to social experimentation as a method. Furthermore, Donald Campbell's interest in quasi-experiments had, by this time, become widely known and several papers had appeared. Accordingly, there was a ready-made nucleus of interest and competence available to the Council at the time that the President's Science Advisory Committee became interested in the gigantic task of measuring the effectiveness of Federal programs in education, welfare, racial matters, urban questions, and poverty. David Beckler, then executive secretary of the PSAC, asked if the Council could offer any help with the task. Henry Riecken, who was president of the Council at the time, proposed a session at the October 1970 meeting of PSAC to discuss the possibilities and opportunities of social experimentation. Rees and Campbell agreed to make presentations and the ensuing discussion was lively as well as enthusiastic. The outcome was a request on the part of PSAC that the Council undertake to correlate and diffuse knowledge about social experimentation more widely. The National Science Foundation was generous enough to provide support for the effort.

Social experimentation may develop into an extremely valuable tool for decision making or it may prove to be too unwieldy in dealing with complex social problems. The availability of this volume aids in maximizing our opportunities for careful experimentation and for requisite tests of its strengths and weaknesses. We are grateful to the authors for a major contribution to our understanding and guidance in current and future efforts.

Eleanor Bernert Sheldon
*President*
*Social Science Research Council*

# Preface

Most social problems are very complex and our understanding of the social processes that create and sustain them is slender. It seems prudent, then, to adopt a tentative attitude toward new proposals for solving a social problem, and, more importantly, to subject such proposals to controlled experimental trials before embracing them on a national scale as if they were certain to work. The idea of using randomized controlled experiments to plan, develop, and evaluate innovative social programs is an appealing one. Experimental comparison of alternative social interventions is feasible, as this book reports; and experimentally designed trials of interventions provide the least equivocal evidence possible regarding the effectiveness of an intervention. Some really novel interventions, furthermore, require experimental trial because no relevant prior experience exists.

The purpose of this book is to consolidate what is known about social experimentation, and to communicate that knowledge to a rather diversified audience. It is frankly aimed at influencing the thinking of policy developers and decision makers in Federal, State, and local governments who must cope with serious social problems and who have an opportunity to deal experimentally with them. At the same time, it is intended to draw the attention of social scientists to some of the basic scientific problems as well as those of technique and method that have not been solved for social experimentation. Finally, it is designed to interest younger social scientists who may not yet have fixed their career objectives or who wish to expand the range of their capabilities to include the use of experimental methods for analyzing, planning, and evaluating solutions for current and future social problems.

Because we have chosen such a broad target audience, the committee that prepared this book has tried to simplify technical issues and to make them intelligible to those who are not social scientists or statisticians. At many points the text goes into only the amount of technical detail that is necessary to illustrate the complexity of issues, and to signal the reader that specialized assistance may be required to resolve them. We believe this approach is justified on the ground that it is important to spread knowledge about social experimentation widely, since it is a relatively new technology with broad applicability to testing effects of social programs.

Nevertheless, there are some guideposts for the various components of the intended audience. Chapters I and II are aimed at the reader who is looking for a general orientation to the nature of social experimentation—its advantages, limitations, and practical possibilities. Chapters III, IV, and V are more technical, being addressed primarily to readers who are concerned with the major scientific and technical issues in design and measurement, or who expect to have such responsibility thrust upon them. Chapter VI considers the principal operating problems confronting managers of experiments in the field. Chapters VII and VIII are addressed particularly to policy-makers and administrators who may have responsibility for deciding whether or not to undertake a social experiment, although we believe that they are of such general importance that they may be useful to every interested reader whether he expects to be directly involved in social experimentation or not.

Responsibility for the contents of the book is shared by the entire committee for, although individual members were responsible for the first drafts of the separate chapters, these were subsequently revised extensively in consultation with the rest of the committee so that they form a composite of each primary author's ideas and those of his colleagues. Because the committee thought the book would be more readable if differences among chapters could be minimized, the editors undertook further revision in order to bring a somewhat similar style of presentation and level of difficulty to all parts of the manuscript, within the limits of the technicality of the subject matter. The book is, therefore, the product of the whole committee, who worked jointly in every respect, and we wish to acknowledge and jointly thank the following individuals whose help in its preparation has been so important.

First we acknowledge the deep debt of gratitude we have to the volunteer consultants who gave so freely of their advice, experience, and views at the first of the summer workshops: Samuel Ball, Peter Bloch, James D. Cowhig, Howard Freeman, Bernard G. Greenberg, David Kershaw, Frank Lewis, William A. Niskanen, Francis H. Palmer, David Parmasel, Peter Rossi, William R. Tash, Robert Voas, Harold W. Watts, Hans Zeisel.

We had help from a number of colleagues who performed such tasks as reading this manuscript and giving us the benefit of their criticisms and suggestions as well as correcting our errors of fact or interpretation: Garth Buchanan, Herman Chernoff, Lee Cronbach, Jerilyn Fair, Arthur Goldberger, Robinson Hollister, William H. Kruskal, Frederick Mosteller, Edward O'Connell, M. Brewster Smith, Leroy Wolins, Melinda Upp.

The committee would also like to acknowledge the very helpful and stimulating participation of Edgar Borgatta, who took part in the first summer workshop of the committee, but was prevented by other commitments from making any written contribution to this book.

We should like to acknowledge a special debt to Mrs. Edna Lusher, who took responsibility during both of the summer work conferences not only for helping us get our thoughts on paper, but also for managing the complex schedule of guest visits, acting as hostess and even as chauffeur for the guests. Her gracious good humor, combined with dedication to the success of the project, merits our deep gratitude. A large share of the burden for typing the final manuscript fell on the shoulders of Margaret Hadley

The major support of the project through a grant (GI-29843) through the Division of Research Applied to National Needs (RANN) of the National Science Foundation. Donald Campbell and Robert Boruch wish also to acknowledge the assistance of the Division of Social Sciences of the National Science Foundation through grant GS-302-73X. John Pratt wishes to acknowledge assistance from grant GS-2994, through the same Division of the National Science Foundation.

Henry W. Riecken
Robert F. Boruch

# Acknowledgments

**Figure 4.9** is modified from Baldus, D.C. Welfare as a loan: The recovery of public assistance in the United States. *Stanford University Law Review*, 1972, **25**, 204, Figure 1. Reprinted by permission.

**Figure 4.10** is from Campbell, D.T. Reforms as experiments. *American Psychologist*, 1969, **24**, 419, Figure 11. Reprinted by permission.

**Figure 4.11** is reprinted from Ross, H.L.,Campbell, D.T., and Glass, G.V. Determining the effects of a legal reform: The British breathalyser crackdown of 1967. *American Behavioral Scientist*, 1970, **13**, with permission of the publisher, Sage Publications, Inc., © 1970.

**Figure 4.14** is reprinted from Ross, H.L. Law, science, and accidents: The British Road Safety Act of 1967. *Journal of Legal Studies*, **2**, copyright 1973, by permission of The University of Chicago Press.

**Figure 4.16** is from Weiss, C.H., *Evaluation research: Methods for assessing program effectiveness.* © 1972. Reprinted by permission of Prentice-Hall, Inc., Englewood Cliffs, New Jersey.

**Figures 4.18 and 4.19** are from Lohr, B.W. An historical view of the research on the factors related to the utilization of health services.

Duplicated Research Report, National Center for Health Services Research and Development, Social and Economic Analysis Division, Rockville, Maryland, 1972; and Wilder, C.S. Physical visits, volume and interval since last visit, US 1969. National Center for Health Statistics, Series 10, No. 75 (DHEW Pub. No. (HSM) 72-1064), Rockville, Maryland, 1972.

# I

## *Experimentation as a Method of Program Planning and Evaluation*

In 1961, the Vera Institute of Justice, in collaboration with the criminal court judges of the Borough of Manhattan, New York, began the Manhattan Bail Bond experiment. The experiment was motivated by a desire to alleviate the situation of a great many criminal defendants who remained in city jails for many months while awaiting trial simply because they were too poor to make bail. Judges and lawyers generally believed bail to be the only satisfactory method of binding the accused person to an agreement to appear for trial, which might occur as much as a year or more in the future. On the other hand, some criminologists contended that an accused person who had substantial links to the community through employment, family, residence, friends, or social institutions could be successfully released prior to trial *without* bail. The Vera Institute proposed an experimental test of this contention. The experiment defined a target group, namely persons accused of felonies, misdemeanors, and certain other crimes (but excluding individuals charged with homicide and other serious crimes). The defendant's records of employment, residence, family structure, personal references, and criminal charges were reviewed to make a judgment about eligibility for pretrial release without bail. The next step was to divide the total group of eligibles randomly into an experimental and a control group. All members of the experimental group were recommended to the court for release without bail, while members of the control group were not so recommended. Judges were, of course, free to accept or reject the recommendation; it was accepted in a majority of cases. The results were clear cut. Between 1961 and 1964, when the experiment ended, less than 1% of the experimental group had failed to appear in court for trial—a rate that was lower than that for similarly charged defendants who had posted bail. Following the experiment, the New York Department of Corrections extended the program to all five boroughs of the city; and similar projects were launched in other cities. The idea of bail-free release was extended to Federal defendants and written into the Bail Reform Act of 1966. A social policy had been shaped by an experiment conducted to test its effects before incorporating it into normal social processes.

The shaping of social policy involves a combination of value judgments and information in a variable mix. Some debates about social policy have a heavy loading of value judgments for they pivot around the question of whether it is socially valuable to achieve or sustain a particular state of affairs in society: for example, whether involuntary military service should be required of young men. Other debates rest more on information, for they are concerned with the relative effectiveness of alternative measures for achieving an effect on whose desirability there seems to be substantial consensus: For example, would drug addiction be lessened by more stiffly enforced laws to control drug traffic, by educational and therapeutic programs, or by other measures? Whatever the particular mix of values and information on any given question, the making of public policy requires both some consensus on the goals to be sought and as much knowledge as possible about the feasibility, the cost and effort, and the effectiveness of various means of attaining those goals.

Getting knowledge about the probable effectiveness of various means for attaining desired social goals is what this book is all about. It is not an easy task, yet it is a crucial one because, increasingly, the nation is attempting to solve its domestic problems through planned programs of social intervention. These attempts are usually handicapped by the lack of two kinds of knowledge: On the one hand, there is insufficient information of a "base-line" character about the extent of a problem—the kinds of people affected by it and its indirect consequences or associated phenomena. On the other, we suffer from a meager understanding of the complexity of relationships among social forces. For both of these reasons it is always difficult to forecast accurately the effects (both direct and incidental) of an attempt to solve the problem—that is, the effects of a program of deliberate social intervention. Too little is known factually about the problem to begin with;

and good theoretical models of the social processes involved in intervention are lacking. It is essential to enlarge empirical experience with intervention in such a way as to learn as much as possible about the social problem and the various possibilities of intervening before initiating a full scale program. Accordingly, this book focuses attention on one method for obtaining a dependable knowledge base for *planning* and *evaluating* social programs—namely social experimentation.

The position taken in this book is that *systematic* experimental trials of proposed social programs (interventions into normal social processes) have certain important advantages over other ways of learning what programs (or program elements) are effective under what circumstances and at what cost. By *experiment* is meant that one or more *treatments* (programs) are administered to some set of persons (or other units) drawn *at random* from a specified population; and that observations (or *measurements*) are made to learn how (or how much) some relevant aspect of their behavior following treatment differs from like behavior on the part of an untreated or control group also drawn at random from the same population.

To concretize some of the terms in this definition without defining them formally, consider the example of an experiment in teaching children to read by the "Omega method." The *treatment* administered is whatever the Omega method of teaching includes: computer-assisted instruction, word recognition, syllable drill, money incentives for improvement, or a low pupil-to-teacher ratio. (Systematic variations in a treatment might deliberately alter some elements of the Omega method—e.g., eliminating the money incentives for some pupils in order to do a refined test of which components of the Omega method are contributing most to its effectiveness.) The units to be taught by the Omega method might be drawn *at random* from the population defined as "all first-grade classes in the public elementary schools" of a given city in a particular year.

To be "drawn at random" means that the choice is made through a procedure which is blind to the personal characteristics of first-grade pupils. The easiest case to explain is simple random sampling with 50–50 probability, which operates on a chance basis such that each pupil is just as likely to end up in the experimental (treated) group as he is in the control (untreated) group. The requirements of a particular experimental design can alter probabilities (and randomization procedures) so that, for example, 40% of pupils would be placed in experimental treatments and 60% in controls. This would not change the chance (random) character of the assignment process. Commonly used randomizing procedures are discussed in Chapter III, and in a number of texts on applied statistics. Randomization has clear rules and a very explicit technology, and it requires meticulous attention to detail. It is not the same as haphazard choice, in which the chooser does not make his premises or his operating rules explicit.

*Random assignment* of study subjects (pupils in this case) to experimental groups or control groups, is the essential feature of true experiments because it provides the best available assurance that experimental subjects (as a group) are so much like control subjects in regard to ability, motivation, experience, and other relevant variables (including unmeasured ones) that differences observed in their performance following treatment can safely be attributed to the treatment and not to other causes, with a specific degree of precision.

To continue the example, we presume that in this instance the pupils in the control group are to be taught reading by some method other than Omegation (although it is conceivable that the control group subjects in some kinds of experiments might not be given any "treatment" whatsoever). At the end of the period of Omega treatment, both the experimental and the control groups are given some appropriate test. If the Omega method purports to teach pupils to read faster, a reading speed test would be appropriate; whereas if the method aimed at increasing comprehension, the relevant behavior to be observed might be changes in pupils' ability to understand complex printed material. Whatever the measure or observation used, the final and critical question which an experiment attempts to answer is: Are there differences in reading proficiency between experimentals and controls following the treatment? If so, are these differences greater than might have arisen through chance, that is, through sampling fluctuations and errors in measurement? If so, do the differences favor the experimental group and thereby demonstrate the superiority of the experimental method?

Randomization in social experimentation calls for the utmost ingenuity, resources, persuasiveness, and care because randomness of subject assignment gives the best possible assurance that nothing but the treatment administered is responsible for any observed differences between experimental and control groups. Achieving randomization is sometimes difficult for a variety of reasons: legal, ethical, political, and administrative. For example, in an experiment designed to determine the effect of pretrial conferences among counsel and judge upon the outcome of the litigation (Rosenberg, 1964) it was impossible to make random assignment of all litigants in the jurisdiction to experimental or control treatment because every litigant had the legal right to a pretrial conference and could not be required to forego it (i.e., could not be involuntarily assigned to the control group). So randomization was limited to the invitation to waive the opportunity for a pretrial conference. The result is the introduction of possible bias which is discussed in Chapters III and IV. Ethical constraints would prevent the random assignment of trauma patients in hospital emergency rooms to an experimental and a no-treatment control group because of the generally held conviction that medical assistance should be available in proportion to the life-threatening character of the disorder. Sometimes administrative procedures are hostile to random assignment—often illegitimately so, as is illustrated by the experience of some parents in a metropolitan ghetto whose first day-care center, for a mere 70 children, was fully enrolled some weeks before its opening had been officially and publicly announced. Aggressive managerial policies on the part of those conducting experiments can overcome such obstacles to randomization, which are usually less formidable than legal or ethical constraints against it.

We are inclined to emphasize the role of experimentally gathered information in the shaping of social policy because such information is most helpful in learning the causal relationships among program elements and outcomes. If an effect can be demonstrated in a group of units (persons, places, or institutions) chosen at random and subjected to a specified treatment while a similar group that is not treated does not show the effect, one can be reasonably confident that the treatment produced the effect. Such confidence cannot so readily be reposed in nonexperimental evidence, even though sophisticated methods of analysis can be used to reduce the ambiguity of casual inference. The superiority of experimental method lies in the fact that in a true experiment the differences between a treated (experimental) group and an untreated (control) group can be attributed entirely to the effect of the treatment plus an accidental (random) error component which can be accurately estimated and which will be evenhandedly distributed across the control and the experimental groups alike. Furthermore, all the other factors which augment or suppress the outcome variable occur evenhandedly in both the experimental and the control groups.

There are, of course, ways of estimating the effect of some social event or constellation of circumstances without doing an experiment. For example, one might analyze historical records and attempt to find statistical relationships between, say, changes in children's height and weight on the one hand and the price of available sources of protein, if one wanted to examine the effects of protein nutrition on physical growth. It would be unusual to find, in such data, measures of all of the variables (parental stature, socioeconomic status, dietary habits, etc.) that might affect physical growth and might be correlated in unknown fashion with the gross indices available through records. Thus a number of uncontrolled (and uncontrollable) factors that might also be affecting height and weight would not appear in the analysis, and these uncontrolled sources of variance would lessen confidence in the interpretation of the correlations obtained. Alternatively, one might design a prospective study to follow a cohort (a group all born in the same year) of children for a period of years in order to observe changes in height and weight as well as measuring their dietary intake (and the price of protein). Other variables that were hypothesized to be related to physical development, such as those mentioned earlier, could also be measured. While such a design would be a vast improvement over the study of historical records, and while the best methods of multivariate statistical analysis might be applied to the data, the results would still be correlational, indicating the presence and the strength of a relationship but not unequivocally establishing the casual direction: Does a relationship between a child's weight and the number of visits to a physician indicate that frequent medical attention improves children's nutrition? Or, are well-nourished children found in families that can afford medical care for even minor illness?

Experiments not only lead to clearer causal inferences, but the very process of experimental design helps to clarify the nature of the social problem being attacked. The sheer volume of information available about a particular area of social life can swamp decision-makers unless they can sift out relevant from irrelevant data. True experiments may simplify the sifting process because of the requirements of design. Designing an experiment, in contrast to analyzing existing bodies of data, focuses attention on the variables of specific interest, forcing administrators and social scientists to specify objectives and operations, thus linking the data to be collected with the policy decision that is to be made.

This stance does not negate the value of having some kinds of baseline data available prior to conducting an experiment. Such data can be helpful in estimating the order of magnitude of parameters before designing the treatment or the outcome measures; can help appraise the reliability or credibility of evidence gathered in the experiment, as well as the validity of the sampling of subjects or occasions in the experiment; and, in the case of very stable phenomena, may even allow the prediction of what the state of the social system would be (or would have been) in the absence of special intervention programs. Lastly, as we shall see, regularly collected data can sometimes be exploited in quasi-experimental designs when true experiments are impossible or unfeasible.

Everyone would agree that it makes good sense to try out important social changes on a small scale and in such a way that one can dependably assess their effects. The justification for writing a book to explain the methods for doing so are the commonly observed defects in more casual and unsystematic observation. All of us, not simply program managers, are inadequate or biased observers of the social scene. We rarely (unless we take special trouble to do so) obtain an unbiased sample of the relevant behavior that we ought to observe in order to assess effects of a social intervention. We frequently lack any kind of comparison between the behavior observed following a treatment and that of a comparable person or social unit which has not been given that treatment. That is, we often do not know whether an untreated or control group would have shown the same kinds of behavior as the treated group without having received the benefits of the program. Changes that are just what we would have expected from the treatment can occur as a result of forces outside of the social program. For example, if we simply observe that 80% of a group of previously unemployed persons who receive job training subsequently become employed, it is not possible to assert that the job training was effective unless it can also be assured that similar persons who did *not* receive the training did *not* become subsequently employed at such a high rate. Perhaps the observed effect was not due to the job training after all, but only to a change in the economy and a decrease in the overall unemployment rate or to some other event unrelated to the training.

Furthermore, if it is decided to make the appropriate observation of an untreated control group, it is not sufficient to compare those who volunteer for job training with a group of unemployed who do not. There is strong evidence that such a comparison would involve some sort of *bias* or *systematic error* in selecting the subjects for the experiment. Those who volunteer for training may be better motivated or more desperate or perhaps more hopeful of success than those who do not. Or they may be more intelligent. Sometimes they are younger, at other times, older. Whatever the case, there is almost bound to be some systematic difference between treated and untreated groups, and it is sure to make the conclusions about the effectiveness of a treatment dubious, since the groups might well have performed differently regardless of treatment. (These remarks do not impugn the strategy of employing only volunteers in an experiment and alloting volunteers randomly to experimental or control treatments.)

From the foregoing description it should be evident that we are using the term *experiment* in a restricted rather than a loose sense. Our usage does not encompass "demonstration" programs, which are organized try-outs of social mechanisms to test the feasibility, for example, of a different means of delivering social services or a different incentive structure for providers. Nor do we count as experiments those pilot or prototype projects undertaken to test detailed program procedures so that erroneous assumptions and mistaken notions about how to administer a program can be eliminated. Such studies are useful, although their purpose is also served by well-designed experiments. Unless provision is made for measurement of outcomes, for controls, and, above all, for random assignment of subjects, we do not count demonstrations and prototypes as experiments.

When randomization cannot be achieved, or when a control group is not feasible, a variety of quasi-experimental designs may be substituted—with greater ambiguity in the interpretation of results but still considerably more dependable information than is ordinarily obtained from analysis of nonexperimental data. Quasi-experiments correspond to certain natural social settings in which the experimenter can approximate experimental procedures for collecting data even though he lacks full control over the delivery of the treatment. When no control group can be arranged, a time series quasi-experiment can sometimes be constructed by taking periodic measurements of relevant behavior of a single group and introducing one or more instances of treatment into this time series of measurements. There are other occasions when a control group can be constructed but individual subjects cannot be randomly assigned to treatment or nontreatment, for example, when naturally occurring collectivities such as neighborhoods or classrooms cannot be broken up and rearranged; and when the collectivities themselves cannot be randomly assigned. The more similar the two groups are on a pretreatment test, the more confidence can be placed in observed differences following treatment; but this design still has some serious weaknesses. Still other circumstances can be fitted by a variety of other quasi-experimental designs, which are discussed in Chapter IV.

It is reasonable to encourage policy strategists and program managers to adopt an experimental attitude toward their work, employing experimental designs or experimentlike approaches, because some experimental or quasi-experimental design can be devised for nearly every social setting and nearly every kind of social intervention with which a policymaker may be concerned. No quasi-experimental design yields results that are quite as convincing as those from a true, randomized, controlled experiment. Each quasi-experimental design has specific weaknesses (as well as strengths), which must be carefully considered before deciding upon it as well as in the interpretation of results; but all of these designs yield information that is superior in at least some respect to wholly nonexperimental, observational studies.

What then are the advantages of experimentation? Its primary advantage over simple observational or retrospective studies is, as already emphasized, that an experiment generally allows inferences of superior dependability about cause and effect. In the case of almost any social phenomenon, there are likely to be several plausible explanations competing for acceptance. For example, if mothers who voluntarily seek prenatal care have healthier children at 1 year of age than mothers who do not get prenatal care, is this the result of the care itself? Or was it the more intelligent, able, "socially competent" mothers who sought out the prenatal care program? A systematic experiment virtually rules out the possibility of "causal displacement" or the error of attributing to treatment an effect that is produced by some uncontrolled variable such as a characteristic of the persons treated. True experimental design eliminates the possibility of causal displacement by assuring that the ability, motivation, or suitability of participants is approximately evenly distributed between the treated and untreated groups (with a specifiable amount of chance error).

Second, an experimental design has the advantage of allowing a comparison to be made between the effectiveness of two perhaps equally plausible kinds of treatment, i.e., two programs that are in competition for acceptance and with a prima facie equality of claim to effectiveness. An *experimental* comparison of two such programs is to be preferred to a merely casual observation of each or both in operation.

An experiment can include multiple and complex treatments designed to induce intensities of treatment influence or combination of forces that would never occur naturally (or would occur too infrequently to be noticed) in the ordinary course of events. For example, in an experiment on nutrition and mental development being conducted in some rural Guatemala villages, the experimental treatment produces a level of protein–calorie nutrition that would not normally be observed in most of the population under 12 years of age. An attempt to relate nutritional level to intelligence tests which depended on naturally occurring variation in nutritional status in this environment would miss a most important portion of the distribution of nutritional status, namely, the protein well-nourished.

Experimentation usually has some serendipitous advantages, too. Designing an experiment forces one to confront certain problems that might otherwise be ignored or left in ambiguity. It forces one to define clearly in operational terms what the objectives of the treatment (the intervention program) are, what effects are expected, and how effects are to be measured. Further, one is forced by design requirements to spell out rather explicitly what the treatment will consist of, i.e., what particular actions and operations will be carried out. Then, when the treatment is actually carried out for experimental purposes, program operators will learn much about how to implement their purposes and what some of the obstacles and problems are. Many of these will foreshadow the problems of establishing a nationwide program and will reveal facets and consequences—both positive and negative—that program proponents did not anticipate or intend. The experimental operation of an intervention can also increase public understanding of a particular social policy and help to focus discussion on real, rather than imaginary, issues. It may also have the effect of removing some issues from the purely political arena and placing them in the more neutral zone of science. To the extent that arguments over what would be the effects of a proposed intervention can be settled by experimentation, the true experiment can be treated as a laborsaving device that allows statesmen and the concerned public to spend their time more usefully making value judgments.

Finally, the experimental approach to understanding social phenomena brings the reassurance that any deliberate intervention a priori brings, namely, if one can intentionally and successfully produce (or prevent) a phenomenon, one has a surer sort of knowledge about its causation than can be obtained in any other way.

Experimentation also has its drawbacks and difficulties—which lead us to refrain from an unqualified prescription to use this approach for every situation. Primary among these are the problems of cost, complexity, and delay in getting an answer. Although the cost of social experiments may be small by comparison with such applied experiments as underground atomic explosive tests, moon shots, or weather modification experiments, nevertheless they are often more expensive than other forms of social research. An experiment being carried out in New Jersey to test the effects of a "negative income tax" form of welfare will cost more than $10 million, including the outlays for income maintenance payments. An experiment in rural Guatemala to examine the relationship between nutrition and mental development will average about half a million dollars per year over a 7-year period (again, including costs of treatment administration). Expensive as they may be, such experiments are often the best way to obtain dependable knowledge and for this reason alone are a bargain.

Not all experiments are so expensive. The Manhattan Bail Bond experiment cost less than $200,000 for a 3-year period, and many educational experiments have been even cheaper. Welch and Walberg (see

Appendix, Section IV) estimate that the main body of their experiment on the effects of a novel curriculum on students' interests and skills required approximately $50,000 over its 2 years (not including teachers' salaries); while Earle's (see Appendix, Section II) 2-year experiment on police recruit training involved almost no direct expenditures, since the treatment was also actual training legitimately chargeable to police department operations and the experimenter voluntarily contributed design and analysis time. Experiments conducted in less developed countries can be extraordinarily *in*expensive. The Taiwan experiment on acceptability of birth control devices reported spending only $20,000 for a full year of treatment and on-site measurement (Ross, 1966).

Besides money, some experiments have requirements for manpower, time, managerial skill, and ancillary services that the academic social researcher does not ordinarily need. Ordinary social research requires the development and application of measuring instruments, data analysis (including computational facilities), and a certain amount of professional time for formulating the conclusions and writing the report. In addition to these requirements, experiments must provide the treatment offered to the experimental (and sometimes to the control) subjects. Such treatments may require a large nonresearch staff and also some skills and materials quite different from those with which the academic researcher is accustomed to work. In the rural Guatemala experiment, for example, it proved necessary to offer medical care as well as food supplementation to the experimental population in order to keep the experiment going. Both the food supplement and the medical care required additional and different personnel, vehicles, buildings, material, and above all managerial supervision. In some sense, running an experiment of this sort is akin to managing a live-in educational or custodial institution. For its management, the New Jersey Negative Income Tax experiment has many of the characteristics of a full-scale welfare plan. Moreover, experiments present larger and more extensive problems of data management and data processing than are encountered in much social research. Still other organizational and managerial requirements, including those of training paraprofessionals, maintaining their interest and skill and the quality of their work, keeping the attrition rate low by making sure that subjects do not drop out of the experimental treatment—all of these matters are covered in Chapter VI.

A second drawback for many experimental treatments is the time delay involved in obtaining the information necessary for planning or for an assessment of the effectiveness of the program. It may require many months to design the experiment, pretest its procedures, assemble the staff, and put it into operation. It must then run for a sufficiently long time to allow the treatment to produce its presumed effects. Finally, there is bound to be a period of analysis and interpretation of results that will extend the delay by still more months. The New Jersey experiment was planned in 1967 and results became available late in 1973. The Guatemala experiment began pretesting in 1969 and the final testing of children will not take place before 1975 at the earliest. Shorter experiments have been conducted in different areas, of course. For example, the Manhattan Bail Bond experiment took less than 3 years. Experiments on administrative procedures and curriculum innovations have taken less than 6 months. However, the time delays characteristic of tests of large programs suggest that experiments should be undertaken only after strategic consideration has been given to the time at which results are needed and the likely costs of either taking no action in the interim or taking actions which are stopgap and of uncertain efficiency.

Finally, experiments pose particular ethical problems which may be present in all social research and all policy decisions, but which become exacerbated in experiments. These are covered in Chapter VIII and will only be touched upon here. They include questions of fairness in selecting and assigning participants to experimental and control treatments of protecting the anonymity and confidentialilty of subjects' records, and of how to terminate the experiment without unjustified disruption of the subjects' lives.

This list of the difficulties and drawbacks involved in experimentation is formidable, but it must be weighed against the corresponding list of advantages to be obtained from data collected through experimental methods. When conditions are not problematic or when the creativity and ingenuity of the research designer can resolve difficult problems, then experimentation is the *method of choice* for obtaining reliable and valid information upon which to plan social programs.

# II

# Why and When to Experiment

In the introduction to this volume, the advantages and some of the costs of social experimentation were set forth. But the brevity of the exposition may well have left some readers in doubt on more specific questions, for example: Under what institutional and political conditions is an experiment advisable? What are the scientific requirements for a successful social experiment? How can experimentation be used specifically for program planning? For evaluation? What are some of the factors and conditions that program managers ought to note before engaging in social experimentation? This chapter will attempt to answer some of these questions with the intention of providing initial practical advice rather than detailed technical comment on the issues involved. Where these issues do have technical aspects, or where topics have more complexity than can be conveniently touched upon here, reference is made to later chapters in the volume.

## Why Experiment?

Experimentation should be viewed as a cycle that begins with problem analysis; proceeds through the planning of an intervention, its development, experimental trial, and evaluation; and ends in either program implementation or in replanning the intervention. The cycle is dominated by the notion of an experimental design. Ideally, a proposed social intervention would be tried out as if it were an experimental treatment; and the means of deciding whether or not it is an effective intervention would be built into the experiment at the very beginning. The trial of the proposed intervention would be *designed* to yield information for *evaluating* it and for *planning* how to improve it if, as is likely, the intervention is imperfect. If the experimental trial shows no evidence that the intervention is effective, then, of course, the replanning phase consists of a fresh analysis of the problem and attempts to invent an alternative solution in the form of a new intervention. If a satisfactory effect has been achieved, the replanning phase is concerned with implementing or installing the full-scale intervention. The important point is that social experimentation not only includes one form (probably the most useful form) of evaluation, but makes evaluation an integral part of a design that starts with a planning phase and ends by using the information derived from the evaluation phase. That information may result in a decision to accept the intervention and implement it on a larger scale; to reject it as ineffective; or to modify it.

We stress the idea of planning in this chapter because, as pointed out in the introductory material, many of the major national social programs of the 1960s in education, manpower, and community action apparently failed to produce the effects that had been intended. The first reaction to this appearance of failure was to attempt to examine the strengths and weaknesses of programs through evaluative research. Beginning in 1967 or 1968, a number of efforts to evaluate social action programs were initiated, especially in the Office of the Assistant Secretary for Planning and Evaluation in the Department of Health, Education, and Welfare, and in the Office of Research, Plans, Programs, and Evaluation in the Office of Economic Opportunity.

These nonexperimental evaluations, by and large, provided little support for the belief held by program operators that their programs were great successes (Rivlin, 1971). But, perhaps more important, these evaluations after the fact provided precious little guidance for program improvement or development. The studies could say a little about differential effects of the program upon different population groups, but nothing about which avenues of program development would hold out the greatest promise for success. Moreover, even in looking at the simple impact question, Did the program work? these studies were able to bring only weak methodology to bear because of the timing of the inquiries (generally after the fact) and because the broad availability of the programs precluded the use of really credible control or comparison groups.

One might think that ordinary, everyday experience with a social intervention program would provide a sufficient basis for developing and improving it, but this is rarely the case. An operating program frequently does not encompass a wide enough variation in treatments to permit conclusions to be drawn about alternative combinations of treatment components or alternative intensities of their application. Unless deliberate efforts are made to plan informative alternative versions of the programs, the range of variation is likely to be narrow and to be determined by administrative convenience, budget, custom or site-related factors. Accordingly, even when such variations do occur, the treatment effects may be confounded by special characteristics of the recipients, by geography, or by the way the program was administered. One cannot be sure, on the basis of such casual experience, whether the program was a success; and if one could be, there would be no way of telling whether it succeeded because of the inherent effectiveness of the treatment, the charisma of an administrator, or some attributes of the treated units.

Last, after-the-fact evaluation of operating programs is often ineffective in changing them. Once a program has been established, with the announced purpose of social amelioration, it is perhaps more difficult to redirect it than to abolish it. Organizations have been formed, institutional accomodations to the program have been made, and individuals have made psychological and occupational commitments to it. As will be pointed out later (in Chapter VI) the "action team" operating a program is usually convinced of its effectiveness and resists changing it in response to research findings.

All of these factors lead one to a belief that learning about an intervention and evaluating its effectiveness should start prior to the time when a major program is initiated. If a small set of projects is sytematically put in place for the explicit purpose of learning, the results may be persuasive in guiding the subsequent development of a full-scale program and its subsequent modification in response to changing conditions. This then is one of the major motivations for social experimentation—the initiation of more systematic program development. It is not the only reason, however. It is well to recognize that there are many purposes for experimenting even though the current interest in the subject derives largely from a desire for better program development, since recent experience has demonstrated that successful social innovations cannot be guaranteed in advance of trying them out.

THE PURPOSES OF SOCIAL EXPERIMENTATION

The following list of purposes for experimentation is not intended as a scientific taxonomy of mutually exclusive alternatives but rather as a useful list of major objectives that may help to clarify the question, Why should one experiment?

*Hypothesis Testing.* The type of social experiment that comes closest to the classic laboratory experiment is one that is intended to test a plausible hypothesis as a precursor to the development of a social program. The emphasis in such an experiment is on the alleged relationship between a particular factor (which might become an element of a treatment or a social program) and some desired effect. A clear example is provided by the experiment conducted through the Instituto de Nutricion de Centro America y Panama (INCAP) which is testing the hypothesis that protein supplements in the diets of pregnant women and preschool children can reduce or eliminate retardation in cognitive ability at school age (Canosa, Salomon, and Klein, 1972). More specifically, this experiment is testing the hypothesis that such effects will be obtained through the manipulation of the biochemical and nutritional conditions without altering the sociocultural, educational, and economic circumstances of the population, and without providing additional services. The experiment seeks to disentangle the effects of the nutritional and health variables *per se* from the sociocultural.

Typically, the designs involved in testing hypotheses prior to social program development must be carefully systematic, rather tightly controlled, and especially attentive to unintended consequences of the treatment. The documentability of the treatment is of great importance and hence it is necessary to observe and identify components of the treatment very carefully. Of less concern are such practical questions as the cost of providing the treatment, the managerial and personnel requirements, the necessary institutional auspices, and a variety of practical matters which would certainly be of concern to program managers. The focus of the hypothesis-testing experiment, however, is not on program so much as it is upon the truth or falsity of an alleged relationship, as a basis for proceeding further with, abandoning, or modifying a particular direction of thinking in social policy formulation. If protein nutrition is not an effective way of reducing retardation in cognitive ability, then some other line of social intervention must be sought (or some other justification for a protein supplementation program). The purpose of the hypothesis-testing experiment is to give preliminary confirmation (or disconfirmation) to a general proposition about human behavior in society that might subsequently become the basis for the development of a social program. As intimated earlier, such experiments can sometimes be successfully performed in a laboratory when appropriate conditions can be created there. When they cannot, it is necessary to undertake a field experiment.

*Developing Elements of a Social Program.* If some proposition about human behavior or about society is accepted sufficiently to have led to a decision to base some social intervention on it, then experiments can be useful in developing elements of that social intervention program. Typically, such elements are propounded on the basis of experience and/or theory that leads the program developer to believe an efficacious set of operations can be devised to realize the general proposition. For example, if the proposition is accepted that the "discovery method" of teaching physical science to elementary school children is superior to didactic instruction and conventional textbooks, then the task of developing a "discovery curriculum" is one element of such a program. The program developer needs to identify a list of physical science principles to be learned through discovery; to invent or modify existing scientific procedures for discovering these principles; and to invent, modify, or borrow appropriate materials for the discovery experiences.

In such experiments there is still considerable attention to the validity of the general proposition about the superiority of the discovery method for learning, and the ultimate payoff variable is likely to be an assessment of how much the children learn under the new, as against conventional, methods; or how long they retain it; or how well they are able to generalize or transfer their knowledge to novel situations. Almost equal attention is likely to go to the material and mechanical aspects of the operation. Were the materials sufficiently manipulable by the children? Did they stand up under ordinary usage? Were they safe? Were they clearly understood? Did they have unanticipated properties or aspects? Still a third focus of attention is also operational: whether the teachers were able to work satisfactorily with the innovative curriculum. Did they understand the principles to be taught, the purpose of the discovery method? Were they able to work with the individual lesson plans? And finally, some attention is sure to be paid to differentiations within the curriculum development experiment. Were some phases of the instruction more successful than others? Is there some hint that this method needs to be supplemented by more conventional ones or broadened in some respect?

Pragmatically oriented as such experiments are, they still leave many aspects of program development unexplored. These are generally encountered in the larger-scale experiment which we have called comprehensive program development.

*Comprehensive Program Development.* Experiments of this magnitude are less common. They involve a total program, including, for example, staff training, program materials, administrative procedures, project leadership, institutional sponsorship, and in some cases legal and administrative changes necessary to make the program work successfully. This type of program development has occurred in the area of early childhood education (for examples, see Stanley, 1972). The aim is usually to produce a complete package, including educational materials, teaching methods, teacher training, and other components that, taken together, form an integrated program for the early education of children which is presumably ready to be installed in its entirety in a school.

Experimentation is employed as an integral tool of program development. The various components are tested experimentally against the conventional educational methods, which are used in the control groups. Alternatively, two or more innovative (experimental) versions of a curriculum or a method can be compared in an experiment, with or without using an "untreated" control group. In principle, differing levels of intensity of a treatment can also be compared against each other and against an untreated condition. Likewise, the effects of multifactor treatments (e.g., various combinations of curriculum, teacher training, and materials) can be experimentally compared in order to learn whether one factor produces greater effects than another as well as whether interaction effects arise from some combinations.

The development of such a comprehensive program usually requires a degree of control over circumstances and personnel that can best be obtained in a laboratorylike situation. The specially selected and trained staff of an experimental program are likely to be of higher quality than one would expect to find as the average in a national program. Facilities may be exceptional or unrepresentative. There may well be some special effects attributable to the very novelty of the experimental procedures (see Chapter V for a discussion of "Hawthorne effects"). As a consequence, the results of such experimentally developed programs may not be replicated under ordinary operating conditions when the program is installed in an average school, for example. There may indeed be a trade-off between the precision obtained in a highly controlled experimental development process and the generalizability of its results. It is sometimes argued, on largely pragmatic grounds, that experiments ought to be conducted in more realistic settings even if that forces them to be less neat and precise. This point of view is represented in the following section.

*Choosing among Program Designs.*    Another approach to program development allows for many variations to be examined simultaneously. Ideas about early childhood education that stemmed from experiments in psychology laboratories and child development institutes did not, in general, provide detailed guidance for the development of practical programs in this area. Furthermore, there are a number of competing points of view and methods of teaching with strong claims for effectiveness that seem to call for comparative evaluation. These considerations led to the development of the notion of "planned variations" on the part of the Follow Through program in the United States Office of Education. While Follow Through was not itself a true randomized experiment its approach represents a compromise between the rigor of a highly controlled and tightly designed laboratory experiment with the popular and politically appealing feature of community participation and local control of compensatory education. The planned variations thrust in Follow Through drew upon the professional ingenuity and the diversity of educational claims by a dozen or so "program sponsors." These educators, child development specialists, and psychologists were encouraged to put together a package of curriculum materials, teaching technology, and so forth, which could be offered as options to a local community wishing to participate in the Follow Through program. The community had an opportunity to choose among the products of a number of program sponsors and had to agree to conduct its local program in accordance with the specifications and procedures laid down by the sponsor. To the extent that these conditions were fulfilled, there was a series of comparisons possible among communities and among sponsors of different sorts of compensatory programs. Presumably such experiments represent rather realistic comparisons of program designs when employed by types of staff and in physical settings that are typical of local projects. While the extent of control over program execution is probably much less than a laboratory scientist would like, a counterargument can be made that the programs are probably more representative of what would actually happen if any particular variation were to be regularized and offered as a national program.

Efforts to test planned variations have experienced many problems. Holding treatments constant is all but impossible, and obtaining good controls is difficult. The feature of local determination and community control may raise obstacles to randomization. The process by which local schools and program designs are brought together provides numerous opportunities for self-selection bias to enter. The projects mirror the now classic conflicts between project operators attempting to deliver services; clients receiving these services; evaluators; and program developers. The result is no doubt poorer as regards experimental design, but perhaps of greater immediate program relevance than "hot house" experiments.

*Estimating Critical Parameter Values.* Of comparatively recent vintage are a group of experiments that are more similar to physical science experiments than those previously discussed. Best exemplified by the Income Maintenance experiments, these seek to use experimental means to establish critical values of parameters in the models of individual behavior. In the Income Maintenance experiments, the intent is to examine the effects which various levels of payments together with "tax back rates" on individual earnings have on the work behavior of the recipients. Random assignment among treatments was possible because of the design and treatment which allowed individual families to be dealt with in isolation from one another. Since some of these experiments are still in process, many questions concerning their outcomes remain unanswered. Clearly, there are important questions concerning the manner in which behavior of persons who are isolated (as in these experiments) compares with their behavior when an entire community is eligible to receive benefits. The problem of inferring "permanent" behavior from an experiment of 3 to 5 years duration remains largely unexplored. Thus, while the Income Maintenance experiments are frequently held up as an exemplar, which they are in many respects, they may suffer from unavoidable limitations.

While the Negative Income Tax experiment represents a relatively refined instance of parameter estimation there are perhaps some more common conditions under which parameter estimation can be a useful function of experimentation. In general, these are likely to depend upon variation in the intensity of a treatment. It is worthwhile to remark here that many social interventions are weak in comparison to the naturally occurring circumstances and forces of daily life which may work against intervention or at least not favor it. For example, in programs to treat delinquent youth, or to give occupational counseling to high school dropouts, or job retraining to displaced workers, the psychosocial force supplied by a few hours of companionship, sympathetic listening, good advice, and helpful factual information may be trivial in comparison with the socioeconomic resistances to change supplied by employer prejudices, union regulations, licensing requirements, wage differentials, worker boredom, or social pressure from peers. The question ordinarily asked about social work or counseling, for example, is, Does it do any good? A more penetrating question would be, How much social work or how much counseling would be necessary to accomplish some good? Perhaps the answer is that no amount of social work alone, or no amount of counseling, will achieve the intended effect—perhaps because the treatment is inappropriate for the problem. Or perhaps the answer is that the cost of the amount of treatment required to achieve an effect would be prohibitive. On the other hand, the answer might simply be that doubling the conventional amount of attention would be sufficient to accomplish a great deal. Until systematic variations in the intensity of treatment are tried, it may be a mistake to discard a treatment that one single-level experiment has failed to show to be efficacious. The intensity of treatment usually should not exceed by very much a programmatically feasible level, but there may be occasions when the inherent efficacy of a procedure is under question and the treatment level should be extended to its absolute maximum for one of the experimental groups.

*Evaluating a Concept or Claim.*   Just as an experiment can be a useful method of testing the efficacy of a claimed improvement in the conventional method of performing some social action such as teaching or giving welfare, advice, or counseling, it can sometimes serve to resolve conflicting claims of efficacy between two or more such alternative methods. While it bears some resemblance to the hypothesis-testing purpose mentioned earlier, this use of experimentation has more in common with product or materials-testing of the sort undertaken by consumers' organizations or the National Bureau of Standards. Ordinarily, however, the experiment is undertaken in a comparative context in which the new method is contrasted with existing techniques. Ordinarily too, each method is a complex treatment package, not a pure variable, as it would be in an hypothesis-testing experiment.

An example is "performance contracting" in the field of teaching compensatory reading and mathematics. The claim had been put forward that commercial or nonprofit agencies outside of the conventional public education system could outperform that system in the teaching of reading and mathematics to young children through the use of an accountability procedure in which the contractor would sign an agreement to improve students' performance in certain basic skills by specified amounts and would be paid according to his success in achieving such levels. Within the guidelines provided by the local school board, the contractor would be free to use whatever instructional techniques, incentive systems, and audiovisual aids he felt were most effective. Limited experience with one such program suggests the desirability of an experimental trial of the concept in several different schools. This experiment was mounted by the Office of Economic Opportunity in the 1970–1971 school year (OEO, 1972). Eighteen school districts contracted with six private firms to teach mathematics and reading to students in two sets of grades: first through third, and seventh through ninth. About a hundred students in each grade at each site received instruction for about half an hour daily per subject for the full academic year, while a similar group of students in traditional class-room settings was selected and tested but taught only by conventional methods. These children attended nearby schools and were matched as closely as possible to the children in the experimental program. Because of the absence of random assignment of pupils to experimental or control groups, this study is properly termed a "quasi-experimental" design, but in other respects it approximates the desired experimental form. The school districts involved constitute an illustrative range of kinds of schools in low-income areas; the range of programs offered by the performance contractors is wide and substantially exceeds the range of teaching techniques ordinarily appearing naturally in these schools. On the other hand, of necessity, the design is too simple to test the effects of different forms of incentives or curricula. In a sense ths experiment represents an improvement over classic program evaluation in that it was undertaken before the "program" was under way and was more carefully controlled.

The number of experiments undertaken to test a claim has not been great, perhaps because the advantages offered by an experimental test of a plausible claim have not been well recognized. Perhaps a more common happening has been that a plausible and persuasive idea for social innovation has been adopted wholesale without adequate pre-test and experimentation or with only a demonstration phase to examine the administrative and mechanical feasibility of the idea. Recognition of the advantages of experimentation, of testing a plausible claim on a relatively small scale experimentally, may be expected to increase the use of experimental technology for this purpose.

FURTHER REASONS FOR EXPERIMENTING

As this chapter began by saying, the various purposes for which experiments may be conducted are seen as integral parts of a planning, implementation, testing, and replanning cycle for the development of social intervention programs. This conception of the planning process is not in itself novel, and experimentation is only one of several methods for informing the planning process.

Perhaps the most important consideration in answering the question, Why should we experiment? is the fact that experimental results are convincing. In comparison to all other research designs, experimentation is more convincing because the capacity to produce a particular outcome deliberately in a randomly assigned group of persons is the surest testimony of the effectiveness of the treatment. This assertion does not mean that other designs and other approaches to the analysis of behavior can never provide useful information. Indeed, analyses of records, and, sometimes, prospective surveys or observational studies can often be used effectively prior to beginning an experiment, by serving to narrow the arena of plausible treatments and to focus attention on relevant variables. Furthermore, there may be situations in which experimentation is impossible, dangerous, or unethical, but where analytical methods can be applied to data that are routinely or specially collected. (See Chapter IV on quasi-experimental designs.) In addition, there are situations in which the cost of experimentation in money or in delaying social amelioration seems not to produce sufficient benefit to justfy it. This calculus is necessarily crude because it is hard to estimate the value of the increased confidence in findings that experimental procedures bring to a policy-planning dilemma. That they are more convincing and their results more dependable cannot, however, be doubted.

Experiments also have certain secondary advantages over other forms of research—advantages that are not trivial. For instance, the very execution of an experiment forces one to think through a very large number of the implications of a general plan. As anyone knows who has attempted to realize in concrete terms an intervention concept or general plan, there are many ambiguities to confront and many decisions to make. For example, in the New Jersey Negative Income Tax experiment, a decision had to be made as to what accounting period would be used to calculate payments to participants. The choice among a weekly, monthly, yearly, or other period confronted the problem of balancing equity to the participants against responsiveness to their needs as well as administrative feasibility and the fiscal responsibility of the project. The choice was complicated by the differences in patterns of income receipt among participants. Those who had earnings that fluctuated markedly because of intermittent employment might have been disadvantaged or inequitably treated by the same accounting period that fairly treated others who had low wages but steady employment.

Furthermore, in trying to mount an experiment, one may discover that an assumed state of affairs is fictitious; or that an important condition of the intervention plan cannot be met; or that a plausible way of administering the treatment is administratively unfeasible. The practical value of trying out an intervention experimentally is that it provides some reality testing on a relatively small and inexpensive scale. Finally, during the course of the experiment one may often learn, incidentally, some important things that he did not go looking for at all. For example, the New Jersey Income Maintenance experiment was designed primarily to measure labor force participation, but made an interesting incidental discovery about residential mobility. One might plausibly have expected the experimental groups to move less often than the controls on the ground that the noncontingent income payments would increase their ability to meet rent payments. The actual finding was, rather surprisingly, that experimentals and controls were equally mobile. Further analysis turned up a difference in the pattern of mobility with implications for income disposition. While the mobile control group members moved from one rented dwelling to another, a large proportion of the experimental group who moved were buying their own homes.

This sort of serendipity is not unknown in research using nonexperimental methods, but experience suggests it is more likely when one is deliberately trying to produce an effect instead of simply examining the outcomes of normal social processes. However, since large-scale true experimentation can be difficult, expensive, and time-consuming, some attention ought to be given to the conditions under which experimentation, rather than alternative ways of getting knowledge, should be undertaken. The next section of this chapter addresses itself to that range of issues.

## When to Experiment

Experiments are ordinarily undertaken after a rather careful analysis suggests that an experiment is the best way to get dependable knowledge about some social intervention—a new way of dealing with a familiar social problem or an attempt to cope constructively with a problem that has recently been identified and around which a degree of public or governmental concern is arising.

Social problems become candidates for experimentation as needs for amelioration or reform are perceived, identified, and publicly discussed. The problem of poverty well illustrates the process. Until the late 1950s little or no attention had been paid to the "one-third of a nation" (as Franklin Delano Roosevelt referred to it in 1934) that was "ill-fed, ill-clothed and ill-housed" since World War II. Then two influential books and a number of articles in magazines read by "opinion leaders" called attention to the continuing poverty of a substantial number of Americans. These concerns began to be discussed by administrative officers of the Federal government, by legislators, and by journalists. Questions arose and data were found lacking about how many poor there were as well as about their characteristics and distribution.

Even before such questions were being asked, proposals were being put forward to alleviate poverty. The reform of welfare laws and administrative processes; the provision of jobs and job training; the provision of food subsidies; and the offer of "compensatory" educational opportunities for "disadvantaged" children—all were offered as remedies for poverty.

Many proposed remedies were based on wholly or partially faulty diagnoses, which in turn arose from a dearth of information—either about the facts of poverty or about the likely consequences of any given intervention. Would food stamps improve the nutrition of children? Would "head-starts" improve their intellectual functioning? Would housing allowances improve their health? Would job training decrease unemployment and raise the incomes of their parents? Would a guaranteed minimum income serve to raise the total level of living of a family or would it merely substitute for the income produced by the work of the household head? Both solid data and a confident forecast of outcomes were wanting.

Such conditions are essential and set the stage for experimentation. But they are not enough. There must be, in addition, the organized capacity, through governmental or private agencies, to devise an experiment intended to enlighten policymakers and program planners about the probable effects of proposed schemes for social amelioration.

In the case of poverty, the variety of interventions proposed was quite large, but some of them were particularly strongly urged. One, at least, seemed to the administrators of the Office of Economic Opportunity to be susceptible of experimental testing. The guaranteed minimum income plan, which involved government provision of enough income to make up the difference between the earnings of the head of the household and the "poverty line," presented a specific perplexity: If a minimum (survival) income were guaranteed, would this assurance result in a reduction of work effort on the part of the wage earner(s)? Would the heads of poor families prefer to refrain from work and simply collect their guarantee? Or would they continue (even, perhaps, increase) their work effort with the knowledge that, as their earnings from work increased, their government subsidy would decline at a predetermined rate.

Available information from studies of income distribution, unemployment records, and other labor market behavior was not sufficient to answer this question. Debate over the negative incentive feature of a guaranteed income continued among economists, public officials, legislators and others concerned with poverty. It became apparent that only direct investigation of the question was likely to yield a convincing answer. The Office of Economic Opportunity accordingly decided that the importance of the problem, with its implications for public policy in the arena of welfare, justified an experiment of limited dimension to discover whether such a guaranteed minimum income would indeed alter the incentive to work. Furthermore, the Office decided, the experiment could also assess the differential effects of various levels of guarantee and various rates of "tax" (i.e., the rate at which guaranteed income declined as wage earnings rose) upon work behavior. Out of these considerations the so-called Negative Income Tax experiment was undertaken in 1968. This experiment is mentioned frequently in the pages of this book for it exemplifies many of the features that future experiments with social intervention may share. It happens to be a particularly well-documented and carefully planned experiment although it is not unique.

Other social interventions have also been the subject of experimentation and it seems likely that still more will be done in the future. Subjects that are of central concern to society, such as education, social welfare, health, crime, environmental pollution, and other large matters are likely to be almost continuously under examination and debate as poverty has been, and this scrutiny is sure to give rise to new proposals for amelioration. Almost as surely, these proposals will encounter doubts, questions, and challenges that cannot be satisfactorily met by rational argument or inference from existing information. Many proposals, seemingly plausible, will contend as solutions for a particular problem; and some will be so novel, or their consequences so unknowable a priori that their effectiveness can only be estimated through careful, systematic trial under controlled conditions on a small scale—in other words, through experiment.

This forecast has many implications. For social scientists, one at least stands out. There will be an even greater need in the future for tests and other measuring devices that can estimate the effects of various social interventions upon such matters as human development (both intellective and social–emotional), motivation, family integrity, employment performance and satisfaction, personal fulfillment and satisfaction, health (in contrast to illness and disease), and those as yet ill-defined properties that underlie the equally vague notion of a satisfying society. The state of scientific knowledge in these areas is deplorably weak. Yet, as the attention and the energies of men are increasingly devoted to deliberate interventions to achieve a more satisfactory society, there will be a corresponding need for instruments to measure the effects of their experimental attempts. It would be hard to conceive of a more significant area in which to invest energy in methodological research and development.

Although it must be clear that the general stance of this volume is to endorse experimentation as a superior means of getting dependable knowledge about social interventions, it does not advocate indiscriminate and exclusive use of the procedure. First, existing knowledge should be fully exploited before an experiment is planned. Not only is it economical to do so, but technically necessary in order to make intelligent decisions about experimental design and measurement. For instance, until one knows something about the naturally occurring variability in a phenomenon, it is difficult to know how large an experiment will be required. Second, there are, no doubt, many situations in which the adoption of a social intervention, or its rejection, will be determined by overriding political, humanitarian, or economic considerations. It is nevertheless possible to develop here some suggestions to help the policy planner decide whether or not to undertake an experiment in connection with some proposed social intervention.

## SOME CONDITIONS FOR THE DECISION TO EXPERIMENT

The sections which follow review some particularly important conditions, of a political, ethical, administrative, and technical character, on which a decision to experiment ought to rest. Because of the enormous variety of situations, types of intervention, institutional auspices, and program substance it is impossible to provide detailed rules and absolute strictures. Furthermore, experience with different types of experiments is still accruing; and practical experience, together with informed judgment and some scientific knowledge, is the basis for the views expressed in the next pages. Lastly, the various considerations to which attention should be given in deciding when to experiment are not without potential internal contradiction. The weighting of various factors requires experienced administrative judgment. Sometimes humanitarian reasons for conducting an experiment will outweigh technical difficulties. Sometimes, the political importance of taking an action will loom larger than the inadequacy of the administrative and managerial factors that counsel caution and delay. Sometimes the costs of experimentation and the delay involved will be so trivial compared to the potential waste of human resources if a misguided or harmful "ameliorative" action is taken that no argument against experimentation should be conclusive. In any concrete, specific case, the decision can be difficult. The following sections may serve to focus the thinking of those who must decide upon issues that we consider most central.

*Political Conditions.*    Perhaps the prerequisite condition should be that experimentation be undertaken when there is a possibility of influencing the fact, form, or substance of the proposed intervention. Even when overwhelming political or social forces dictate the taking of a social action and it is apparent that something must be done regardless of the adequacy or inadequacy of the informational base, there may be some point in undertaking an experiment if the outcome can influence the shape of the program. Certainly the reverse is true. When there is a good opportunity for influencing a political or social decision; when there is considerable ambiguity about the effectiveness of a proposed intervention; when there are several competing alternative "solutions" for a social problem; and when there is sufficient time between the undertaking of the experiment and the making of the political decision to allow its results to be fed into the planning process, then the conditions for experimentation are enhanced. Fortunately, very many political decisions are of this character. This is especially true when some realm of social life is in disarray and there is widespread dissatisfaction but no clear consensus on the remedy for the difficulty. This state of affairs is well illustrated by the condition of welfare programs in the United States in the late 1960s and early 1970s. The proposal for a negative income tax was only one of many competing alternatives for reforming the welfare system. Furthermore—and this is not trivial— it was one to which only a few thinkers and planners (albeit influential ones) were willing to give serious consideration at the time the experiment was planned. Under such conditions it was possible to conduct an experiment and to have time enough to carry it out before a decision had to be made. The fact that rather few people, principally academicians and policy planners, took the idea seriously meant that it was in little danger of being captured by political forces and concretized into a total national program without adequate information. The fact that it was plausible and not wholly ridiculous or impossible meant that the proposal for an experiment could be taken seriously.

A second political consideration is that the proposed intervention be something of sufficient importance in the life of the individuals affected to justify the investment of considerable resources, both human and financial. When large sums of money are to be expended, when the life conditions of very many people are to be affected, when substantial changes are to be made in institutional arrangements, the matter is weighty and deserves the weightiest consideration. If pressures of time are not overriding, perhaps a good guideline to follow is to experiment with those kinds of social intervention which appear most prominently in the national budget and in the popular consciousness.

A third consideration, not so obvious, perhaps, as the former, is that the substance of the intervention or the resources to be used in effecting it be in short supply. A good illustration of this condition is the planned variations format of the Follow Through program. Although originally conceived as a nationwide project, the funds allotted for its execution were so limited that it could be undertaken in only a small number of school districts. Since there was no possibility of everyone sharing in this boon, it was possible to conduct selected experiments while minimizing the envy of those who might be excluded. A parallel, though converse, situation obtained at the time of greatest crisis in the flying training commands of the United States Air Corps during World II. An extensive battery of psychological tests designed to pick candidates with the highest aptitude for positions of pilot, bombardier, and navigator were administered to a large number of cadet recruits. In order to test the validity of this psychological battery it was essential to allow all of the cadets (those with high as well as those with low scores) to complete air crew training. By comparing success or failure in training with aptitude scores, the test developers could determine which, if any, tests were useful in predicting training success. From one point of view it was fortunate that pilots were in short supply, and administrative officers in charge of training were not impressed by scores on a mere psychological test battery. Accordingly they were easily persuaded to allow all of the first thousand candidates to go through training and, on the basis of this experience, it was learned that the psychological battery could predict failures in training.

While shortness of supply is an almost accidental ingredient that abets but does not guarantee success in experimentation, a more essential feature of a successful experiment is that the cost of delaying the introduction of a solution to a pressing social question be small relative to the cost of proceeding with an intervention based on less information. This requirement obviously combines three elements: the length of time it will take to obtain satisfactory results from the experiment; the amount of delay that is politically, socially, and ethically defensible in obtaining that answer; and the extent of agreement among experts and decision-makers about the value of the intervention. All three are matters of judgment. Most elements of the educational curriculum can be satisfactorily tested, at least for short-run effects, in a single academic year or two. The experiment on performance contracting in a number of elementary schools required but 1 year to yield an answer that was sufficiently conclusive to prevent adoption of such programs in the form tested (OEO, 1972). Furthermore the resilience of students and pupils in the face of bad teaching, outmoded curricula, and daft inventions suggests that it is not unreasonable to "deprive" the subjects in a control group of the "benefits" an alleged advance in methods until the quality of that advance can be assessed experimentally. Other judgments may be harder to make. Would it be worth-while to delay reform of the welfare system in the United States until the results of work incentive experiments now in progress are known? It is more difficult to believe that much could be gained by deferring a program to provide supplement protein feeding to infants until the results of an experiment on the relationship between malnutrition and mental development could be made available. The outcome of such an experiment might reinforce, or, indeed, might remove one of the justi-fications of the feeding programs, but in either case would leave the program still with a strong humanitarian rationale.

It is not, of course, always necessary to defer social action until all the answers are in. We agree with Rivlin: "Action and experimentation are not mutually exclusive. A community or a nation that wants to act can act and experiment at the same time (Rivlin 1971, p. 118)." What is required is that the action be taken in such a way that something can be learned from it—in other words that it be undertaken systematically, with designed variation, rather than haphazardly—a point to which we shall return. Sometimes the pressure for intervention, as social reform, is so great that it cannot and should not be resisted. Yet few important reforms are without defects and unintended negative consequences. If experiments with variations in the reformist program can be under-taken even in the wake of its institution, their results may still contri-bute to reshaping the program for the better.

*Ethical Considerations.*    A full discussion of ethical aspects of social experimentation appears in Chapter VIII. For the purposes of the present section it is assumed that the ethical desiderata of all experi-ments (such as protection of subjects' privacy, confidentiality of data, avoidance of harmful treatments or side effects, and so forth) can be achieved. If they cannot, then an experiment should not be begun. But the question, When should one experiment? must confront two other considerations.

The timing of an experimental intervention is consequential. In the first place, an experiment ought not to postpone the installation of a reform of already agreed-upon value. Experiments should not be used as an excuse for delay or political inaction when the desirable course is clear. Second, an experiment should hold promise of learning some-thing useful for future program planning in time to affect that planning.

Furthermore, from an ethical as well as a political point of view it seems important that the general nature of an experiment ought to be agreed to by the persons actually involved as participants in it, and perhaps by the public at large (or their elected representatives) as well. To what extent the subjects in the experiment should be given a complete and wholly revealing explanation of what is being done is a problem, for technical as well as ethical reasons. Many social experiments are concerned with human behavior that is, to a greater or lesser degree, under the voluntary control of the individual. In many situations a full understanding of the experimental purpose could lead to voluntary changes in behavior, which could have the effect of artificially depressing or enhancing the effect of the treatment. One must set against this technical difficulty the ethical requirement that a subject in an experiment has the right to a full explanation ("informed consent") of what he is about to experience. Guidance as to how to manage this conflict between a technical and an ethical requirement is extremely difficult to provide. Perhaps the best suggestion is that counsel in difficult cases be sought from a broadly based group of persons, acquainted both with the experiment and with the participant population, to assist in making a judgment. If such advisors feel that the loss or damage incurred in withholding explanation is trivial or nonexistent, whereas a full explanation would probably damage the validity of the experiment, it seems reasonable to limit information on the experiment's purposes. Where the reverse is true, full explanation is strongly advised. Where the two principles are in direct and strong conflict, perhaps the experiment should not be done at all.

*Technical Requirements.* It is important to understand the point of view implied in the notion of experimental *design*. An experimental design is a detailed plan for executing the experiment, including a procedure for deciding who shall be in the group that receives the experimental treatment and who in the control group, for administering the treatment, for making the observations (tests, interviews, etc.) of behavior needed to estimate the effect of the treatment, and for other features of the experiment, as detailed in the next chapter. Implicit in the idea of an experimental design is the capability or power of the experimenter to control such matters as the design requires. Unless an experimenter has that power or can obtain it through negotiation and agreement on the part of everyone else involved, it will be impossible to carry out a properly designed experiment. As will be seen in later chapters, the failure to adhere to the design is the major threat to the integrity of an experiment. Some compromises with the requirements are more serious and more damaging than others. Almost all compromises involve some loss of information obtained from the experiment, but if the nature and extent of deviation from the design are known (and measurable), it may be possible to make adjustments in the analysis which will partially reduce such losses. On some occasions when an experimenter cannot exercise control over the situation, he can substitute a *quasi-experimental* design. Such designs are particularly appropriate when randomization of persons to treatments is partially compromised or unavailable.

Also important is the "answerability" of a question by an experiment. This breaks down into two components: the clarity and specificity of the treatment; and the reliability, validity, and relevance of the measures of outcome. Both of these, of course, assume the existence of a theoretical model of the intervention process, which guides the specifications of treatment and the contents of outcome measures.

Turning to measures, it seems clear that the more reliable, valid, and relevant a set of measures, the more dependable the answer yielded by the experiment will. *Reliability* refers to the consistency with which some behavior is measured from time to time in the same person, while *validity* refers to the extent to which a measure tests what it professes to test. *Relevance* calls attention to the fact that a valid test is not necessarily pertinent to the purposes of the experiment. In the absence of reliability, errors in measurement can be so great as to obscure real differences. In the absence of validity the test may be measuring something quite different from what it purports: response speed, for example, rather than comprehension of arithmetic principles. Even if comprehension of arithmetic principles is being measured, that measure may not be relevant to a program which purports to teach secretarial skills. There are many kinds of personal and social behavior for which reliable and valid measures are not currently available. Some concepts intrinsically defy operational measurement, whereas others are so complex that they must be decomposed into elements before they can be accurately measured. Social interventions may have purposes which exceed the grasp of social scientific measurement devices. Should one conduct experiments when the measurement outcomes are guaranteed to be uncertain? Probably not. On the other hand, one may ask whether some indirect measures of slightly lower relevance but of higher reliability and validity might be substituted for the unavailable measures. These would give some guidance that would point in a satisfactory direction, though falling short of perfection.

In regard to the specifiability of treatment, there is again an area of uncertainty. To the extent that one can state rather precisely what a particular treatment is intended to do and what its effective elements or components are believed to be as well as the theoretical grounds for holding such beliefs—to that extent one approaches almost an ideal state for experimentation. Such a well-specified treatment permits not only more sophisticated combinations of program elements, but also much more elaborate analysis of outcomes in relation to them. Sometimes, however, such specification cannot be achieved. The social intervention is of the character of a "black box" whose exact operation cannot be described, or for which there exists no suitable and convincing theoretical rationale. Would experiment still be justified in such a case? In general the answer is yes, provided that the cost of discovering whether or not a particular "black box" works is justified by the administrative, political, or institutional information that it provides. One may be quite willing to pay for the cost of learning whether performance contracting works or not, without, at the same time, learning why it does or does not work. This assertion does not minimize, however, the importance of experimenters trying to make explicit the theoretical and procedural rationale of social interventions. A specified treatment allows a much more powerful experimental test than does a "black box." Furthermore, specifying treatments helps to achieve comparability between different experimental sites or to permit exploitation of necessary variations from site to site for useful learning purposes. In other words, when an experimental treatment is repeated (replicated) it should be kept the same or deliberately and sytematically altered, rather than being allowed to vary haphazardly.

The idea of close and systematic control over what is done in a social experiment derives, of course, from the laboratory model of the scientific experiment in which the aim is to get as pure a test of the effect of a given variable (or combination of variables) as is possible. As pointed out previously (p. 18), the benefits reaped from a closely controlled "pure" test may incur some costs that a looser design may not. The latter may be more realistically representative of the actual treatment if and when it is instilled as a routine program, and, hence, the effects observed in the looser design will be more generalizable. Informed and expert opinion is not homogeneous in this matter. Whichever design is used, it is highly desirable that the treatment be specified in as much detail as possible.

Finally, the decision whether or not to do an experiment should depend upon whether available treatments are strong enough to produce measurable effects. As we have observed elsewhere (p. 20 and in Chapter VI), a great many social interventions seem, disappointingly enough, to have no effects—their thrust is dissipated, their effect negated by more powerful forces, their weight too little to counterbalance the social forces they are trying to overcome. An experiment probably should not be undertaken unless there is some reason to believe that the treatment proposed will have a detectable effect. Perhaps an exception to this rule should be made when there is considerable enthusiasm for an intervention about which there is little evidence (or dubious evidence) and it appears that a considerable social investment may be about to be made in it—as was the case of performance contracting in education.

Furthermore, in such cases, as in many others where the effect of the proposed treatment may be small, the intensity of treatment in the experimental version should not be limited to what is politically feasible or judged "reasonable" by common sense; for, if treatment effects are monotonic they should be easier to detect if a wider range or a bigger dose is used in the experiment. In other words, it may be important to find out whether a given treatment in any magnitude is effective, meanwhile recognizing that the effective level of treatment intensity may be administratively or politically unacceptable. Where there is any doubt, at least one treatment variation should be included which greatly magnifies the strength of the treatment under consideration. If in a remedial education program a pupil–teacher ratio of five to one is proposed, let there also be one variation in which the ratio is two pupils to one teacher, for example. Social ameliorists characteristically underestimate the strength of opposing social forces and overestimate the effectiveness of the treatments they propose.

*Administrative–Managerial Factors.*   In this section we turn our attention to the resources, both human and financial, that are necessary for the successful conduct of social experiments. The adequacy of the available resources is an essential consideration in deciding whether to experiment.

Since social experimentation is a relatively underdeveloped art, there is not a large body of experienced experimenters available, and correspondingly an even smaller number of organizations capable of mustering the scientific talent and managerial skill required. The range of talent needed is likely to be quite extensive. Personnel with skill in applied statistics and experimental design are of the essence. The experimental team should include at least one senior person who has had extensive experience in this area, though he need not have acquired it entirely in *social* experimentation. Statistical skills tend to generalize and if the statistician is coupled with another senior person who has substantive experience in the kind of social action (educational, welfare, criminal rehabilitation, psychotherapy, or other) under study, their combined talent may suffice. Since most social experimentation involves measurement of outcomes, it is important to have someone on the team with skill in econometrics, psychometrics, or a similar relevant topic.

A great many social experiments call for the use of sample survey techniques, and, in such cases, one member of the team should be experienced in this area. Ordinarily social experimentation requires a large team effort with a substantial body of paraprofessionals to conduct interviews, to administer psychological tests, or to collect other kinds of data. Managerial skill is required to recruit, train, and supervise such a team of paraprofessionals. In addition, the manager of field operations must have experience in record management, so the data can not only be collected and stored in a technically adequate way, but made available for retrieval and analysis. The technology of managing the storage and retrieval of a large quantity of records, especially on a longitudinal basis, is itself underdeveloped. It appears difficult to overemphasize this point. Virtually all professionals who have been directly associated with a large, longitudinal experiment have cautionary tales to tell about the difficulties, costs, and opportunities for error that data systems experience in such experiments. They are unanimous in concluding that someone with a great deal of experience in computerizing record storage and analysis is an essential member of the team. Finally, the leader or some other member of the research team must be capable of conducting sometimes lengthy and extensive negotiations with the action team that will develop and administer the experimental treatment, in order to maximize the amount of agreement on objectives and on the technique of assessing outcomes.

At least three identifiable parties are involved in most social experiments. One party consists of the developers or executors of the treatment (the treatment administrator or "action team"). Ordinarily they are identified with the treatment and hopeful of its success, if not convinced a priori of its effectiveness. If they are not so at the beginning, they very often become so before the experiment is over.

Because of their involvement, the action team should not be given the responsibility for measuring the outcome. Rather, this responsibility should be assigned to a second party, which we identify, for the sake of convenience, as the "designer–researcher team." It should be administratively separated from the action team, either through being located in a totally separate organization or in a different compartment of the agency in whose interest the experiment is being carried out (the "sponsor"). The relationship between the action team and the research team is treated extensively in Chapters VI and VII and the intricacies of that nexus are summarized only briefly here. It must be at one and the same time intimate and distant—close enough to negotiate a mutual understanding of treatment objectives and agreement on how they are to be measured; yet distant enough to maintain the objectivity of measurement and the integrity of the research design. This posture leads to the necessity to negotiate operational definitions of treatment objectives so that all three parties to the experiment enter it with as much agreement as possible on these major issues. Finally, a clear and enforceable agreement should be negoiated which specifies how the treatment is to be administered and under what conditions deviations from that set of specifications will be allowed by the research team. Experience with social experiments has shown repeatedly that, as the a priori ideas of treatment are tested in the actual administration of treatment, the expectations, convictions, and knowledge on the part of the action team change considerably, with the understandable result that they wish to change ("improve") treatment. Whether such changes are tolerable from the point of view of experimental design depends too much on the specific details of the experiment to offer a judgment here. Sometimes it is possible to reach a compromise in which the original treatment is retained for some subset of the treated population, while a revised treatment is added to the experimental design and this permits both preserving the intactness of experimental design and allowing for creativity and revision on the part of the action team.

The sponsoring agency also has some tests of adequacy which it must meet before it engages in social experimentation. It should have on its in-house staff some competence both in experimental technology and in the substance of the behavioral realm to be studied. Such competence is necessary in order for the sponsor to be able: to prepare intelligible and realistic requests for proposal; to evaluate or to establish adequate evaluation machinery for the review of proposals received; and finally, to monitor the performance of the research and the action teams during the course of the experiment to make sure that both are living up to specifications. Without such in-house competence, the sponsor can be victimized by inadequately prepared proposals, pretentious claims, unrealistic aspirations, and inadequate performance. The art of social experimentation is young and its competent practitioners few; there are bound to be inadequately qualified individuals and organizations who rush in to fill the supply vacuum when the demand rises.

Finally, a comment on the competence of academic social scientists to perform applied experiments. The fact that an individual has eminence as a contributor to a disciplinary field in social science is not a guarantee that he will possess the range of talent, skill, and experience required for successful social experimentation. Sometimes, in fact, individuals of lesser *academic* distinction but with a broader range of interests in social policy and applied research may be a better choice. Unfortunately, at the present state of development of social experimentation, it is difficult to attract and retain first-class intellectual talent in organizations that might perform social experiments. There is not a clear career line; there is no dependably continuous employment; and perhaps most significant of all, there is no prestige and recognition structure analogous to that which attends outstanding performance in academic social science. For these reasons we have recommended that there be supported on a substantial professional and financial basis some independent research institutions whose personnel would be composed of the kinds of talents and skills outlined earlier and which might be expected to engage serially in a wide variety of social experiments for various sponsoring agencies. The character of such institutions is specified in Chapter VII; unless or until they are created, the burden of first-class work in social experimentation will fall on the very small number of government research agency divisions, academically based applied social research institutes, and independent profit or nonprofit corporations with the primary mission of social research. Some of the existing organizational resources are entirely adequate, though many are overburdened; others are technically underdeveloped; almost all are financially insecure. We recommend that the best of these should be strengthened, both professionally and financially, and that consideration be given to creating new institutions.

It is difficult to give detailed advice on financial requirements for social experimentation because of the very considerable variability in major components: the costs of central scientific and managerial staff, which may run from 3 or 4 to as many as 15 or 20 senior professionals; the costs of data collection, which vary with the extensiveness and frequency of surveys, tests, or other observations; the costs of administering the treatment per se, which can vary from highly sophisticated operations performed by trained professionals, or substantial money payments or other material provisions, to very simple and inexpensive treatments administered by paraprofessionals of modest skill and training; and, finally, the length of time over which the experimental treatment is continued, and the number of subjects as well as the number of sites on which treatment and measurement of controls are carried out. Efforts to secure dependable information about costs in recent social experiments have been frustrated by the absence of a commonly used accounting method as well as by complex interinstitutional arrangements for the financing of treatment administration separately from data collection. Accounting for the costs of central professional, managerial, and administrative staff is one difficult problem, for these costs are sometimes hidden in institutional subsidies, as are some kinds of facilities costs. In like fashion, the costs of treatment administration are partially absorbed or hidden in routine institutional operations; examples of this are found in educational experimentation. Accordingly, we make no attempt to report here the rather uneven data we have obtained, but make one further comment based on examining a number of social experiments.

It appears that the principal difference in cost between social experiments and nonexperimental social research is in the cost of treatment administration. Whatever it costs to make welfare payments to experimental groups, to counsel, instruct, feed, or play with them is the principal additional cost of an experiment. Such costs would, of course, be incurred in a "demonstration" project instituted prior to installation of a national program. Most of the *research* costs in a social experiment are geared to the character of the data collection process and the time over which it extends, rather than to any special feature of experimentation as a method.

It is, of course, possible to conduct useful experiments at quite low cost. As pointed out earlier, the Manhattan Bail Bond experiment cost less than $200,000 and numerous short-term educational experiments have cost less than $50,000. The idea of social experimentation should not be automatically associated with a high-cost, long-term operation. Many experiments that are concerned with weighty matters will (and should) cost very nearly what experiments in medicine and physical science cost. Information on which major social decisions are partly based should be as dependable and as accurate as we know how to make it. It is unwise public policy to save dollars at the risk of having to rely upon undependable knowledge.

REANALYSIS AND REPLICATION

Finally we suggest some guidelines for the reanalysis and replication of social experiments. When an experiment is concerned with a socially significant matter, and when it produces results that are controversial, we strongly recommend a policy of freedom of information needed for reanalysis. Experimental results should be available in a timely fashion and access to data should be permitted to responsible and competent professionals for use in reanalysis. While recognizing that the original principal investigator has limited proprietary rights to the data, it is our conviction that free access for reanalysis will not only serve to increase the original investigator's sense of responsibility for careful and competent work, as well as exposing distortion and misrepresentation if it should occur, but will also help to advance the state of the art. We recognize that there are many technical aspects of data collection and analysis about which experts genuinely and honestly disagree. There may be unknown and unobserved errors in interpretation, and there may even be effects and outcomes that are undetected in the original analysis. The same line of reasoning suggests that in crucial decisions, provision should be made for replication of the original experiment (or replication with systematic variation), if that is possible, by responsible and competent alternative investigators. At the same time, we would defend the right of the original investigator to resist pressures to make data available in midexperiment if, in his judgment, this would damage the subsequent course of the experiment, or if there is good reason to believe that preliminary data are incomplete and might result in misleading conclusions. Because social experimentation is designed to shape public social policy, the public has a corresponding right to know whether the experiment has been well conducted and whether its results are dependable. But this right to know should not result in harassment or interference with the ongoing experiment. Clearly, some more detailed guidelines should be developed for the release and reanalysis of data arising from social experiments.

One further comment on reanalysis and replication is appropriate. It is important to undertake "cross-validation" after a social experiment has been successful and a policy decision has been made to institute the program on a national scale. At this point, a monitoring operation in the form of a quasi-experiment (See Chapter IV) should be designed to check whether the treatment effects observed during the experiment persist into the routinization phase of the program. Such a check may substantiate the findings of the experimental phase, but it may also lead to discovering additional conditions and contingencies that were unnoticed in the experiment or help to detect flaws and failures in the administration of the ongoing program.

# III

# Experimental Design
# and Analysis

An experimental *design* is a plan for conducting an experiment. The plan includes deciding how to assign experimental *units* (e.g., persons, classrooms, cities) to *treatments* (e.g., to welfare programs, or educational innovations) or in each case, to a no-treatment (i.e., "control") condition; and deciding what measurements to make of the behavior of the units; especially, how to measure their responses to the treatment. The techniques for making such assignments and some of the matters to be considered in making such decisions are the subjects of this chapter. It is also concerned with how to analyze the data collected during the experiment, and how to interpret results.

The intent of what follows is to provide a general introduction to experimental design for administrators and managers of social programs who may be considering social experimentation and who wish to have a grasp of general principles but do not need to master the technical details. The chapter also tries to dispel some erroneous ideas and to discredit misleading notions. What follows is as accurate as we know how to make it without being overly precise and pedantic; at the same time it is necessarily incomplete, and almost guaranteed to provoke criticisms of omission from statisticians and other professionals. We have chosen to aim at a nonprofessional audience, however. We have tried to make the exposition clear and informative enough to let the members of that audience know when they will need competent professional advice, why they need it and, as far as possible, how to interact more effectively with professionals and technicians in experimental design and analysis. The chapter introduces and illustrates some of the major ideas in experimental design and analysis, as well as explaining why certain technical issues are important and need special attention.

We note, also, that the prescription for experimental design is idealized. That is, in practice experimenters will encounter operational problems in implementing it and perhaps economic or political obstacles as well. The recommendation therefore must be to come as close as possible to the ideal requirements of design, especially in regard to randomization.

The design of an experiment and its analysis are interrelated. Indeed it is often said that one should not do an experiment without knowing how it is going to be analyzed. In most large and lengthy social experiments, this dictum certainly cannot be obeyed literally, but it becomes all the more important to be as foresighted as possible. Careful thought, in the design phase, about the analysis, even though it may be several years off, may vastly improve the experiment, or even save it from being unanalyzable waste. Someone competent in the field of statistics should be involved from the beginning in any serious experiment.

It might seem logical, in view of these comments, to discuss analysis before design. In fact, however, the ideas of design can be understood qualitatively without discussion of analysis, while the latter has much more substance if design has been discussed first, as it will be here.

The first section describes the essential nature and components of an experiment. The second section discusses experimental error, and distinguishes between systematic and random components of error. It also distinguishes between two purposes in experimentation: fairly comparing two or more treatments on the one hand; and, on the other, accurately measuring the average effect of a treatment in some very specific population. The aim of experimental design is to reduce both the sytematic and random components of the relevant experimental error. The third section explains randomization while the fourth presents the main ideas behind blocking, factorial designs, and covariates. A brief discussion of how big an experiment to do constitutes the fifth section. The remainder of the chapter concerns statistical analysis, in particular, statistical inference and the analysis of bias in attrition.

## Components of an Experiment

As pointed out in Chapter I, the essence of an experiment is that two or more treatments are applied to experimental units in accordance with some chosen plan; that one or more response variables are measured; and that randomization is employed in the assignment of units to treatments in such a way that inferences can be drawn about the treatment effects without fear of systematic error due to the assignment, and the level of uncertainty in the inferences can be calculated.

For example, to compare two types of day care (the treatments), we might set up 10 day-care centers (the experimental units) and separate them into five pairs (perhaps on the basis of convenience); pick one center of each pair at random for type A day care by flipping a coin; assign the other to type B; and measure some response on the part of the children in each center (for example, a measure of intellective performance). (See Table 3.1.)

The first question the experimenter is trying to answer is which type of center produces superior results on the response variable, but he typically puts the question in the following form: If the two treatments were equally effective, what is the likelihood that one of them would show consistently better outcomes? If that likelihood is small and if one type does show consistently better outcomes, then the inference is justified that they are not, in fact, equivalent but one type is better.

Thus if, in the example, it turned out that in every pair the type A center produced better results than the type B, it would be reasonable to conclude that type A was really superior because the probability of getting a result so favorable to A would be only 1/32 if A were in fact equivalent to B (because there are 32 possible outcomes of the experiment but there is only one in which type A is better than type B in *every*

**TABLE 3.1**

**Possible Day-Care Experiment**

| | Pair 1 | Pair 2 | Pair 3 | Pair 4 | Pair 5 |
|---|---|---|---|---|---|
| | Center 1 Treatment B | Center 3 Treatment A | Center 5 Treatment A | Center 7 Treatment B | Center 9 Treatment B |
| | Center 2 Treatment A | Center 4 Treatment B | Center 6 Treatment B | Center 8 Treatment A | Center 10 Treatment A |
| Coin: | Tails | Heads | Heads | Tails | Tails |

pair). This probability measures the security of the inference that A is better than B, or the confidence one can place in the obtained result of the experiment. If, on the other hand, the type A center turned out to give better results in only four of the five pairs, one could place much less confidence in the superiority of A, for the relevant probability is then 6/32. In fact, a cautious analyst would conclude that the superiority of A had not been demonstrated and that the inference: "no difference between the types" (called by statisticians the "null hypothesis") was tenable. It is important to emphasize that this kind of thinking about the problem, and the calculation of such probabilities, relies on the random assignment of units to treatments. With any other kind of assignment there would always be the possibility that the apparent superiority of A merely reflected some bias in the assignment, and there would be no convincing way to relate a probability to the inference that A is superior.

This example illustrates only the bare essentials of the experimental model. A real experiment would be more complicated. The pairs of centers would be chosen to be as well matched as possible, and the design might be more elaborate, to allow, say, for comparing the effects of treatments on children from different socioeconomic classes, or for the length of time treatment was applied. It would be prudent to measure a number of responses—the health, physical vigor, and emotional responsiveness of the children as well as the employment and earnings of mothers and the stability of families. Inferences about outcomes would be multiple and might have to be qualified by the possibility of biases in measurement, for instance. The experimenter might also be interested in the amount by which one treatment was superior. But his aim would be to approximate as closely as possible in the real experiment, the essential features of random assignment of units to treatments and the unbiased measurement of responses.

The reader's understanding of the design of experiments will perhaps be enlarged by a fuller discussion, with illustrations, of the principal components of an experiment.

The *treatments* might be, for example, special rehabilitative programs involving therapy, drugs, or education; income supplementation schemes, as in the Negative Income Tax experiments; alternative judicial or administrative procedures, as in the Manhattan Bail Bond experiment; educational programs, as in the performance contracting experiment to accelerate first graders' learning to read; alternative day-care arrangements in a possible day-care experiment.

Care is required in deciding how the treatment is to be defined in order to appreciate the limits to which it can be expected to apply if repeated or extended into routine programmatic use. It is not appropriate simply to record exactly what was done in a particular situation (even if this were possible) and to call that the treatment, for such a record might well incorporate both accidental and idiosyncratic events as well as the constant, intended features of the treatment as designed; and inferences about the effects of such a "treatment" would validly apply only to a detailed copy of the original version. The definition of the treatment should include the essential features of whatever procedure is employed—"essential features" here being understood to be those elements of the treatment procedure which remained constant in the experiment and would in future application, and which are intended to bring about the effects sought. For example, the essential features of the treatment in the Negative Income Tax experiment consist of the income supplement, the rate at which it is reduced as earned income rises, the requirement that subjects report income periodically, and the structure of the households participating (intact families with employable male heads).

The treatment is not defined to embrace any differential influence that particular interviewers of the participants may have on how they dispose of income, or any attitudes or conduct that participants'neighbors may display, or any systematic variation in participants' ethnicity. Such factors (and others excluded from the treatment definition are presumed to vary randomly and to be handled by randomization in assignment; or to be unimportant or uninfluential in affecting the outcome of the experiment.

One need not necessarily specify all aspects of the treatment rigidly in advance. For example, the treatments might be simply sets of instructional materials which each teacher is allowed to adapt at will. If two such sets of materials are assigned at random to classrooms, each classroom having its own teacher, an inference could be made about the difference in effectiveness between the two sets, which might reasonably be thought to carry over to other teachers in other classrooms. One could not, however, infer that adaptations made in response to the particular situation in the experimental classrooms would spontaneously arise in other situations, so these adaptations should not be made part of the treatment definition. Adaptations made in response to recurring problems which will ordinarily be handled in the same way, such as failing to repeat lessons missed by pupils absent for illness, may be made part of the treatment definition, since their effect can be assumed to be the same in other situations. One must use judgment in this matter, and be cautious about making the latter assumption. Adaptations which neither are made on a unit-by-unit basis nor are constant in their effect may contribute to systematic error and/or underestimation of inferential uncertainty. Avoiding this generally requires careful advance specification of the treatments.

The word "treatment" applies to the control treatment as well as to the active treatments. It is usually necessary to include *controls* in an experiment—that is, some units receiving a *control treatment*. This may be either no special attention at all but simply retaining the status quo; or a "placebo" (dummy) treatment which might include observation or measurement of characteristics and behavior but no deliberate effort to influence them; or some other minimal treatment. For example, in an educational experiment to teach children concepts of spatial relations, the minimal treatment used as a control was to have a teacher spend a period in play with the child but not engage in any didactic activity. The control treatment for a Negative Income Tax experiment is simply to interview families that are not receiving income supplements.

*Control units* are essential to permit the inference that an observed treatment effect would not have occurred even in the absence of the treatment, and to provide a base line from which to measure treatment effects. If random assignment is to serve its purpose, it must apply to the control treatment as well as the active treatments. The power of an experiment can be greatly enhanced by clever choice of controls. (See, for instance, the discussion of "blocking" in the section of this chapter entitled "Reducing Random Error.") This does not mean that a treatment effect can be increased, but that it can be measured more accurately for the same cost.

Sometimes considerable thought is needed in defining a suitable control. For example, is the control treatment for headache remedies no treatment, a placebo, or aspirin? In a day-care experiment for children of working mothers, is it minimal day care at a center, the mother's normal arrangement, the arrangement she would make if given cash equal to the cost of minimal day care, or something else? There may be more than one benchmark of interest, and hence more than one control treatment may be needed. Notice that control is not simply the absence of treatment. In a nutrition experiment, starvation is not an appropriate control treatment.

Sometimes there is no way to avoid partially treating the controls in the process of selection or measurement. For example, the interviewing or compensation of controls may itself be a relevant treatment for the responses being measured. Nevertheless, such controls may be a reasonable benchmark, and are much better than none.

Occasionally no control is possible in the ordinary sense, as when a program must be made available to all eligible units. It may still be useful and possible to conduct an experiment in this context by deliberately varying the intensity of treatment. If greatly increasing the intensity of treatment beyond the standard level has no additional effect, then it may be doubtful whether the standard treatment has any effect. Similarly, it would be wise to include a *less* intensive variation in the design to learn whether lowering the intensity of treatment somewhat would appreciably reduce the effect. No matter how the experiment may turn out, it would seem prudent to vary the intensity of treatment over at least a range that illustrates what is programmatically feasible.

The purpose of an experiment, as opposed to a demonstration, for instance, is to test whether the treatments really have any appreciable effects, and if so, to measure them. For this purpose, some *response* variables must be chosen and measurement methods set up. (This important topic is discussed extensively in Chapter V.) The *effect* of a treatment with respect to any particular response variable is ordinarily measured as a difference from the control treatment. Treatments may have, and often are expected to have, several types of effects, so it may be in order to measure many kinds of response, including unwanted side effects. If, however, the responses which can be measured and the statistical power of the experiment are such that the result of the experiment—be it the apparent presence or absence of measurable effects— is unlikely to change the opinion of any important audience, then it is doubtful that the experiment should be done at all.

The experimental *units* may be people, households, city blocks, schools, or even whole states. For example, in certain proposed experiments with police behavior, experimental units are precincts; in many educational experiments the actual experimental units are classrooms; and in the Manhattan Bail Bond experiment, people were the units of analysis. Geographic areas may constitute experimental units, with entire villages being used as experimental units, for example, in experiments on nutrition and mental development.

The essential point is that is should be possible to assign a particular treatment to one unit without restricting the choice of the treatment of any other unit. This is necessary to permit random assignment of treatments to units. For example, a driving safety campaign involving newspaper or radio advertising cannot ordinarily be carried out on less than a citywide basis. If such a campaign is one treatment, and, say, the status quo is another, then the experimental unit is not an individual driver, even though he receives the treatment, because the treatment of one driver cannot be changed without changing that of all other drivers in the same city. The experimental unit would therefore be a city, and a true experiment would involve random assignment of whole cities to the two treatments. Furthermore, it is essential that units be capable of responding independently (of each other) to treatment. For example, if 200 soldiers are randomly assigned to view one of two training films, but there are obvious audience influences on the way the films are perceived, attended to, or evaluated, then the experiment may truly consist of 2 rather than 200 units. The individual soldiers have probably not responded independently of their neighbors' responses.

It is also essential that the response variables be measured separately on each unit, or at some level below the unit. For example, one could measure the birthrate of individual families within neighborhoods, provided the analysis recognized that the experimental units were still neighborhoods and did not treat the families as independent units. One could not, however, aggregate neighborhoods in measuring birthrate without also enlarging the experimental units to the neighborhood (i.e., the aggregate) level. The influence of the choice of experimental units on measurement methods will be discussed further in Chapter V.

A large number of small units ordinarily provides a more powerful experiment than a small number of large units, even though the total number of persons treated is the same. It is therefore generally desirable to make the experimental units as small as possible, subject to the requirement that independent (of each other) units can be randomly assigned to separate treatments, because more independent information will result. Furthermore, for purposes of statistical analysis, the size of an experiment is the number of units, not the total number of people involved. Thus, if 4000 fourth grade pupils are to be involved in an experiment, a statistician would prefer that they be assigned as 4000 units in the randomization, rather than as 160 classes of 25 each, or 32 schools of 125 each.

The statistical desideratum of large numbers of randomized units often has to be compromised in favor of other considerations. To randomly withdraw some pupils from a classroom creates an awkwardness and awareness of special treatment which may reduce comparability with those future regular classrooms one wants to be able to generalize to. Such a process also requires extra classroom space, and more supervisory help. There are thus good practical and scientific grounds for randomization at the classroom level, assigning whole classrooms to one treatment or another. In this case, randomization by classroom seems the desirable option, although randomization by child is also feasible. In other instances the alternative of randomization at the person level may be essentially impossible.

Take the day-care program example. One might well end up with *nine* separate experimental programs to be compared: three instructional modes each tried out at three levels of staff–child ratios. Each is to be located within walking distance of the children it serves. It is inconceivable to set up all nine experimental programs in each experimental neighborhood and randomly assign applicant children (by family) to each. One might set up two in each neighborhood and in 36 neighborhoods achieve a pairing of each type with each of the others. But juxtaposition of centers with such different levels of funding would cause parent and staff complaint sufficient to jeopardize the program. In the end, one is forced to a random assignment of sites to treatments, blocking prior to randomization on city (where large enough to contain all nine), poverty level, type of economy, etc. One might hope for four exemplifications of each of the nine treatment combinations, for a total of 36 day-care centers.

The type of effects one is examining also affects the type of unit selected. If individual effects are under study, then the individual person is usable as a unit, but one can also, as we have seen, use larger units, such as classrooms or centers. But if a group effect or a neighborhood effect is under study, then the unit of randomization must be at least equally aggregated. For example, one of the issues in the New Jersey Income Maintenance experiment was the effect on neighborhoods, on local retail sales, and on employment. Another problem was the probable differential reaction of a recipient when he was the only one of his equally poor neighbors receiving the treatment, as opposed to a setting in which all of his eligible neighbors were likewise receiving equivalent income transfers. Both of these considerations argued for random assignment of compact poverty communities to treatments, rather than families. This alternative was not feasible because of a combination of design, statistical, and cost considerations. With eight different experimental treatments (various combinations of income maintenance levels and taxation rates), with the available discrete communities often having as many as 100 eligible families, and with funds projected for only some 600 experimental families, there was not a sufficient number of units to make randomization effective. Hence, a judgmental selection was made of several poverty areas, and families resident therein were randomly assigned to treatments. It may also be worth noting that compact treatment areas would have represented larger political plums for the recipient cities, and this would have been more of a political bone of contention in the site selection process.

It may be possible to use smaller units than at first appears. For example, birth control programs have been conducted in special areas within large cities of nonmobile populations. An experiment on family planning in Taiwan (Freedman, Takeshita *et al.*, 1967) made successful efforts to randomly allocate different combinations of birth control information and services to some 2400 neighborhoods in one province.

A final remark on choice of units points to something which is obvious once it has been said. Many social interventions (and their experimental treatment counterparts) are believed to vary in effectiveness depending upon some characteristic of the experimental unit. For example, a program to teach children to read through monetary rewards for performance might reasonably be expected to be more effective for children from poor families than from rich families and most effective for children who have the smallest disposable incomes. An experiment to test the effects of money incentives should be designed to include a large enough (for statistical purposes) group of children from very poor families, even if this requires special efforts to locate such children and recruit them into the experiment. (These specially recruited children would, of course, be randomly assigned to experimental and control treatments.) If the treatment is shown not to be effective for those units judged to be most susceptible, it is probably not effective at all.

The advice to include such a specially selected group of units in an experiment runs parallel to the idea of including, as well, an extremely intensive treatment in order to learn whether the treatment is at all effective under the most favorable circumstances. Past experience with social intervention programs suggests that often the treatment is weak in comparison to the restraining forces of everyday life which affect the treated units—a little job counseling is a weak counterforce against lack of skill, poverty, low morale, and a tight labor market, for example. Accordingly, it may be worthwhile to experiment with a greatly increased intensity of treatment—even if such a level of treatment could not be provided on a regular basis in the program—just to see if it is effective. Extreme treatments and extremely susceptible units will not give an unbiased estimate of an "average" treatment effect, but they may be useful in detecting completely ineffective treatments.

## Experimental Error

If everything could be held constant except the treatments, and if the treatment effects could be measured perfectly, then one could determine exactly what the treatment effects were under the experimental conditions. Unfortunately, reality is not so simple, at least in the social sphere. Even without special problems such as attrition (i.e., the loss of subjects from the experiment during its course), the experimenter usually faces variability among the experimental units, in environmental conditions, in the actual application of the defined treatments, and in the measurement of the responses. That is, all the pupils in first grade classrooms are not alike in ability, nor are the physical conditions of their classrooms the same, and teachers will vary in the way they execute the treatment program of the experiment. Besides these sources of variability, there may also be systematic errors arising from the introduction of bias into the experimental design—for example, providing experimental treatment to volunteers and allowing nonvolunteers to serve as controls; or using tests and measures that favor higher socioeconomic status groups; or selecting experimental units that do not represent the target population of the experiment.

All of the sources of variability contribute to error in estimating the effect of a treatment, but statisticians distinguish between purely accidental sources of error (*random error*) and systematic sources of error (*bias*). The random components of experimental error do not consistently favor one treatment over another. Consequently, for example, no matter how the intellectual ability of first graders is distributed among the children of a city, an experiment in which first graders are assigned at random to experimental or control treatments is likely to wind up with quite similar distributions of intellectual ability in both treatments, provided the number of children is fairly large. Any difference between the groups in intellectual ability would be attributable to chance, or random error. It is this kind of error that statistical analytic procedures can handle by providing an estimate of it and putting "confidence limits" around the estimate of treatment effect.

Systematic error, or bias, however, cannot be so easily handled statistically at the end of the experiment, but requires thought and care in the design stage. In fact, standard methods of statistical analysis ignore biases and cannot detect the presence of constant measurement errors. For example, it has been repeatedly found that some kinds of wording of questions in an interview or questionnaire will bias responses: negatively phrased questions tend to elicit more negative material than positively phrased questions. Another frequently reported source of bias is a seeming tendency on the part of respondents to agree rather than disagree with a consistent positive or negative tone of a series of questions—acquiescence bias. Such biases as these can be prevented or minimized, but not through the application of any purely statistical technique. They call for careful design of measuring instruments and familiarity with their problems.

For many sources of variability, the experimental design affects how much of the variability goes into systematic error, how much goes into random error, and how much is eliminated. For example, if an experimental program were tried in first grades in one part of a city, with the rest of the city as control, then differences between schools in the two parts of the city would contribute to systematic error. The reason is that family income (hence, socioeconomic status and its concomitant variable, educational level of parents) is not distributed at random to the geography of a city. If experimental units are chosen from only one part of a city a systematic error will be introduced into the estimate of treatment effects because of the biased selection of units. If the experimental group were chosen randomly from all first grades, then differences between schools, including differences between parts of the city, would contribute to random error but not to systematic error. If pairs of first grades in the same school were assigned randomly, one to treatment and one to control, then with an appropriate analysis, the main differences between schools would be eliminated entirely from the error in the treatment–control comparison. In all three cases, any variations in the treatment effect from school to school would contribute to error, as would differences between first grades in the same school.

How important is it that the units in an experiment be an unbiased sample of the target population? We speak now not of random assignment of units to treatments, but rather of random selection of the participants (whether experimentals or controls) from the population toward which a social intervention program is aimed. Should an experimenter take pains to obtain a representative sample of the target population?

The answer depends upon the purpose of the experiment: Is it concerned purely with making a fair comparison between treatments? Or is it concerned with estimating the average size of the effect in the specific target population? If the latter, then the representativeness of the experimental population is important, and this leads to difficulties. In most large-scale social experiments it is infeasible to sample randomly from the ultimate target population of the treatments being studied, and hence to obtain statistical representativeness. Fortunately the main purpose of such experiments usually depends on comparison rather than representativeness, for the purpose is to see whether a treatment does or does not have an effect of practical importance. For this purpose it suffices to make a fair comparison of the treatment with a control treatment in circumstances favorable to the possibility that the treatment has an effect. If its effect under these circumstances appears nonexistent, or too small to have practical importance, then lack of representativeness has not hurt. If it seems to have an important effect, the experimenter will ordinarily be concerned with what kinds of people it can benefit by how much, but very rarely would he be so far along in a cost–benefit calculation as to need an experimental design and analysis strictly representative of a specific target population.

In general, however, we believe that social experiments are likely to be concerned with making fair comparisons between treatments rather than making population estimates of effects; accordingly we shall assume in the remainder of this book that representativeness of the experimental sample is not likely to be an important consideration in experimental design.

## *Randomization*

Earlier portions of this book have stressed the importance of randomization in order to eliminate bias in assigning experimental units to treatments, and an earlier section of this chapter illustrated a particularly simple instance of a randomized experimental design, as well as calculating the probability of an assumed outcome. In that illustration, the 10 day-care centers were divided into pairs, and the experimenter flipped a coin to decide which center in each pair received the experimental treatment. (Had the pairs been composed by matching them in respect to socioeconomic status of their catchment area, the power of the experiment could have been improved without affecting the fundamental randomization requirement.)

If the design had called for five sets of three centers each, with two control centers and one treated center in each set of three, random assignment would have meant picking at random one from each set of three to receive the treatment, with the other two as controls. In this case it might have been more convenient to use a table of random numbers instead of flipping a coin to make the assignment. Each center in a triad would be numbered 1, 2, or 3. Starting anywhere in the random number table, the experimenter might have followed a rule directing him to assign the experimental treatment to whichever unit number he next encountered in the table. Thus for the random number sequence 71803 26825 05511 and triads A B C D E, the experimental units would have been A1 B3 C2 D2 E1. With still more complicated designs, the randomization process is more complicated, but the idea is the same. In every case, no one can doubt the fairness of the process by which the units are assigned to the treatments, and no bias is involved.

The primary source of variability in most experiments is the variability among the experimental units. Correspondingly, the primary randomization is the random assignment of units to treatments, including the control treatment. This insures that the treatment groups are comparable, except for chance variations, and that such variations will not systematically favor any treatment over any other. Moreover, if other sources of variability (including events occuring *after* randomization) are linked exclusively to the experimental units but not to the treatments, these sources will also contribute to random rather than systematic error as long as there has been random assignment of units to treatments. For example, if the units are day-care centers and some are closed for part of the year because of bad weather, or if there is turnover in the staff, then as long as these events would have occurred regardless of the treatment, their contribution to error will be random as a result of the random assignment of units to treatments.

On the other hand, if staff turnover is consistently higher in one treatment, it is likely to be attributable to some feature of the treatment which the staff dislike. It should then be considered either as a treatment effect or as a source of systematic bias rather than as random error. Likewise, if the staff of a day-care center are recruited before treatments are randomly assigned to centers, then variation in quality of staff can be considered to have been randomly distributed in relation to treatment and this source of variability can be considered random error. Whereas, if the staff are recruited *after* assignment of treatments, and if one treatment appears to attract a higher (or lower) quality of staff, then this source of variability must be considered systematic.

Furthermore, introducing randomization into any other component of the experiment (not only into assignment of treatments to units) will shift some errors from systematic to random. Thus, sources of variability not linked to the experimental units, whether related to environmental conditions, the process of delivering the treatment, or the measurement of effects, can sometimes be made purely random rather than partly systematic by additional randomizations. For example, the time or place at which the treatments are carried out might be randomized if it is neither determined by the experimental units nor part of the definition of the treatments. Similar considerations apply to the measurement process, especially if it is partly subjective. Even apparently quite objective questionnaires may give results which differ systematically depending on the interviewer's expectations, sex, race, friendliness, etc. Randomness in the assignment of interviewers to subjects may greatly reduce or eliminate bias from these sources.

It may be possible to do still better by a carefully designed nonrandom assignment which equalizes the treatments in regard to time or place of application or to interviewers and thus eliminate their effects from the random error as well as from the bias. Not all bias can be eliminated by either means: If most interviewers favor one treatment and they know the treatment received by the respondent, then a bias may well arise which neither randomization nor equalization will eliminate. Such problems, and in particular "blind" measurement, are discussed extensively in Chapter V.

A further benefit of randomization in comparative experiments is that it reduces the plausibility of alternative explanations and increases the plausibility of the inference that the treatment was actually the cause of the effect observed. The argument is this: Suppose again that in each of five pairs, one unit was chosen at random for treatment and, that, in every pair, the unit thus treated gave the higher response. This observed effect is beyond what could reasonably occur by chance in the absence of any true effect. If this is to be explained in some alternative way, not as cause and effect, there must have been a remarkable coincidence (probability 1/32) between the random drawing and the alternative explanation. Of course, this does not rule out explanations in terms of components of error arising in such a way that they were not subject to randomization. This illustrates, again, the reason why the reduction of systematic errors requires so much attention.

Not only do those components of error subject to randomization contribute solely to random and not to systematic error, so that they are fully reflected in the statistical analysis, but randomization also plays a role in the justification of the resulting probability statements expressing the uncertainty of the inferences drawn from the experiments. In the foregoing example, the randomization played a direct role in the probability statement through a statistical procedure making overt use of it. More often it plays an indirect role in the probability statements of statistical inference by helping assure that the assumptions upon which the statistical analysis is based are at least approximately satisfied. (See also the "Statistical Inference" section later in this chapter.)

IMPLEMENTING RANDOMIZED ASSIGNMENT

The procedure described previously for randomly assigning 10 day-care centers to experimental or control treatment is appropriate for a simple situation with a small number of units to be treated. When assignment must be made from a larger pool of eligible units, or when the individual units are grouped in some fashion (e.g., by geographical location, age, grade, etc.) the process is mechanically more complicated but fundamentally identical to the simple procedure. Two broad strategies of randomization are important where these natural groupings occur: batch randomization and sequential (or trickle) randomization. Batch randomization, the more simple process, is described in the next few paragraphs; the need for sequential randomization is determined primarily by managerial constraints on the experiment, and is discussed in Chapter VI.

The first requisite for randomized allocation from an available group is to get as *complete* a list as possible of the eligible units, for example, a list of persons, families, classrooms, schools, precincts, or whatever is applicable. If a reasonably *complete* list does not exist, it will have to be created, perhaps through direct enumeration, for incomplete lists are usually biased (see also Chapter VI).

Assume for the moment that such a list is available, whether a voter registration list, a school attendance roster, or a list of administrative units; each unit in the list must have or be given a unique number. Identification numbers are acceptable and so are addresses even if there are gaps in the numbering system or if only a few of the possible numbers are used, for the only requirement of the numbering system is that there be no duplications or repetitions. If such unique identifying numbers have to be created, this may be done in the easiest way possible. For example, if there were 25 short lists already numbered within each list, with list length ranging from 12 to 57, one would assign 2-digit numbers to the lists (1 through 25) and combine these with the already existing within-list numbers to create 4-digit identification numbers (with many gaps). In this manner, street numbers, office numbers within buildings, and so forth can be used as components of identification numbers.

The next step is to use a table of random numbers (Kendall and Smith, 1954; Rand Corp., 1955) to guide the selection of the sample from within the lists. Instructions for the use of random number tables are provided in the tables themselves or in texts (e.g., Kish, 1967).

The use of the prepared tables of random numbers is usually superior to mechanical randomization processes such as dice, shuffled cards, spinners, roulette wheels, and urns of balls. These mechanical devices frequently do not yield the near perfect randomization necessary in high quality experiments. In the 1970 Draft Lottery, for example, there is strong evidence that the capsules had not been well stirred, that birthdates in the early months of the year were much too frequent among early numbers drawn (Fienberg, 1971).

Where public drawings by participants or their representatives seem useful in securing acceptance of a random decision process, extreme care should be taken to devise one unlikely to be biased by inadequate shuffling or stirring. We do recognize the value of such public procedures. If the lists involved are already haphazard initially and a mechanical randomization is superimposed, the total procedure has minimal likelihood of being biased. If a list is technically random, so is the total procedure. Alphabetized lists are often essentially random for some purposes. Fienberg (1971) discusses the several procedures designed to improve the randomness of public drawing of draft numbers.

Sometimes randomization may produce an assignment which seems too unbalanced to be suitable. For example, in an experiment assigning 90 parolees to a supplementary counseling program, it turned out that all 8 of the drug offenders among the 90 ended up by random assignment in the 45-man control group. Drug offenders were believed to be so atypical that this would undermine the credibility of many comparisons. To avoid this bias, the designer should have restricted randomization or the design so as to assign 4 drug offenders to the experimental group and 4 to the control group (e.g., by blocking as described in a later section). More generally, if background data are available with the lists, or if attributes of program participants are ascertained in pretreatment tests, the experiments may be designed to have balanced groups.

REFUSALS AND THE ORDERING OF RESEARCH OPERATIONS

The discussion so far has gone on as though each person or unit accepted the treatment condition which his random assignment brought. Such uniform acceptance is decidedly *not* the usual case, and there arises, therefore, the practical issue of the order in which the operations of randomization, measurement, and invitation to treatment are scheduled.

The operations involved can be itemized as follows, although not all occur explicitly or separately in every instance.

1. Achieving a list of eligible units (as illustrated later, this can involve several steps)
2. Asking for cooperation in the measurement activities (pretests, posttests, etc.) which are to be shared by the experimental and control groups
3. Randomly assigning units to the treatments
4. Asking for the acceptance of the assigned experimental and control treatments

While not all orders are conceivable, many reorderings of these operations are possible, and they have different implications for the appropriateness of statistical models. Stages 1, 2, and 4 involve losses of cases. Random assignment can occur any place in the sequence, and the later it comes, the less bias is likely to result from differences among control and treatment groups, and the more applicable the statistical model for experimental comparisons becomes.

Let us make these steps explicit by illustrating them from the New Jersey Income Maintenance experiment. An early decision had been made that the experiment could not be distributed randomly on a nationwide basis, but had to be concentrated in a single area where it could be serviced by a single delivery and research staff. Representative sampling of sites was thus precluded; instead, a judgmental sample of several sites was chosen, designed to exemplify a wide range of eligible recipients. Within the several New Jersey and nearby Pennsylvania cities thus chosen, the universe for sampling was all the poverty areas designated by the 1960 Census plus all other areas judged to have become poverty areas since then. Within these areas, modern public opinion polling procedures of randomized cluster sampling were employed. Residential blocks were chosen at random. For these blocks, all residences were listed. From these listings individual households were selected at random, in numbers estimated to be sufficient to find enough eligibles. Members of these households were then approached for a screening interview to ascertain the eligibility of the family for the program. At this stage, 20% refused to be interviewed and 21% could not be found at home after four tries. Of those who completed the screening interview, 18 % were judged eligible and were then approached for a detailed preenrollment interview; 7% of the interviews attempted resulted in refusals at this stage, and 14% were lost through changes of address and so on. As a result of this process, a list of eligible families was achieved.

From this list, random assignment was used to create eight experimental groups ranging in size from 48 to 138 families, totaling 725 families, and one control group of 632 families. Those assigned to the experimental groups were then approached with a request to cooperate with the income supplement system, the required record-keeping, and the quarterly interviews. At this stage, 8.6% declined, with more declining in the less remunerative treatments. Those assigned to the control group were later approached for cooperation on the occasion of the first quarterly interview, at which time 7.9% declined.

This brief scenario serves to raise the issue of scheduling the point of randomization. The experimental groups could have been designated within the first stage, at the point where residences had been selected for the initial interviewing. But the occurrence of refusal and noneligibility would have given opportunity for the assigned groups to have become dissimilar, and a later point was therefore chosen. Nevertheless, there were opportunities for bias. For example, losses from the control group were probably due mainly to low economic motivation to cooperate, while the experimental losses were in some part due to unwillingness to accept charity. Hence, differential rates of noncooperation or essentially the same crude rate of refusal but for different reasons (as in this case) may operate to undermine the randomization. Thus, the experimental statistician might prefer to move the point of randomization to a still later place in the sequence.

Two alternatives suggest themselves. First, since both experimental and control groups share the same measurement framework of quarterly interviews, one could first ask the entire sample to agree to this interviewing procedure, and then randomly assign those agreeing to experimental and control groups. Subsequently, the experimental groups would be invited to participate in an income support plan. If all accepted, the comparability would be maximum. The reports of the New Jersey researchers indicate, however, that a small number refused on grounds of unwillingness to accept charity. This could produce a bias, although similar persons might remain in the control group. Had things been scheduled in this way, it would have been desirable to keep those that rejected the experimental treatment in the repeated measurement study which they had agreed to. In later analyses, if one wanted to be absolutely sure that such differential dropout did not explain the obtained results, one would analyze these households *as though they had received the treatment*, that is, according to the random assignment, even though they rejected the treatment. A strong effect would survive such dilution. The analysis is conservative, leaning over backward to avoid a pseudo-effect due to selective dropout, as is discussed in detail later.

This discussion serves to point up the trade-off between disadvantages of early versus later randomization from the experimental designer's point of view. Other considerations are involved as well. Chapter VII discusses some of the political aspects of site selection, while Chapter VI considers the practical managerial tasks of enlisting cooperation and minimizing attrition among the experimental population. There are also ethical considerations in allocating an experimental boon (treatment benefits) to some eligibles while placing others in a control group that may confer only an administrative burden. These issues are taken up in Chapter VIII. Later, we return to questions of design as such.

## Reducing Random Error

Experimental designs can be made more complex (and experiments more powerful) than the simple illustrations we have given earlier by making use of various statistical devices which rest on three main ideas: *blocking*, adjustment using *concomitant observations*, and *factorial designs*. These ideas are easily understood and can be explained without getting into the technical statistical details whose mastery is required for their actual application in an experiment. Should the use of one more of these approaches seem appropriate for what the prospective experimenter wants, he should either have such mastery or seek help from a competent statistician. One further word of caution is in order. Blocking, adjustment by concomitant observations, and factorial designs are primarily aimed at reducing random error through increasing the uniformity (homogeneity) of analytic units. It is often more important, however, to increase the accuracy of an experiment by reducing bias (systematic error) rather than by trying for the nth degree of refinement in random error reduction. Effort might better be spent in reducing bias by vigorously following up nonresponsive units rather than by measuring yet another concomitant variable to use in adjustment. When reduction in random error is sought, the following techniques are useful.

### BLOCKING

In blocking, the idea is to select *groups* of units that are as homogeneous within a group as possible, allowing possibly large differences between groups, and to randomly assign different treatments to units in the same group. The treatments can thus be compared within homogeneous groups even though, over all, the units are highly variable. The groups are called *blocks*. Randomization should of course be used in the assignment of units to treatments within blocks. The design is then called a *randomized block design*.

For example, in the day-care experiment described earlier, the blocks were pairs of day-care centers, presumably chosen to be as well matched as possible, and the two treatments were assigned randomly to the two centers (units) within each block. (See Table 3.1 on p. 43.) Another example of blocking is the assignment of students within institutions (i.e., within blocks) at random to treatment groups in an experiment on the effects of special career education programs (Zener and Schnuelle, 1922).

Where blocking is involved, the listing and randomization process would be done separately for each block or stratum of the population. The blocks may be formed so that the units within a block are homogeneous with respect to many factors simultaneously, if such units can be found. They may be formed on the basis of qualitative judgments that certain units are "like" others for the purpose at hand. But the actual assignment of treatments to units *within blocks* must be random. The selection of comparison, or control, units after the treatment units have already been selected would *not* be a true experiment, and the outcomes of such an investigation are difficult to interpret statistically.

If each block has exactly as many units as there are distinct treatments and each treatment is used on only one unit in each block, then the experimental design is called a *complete block design*. To keep the blocks homogeneous, especially when the units occur naturally in small groups, it may be desirable to have fewer units in each block than the number of distinct treatments, in which case the blocks must be *incomplete*.

## CONCOMITANT VARIABLES

A second method of reducing variability in an experiment is the adjustment of the experimental results in the analytic stage by taking into account *concomitant variables*—observable or measurable phenomena that are statistically associated with the responses of principal interest. Its usefulness depends upon the existence of a degree of association or correlation between some measure of experimental effect and some extrinsic element of the situation, for example, the employment record of a subject following a job training program and his general physical condition. One might plausibly expect some correlation between these two variables, with generally healthy persons having better employment records. Since state of health might affect employment independently of an effect of the training program, the experimenter would want to take this influence into account in order to reduce error in estimating the treatment effect, but he might not be able to do it by blocking or other adaptations in the assignment-to-treatment process. Instead, the experimenter would obtain a measure of all participants' health that he could use in the analysis to remove statistically the error associated with the commingling of robust, average, and sickly participants.

In other words, the response being measured may often be statistically associated (correlated) with some other quantifiable phenomenon that can be observed. It is then natural to make such supplementary observations and to use them to try to reduce the unpredictable variability and thus increase the precision of the treatment comparisons. Observations used for this purpose in true experiments are called *concomitant observations*. An obvious choice is the response variable itself measured before treatment begins. The pretreatment employment record of a job trainee will probably be correlated with his posttreatment record. This suggests that the posttreatment measure should be adjusted by taking into account the fact that trainees with a better employment record before training will probably have a better record afterward.

The stronger the statistical relationship between the concomitant variables and the response variable, the more their use can reduce the uncertainty of the treatment comparisons. Concomitant variables must, however, satisfy one essential condition if the meaning of the comparisons is to be preserved: They must not be affected by the treatments. Thus observations made before the treatments begin may always be used. For observations made later, one must be entirely satisfied that they would not have been affected, directly or indirectly, if the treatment assignments had been different. Age could hardly present a problem, even if not measured until the end of the experiment, nor would a measure of mental ability in an income maintenance experiment.

The statistical technique to accomplish this adjustment is most commonly called "covariance analysis." It does not measure differences in response *caused by* the concomitant variable, but it eliminates variability in response associated with that variable. In true experiments, adjustment for concomitant variables simply increases the precision of treatment comparisons. It neither lessens the need for randomization nor vitiates its virtues of eliminating biases and justifying causal inferences. It cannot transform a quasi-experiment into a true experiment. One sometimes does encounter research designs that attempt to use covariance analysis to adjust for real differences in nonrandomly assigned treatment groups. This usage is not acceptable since, if the covariate contains error or unique variance, the adjustment will only partially remove such differences and the underadjusted residual is likely to be mistaken for treatment effects. (See Chapter IV for an illustration of the biases involved.)

It is usual to assume that treatment effects are constant and do not vary as the concomitant variables vary, in other words, that the treatment effects do not differ systematically from one part of the target population to another. If there is just one concomitant variable, for instance, this means that the difference between treatments at high levels of the concomitant variable is the same as the difference at low levels. This assumption is called additivity, because the average treatment response can be calculated by adding two quantities—the treatment effect and the amount of response associated with concomitant variables. When the assumption of constant treatment effects is false, however, concomitant variables can still be helpful because they permit detection of systematic variation in treatment effects, which is ordinarily information of great interest. In short, if the usual assumptions are satisfied, concomitant variables can increase experimental precision, and if not, they permit a much clearer picture of the situation to be obtained provided the analysis takes note of it. When designing an experiment, one should, therefore, consider carefully what measurements might be taken for use as concomitant variables, for either reason.

## FACTORIAL DESIGN

Sometimes a treatment involves several *factors* which it is natural or useful to think of separately. For instance, in a nutrition experiment, the subjects might receive a 1000 calorie per day diet supplement providing protein, iron, various vitamins, and so forth. These components (factors) can be given in combination, with the levels of each varying separately, so that different people receive different combinations. Thus some people might receive 20 gm of protein, 5 mg of iron, and 2 mg of Vitamin A; others no protein, 2 mg of iron, and 2 mg of Vitamin A. A treatment would then be any such combination of factor levels. Factors that are not part of the treatment, such as age or family income, may also be considered, as may nonnumerical factors like sex or presence–absence of the father in the home.

Under some circumstances, a well-designed experiment may provide as much or more information about several factors simultaneously as could be obtained with separate experiments of the same size devoted to each factor individually. For example, consider a nutrition experiment with 24 experimental units arranged as in Table 3.2. Suppose that the effect of protein does not depend on the vitamins or iron also supplied. Then each group of three units in a column of the table supplies information about the effect of protein, and the whole experiment could be viewed as a randomized block experiment with three treatments (0, medium, and high protein) in eight blocks of three units each (the eight columns). At the same time, however, it might be viewed as an experiment on four vitamin mixes in six blocks of four units each, and also as an experiment on iron in twelve blocks of two units each. Thus we have three experiments in one. So-called "fractional factorial" designs can have essentially all the desirable features of full factorial designs without the size implied by multiplying together the number of levels of all the factors. By omitting certain combinations of factor levels chosen on the basis of carefully assessing the information provided by certain combinations, the size of the experiment may be reduced to one-half, one-quarter, or even smaller fractions of the full factorial design.

In the interpretation of effects, there is a fundamental difference between those factors that are controlled by the experimenter and randomly assigned to units (e.g., in the nutrition experiment, the composition of the diet and the frequency of its administration) and those factors, on the other hand, that are inextricably linked to the units and may be used only to select or classify them (e.g., the age and sex of the subjects, their family income, or employment). Differences in the response to treatment may be associated with different levels of these "classificatory factors" but cannot be assumed to be caused by them. Inferences about effects associated with the "controllable" factors (i.e., those subject to randomization) are, on the other hand, on much stronger ground.

A crucial question in the interpretation of the results is whether the effect of each factor is the same at all levels of all other factors. If so, as assumed in the preceding paragraph, the effects are called *additive*, the concept being the same as that discussed earlier for treatments and concomitant variables. A factorial experiment ordinarily provides a lot of evidence about additivity, and the data should be examined for it.

**TABLE 3.2**

**Nutrition Experiment (Factorial Design)**

| | NO IRON | | | | | IRON | | | |
| | Vitamin mixture | | | | | Vitamin mixture | | | |
| Protein | I | II | III | IV | Protein | I | II | III | IV |
|---------|---|----|-----|----|---------|---|----|-----|----|
| None | | | | | None | | | | |
| Medium | | | | | Medium | | | | |
| High | | | | | High | | | | |

When the effects are additive, each factor has an effect, and the effect of a combination (treatment) is obtained simply by adding the relevant factor effects. Furthermore, the factorial experiment has served as a full experiment on each factor. Each unit has done multiple duty, serving once for each factor. Also the generalizability of the experiment is enhanced because each factor is examined under a variety of conditions.

The more complicated, nonadditive situation is again important to recognize, and factorial experiments are particularly good at detecting it. An exposition of this point would exceed the scope of this chapter, as would a complete treatment of the various refinements of factorial design of experiments, but the reader should be aware of the advantages of such a design. It examines all its factors under a variety of conditions, enhancing generalizability. If the factor effects are additive, the design provides several experiments for the price of one. If they are not, it provides good information about how the effects of each factor vary with the levels of the other factors.

## COMBINATIONS, EXTENSIONS, AND LIMITATIONS

The basic designs just described can be combined, extended, and ramified in many useful ways. Adjustment for concomitant variables can be carried out in conjunction with any design. Factorial designs can be partitioned into incomplete blocks and can be combined in special ways. One particular combination, for example, can be useful and might easily be overlooked. The design can block on two or more factors simultaneously, in a cross-cutting manner. For example, one might wish to try several treatments in several cities and several school grades, blocking on city and on school grade, without trying every treatment in each grade of each city. Table 3.3 shows one way this can be done. Each treatment appears once in each grade, so each grade forms a block. Similarly, the cities form blocks, which cut across the blocks for grades.

Sometimes it is possible to use smaller units for some factors than are feasible for others. For example, suppose that in a day-care center experiment, the level of Federal subsidy can be varied from city to city (but not within a city) while hours of care provided can vary within a city. Then the units are pairs of centers in the same city for the purposes of the subsidy factor, whereas the units are individual centers for the hours-of-care factor. This type of design is worth using for the gain in precision it provides.

Such combination designs recommend themselves on grounds of statistical elegance and economy but give trouble if some data are

**TABLE 3.3**

**Latin Square Design for Treatments A, B, C, D**

| Grade | City | | | |
|---|---|---|---|---|
| | I | II | III | IV |
| 3 | B | D | C | A |
| 4 | D | A | B | C |
| 5 | C | B | A | D |
| 6 | A | C | D | B |

missing or if the design cannot be completed. Furthermore, the gain in precision from an elegant design may be purchased at the cost of a larger experiment. Since a complex design will have many cells, each possibly requiring several measurements, it is easy to see how enlarging the number of cells rapidly expands the size of the experiment. This penalty may be partly mitigated by fractional or irregular designs. Complex designs also carry an important statistical constraint. The more complex the design, the greater the loss in "degrees of freedom for error"—that is, the sample size effectively available for estimating the size of the residual variability, and hence the accuracy of the estimates of treatment effects. Each block after the first, each concomitant variable, and each factor or treatment category uses up at least one "degree of freedom"—more than one if nonadditivity or curvilinearity is to be investigated. To take an extreme case, if we fit a straight line to just two data points, the sample fit will always be perfect, and although we know it is not truly perfect, there is no apparent way to assess its probable imperfection. Similarly, if we use enough concomitant variables, we can always obtain a perfect fit, but it will be spurious and useless. In these extreme cases, the "degrees of freedom for error" are 0. Any experiment with less than, say, 10 degrees of freedom for error should be carefully scrutinized, and less than 5 degrees generally calls for special techniques. It follows therefore that the more complex the design, the larger the number of units required for a meaningful estimate of treatment effects and their uncertainties.

The statistical literature emphasizes designs having various properties of symmetry, balance, or regularity. This used to be essential for hand calculation, because it permits special shortcuts in the analysis.

Now, however, by computer, unbalanced designs can be analyzed about as easily as any others, and by and large they permit estimates of the same quantities and tests of the same hypotheses under the same assumptions. They may be desirable because the balanced designs which fit a given situation may be much larger than the budget permits or precision requires. Furthermore, natural block sizes may vary, and inequalities of cost, variance, importance of different treatments, and so forth may suggest unequal emphases in the design. Unbalanced designs should nevertheless be chosen with great care, if at all, because different designs can lead to great differences in the precision of the treatment comparisons, and unbalanced designs may be extremely inefficient in their use of the observations, compared to balanced designs. Balanced designs also permit some simplification in the presentation of certain results, and a more intuitive estimation procedure which may find readier acceptance.

## CHOICE

The choice of a design for a social experiment cannot be reduced to a simple, mechanical process, for many considerations enter into the decision. The feasibility of a given design is determined by the facts of a particular situation. The experimenter must weigh the relative importance of testing the mere existence of treatment effects against measuring variations in intensity of treatment and interactions among factors. The generalizability of the results may outweigh the efficiency of the design, or vice versa. The possible gain in efficiency through changing the size of the experiment and the cost of so doing; the flexibility of various designs in case change or cessation of the experiment becomes necessary; and the simplicity and understandibility of the analysis all must be considered in making a complex judgment.

About the only rule that can be given to guide the choice of a design is that the designer should be thoroughly familiar with the purpose of the experiment, the situation(s) in which it is to be carried out, and the topic to be investigated, as well as familiar with experimental design. The last item cannot substitute for the others, but a professional statistician can learn about them by immersing himself in the situation.

It may be helpful to start by thinking in terms of, and indeed making, a list of all important variables, or factors in the ordinary sense of the word, without worrying about whether they will be treated as factors in the statistical sense or even whether they will or can be measured. The variables can usefully be subdivided into those associated with treatments, with the environment, and with the experimental units. Less obvious but equally significant are certain questions about their control or measurement, as will become clear.

*Factors.* Factors in the statistical sense are controlled at specified levels. A variable is a possible factor, then, only if either (1) it can be controlled directly or (2) it is known in advance and can be controlled through selection of the units. Recall further that causal inference is possible, on a statistical basis, only for variables that are controlled directly and subject to appropriate random assignment of units. Ordinarily the variables of most interest will be treated as factors if possible. In particular, the treatment(s) (which always represent at least one factor in a true experiment since they are directly controlled and randomized) are prime candidates for defining in terms of (or breaking into) several factors. Other variables, especially environmental ones, are sometimes usefully treated as factors if they are important and it is feasible to do so. Unless they are directly controlled and appropriately randomized, however, their effects are not interpretable causally and they might perhaps be better viewed as "blocking" variables.

In general, then, the most important variables will be treated factorially if possible, and in particular, they must be if causal inferences about their effects are sought. The remaining techniques are for the reduction of errors in inferences about these primary factors and further variables may be introduced for this purpose as well as for examining interaction effects with the primary factors.

*Blocks.* Blocks must be formed before the experiment starts: For instance, by selecting units in specified ranges of a variable that is known in advance, such as age, sex, or education, and assigning units within blocks randomly to experimental or to control conditions. If a variable desired for this purpose is not known in advance, it may be worth while to seek a "proxy" that is. For example, if the educational level attained by an individual cannot be determined in advance of the experiment, it may be sufficient to use his income as a "proxy" because education and income are so highly correlated. If blocking were to be carried out on many specific variables, however, it would rapidly become difficult to select units, since they must satisfy requirements on all the blocking variables simultaneously. Accordingly, the direct use of variables for blocking must ordinarily be restricted to a very few, important candidates.

More commonly, blocking is based on simultaneity, contiguity, or other similarity which, it is judged, will eliminate in one fell swoop much of the variability associated with many variables. This can be effective even for variables which are unmeasured or unmeasurable. It does not mean that one should forget entirely about such variables, however. They are relevant to thinking about the formation of the blocks. Blocking is especially likely to be useful in connection with environmental variables, since they affect many units similarly.

*Concomitant Variables.* Concomitant variables require no ability to control or select, but they must be measured. Recall that they must either be measured before the treatments are applied or be unaffected by the treatments. (Again, if the measurement cannot be made directly, a "proxy" may be worth seeking and using as a concomitant variable.) Like blocks they are used for the reduction of errors in inferences about the treatments and examination of interaction with them. Their chief weakness is that the appropriate adjustment must be estimated, either judgmentally or statistically, and error in this estimate lessens the error reduction achieved in estimating the treatment effects.

Variables associated with the units are particularly likely to be best treated as concomitant. In selecting concomitant variables, it is statistical association with the responses, not causation, that counts. Furthermore, to the extent that the concomitant variables used are associated with variables not used, they will partially take account of the latter. Thus, when contemplating adding a concomitant variable, the relevant question is not what association it alone has with the response, but what association it has independently of concomitant variables already included. Similarly, if the experiment is in blocks, the associations within blocks are what count, and these may be much weaker than the overall association.

To summarize, ordinarily the variables of primary interest, about which inferences are to be made, in particular the treatments, will be handled as factors. Blocks will be formed before the treatments are applied on the basis of the most important remaining variables then available and/or on some general basis designed to eliminate, as far as possible, variability of all kinds. Concomitant variables will be chosen from those remaining variables which can be measured before the treatments are applied, or later if they are still unaffected by the treatments. Variability not eliminated by these means will be thrown into random error by randomization.

## How Big Should an Experiment Be?

In deciding on the right size for an experiment it is helpful to have a clear idea about two things: How big must an experimental effect be to compel the conclusion that the treatment has *practical* or *social importance?* and How confident must one be in the correctness of the conclusion drawn from the experiment? These two points are interrelated, but they are distinct, and they direct attention to different aspects of the experimental design and analysis.

If there is reason to expect that the observable effect of an experimental treatment is too small to be of practical (or policy) importance, then the proper size of the experiment is zero—no experiment is worth doing. Furthermore, if the expected effect, though practically significant, would be so small relative to natural variability that one could not draw firm conclusions except from an experiment of an unacceptably large size, then again no experiment is worth doing.

When innovative social programs are concerned, it may not be easy to get the evidence upon which such judgments partially rest. The innovators are likely to claim that there is nothing like their treatment anywhere else and it cannot be compared to previous attempts to deal with, say, unemployment, failure to develop normally, or retardation in learning. Nevertheless, many behavioral phenomena of interest in social experimentation have been studied, and evidence exists about their normal occurrence and variations in it. The time of life at which children learn various skills or capacities is known as well as the normal range of variation in these acquisitions. The rate of unemployment by age, race, sex, and skill categories has been established, though the evidence is firmer for a longer period in some areas than in others. From such bases as these a rough estimate can readily be made of what sort of change or variation in the phenomenon might reasonably be expected to occur naturally, and, accordingly how large the effect of an experimental treatment must be in order to enable conclusions to be drawn from an experiment of acceptable size.

Judgment as well as evidence enters into the decision about practical importance. A drop from 30 to 25% in the unemployment rate of disadvantaged youths would be considered an imposingly successful effect of an experimental job-training program; whereas it would require a 40 or 50% increase in reading speed before educators would be much impressed by an experimental treatment in this area. Furthermore, such judgmental factors may be compound rather than simple. An increase of 10% in the number of overtime parking fines collected might be considered evidence enough for the effectiveness of a stricter enforcement program; but if labor costs for enforcement increased by 8%, the municipal administration might well consider the net effect too small to be of practical importance—especially if the administration believed it could also expect an increase in motorists' complaints about police harassment.

Sometimes, of course, the alleged or intended effects of a program that is proposed for experimental testing have no direct precedent, and even relevant evidence may be scanty. This clearly was the situation for the Manhattan Bail Bond experiment, and in such instances the decision whether to experiment or not becomes purely judgmental, taking into account the importance of the topic, the feasibility of doing any experiment, and the best available estimates about the magnitude of effect that would be of practical importance. We stress the value of coming to some specific estimate of desired or expected treatment effect before designing the experiment, even when relevant prior evidence is weak and uncertainty is great. There are two reasons for this recommendation. The first is statistical and we shall explain it in the paragraphs that follow. The second is strategic. Nothing helps as much to clarify thinking about the development of an experimental treatment and an experimental design as does an attempt to state in some form the magnitude of the outcome to be expected. Even crude calculations of effects can help to increase agreement among the various parties to an experiment as to their purposes; their beliefs about the dynamics of the treatment; the characteristics of the experimental units, and their environment; and even, indeed, their assessment of the problems of managing the experimental procedures and the possible usefulness of its results.

The statistical reason for being interested in estimates of the size of experimental effects is that this magnitude is intimately related to design requirements, to the sensitivity of measures to be used (see Chapter V), and to the size of the experiment—the question with which this section began.

The important technical fact about the size of an experiment is that a "square-root" law operates. For instance, roughly speaking, doubling the size of an experiment will not halve the uncertainty (double the precision) but will reduce it by only 29% to $1/\sqrt{2} = .71$ times its former value. To reduce the uncertainty by a factor of two, it is necessary to increase the size of the experiment by a factor of four. Since many experimental costs are directly proportional to the size of the experiment, this means that generally, as the size is increased, the cost goes up very much more rapidly than the uncertainty goes down. This makes other methods of increasing precision all the more desirable.

One other method is to increase the treatment effect by increasing the strength of the treatment and/or by choosing units or conditions for which the treatment effect is expected to be greatest, as mentioned earlier. This possibility should not be ignored, because its effect is squared in relation to the size of the experiment. For instance, doubling the effect is as good as quadrupling the size of the experiment and permits quartering the size with no change in sensitivity (if the design can be quartered). Increasing the effect by 10% is as good as increasing the size by 21% (because $(1.10)^2 = 1.21$) and permits reducing the size by 17% to 83% of the original ($1/1.21 = .83$).

The classical statistical approach is to choose the size so as to satisfy one or two specific statistical requirements on, for example, the standard deviation of the estimates of treatment effects, the length of confidence intervals, or the significance level and power of a statistical test. Such procedures are at least explicit and recognize the existence of uncertainty, but they also take into account only indirectly—through the choice of the specific requirements to be satisfied—many important, relevant factors and the way these factors change marginally with the size of the experiment.

The general purpose of optimizing size is to reduce uncertainty in comparing treated versus control groups, subject to certain constraints. Under some conditions the size of the experimental group(s) will differ from that of the control(s) because of considerations of cost and of policy-related constraints on the experiment.

For example, in the Negative Income Tax experiment, the design conditions most important for policy purposes were first identified. These conditions included not only alternative tax rates, but also benefits paid under unemployment, and normal preexperiment earnings. The experimenters' objective was to allocate the number of families to each of 27 design conditions so that variability was minimal. The primary constraint on the allocation process was cost (fixed budget but variable cost for each treatment and design condition).

In the Negative Income Tax experiment, the allocation process resulted in the major portion of the budget being taken up by high-benefit treatment conditions and a majority of the total number of families being allocated to low-benefit and control conditions. Having a large number of units allocated to control conditions was (and often is) useful on grounds of economy—since control group members generally cost less to monitor; and the strategy is often useful on statistical grounds to improve precision of program comparisons. Note that having a larger control group will *not* in general resolve problems of attrition, since the character of attrition may differ considerably among treatment and control conditions and consequently undermine the equivalence of the two groups during the experiment. It is usually practical to explore several different sizes of experiment, with respect to various objectives, statistical measures, and so forth. This makes it relatively easy to duck the judgments no one wants to make, to allow multiple purposes, to explore changes in assumptions, etc.

Exploration of a few sizes, not just one size, is suggested because it is the most feasible way of discovering whether a *change* in size will result in a *change* in precision which justifies the *change* in cost. The fact that an experiment is (or is not) clearly worth its cost says nothing about whether a smaller or larger one would be better. There is usually no need, however, to explore many possible sizes, because of the one happy aspect of this whole messy business: Modest variations around the theoretically optimum size seem generally to have a very minor effect on the total gain, because of the way a change in the cost of the experiment is offset by a corresponding change in the value of the information gained.

Our final point is that the foregoing discussion has been concerned entirely with random error and has not mentioned bias, or the trade-off between reduction of bias and reduction of random error. It has been implicity assumed that all feasible steps would be taken to eliminate any biases not automatically eliminated by randomization. If, however, a contemplated experiment is large enough to reduce random error to a very low level, then it is worth asking whether the resources released by allowing a slight increase in random error could be effectively employed in the reduction of bias. Only in small experiments is one likely to accept a larger than necessary bias in order to reduce random error.

## Statistical Analysis

Having carried out an experiment, what should be done with the masses of data which typically result? Statistical analysis is a kind of digestion of the data. It has two main purposes. One is to get a feeling for the shape of the data. The second is to tell the experimenter how unreliable those feelings may be—specifically, how much of what he sees in the data may actually be the product of random variation and self-delusion (or rose-colored glasses).

Traditionally, data analysts have practiced the art of "grubbing around" in the data, following hunches suggested by inspecting the gross tabulations of results; making various cross-tabulations, graphs, scatter diagrams, and so forth—in short examining the evidence under different assumptions and by a variety of techniques. Such grubbing around often reveals unexpected findings and suggests leads for further analyses which would not have been thought of if the analyst were simply applying the statistical model (see later) of the experiment to the data. For example, after searching data on *Sesame Street* for interesting phenomena, one may find that, within a control condition, children who watch adult talk shows perform better on achievement tests than children who watch simple cartoons.

Because "grubbing" is, in effect, the practice of examining results of experimental (or other research) data to test hypotheses which the experiment was not designed to handle unequivocally, two kinds of problems arise. First, because the children have not been randomly assigned to adult shows versus cartoons, it is possible that children's pre-viewing performance levels coincide with their choice of show; differences among performance levels may then be attributable to natural differences among the children rather than to differential impact of the TV programs.

Second, if there are no pre-viewing differences between groups, the finding of a post-viewing difference may be attributable entirely to chance if the finding is made after a long search program. That is, if one looks at enough data, one can always find an interesting, "important," and thoroughly accidental effect. This problem is akin to legal search of circumstantial evidence; it is easy to find evidence which appears to verify a contention (given a diversity of information about a phenomenon) despite the fact that the evidence is irrelevant to the contention at hand. It is, furthermore, usually impossible to calculate the probability of chance findings (in the absence of a genuine effect) under the ordinary conditions of grubbing.

This sort of problem cannot be avoided in sequential searches of the data, but it can be ameliorated. If, for example, the finding is legitimate rather than gratuitous, it should be replicable. It has become common practice in industrial experiments as well as in quantitative exploratory research in psychology to randomly select a holdout (or validation) sample from the main body of data, so as to verify inferences and findings obtained in grubbing. Of course, side experiments can be conducted or new data collected to assist in verifying earlier grubbing.

The fact that statistical analyses of large bodies of data are nowadays ordinarily done on a computer means that analysts have a different problem in grubbing around in the data then they did in the era of desk calculators and countersorters. Because computer usage patterns in a given center may be oriented toward batch processing and standard analytic program packages, analysts may not have such natural occasions for grubbing around as they used to. On the other hand, with the right kind of flexible software, the computer permits grubbing around on a vastly grander scale than could be dreamed of before computers, but only by remote control—which necessitates time-sharing modes or frequent return to the machine in a step-wise process.

The second purpose of statistical analysis as mentioned earlier, is to give the analyst some idea as to the reliability (or unreliability) of the outcomes he observes in the data. A discussion of this purpose takes us to statistical inference, the subject of the next section, but it is convenient to preface this section by introducing the notion of a *statistical model* which guides the analyst in his formal search through the data (and which indirectly guided the design of the experiment). In other words, besides grubbing around in the data, the analyst ordinarily has a more or less explicit idea about how the experimental treatment is supposed to work; and this idea can be formalized in a statistical model which informs the procedures the analyst employs in testing whether the expected outcomes actually occurred. For example, a "linear model" of an educational program might be written as: $y = a + bx + e$ in which $a$ depends upon the treatment given and represents the treatment effect; $x$ stands for the subject's score on an educational test prior to treatment; score following treatment is represented by $y$; $b$ measures association between $y$ and $x$; and $e$ is an error term. Within such a model, hypothetical values of the treatment effect could be tested against the data by a $t$-test, for instance. A more complicated model of the treatment might involve the supposition of differential effects according to the subject's measured intelligence or socioeconomic status; or according to the intensity of treatment, experience level of teachers, etc. Such a model might well be tested by analyses of variance or multiple regression techniques. Whatever the details, the point is that the model employed directs the attention of the analyst to certain features of the data and suggests the statistical procedures he will want to use in drawing inferences from the evidence.

## STATISTICAL INFERENCE

Statistical inference is the process of drawing conclusions from uncertain (quantitative) evidence. Included under this rubric are methods of estimating the true value of the treatment effect, placing limits on the uncertainty of such estimates, and tests of statistical significance.

The various statistical tests mentioned in a preceding paragraph are ways of making allowance for the random variation in the data and, thus, for allowing the analyst to say with some accuracy how sure he can be about the results of the experiment.

The first question one might ask is: Has the treatment had any effect at all or might the observed differences be entirely a result of chance? The classical statistical method of answering this question is a test of significance. It says, Suppose that in fact the treatment had no effect at all (the null hypothesis, introduced on p. 44 in connection with the day-care experiment example). What then is the probability of observing as large an effect as was obtained or a larger one? If this probability is quite small (say less than 1 chance in 20, or 5%, as in the day-care example) then either some unusual accident occurred in the data or the treatment really did have an effect. If the probability is larger, say one chance in five (20%), the statistician believes he cannot safely reject the null hypothesis. That is, there is not adequate reason to presume that the null hypothesis is false: There may or may not be any real treatment effect, for all we can tell from the data. There is so much "noise" (random error) in the evidence that we cannot detect even the direction of the signal with assurance.

Conventional significance levels chosen to judge the outcome of an experiment are the 5% and the 1% levels—that is, 1 chance in 20 or 1 chance in 100, depending upon how much assurance one wishes to have that the null hypothesis will not be rejected when true. A significance test concerns itself with the probability of outcomes at least as extreme as what was observed. This probability itself, usually called either the observed significance level or the $p$-value, is of some interest. If one knows the $p$-value, one can carry out a test at any significance level one chooses, rather than only at the level chosen by the experimenter. If one knows only whether it was significant at the 5% level, one does not know whether it was just barely significant or would still have been significant if a more extreme level had been chosen, such as 1% or .1%. The $p$-value is more informative in this respect. Furthermore, it seems to provide a kind of measure of the extent to which the null hypothesis is discredited by the data. One must be very careful about both these interpretations, however. First, the method of calculating significance tests assumes that the experimenter has chosen in advance the level of significance by which he is willing to be bound in evaluating experimental evidence; if one were to choose the level *after* the data had been analyzed, this would vitiate the assurance the method is intended to provide. Second, the $p$-value is emphatically *not* the probability that the null hypothesis is true, given the data. No such probability exists in the classical language, and in a language where it does exist, it is quite different from the $p$-value except in a very special situation.

It is important to emphasize that tests of *statistical* significance say nothing about *practical* significance. It is perfectly possible to find a statistically significant difference that is so small as to have no practical importance. For statistical significance does not mean that an observed difference (between experimentals and controls, for instance) is a big difference, but only that it is unlikely to have arisen by chance. On the other hand, a practically significant observed difference between experimental and control treatments may turn out not to be statistically significant, that is, the random variation in the data may be so great as to allow the possibility that even a very large apparent effect could have come about by chance.

The prime purpose of a test of statistical significance is to protect experimenters and policy makers from drawing the false inference that a treatment has had an effect when in fact it has not. But such false positive ("type I") errors are only one of two ways to be wrong. An experimenter might also err in concluding that a treatment had had no effect when in fact it did. Significance levels are not useful in protecting against this second type of error. But, ordinarily, such "type II" errors in social experimentation are less important since, in general, the more important policy problem would seem to be how to avoid the disappointment, frustrated effort, and wasted resources caused by making a type I error, that is, adopting an ineffective treatment as a social program. To be sure, one should not do an experiment if the probability of a type II error is so large that one is unlikely to be able to detect an effect. The capacity to avoid type II errors is technically called the "power" of a test and an experimental design. This facet of statistical inference is less well known and more complex than the areas we have already covered and, to learn about the power of available procedures, the experimenter should seek expert advice.

Tests of significance provide very limited information. Failure to reject the null hypothesis does not justify concluding that the true effect is not substantial. Rejection says nothing about the size of the effect (except that it is not 0). Especially in the latter case, one would usually like to have more information than tests of significance provide. Estimation techniques and confidence intervals provide additional information as we explain later.

Sometimes an experimenter is less interested in whether the experimental groups differ from controls in respect to some outcome measure than he is in estimating the size of the treatment effect: For example, How much was reading speed increased by a training program? or How much was employment decreased by welfare payments? Analysis of an experiment may yield a number which a statistician regards as a more or less reliable *estimate* of the true value of the effect.

If, however, the experiment were to be repeated even under highly similar circumstances, the number yielded by analysis of the second experiment would differ from the first. Thus, the statistician also has the problem of estimating how much variation there might be in successive experiments and describing the uncertainty consequent upon this variation. He might, for instance, place some reasonable boundaries around the estimate of effect and convey some measure of (his assessment of) fhe confidence one may have that its true value lies within these specified boundaries.

Establishing *confidence intervals* is the standard method of doing this. It is technically the inverse of testing the null hypothesis. It starts with choosing the level of confidence the experimenter wishes to have in the confidence interval he will establish; for example, the 95% confidence level places the probability at 19 chances out of 20 that the confidence interval constructed will include the true value of the result being estimated.

The procedures for constructing confidence intervals are well standardized and the conventional levels for confidence intervals (95% and 99%) are the complements of significance levels for statistical tests. Confidence intervals provide more information than tests, however, and their interpretation is relatively straightforward; the confidence level is the probability (beforehand) that the confidence interval obtained will *contain* the true value being estimated. This does not mean that the true value lies at the middle of the interval; or that extreme values within the interval are necessarily less likely than values near the center; or that the probability applies to a particular interval after it is obtained. If the confidence interval includes zero (indicating say, the absence of any difference between treatment and control groups) then the null hypothesis cannot be rejected. Conversely, a narrow confidence interval containing only large-size estimates of effect coupled with a high confidence level supports the conclusion that treatment was effective. The larger the sample and the more homogeneous the groups of experimental units, the narrower the confidence interval will usually be.

ANALYZING FOR BIAS IN ATTRITION

Among the very many statistical topics that recommend themselves for consideration in this book, perhaps none is more germane to the special statistical problems of social experimentation than the various techniques for dealing with *attrition*, that is, the loss of units from the experiment, for whatever reasons. There is much to be said about attrition, and later chapters will suggest some ways to minimize it. Here we attend to the question of looking for evidence of systematic biasing of results through differential attrition (e.g., from the experimental compared to the control treatment).

Ordinarily the rate of attrition will differ between experimental and control treatments, either because the experimental situation is more attractive and rewarding than the control treatment (as in a money transfer experiment such as the Negative Income Tax) or because it is less attractive, perhaps even painful (as in treatments for weight control). Those who drop out of the experiment are almost certainly different in a variety of characteristics from those who remain as participants. Furthermore, this is likely to be the case even if the rate of attrition is the same in experimental and in control treatments.

Thus, it is important to look for evidence of differential attrition. Three classes of data should be considered. First, reasons for attrition: Are these different for experimental and control groups? Second, prerandomization data on the units (blocking variables, covariates background data). Third, pretest measures, that is, that subset of covariates that are measured prior to treatment and will subsequently be used as outcome measures. The latter two categories should be examined for evidence of differential attrition, recognizing that the more of these that are examined, the more apparent differences will occur by chance. A further analysis with pretests is suggested, which is the complement of this: Delete from the pretest all of those who have dropped out by the end of the experiment; analyze the remaining pretest data as though they were posttest data. If these analyses produce significant effects, this provides a direct demonstation of the fact that attrition can produce pseudo-effects. Under the assumption that attrition correlates equally with pretest and posttest measures, this is also the best available estimate of the pseudo-effects that differential attrition might have caused on the posttest.

It might be thought that use of the pretest scores as covariates in analysis of posttest scores would remove the possibility of differential attrition producing a pseudo-effect. However, this procedure will produce an underadjustment (Lord, 1967, 1969; Porter, 1967), unless the correlation between pretest and posttest scores is perfect. The smaller this correlation is, the larger the underadjustment. In practice of course, pretest and posttest scores are never perfectly correlated, so the use of pretest scores as covariates will generally leave some underadjustment.

Where matched pairs have been randomized, it is a good practice to drop both members of a pair when one is missing. This becomes more important the more highly the variables used in pairing correlate with the measure of effect, and the more differential the attrition. But it does not completely correct for differential attrition inasmuch as there is a selective elimination of those pairs in which, by chance, the control group differed from the experimental group in an attrition-producing direction.

*Attrition from Treatment but Not from Measurement.* Experiments are often done in the context of an encompassing record-keeping or measurement framework independent of the experiment per se. For Rosenberg (1964), Stapleton and Teitelbaum (1972), and Empey and Lubeck (1971), and others, the records of the courts provided such a frame. The use of withholding tax records is another example. Under such conditions, an experimental subject may drop out of the experimental treatment, or refuse it from the beginning, and still be included within the measurement system.

In response to increased emphasis upon voluntarism and informed consent in social experimentation, more and more experiments will be using randomized *invitations* to treatments rather than randomized *assignment* to treatments, as indeed was the case for Rosenberg and for Stapleton and Teitelbaum. Where this is done in the context of an encompassing measurement framework, there result at least three groups: invited–treated, invited–untreated, and controls. A widespread error in analysis is to compare the treated with the controls (or with a pool of untreated and controls), which can produce pseudo-effects due to selectivity in accepting the treatment.

To avoid such pseudo-effects, a conservative approach is to analyze all of those randomly invited as though they were treated, that is, to keep them in the experimental group, even though the evidence of treatment tends to be swamped out by the dead weight of those invited who did not get the treatment. Experimenters are understandably reluctant to so underestimate effects; Rosenberg, Stapleton and Teitelbaum, and Empey have shown examples of methodological insight and commitment in so doing.

An encompassing measurement framework provides some greater ability to estimate the effects of attrition, or to estimate treatment effects uncontaminated by attrition, even though such an estimate may have to be conservative. Recall an earlier suggestion regarding the scheduling of randomization: namely, that where practical, invitation to repeated interviews be tendered prior to the randomized invitation to the treatment, in order that the interview series provide to some extent an encompassing measurement framework for following up those who declined the offered treatment as well as those that accepted.

In the end, there is no purely statistical way of correcting precisely for differential attrition. The violation of randomness involves the violation of assumptions underlying the tests of significance. We may correctly judge that these violations are of trivial importance in our particular case, but such judgments are made on the basis of scientific hypotheses about the real processes involved, not on purely statistical grounds. It will improve our practice if we make these hypotheses explicit and illustrate them in detail in the context of our own data.

One approach is to do a variety of analyses under different assumptions about the nature of the attrition, with some of the analyses designed to illustrate possible but implausible interpretations—as a precaution. As a result of such a set of analyses, one has a range of estimates of effect. In some situations all will be in essential agreement. In others, they will bracket a range of contradictory outcomes and will thus warn of the possibility of attrition artifacts simulating treatment effects. Such bracketing studies will drive home the point that adjusting for attrition involves hypotheses about the nature of the process. The plausibility of these hypotheses needs to be examined on the basis of whatever evidence can be assembled, both statistical and nonstatistical, and it is *always* important to scrutinize the data of an experiment for evidence of biasing due to attrition as well as, or along with, other kinds of bias.

## STATISTICAL ANALYSIS: SOME CONCLUDING REMARKS

The formal statistical analysis of an experiment, done by classical methods, treats it in isolation. However, most experiments are part of an ongoing stream of research and are preceded and followed by related experiments by the same and other investigators. Thus we do not usually decide on the basis of a single experiment whether or not a treatment really has an effect or what range of effect is plausible. Yet statistical analyses often proceed as if we did, and almost never take account of more than one experiment at a time. Statistical analysis of an experiment is vital to its interpretation and cannot sensibly go beyond the experiment at hand, in the first instance. One must remember, however, that it summarizes only one experiment, not the whole of knowledge in its area. This is less of a limitation in typical large-scale experiments on social intervention than in most other situations, however, because such large-scale experiments tend to be few and far between. While this makes formal statistical analysis particularly appropriate, it also makes it particularly desirable to design the experiment so as to answer as many questions as feasible, to keep in mind the future usefulness of the possible experimental findings, and to include within the experiment as much independent replication as possible.

Statisticians regard the evidence from an experiment in much the same way that sports fans regard the results of a particular golf tournament in trying to decide which of a number of players is really the best one. The bigger the winner's lead over other players in a single tournament, the more likely it is that he is better than his opponents; the more tournaments a player wins, the more likely that he is better. There are random and systematic errors in the observations too: All the players do not enter all tournaments; they get hurt, they do not play consistently, and the playing conditions vary from course to course and from day to day. The experimenter usually believes that one program (player) may really be better than another in producing the effect sought (winning). He prefers to run at least one experiment (tournament) before deciding which one it is, unlike the nonexperimentalist who is sure in his own mind a priori that his favorite program (player) is superior.

To be sure, the experimenter would like to run a vast array of experiments (tournaments), comparing many treatments (players) before deciding which one is the best, but he rarely has a chance to study all possible treatments and must usually settle for trying to decide which is the better of two (or some small number of) programs. Furthermore, an experimenter, again like the sports fan, would like to have many matches between contending treatments before awarding the championship, because of chance factors that may affect the outcome of close contests. In real life, however, experimenters and statisticians, like sports fans, have often to settle for just a few trials as their basis for making a decision. The art of experimental design and analysis is in maximizing the confidence one can have in the outcome of a single (let us say) tournament of modest size.

## BAYESIAN INFERENCE

There are several significant schools of thought about the fundamental concepts of probability and statistical inference. We end this chapter by presenting briefly one way of viewing the basic problem and by distinguishing the two currently leading philosophies. Our purpose is to cast a little further light on the now classical methods described earlier and to introduce "Bayesian" thinking, which has perhaps even older roots and has had a strong, durable revival in the past 25 years. We can, however, give only an incomplete sketch from one perspective. As a leader of the Bayesian revival said in a similar context, " [in view of] the intensity and complexity of the controversy over the probability concept . . . [this sketch] is bound to infuriate any expert on the foundations of probability, but [we] trust it may do the less learned more good than harm [Savage, 1954, p. 3]."

Most interpretations of probability in common use can be divided into objective and subjective. In simple cases, which suffice here, objective probabilities are definable as long-run relative frequencies and are physically verifiable in at least some rough sense, but may not be known. For example, the objective probability of serious birth defects for American women taking thalidomide in the first 3 months of pregnancy is the (unknown) relative frequency with which they would occur in the long run in randomly selected births in the United States.

Subjective (Bayesian) probabilities represent the degrees of belief of a person who is perfectly rational in the sense that he is internally consistent. They are supposed to be carefully assessed, if not already available, so in effect they are always known; but they may not be physically verifiable. The subjective probability that Dr. A assigns to Mrs. B's next child's being defective, taking into account such factors as her and her husband's ages and family histories, represents his own considered belief but not a physically verifiable relative frequency.

If Dr. A knew the relative frequency for women of Mrs. B's age and had no other relevant information about Mrs. B, this objective probability would presumably also be his subjective probability.

When seeking to make an inference about a particular hypothesis H, for instance, the kind of question a statistically naive experimenter might ask is: *How probable should one rationally consider* H *to be in the light of the experimental evidence?* He might hope to answer with a probability that is both objective and measures rational degree of belief, without attaching specific meanings to these terms.

Now, posterior opinion depends rationally on prior opinion as well as on the current experimental evidence: If two people received the same evidence but one had a greater degree of belief in H than the other beforehand, then rationally this should still be true afterward (though both should be swayed by the evidence). Thus a full answer to the question as posed depends on what degree of belief in H was "rational" beforehand. An objective and rational prior probability, whether reflecting previous information or ignorance, is a chimera which has been earnestly sought but never found, so some compromise is necessary.

Faced with this dilemma, the classical statistician changes the question to one which has an answer involving only objective probability but whose relevance to the original question is indirect. The probability he gives is therefore not, except coincidentally, interpretable as a degree of belief about H. Thus a test of significance considers the (objective) probability of an extreme event under the assumption of no-treatment effect, say, but it produces no statement about the probability that there is actually no-treatment effect given the event that occurred (the data observed). Subjective judgments are not entirely excluded; they are involved in the choice of design, underlying assumptions, model, test statistic, and so on, even—perhaps especially—in the best practice. As far as possible, however, they should be prevented from degrading the relative frequency property of the probabilities quoted.

The Bayesian chooses instead to answer the question posed, but at the cost of introducing subjective prior (beforehand) probabilities as well. He can argue that there is only one rational posterior probability for any given prior probability (obtained by a theorem which was first stated and proved in a special case by the Reverend Thomas Bayes and published in 1763) and that it is rational to have some prior probability (e.g. Savage, 1954), but not that a particular prior probability is the only rational one to have. He can perhaps justify a particular choice as somehow "neutral." He can investigate the sensitivity of posterior to prior probabilities: If it is low, this means comfortingly that the subjective input has little influence, the data overwhelm prior opinion, and any dispute about the results must be on other grounds than lack of evidence; if it is high, the analysis shows just how the conclusion should depend on prior opinion and where prior opinion and the evidence balance. But he must use some prior probability, and it is not objective, so to this extent his posterior probability is not objective. The Bayesian position is not, however, a license to unbridled subjectivity. Its subjective elements must be made specific and overt and be disciplined by consistency and the data.

The choice between classical and Bayesian approaches to statistical inference ultimately rests on one's view of the significance of the subjective elements of both and of the indirectness of classical methods. Unfortunately a proper view cannot be formed on the basis of such a brief discussion, which can neither avoid imprecision and trespassing on words, nor reflect the technical and philosophical depths of the problem, the many shades of opinion held, and the many arguments advanced relevant to both central and subsidiary, but still important, issues.

The two approaches are not as distant from one another practically as this discussion of their philosophical differences might suggest. For example, confidence levels are often close to posterior probability levels. Furthermore, there is enough sense in both approaches so that they should lead to similar results when sensibly applied to the same set of data. Even a firm believer in one approach should be concerned if his methods are seriously discordant with the other. For example, many of the limitations of significance tests, and their shortcomings when unthinkingly used, which classical statisticians have come to recognize on classical grounds, would have been rapidly brought to light by comparison with Bayesian methods. Bayesian prior distributions which are not true distributions but conventional "neutral" approximations sometimes have an unreasonable consequence which is immediately evident classically.

The two approaches can also abet one another. In the last attrition problem mentioned (i.e., attrition from treatment but not from measurement) for example, Bayesian ideas might be used to guide the choice of an appropriate statistic which then could be analyzed classically.

Finally the two approaches may complement one another: Some problems are difficult or infeasible to handle by one but not by the other. A reasonable analysis by either is far better than unaided intuition.

# IV

## Quasi-Experimental Designs

There are many occasions when a new experimental program is introduced but it is not feasible to assign units at random to produce the control and experimental groups required for a true experiment. In some such situations there may nonetheless be modes of scheduling treatments and measurements, and modes of analyzing data that are useful in evaluating program impact. These modes are treated in this chapter as *quasi*-experimental designs. We can distinguish quasi-experiments from true experiments by the absence of randomized assignment of units to treatments. The boundary between quasi-experiments and correlational studies or descriptive evaluations is harder to define. We focus here on those analyses that come closest to true experiments.

In the area of true experiments there is a substantial methodological consensus among statisticians and experimental social scientists. No such consensus exists in the area of quasi-experimental design. Rather there is a range of possible positions on a scale of tolerance. There are those who, looking at the often unverifiable assumptions which even the best of quasi-experimental analyses involve, reject all such analyses, hold out for true experiments or nothing. Others believe that there are some quasi-experimental designs worth undertaking if a true experiment cannot be done, and this chapter recommends some quasi-experimental designs as useful substitutes which, for all their weaknesses, are much better than current practice. But in presenting the costs in ambiguity of inference that accompany particular designs, this chapter also serves as an argument in favor of the extra administrative effort required to institute a true experiment, if one is possible.

Quasi-experimental designs also represent a useful adjunct to a true experiment and a fall-back position for use in salvaging intended true experiments that fail to be properly implemented. Frequently administrators and operators substitute judgmental assignment procedures where the script called for blind random decisions. The true experiment is damaged or destroyed, but the resulting quasi-experiment may still be very well worth doing if comparable pretests and posttests are involved (e.g., the Pretest—Posttest Comparison Group design which follows). A quasi-experimental adjunct to a true experiment is illustrated in the Sinisterra, McKay, and McKay (1971) (McKay, McKay, and Sinisterra, 1973) study of compensatory preschool education in Cali, Colombia. In addition to the several experimental groups of randomly assigned poverty-level 3-year-olds, this study also includes an upper-middle-class group of 3-year-olds, who provide a quasi-experimental comparison group in terms of which success in "closing the gap" can be measured.

Of the many possible quasi-experimental designs, this chapter focuses on two of the strongest: the Regression–Discontinuity design and the Interrupted Time Series with Comparison Series. The latter provides a convenient introduction to an additional four weaker designs which can be considered as fragments of it. The Comparison Series and its four derivatives are considered in the second section entitled, "Comparison Group and Time Series Designs."

## Regression–Discontinuity Design

The basic ideas behind the Regression–Discontinuity design can be more easily understood if we begin by considering first a strong and then a weak form of a true experiment both of which are applicable to the type of situation which is also appropriate for a Regression–Discontinuity quasi-experiment. Recall an earlier remark that one of the necessary conditions for a social experiment is that the ameliorative treatment be in short supply, thus guaranteeing that there are more experimental units (persons, schools, cities, etc.) available for the treatment than are going to be treated. This condition regularly occurs for pilot programs in which a new program is tried out on a limited population. It often occurs for specialized programs applied to eligible subgroups of the population, such as specialized opportunities based on merit, or compensatory programs based on need. If such programs are in short supply, with more eligibles than program space, it provides one of the conditions for using some of the eligible applicants as a control group.

Under these circumstances, the best strategy would be a true experiment in which random assignment of units occurred *across the full range of eligibility*. Let us consider, for example, a Neighborhood Youth Corps training program in which needy unemployed or underemployed young adults receive training for specific, well-paying jobs. Eligibility for the program might depend (as it once did) on per capita earnings of the applicant's family. If there are a larger number of eligible applicants than the program can handle, the experimentally oriented administrator could randomly select from all those eligible the number for which there was space in the program. By keeping records on the randomly equivalent remainder for use as a control group, he could, at a later time, collect data on earnings of trained and not trained individuals in order to measure the effect of training.

Now, there are many situations in which random assignment of eligibles is not regarded as acceptable. Eligibility, it is argued, occurs in degree, not as a dichotomous quantum: Those most eligible, those most needy, should get the treatment if there are not facilities to take care of all those eligible. This argument against randomization is often stated as though existing assignment procedures *did* meet the equity requirements on which random assignment fails. Careful examination of almost any agency operation will usually show that they do not. There is regularly lacking any procedure for ranking those who are potentially eligible in order of need as a basis for admissions decisions. The casual procedures of recruitment and admission allow ample room for cronyism and administrative convenience. New facilities are deliberately given minimal publicity in order to avoid a surplus of applicants. If a first-come, first-served rule is employed, the most needy will rarely be among those most alert to new facilities. Those first to apply will have learned about the opportunity by informal informational sources prior to public announcement. In contrast with existing practice, a thorough publicizing of program opportunities, resulting in a surplus of eligibles who are then assigned at random to treatment or control status, is a highly moral procedure, over and above the value of making possible experimental evaluation.

Nevertheless, if resistance to full-scale randomization cannot be overcome, it is still possible to give explicit attention to degree of eligibility in a weak form of experiment, namely a *tie-breaking randomi-*

*zation* experiment. Let us suppose that rather than being spread out over the entire range of eligibles, the job training program was instead concentrated on those most in need; and that the program could accommodate all of those with family incomes of $22 per person per week and below, plus half of those with incomes of $23 a week. Even under the constraint to give the treatment to the neediest, it would now be justifiable to assign randomly to treatment or nontreatment those persons who were tied at $23. Thus a small-scale true experiment could be carried out. This is a weak experiment on two counts. First, a very small number of cases may be available and thus a difference reflecting a genuine effect might not be statistically significant, or might even be reversed by sampling fluctuations. One would want to maximize the number of persons who were tied at the cut-off score and a useful way to do this would be to adopt relatively large class intervals within which scores could be regarded as equal for all practical purposes. Thus, in the present example a $2 per week interval would yield a larger number of ties than would, say, a 50¢ per week interval, as well as avoiding the excessive and meaningless precision of the latter calculation. The second weakness of this experiment is that it explores the treatment effect only for a narrow range of eligibility and thus provides a very limited base for estimating the effects over the whole range of treatment (see Figure 4.1). On the other hand, the narrow range that it does explore is presumably similar to the adjacent ranges where expansion and contraction of the program would take

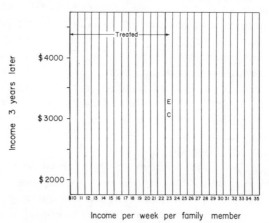

Income per week per family member

**Figure 4.1**  Illustrative outcome for a hypothetical tie-breaking experiment in which some applicants with a per capita weekly family income of $23 are assigned at random to the Neighborhood Youth Corps while others are randomly assigned to control group status. All those with incomes of $22 and below get the training. Means for each group on average earnings subject to witholding 3 years later are indicated by the location of the E for Experimental Group and C for Control Group.

place, and thus it is relevant to an important problem for administrative decision making.

REGRESSION–DISCONTINUITY DESIGN

In considering Figure 4.1, let us ask what might be found if one did a follow-up study of eligibility units adjacent to the experiment. Assuming the training to have been effective, one could expect the all-treated group with eligibility scores of $22 to have later incomes very similar to those of the Experimental (E) subgroup of $23, slightly lower perhaps as a concomitant of their slightly lower starting income, but still higher than the Controls (C) of $23—similarly for scores of $21, $20, or less. On the other hand, later incomes among those with eligibility scores of $24, all untreated, should be very similar to those of the controls of category $23—slightly higher, but not as high as the experimentals of category $23, etc. The hypothetical data of Figure 4.2 extend such a follow-up study across the whole range of income categories.

Comparison of Figure 4.2 with Figure 4.1 suggests that one should be able to infer what the results of a hypothetical tie-breaking experiment would have been from analysis of the effects of nonrandomly assigned treatments across the total range of eligibility. Thus, if the cutting point for eligibility had been set at $22 and below, with all of the $23 group going untreated, and if the outcome had been as in Figure 4.3, we could be quite confident that a tie-breaking experiment would have shown the results found in Figures 4.1 and 4.2. On the other hand,

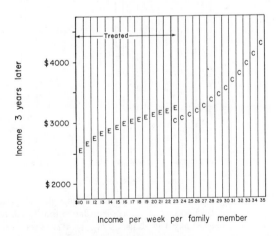

Income per week per family member

**Figure 4.2**  Hypothetical tie-breaking experiment of Figure 4.1 plus values for those in other family income classes, all of whom either got Neighborhood Youth Corps training if at $22 or below, or did not if at $24 and above.

werethe results to be as in Figure 4.4, we could be confident that the treatment had no effect.

Figures 4.3 and 4.4 illustrate Regression–Discontinuity design (Thistlethwaite and Campbell, 1960; Campbell, 1969; and from a different methodological tradition, Goldberger, 1972, pp. 14–21). It is a quasi-experimental substitute for the tie-breaking randomization experiment shown in Figure 4.1, rather than for full-range randomization. The results of Regression–Discontinuity design do not serve as a basis for estimating effects at all levels of eligibility, but only as a basis for extrapolating to the results of a hypothetical tie-breaking experiment at the cutting point. For example, it appears in Figure 4.3 that the income effect drops off among the most eligible, a conclusion which comes from an implicit assumption that without treatment the outcomes would have shown a straight line slope over the whole range. This need not be the case, of course, and curvilinear functions may be at least as common as linear ones in such settings.

The Regression–Discontinuity design is quasi-experimental in that more unverifiable assumptions have to be made in interpreting it than would be required for the tie-breaking randomization. For example, one has to assume a homogeneity of the measurement units on both sides of and across the cutting point. One also has to make assumptions about the underlying mathematical function. A suggested mode of statistical analysis (Sween, 1971) is to fit a curve separately to the two segments of the data above and below the cutting point and to obtain

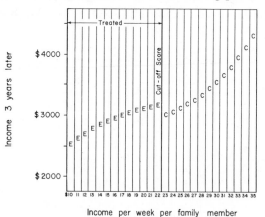

Income per week per family member

**Figure 4.3**  Hypothetical outcome for a Regression–Discontinuity design showing a degree of effect from Neighborhood Youth Corps similar to that illustrated in Figures 4.1 and 4.2. This figure is essentially the same as Figure 4.2, except that there is no randomized category and no tie-breaking randomization. Instead, all at income level $22 and below have been admitted to the program.

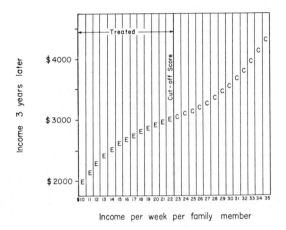

**Figure 4.4** Hypothetical outcome for a Regression–Discontinuity design in the setting of Figures 4.2 and 4.3, but in which the treatment has had no effect.

from each the intercept value at the cutting point, thus literally extrapolating from each side to the cutting point. The magnitude of the difference between these two extrapolated values will obviously depend upon what form of curve is assumed for each of the two parts. If the basic underlying curve is sigmoid, as illustrated in Figures 4.3 and 4.4, then fitting a linear function to a null condition represented by Figure 4.4 will produce a pseudo-effect. One should also graph the results and distrust the statistical results if visual inspection makes plausible a continuous function with no discontinuity at the cutting point. Of course, an arbitrary coincidence of an independent jump in the underlying curve with the cutting point is always a possibility, but an unlikely one if the assumption of equality of intervals in the measurement scale is justified and the variation within intervals is homogeneous.

While the illustrations provided deal with a single dependent and a single independent variable, multivariate versions of the design would often be preferable, as long as the feature of a sharp cutting point on a quantified decision criterion is not lost. Pooling many eligibility variables into a single eligibility score is discussed in the following. Multivariate outcome variables would be usable in several forms. A single dependent variable, such as later earnings, could be statistically adjusted to eliminate differential effects of various socioeconomic background variables, except those used to quantify eligibility. Or, a composite outcome variable constructed by multiple regression techniques could be employed.

PROBLEMS IN QUANTIFYING ELIGIBILITY AND
ADMINISTRATING ADMISSION PROCEDURES

The basic situation is a common one: an ameliorative program in short supply; a basic decision that it should go to the most needy; a desire to see the program scientifically evaluated. For this situation, if random assignment among equally eligible subjects is ruled out, the Regression–Discontinuity design is probably the best one available and thus should frequently be used. To use it requires a quantified eligibility criterion and other special admission procedures and controls.

For some ameliorative programs a quantitative variable is already included among several eligibility criteria. Family income in Neighborhood Youth Corps is but one example. Test scores, as on a reading readiness test, provide another class of examples. Where these exist, a Regression–Discontinuity design can be used among that subsample of applicants who meet all other requirements and for whom this quantitative criterion is thus decisive. In such cases, the Regression–Discontinuity design could be used with present administrative machinery. What is required is (1) adherence to a sharp cutting point, allowing no exceptions for the set of applicants for which the score is to be the sole and uniform decision rule, and (2) keeping full records of eligibility scores and identification data on both those accepted and those rejected by this criterion. Some illustrations of likely biases will help make the admissions procedures clearer.

One source of bias is in the fact that, in most treatment programs, there occur cases which must be admitted to the program regardless of their eligibility as defined by the cut-off score. This may be because of the compelling nature of the person's needs as seen by the staff, because of political considerations, or for other reasons. Such cases should be identified and removed from the research sample without examining their eligibility score and without regard to whether they fall in the treated or the untreated group. Otherwise, they produce bias. The bias arises because administrators typically strive to minimize the number of exceptions to the rules and to invoke special privilege only if the special case would have been rejected for treatment by imposition of the cut-off score. If only those who would have been rejected are then removed from the study, this "purifies" the untreated group without a parallel purification of the treated group. That is, the treated group retains persons who, had their scores fallen instead in the no-treatment range, would have been admitted anyway. Such a process of selective elimination tends to make a compensatory program look good. If these cases cannot be eliminated in advance, one could leave them in the analysis but classify them as their eligibility scores *would* have assigned them, e.g., ineligibles who were assigned to treatment being labeled for analytic purposes as not having received the treatment. While this leads to an underestimate of treatment effects, it avoids letting selection biases produce pseudo-effects. (See the more extended treatment in Chapter III of modes of analysis where not all of those randomly assigned to a treatment accept it.) For the procedure of allowing exceptions by falsifying the crucial scores, there is no methodological cure. One should, however, be able to estimate the direction of bias in many situations. For example, where the program is compensatory, the process would usually exaggerate its effectiveness.

Another potential bias comes from the existence of an official, publicized cut-off score, a practice often followed if there is room for all of those eligible. In the Neighborhood Youth Corps program, the requirement that family income be below the poverty level might have been such a criterion. When this score is something that the potential applicant can ascertain about himself (as income or age), there results a self-selection among ineligible applicants that is not paralleled among the eligibles. Thus, the agency meets and gets initial records on persons in the ineligible region who have not had adequate information about the cut-off point. From this group, therefore, many of the more alert and able have removed themselves. For a compensatory program, this bias is in the direction of making the treatment look good through a sampling bias that reduces the level of competence of the untreated. In the case of a legally fixed cut-off which the applicant cannot himself determine precisely before applying, such as an achievement test score, this source of bias is not likely. Even if there is some tendency in such a case for the alert ineligible not to apply, it is unlikely to produce an abrupt discontinuity in applicant quality right at the cutting point.

The preceding considerations have been presented as though admission were being decided for sizable batches of applicants at one time. Where a new facility is going to open on a specific date or where an instructional program is organized into terms with fixed starting dates, then this is feasible. One can compare the number of spaces with the number of applicants and set the cutting point in a Regression–Discontinuity design. However, the design is also usable for "trickle processing" situations, in which new applicants appear at any time and are admitted or not depending upon their qualifications and the number of beds available—short waits and empty beds being tolerated but kept to a minimum. Under trickle processing, batchlike time periods must be established within which a cut-off criterion is adhered to. If too many empty beds are accumulated or if waiting times become too long, then for the next time period a corrective readjustment is made, for example, by lowering the admission score. Each time period contains a complete quasi-experiment. But individual periods will frequently include too few cases to be interpretable in isolation. Combining time periods or batches requires careful rules to avoid selection biases. Since different cutting points have been used, pooling requires that the data be converted into units above and below the cutting point. (At least four such steps on each side would seem a minimum; more are, of course, desirable.) All batches must contribute in equal proportion to all steps used, otherwise batch-to-batch sampling differences will create bends in the composite curve. But identity in the size of the units from batch to batch is not required.

Many ameliorative programs lack any official quantitiative criteria for admission to treatment. To apply the Regression–Discontinuity design to them, a quantitative ordering of eligibility priority is essential. Two widely useful procedures are ranking and rating. Ranking can only be used if applicants are being handled in large batches. Within each batch, all applicants can be ranked in need by each of the admissions staff and a combined ranking generated. The top $n$ eligibles would be admitted. Alternatively, eligible individuals can be rated as to need by each staff member and the average of all ratings taken. When several criteria are available, they can be combined statistically into a single eligibility score.

In large batch processing the cutting point can be decided after all candidates have been rated, and it can be chosen so as to provide exactly the same number of candidates as there are spaces (randomizing if there are ties at the cutting point). In trickle processing, the cutting point for a given time period must be set in advance on the basis of past experience, including past rate of applicants, typical eligibility, and rater idiosyncracies.

In summary, the Regression–Discontinuity design is an important quasi-experimental analysis, available where program administrators are willing to specify precisely the order of eligibility and to adhere meticulously to it. Because of the requirement of quantifying eligibility, it represents a significant additional procedural burden over ordinary admission procedures, a burden usually as great or greater than that required for randomization from a pool of eligible applicants larger than the facilities can accommodate. Such randomization is to be preferred on grounds of both statistical efficiency and the fewer background assumptions that have to be made. But where randomization is precluded, the Regression–Discontinuity design is recommended.

## Comparison Group and Time Series Designs

The following broad category of quasi-experimental designs is applicable to situations in which a program is applied to all units in a population at once, for example, a new law, a tax, a licensing .provision. The universality of application precludes the establishment of control groups, and only quasi-experimental designs, if any, are available. This section presents a group of five related designs that are applicable to such situations. The strongest of these designs—the Interrupted Time Series with Comparison Series (Comparison Series for short) is explained first, followed by four weaker designs, which can be understood as portions of the first, as shown in Table 4.1.

### INTERRUPTED TIMES SERIES WITH COMPARISON SERIES

Let us consider a specific hypothetical example. In 1957, State A introduced a compulsory arbitration law. State B, with a roughly similar mix of industries, geography, and social structure remained without such a law, nor had it changed any relevant laws in an 18-year period. It is judged, therefore, to be an appropriate "comparison group." For each of the 18 years, the percentage of industrial employment days lost through lockouts and strikes is plotted. If the outcome were as in Figure 4.5, we would be inclined to accept the program as effective. For an outcome as shown in Figures 4.6 or 4.7, we would be less sure but would still consider it as likely evidence of effect; whereas Figure 4.8 would be considered a no-effect outcome. These commonsense considerations, and many of the others that would be invoked with a larger sample of illustrations, can and should be clarified. But such a process cannot be completely formal, for in the last analysis, the inference as to experimental effects has to be judged in terms of the plausibility of the various other explanations available to account for the changes. In generating such alternative explanations and in judging their relative adequacy, local knowledge and local expertise are essential. One of the advantages of graphic presentation is that, unlike many statistical summaries, it allows local experts as well as statistical methodologists to participate in the critical evaluation of results, which is essential in quasi-experimental inference.

Underlying an interpretation of an outcome such as Figure 4.5 is the assumption that States A and B are subject to all of the same change agents—weather, business cycles, historical events, developmental trends, changes in record-keeping procedures, changes in other imping-

**TABLE 4.1**

**Comparison Group and Time Series Designs:
A Series of Quasi-Experimental Designs
Interpreted as Fragments of the Most Comprehensive One**
($m$ = measure, $T$ = treatment, $t$ = time period)

| Design | .... | $t_n$ | $t_{n+1}$ | $t_{n+2}$ | $t_{n+3}$ | $t_{n+4}$ | $t_{n+5}$ | $t_{n+6}$ | $t_{n+7}$ | .... |
|---|---|---|---|---|---|---|---|---|---|---|
| **Interrupted Time Series with Comparison Series** | | | | | | | | | | |
| experimental group | .... | $m$ | $m$ | $m$ | $m$ | $T$  $m$ | $m$ | $m$ | $m$ | |
| comparison group | | $m$ | $m$ | $m$ | $m$ | $m$ | $m$ | $m$ | $m$ | |
| **Single Interrupted Time Series** | | | | | | | | | | |
| experimental group | .... | $m$ | $m$ | $m$ | $m$ | $T$  $m$ | $m$ | $m$ | $m$ | |
| **Pretest-Posttest Comparison Group design** | | | | | | | | | | |
| experimental group | | | | | $m$ | $T$  $m$ | | | | |
| comparison group | | | | | $m$ | $m$ | | | | |
| **One-Group Before-and-After design** | | | | | | | | | | |
| experimental group | | | | | $m$ | $T$  $m$ | | | | |
| **Posttest-Only Comparison Group design** | | | | | | | | | | |
| experimental group | | | | | | $T$  $m$ | | | | |
| comparison group | | | | | | $m$ | | | | |

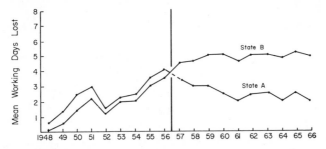

**Figure 4.5** Hypothetical outcome for an Interrupted Time Series design in which State A introduced a compulsory arbitration law in 1957 while State B introduced no such change and, thus, serves as a comparison against which to evaluate the change in State A. Effects are illustrated in terms of mean working days lost per worker per year.

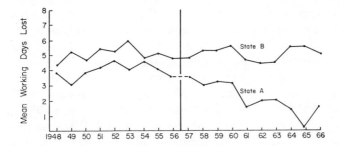

**Figure 4.6** A second hypothetical outcome for the setting of Figure 4.5.

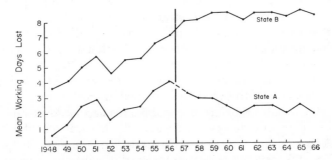

**Figure 4.7** A third hypothetical outcome for the setting of Figure 4.5.

ing laws, and so on—*except for the one law in question*. We know in advance that this cannot be literally so in every detail. The issue becomes one of judging the extent to which an imperfect match plausibly explains away the outcome without necessitating the assumption that the law under study had an effect. Pretreatment similarity is obviously important. Thus, other things being equal, the inference of

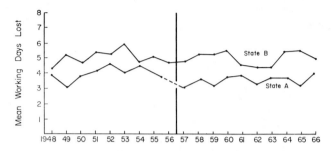

**Figure 4.8**    A fourth hypothetical outcome for the setting of Figure 4.5.

effect is much clearer in Figure 4.5 than in Figure 4.6 because of the generally greater likelihood of other dissimilarities accompanying the larger difference in mean level. Nonetheless, one might well conclude than an effect occurred in Figures 4.6 and 4.7 as well as in Figure 4.5.

Even in a clear-cut case such as Figure 4.5, one should examine the specific plausibility of alternative explanations. Was there a concomitant change in record-keeping rules in State A in 1957? Did new census data change the divisor in the index? Was there a specific local business trend? Is most of the effect due to one industry lacking in B? And so on. For many of these rival explanations, an examination of supplementary evidence will help determine their plausibility. This is an essential aspect of the proper use of the method.

A look at some real data may be desirable. Figure 4.9 (Baldus, 1973) shows the effect in one state of introducing a law requiring repayment of welfare payments from the estate of a deceased recipient. Baldus shows that such laws are regularly effective in reducing case loads, an effect that he judges to be undesirable in that it leads many of the elderly poor to endure inadequate diets and other deprivations so that they can leave their homes to their children. The data of Figure 4.9 are exceptionally untroubled by seasonal trends, secular trends, or inexplicable instability. Note also that Baldus has used several comparison states. This provides a valuable addition to clarity of inference over the use of a single comparison as illustrated in Figures 4.5 through 4.8.

Where the data are available for smaller subunits, various strategies for improving comparability by using selected subsets of the data have been used. Some of these are acceptable, some are misleading. In the hypothetical case of Figure 4.7, for example, disaggregation could be done by type of industry or by county. It would be fine to rework the data by industry, generating a dozen parallel studies within each of which an effect could be examined. However, the smaller actuarial base would increase the instability of each series and might well obscure effects. An averaging of such series would, however, be acceptable,

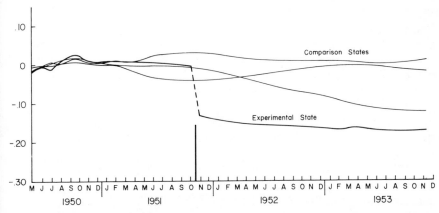

**Figure 4.9**  Effect of introducing a law in State A requiring repayment of welfare costs from the decreased recipient's estate on the old age assistance case loads.
Monthly data have all values expressed as a percentage of the case load 18 months
prior to the change of the law. [Modified from Baldus (1972, p. 204, Figure 1).]

including a "matching" recombination so that industries specific to
one state were eliminated and so that other industries were represented
equally in their contribution to each state's new composite. But
matching subunit scores on the mean working days lost during a specific year is unacceptable in that it can produce misleading pseudo-effects
due to autocorrelated statistical instability. Biases can also be produced
by matching on data specific to a single time period on a series closely
related to the dependent variable.

A subtle form of regression artifact can occur where the extremity
of a single point in the time series determines the time at which a program change is introduced. Consider the example of Figure 4.10, again
based upon real data. State A, alarmed at the rise in traffic fatalities in
1955, instituted a strenuous enforcement effort to reduce highway
speeds. The 1956 fatality figures were better. But in an unstable series
such as this, the statistical expectation is that the points immediately
following an extreme departure from the overall trend will be closer
to the overall trend even with no change in the causal system, merely
as a tautological implication of the fact of instability. This "reversion
to trend" is like the "regression to the mean," and should not be used in
such a setting as evidence of effect of the treatment. Wherever the
choice of point of treatment has been in response to an acute extreme
in the indicator itself (or in a highly correlated series), and where the
posttreatment data return toward the general trend, this explanation of
the outcome is so statistically inevitable (on the average) as to be more
plausible than the hypothesis that the treatment has had an effect. If
in looking at the whole series, it becomes apparent that the period just

prior to the treatment is more unusual than the period immediately following, this regression artifact is to be suspected. The arguments used for justifying the program innovation should be examined to see if the timing of the program change was in fact a response to the extreme prior values. This was indeed the case in the instance reported in Figure 4.10. (While this regression artifact is adequate to explain the drop in 1956, it cannot explain the increased departure from the average of the comparison states in 1957, 1958, and 1959, and this may well be due to the speed restrictions which were kept in force during those years.)

Where a control series from an independent but similar administrative unit or geographical area is not available, other relevant comparison series may be. Ross (1973) (Ross, Campbell, and Glass, 1970) in his study of the British Breathalyser crackdown of 1967, used commuting hours (which were also times when pubs had been closed for several hours) as a comparison for the data on weekend nights, when driving after drinking was common. Figure 4.11 shows his results.

Tests of significance are only a small part of the inference process in such a situation. Most of the threats to validity or plausible rival hypotheses have to be dealt with on more qualitative grounds. Nonetheless, inherent instability in the data series is a rival hypothesis which also deserves being rendered implausible if possible. Because of the autoregressive nature of most such series, ordinary curve-fitting comparisons of slope and intercept may produce inappropriately small error terms, finding a significant shift too often. Appropriate tests of significance are provided by Box and Tiao (1965); Box and Jenkins

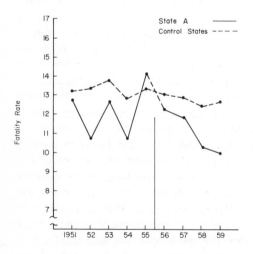

**Figure 4.10** Traffic fatalities per 100,000 of population in State A prior to and after a strong crackdown on speeding initiated in 1956, compared with the average of four neighboring states. [After Campbell (1969, p. 419, Figure 11).]

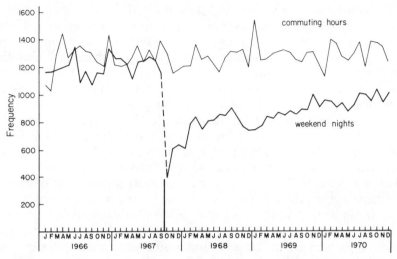

**Figure 4.11**  British traffic casualties (fatalities plus serious injuries) before and after the British Breathalyser crackdown of October 1967, seasonally adjusted. [Modified from Ross, *et al.* (1970, p. 500, Figure 1) on the basis of the revised and extended data reported in Ross, 1973.]

(1970); Glass, Tiao, and McGuire (1971); and Glass, Wilson, and Gottman (1972).

The tests just cited use one observation (often a total, a mean, or a rate) per time period. When these data can be disaggregated into persons, families, factories, schools, precincts, counties, or other units, one is often tempted to apply a test of significance to these frequencies. Thus, in Figure 4.8 one might use the disaggregated data for factories or counties for the year prior and the year following the change and do an analysis of variance of the posttreatment group means with the pretreatment values as covariates. Or one might compute for each county a 1955–1956 gain score and do a test of the significance of the difference between experimental and comparison state gains. The irrelevance of such tests is conveyed by noting that had similar tests been done for other pairs of adjacent years prior to the treatment, each such comparison would usually have been highly statistically significant also. The instability which is revealed by the longer series (as compared with a single Two-Wave Before-and-After design) is usually produced by a succession of very real and significant changes, but ones for which no clear causal attribution can be made. If "statistically significant" changes are happening every year or so anyway, the occurrence of another one coincident with the treatment is not evidence that the treatment caused it.

Replication in a variety of times and settings is important in all experimental designs and is especially so in quasi-experimental ones. Disaggregating the experimental and comparison data into several replications is of dubious value since they may all share a confounding with some local intrastate event that plausibly explains the result. It is most important to replicate at other times and in other settings that are not likely to share rival influences for change.

Note that experimental evidence of effect is valuable even when the political decisions involved are no longer tentative but seem firmly established. The issues are bound to reappear, and controversy over the actual effects deserves to be fed with facts even at some considerable research cost. Thus it is important to measure the effect of extending an accepted program to areas not now having it. In connection with this, it can be noted that a region or group which already has the treatment (e.g., compulsory arbitration) under consideration can be used as a comparison group. Whereas in classical experimental designs and in the examples of Figures 4.5 to 4.8 an effective treatment makes the groups more different; in the case where there is an already treated comparison group, the effective treatment makes the experimental group more similar. Figure 4.12 illustrates such a process. The middle-class comparison group in the Sinisterra, McKay, and McKay study mentioned earlier also represents such a case.

Often a new program requires extensive administrative effort to initiate and, therefore, is most conveniently introduced one region at a time. In such cases, the early and late regions of introduction can serve as each other's comparison groups for a replicated demonstration of effect, as in Figure 4.13. It also seems of social value for future planning to use the occasion of termination of a program as an opportunity to measure its impact. Baldus (1973), for example, has confirmed the deterrence effect of state laws requiring the recovery of welfare pay-

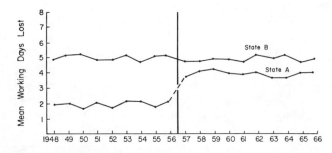

**Figure 4.12** Hypothetical outcome for a setting such as Figure 4.5 in which the comparison state has already had a compulsory arbitration law.

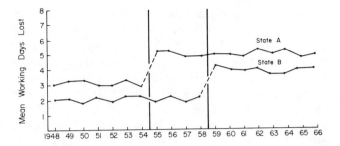

**Figure 4.13** Hypothetical outcome for a setting such as Figure 4.5 in which both states get the law, but at different times, each serving in turn as the control for the other.

ment from the deceased recipient's estate not only from the introduction but also from the repeal of such laws. (His study is also exemplary in examining all of the dozens of replications of onset and termination of such laws.)

SINGLE INTERRUPTED TIME SERIES DESIGN

Often when a new program is introduced nationally, no appropriate comparison series is available. In such instances a single time series may occasionally be interpretable in isolation. The data of Figure 4.14 are, we believe, compelling even without the commuting hours comparison provided earlier in Figure 4.11. In interpreting the September 1967 drop as evidence of program impact one must assume that the prior trend would otherwise have continued both as to general slope, level, and amplitude of fluctuation. Most of these fluctuations are "real"—statistically significant—the product of genuine fluctuations in a variety of causal factors such as weather, traffic density, prosperity, introduction of limited access highways, installation of traffic lights at bad intersections, and so on. One is assuming that the total effect of these heterogeneous influences achieves a stable stochastic character and that no unusual extreme of a past cause, or first appearance of a novel change agent has occurred coincident with the crackdown. Lacking a comparison group subject to the great majority of such possible effectors makes it much harder to rule out extraneous causal agents. However, examination of relevant records for evidence in favor of rival hypotheses, both for the crackdown period and for other periods, can rule out many of these alternatives. In Ross's study, the effects of an increased license fee for two-wheeled vehicles and several other alternative explanations that had appeared in public discussion were effectively ruled out. Hypotheses based on weather and new limited access highways could easily have been ruled out also. It is in the generation and disposal of such rival hypotheses that local subject-matter experts (both advocates and opponents) are invaluable. While this search can never be exhaustive, nor the ruling out of rival hypotheses conclusive, the encouragement of such informed criticism can make this type of applied science more objective.

An important role for the Single Interrupted Time Series design is as a curb on the overinterpretation of transient fluctuations typical of the usual simple before-and-after comparisons (e.g., "compared with this same quarter last year"). On the other hand, it is weaker than the Comparison Series design in that many outcomes interpretable as effects with the latter design would be uninterpretable as effects if only the single time series for the treated state were available. The single series is unable to demonstrate effects of gradually introduced changes or to estimate long-term effects. The single series is also particularly handicapped by seasonal fluctuations, which, if not removed, render the available statistical tests of significance inappropriate and also confuse visual interpretation. Available methods of removing seasonal trends are often unsatisfactory for some bodies of data.

In spite of these problems, this design will often be the only one possible. Used with appropriate caution, it can be much more informa-

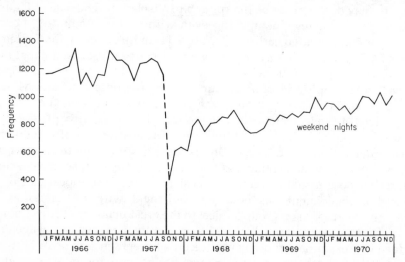

**Figure 4.14** British fatalities and serious injuries combined for Friday nights, 10 P.M. to midnight; Saturday mornings, midnight to 4 A.M. ; Saturday nights 10 P.M. to midnight; and Sunday mornings, midnight to 4 A.M. ; corrected for weekend days per month, seasonal variations removed. [From Ross (1973, p. 33, Figure 10).]

tive than the usual modes of analysis. Where it is being considered as the design of choice in evaluating a planned program innovation, three rules of implementation stand out as particularly important:

1. *Keep the measurement system constant.* Too often a new program is accompanied by reforms in record keeping that produce pseudo-shifts (see Campbell, 1969, for examples). It is usually better to keep an imperfect indicator comparable than to improve it coincident with a program change. (With a multiple indicator approach, it may be possible to do both.) Even without a change in the formal index, an abrupt change in one of its components may produce a pseudo-effect, as when new census figures introduce an abrupt revision of the population estimate used to calculate a per capita rate.

2. *Introduce the new program or policy abruptly.* A gradually introduced program will produce changes that cannot be distinguished from long-term secular trends. In the case of the British Road Safety Act of 1967, shown in Figures 4.11 and 4.14, the starting date for enforcement was set for several months after the legislation was passed and was preceded by an intense publicity campaign which included attention to the starting date as well as the means of enforcement and the penalties involved. Had the new law gone into effect immediately, with gradually increasing enforcement as police were educated, and gradually increasing publicity based upon news of arrests, the abrupt and coincident change in casualties found in Figure 4.14 would have been missing. It is the abrupt and coincident change in the indicator that provides confidence in the causal inference in this very uncontrolled laboratory.

3. *Delay reaction to acute problems.* To avoid the subtle regression artifact problem discussed earlier (Figure 4.10), the introduction of the new policy should not immediately follow a wide fluctuation in the prior series. A quickly introduced corrective measure in response to an acute problem is very hard to distinguish from the ordinary reversion to trend found in any unstable series. Focusing ameliorative efforts on chronic problems avoids this, as exemplified in the British Breathalyser crackdown (Figures 4.11 and 4.14). Where reaction to an acute problem must be made, it is desirable to delay its introduction so that the expected reversion to trend can take place prior to the crackdown. Delaying initiation is also advantageous in providing time for publicizing a starting date, as mentioned in point 2.

All three of these rules are, of course, also desirable for the Comparison Series design, although the latter is sufficiently stronger that inference will occasionally be possible anyway. This reminds us of a fourth rule.

4. *Seek out comparison series,* either from comparable jurisdictions or from content comparisons within one's own jurisdiction. If possible, move up from the Single Interrupted Time Series to the Comparison Series.

### THE PRETEST–POSTTEST COMPARISON GROUP DESIGN

This is one of the most common of quasi-experimental evaluation designs. An experimental group receives a pretest and a posttest. A comparison group of some degree of similarity (but *not* assigned at random from the same pool of respondents) also receives a pretest and posttest, usually timed to coincide with the experimental group testing. Figure 4.15 shows hypothetical data from such a study using states as comparison groups.

The design can be conceived of as a two-wave segment of the Comparison Series design bracketing the point of the application of the treatment. As such, it is much weaker than the Comparison Series. Figure 4.15, for example, presents the same data for 1956 and 1957 as that in Figure 4.8. In Figure 4.15, it looks as though the law reduced days lost from strikes. In Figure 4.8, no such conclusion can be drawn. If the data can be developed for a larger series, they should be, but where new measures are introduced specifically for the purpose of evaluating a treatment, this is rarely possible. However, as long as its potential weaknesses are kept in mind and certain specific traps of analysis are avoided, it is a design well worth employing where randomized assignment is not possible.

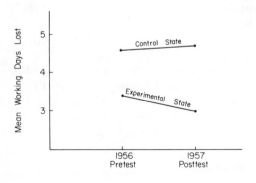

**Figure 4.15** Hypothetical effect of a 1957 law in one state on days lost through strikes, measured by the Pretest–Posttest Comparison Group design. Setting as in Figure 4.8.

Selecting a comparison group is the crucial problem. Commonly, the experimental unit is designated first and a comparison unit searched out later. It is natural to seek a comparison group as similar as possible on all of the various factors that might affect the measures to be used. The problem is to do so in a way that avoids regression artifacts due to selection (Thorndike, 1942; Campbell and Erlebacher, 1970). One should choose such a comparison group on general grounds of similarity but *not* on the basis of the pretest scores. Usually the comparison group and the control group will be different on the pretest in spite of such matching. One should live with such pretest differences rather than try to adjust them away by using matched subsets of the groups or by statistical adjustments. Such adjustments generate pseudo-effects and misleading conclusions that would have been avoided had the whole groups been used with the pretest difference. Thus, in the hypothetical case of Figure 4.15, it is better to leave the comparison as there presented than to present data for matched subsets of metropolitan areas of each state which were selected in order to have equal 1956 strike losses. Figure 4.16, taken from Weiss (1972), illustrates a hypothetical case in which, using the whole groups, it is clear that there is no effect, whereas using matched subsamples selected to produce no pretest difference, a posttest difference results due to the fact that each subsample regresses back part way toward its own mean on the posttest. (The degree of such regression is inversely related to the pretest–posttest correlation: If this were 1.00, there would be no regression. Weiss has used a correlation of .50 in her example. Figure 4.16 assumes, but does not portray graphically, that group variability is the same on the posttest as on the pretest.) Covariance, regression adjustments, and partialing out pretest differences all produce similar effects (Lord, 1960; Porter, 1967; Campbell and Erlebacher, 1970). They all *underadjust* for the latent group differences partly because of the instability or error in the pretest. These underadjusted differences reappear on the posttest or any other measure not sharing the pretest error of measurement.

The regression artifacts are strongest when matching (or statistical adjustment) is based on the pretest. But some degree of such bias will result when adjustments are attempted using any measure which correlates higher with pretest than with the posttest, or vice versa. Thus, in an educational experiment one might be tempted to match on still earlier test results in the school files. However, test scores from adjacent years correlate more highly with each other than do test scores separated by longer periods of time. Therefore, the old tests would correlate more highly with the pretest than with the posttest, and

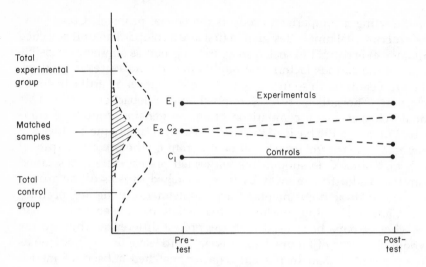

**Figure 4.16** Regression artifacts from using matched samples from groups with different total group means. [After Weiss (1972, p. 71, Figure 4.4).]

matching on them would produce some of the bias shown in Figure 4.16, albeit to a smaller degree.

A qualitative distinction needs to be made between the Pretest–Posttest Comparison Group design involving only two natural groups (e.g., two neighborhood schools) and the stronger quasi-experimental design in which the experimental and comparison groups are each made up from many different natural groups (e.g., the Follow Through compensatory education program, in which many schools receive the experimental treatment and many others serve as controls). In the two-group case, the cause of an apparent effect is ambiguous because there were undoubtedly many differences between the two schools over and above the presence of the treatment. Any of these differences could have produced the differential gains. In the multiple-group version at its best, there are likely to be few differences except the experimental treatment that would operate systematically in the same direction to differentiate the experimental from the comparison schools. (One should, of course, look for such systematic confounding. For example, since the comparison schools usually have to put up with the burden of measurement without the benefit of the treatment, a much higher rate of refusals may be encountered, leading the comparison schools to be more systematically selected for cooperativeness and self-confidence than are the experimentals.)

The discussion so far has avoided another problem present in many quasi-experimental comparisons, namely, differential growth rates. Figure 4.16 illustrates an occurrence that might be expected in an educational study which expressed achievement in terms of a standard score or index analogous to the IQ, on which no growth with age would be expected in the absence of a treatment effect. Such measures are uncommon. For most measures, if the experimental and comparison groups differ at the time of the pretest, almost certainly they differ not only in the mean level at that point but also in growth rate. This differential growth rate has produced the pretest mean difference and, continuing, will produce an even greater difference at any later point in time, including the posttest. In such a situation, the use of any analysis which assumes equal growth rates, such as an analysis of gain scores, will produce pseudo-effects, misinterpreted as due to the treatment but actually due to the differential growth rate. Figure 4.17 illustrates this problem.

Some scaling procedures may avoid the differential growth rate problem, although only at the cost of assumptions about the growth process which need verification in each specific setting. The commonly used grade-equivalent scores on achievement tests do *not* avoid the problem. Figure 4.17 provides an illustration. Raw scores and mental age scores also produce such effects. Scores that are standardized or percentiled by age group, or expressed as a ratio of chronological age to achievement age, such as the traditional IQ, avoid the problem insofar as their assumptions are correct. The major assumption is that the differential growth rate manifest between groups is also going on within groups at later testings. Note that for compensatory education settings in which the comparison group is selected from a population more able than the experimental, both the regression artifact problem and the

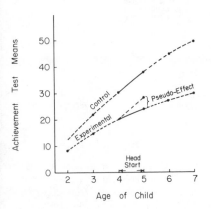

**Figure 4.17** Differential growth rate for two groups differing on the pretest at age 4 (hypothetical data). If the same growth rate is assumed for both and if there is in fact no treatment effect, there will result a pseudo-effect mistakenly indicating a harmful effect of the treatment.

differential growth rate problem will produce pseudo-effects in the direction of making the compensatory program look harmful. When the posttest has higher reliability than the pretest (in both groups), or when the reliability is higher in the comparison group than in the treated group (for both pretest and posttest), similar pseudo-effects occur.

The problem of differential growth rates associated with differences in mean levels occurs for many other quasi-experimental settings, for example, income series and other economic indices. Where the data are available, expanding the design into a Comparison Series design provides a perspective that helps to avoid this error, as Figure 4.7 illustrates.

This is an appropriate place to make an important point about all quasi-experimental designs. Interpretability is in considerable part dependent upon the nature of the results. Thus some outcomes can be explained away as regression artifacts, but others cannot. If the group differences are in the opposite direction from that predicted by regression, or in the same direction but to a larger degree than the test–retest correlation would predict, then the results cannot be explained completely by regression. Indeed, in the reverse-direction instance, regression instead leads us to underestimate effects. Similarly, if a group that started out lowest on the pretest (but which was not selected for treatment on the basis of pretest scores, so that regression is not involved) turns out to gain the most, this results negates the commonly plausible differential growth rate explanation.

Figure 4.18 shows data interpretable as a dramatic quasi-experimental demonstration of the effect of Medicaid on medical attention to the poorest of U.S. citizens (Lohr, 1972; Wilder, 1972). In 1963, this

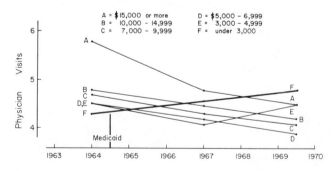

**Figure 4.18** Possible evidence for the effect of Medicaid on the contacts with doctors of persons in low-income families. The first data set is based on weekly surveys carried out between July 1963 and June 1964. The second set come from July 1966–June 1967. The third wave is entirely within 1969. [Lohr (1972); Wilder (1972, p. 5, Table B).]

group is at the bottom in frequency of contacts with physicians, in conformity with an overall pattern for those most prosperous to receive the most help. By 1970, the poorest group is seeing the doctor most frequently, presumably due to genuinely poorer health plus the removal of economic barriers through the Medicaid legislation of 1964. Group E shows a similar 1967–1969 rise, presumably due to the change in eligibility requirements in 1968.

Since there is only one pretest, these data are probably best considered as a Pretest-Posttest Comparison Group design with an extra posttest. They are convincing, in part because the effect of a complete reversal of relative position is so dramatically strong and because there are few, if any, plausible alternative explanations of the result, either in terms of coincidental change agents or in terms of possible methodological artifacts.

Regression artifacts are not a threat in this example. They would have been had the income groups been set up on the basis of the 1963 data and had the 1967 and 1970 data represented reinterviews of the same people, kept in their 1963 classes for purposes of analysis. But these are not panel data. A separate representative sample of persons have been interviewed on each occasion. The measurement process of 1963 also has no relation to the administration of Medicaid. Even if a regression artifact were possible, it would only explain regression toward the mean to the degree of the imperfection in correlation between the measurements in 1963 and 1967 or 1963 and 1969. It would not explain "regression" across the mean to the opposite extreme. Differential trend lines might seem a plausible rival hypothesis if one could imagine that the gap by which Group F trails the other groups was much greater in the decade prior to 1963 than in that year. Lohr judges on other grounds that this is out of the question.

Groups A, B, C, and D are about as dissimilar comparison groups as could be found, yet they do yeoman service here to control for overall trends in access to medical attention. In Figure 4.18 such access seems to be decreasing for these groups, although this may be in part an artifact of inflation, which lends quite different significance to the same dollar income in 1969 than in 1963. But with an essentially fixed number of doctors' hours per citizen, increased attention to Groups F and E, even though they are a small portion of the population, would result in some decrease in attention to the other groups.

THE ONE-GROUP BEFORE-AND-AFTER DESIGN

In this design there is only the experimental group and it is measured twice—once pretest and once posttest. The lower line in

Figure 4.15 illustrates such a design. It can be conceived of as a Single Interrupted Time Series which has been shortened to the limit or as a Pretest–Posttest Comparison Group design which lacks the comparison group. These drastic curtailments have costs in greater equivocality of causal inference. It and the design that follows are so weak that they perhaps should be classified as pre-experimental rather than even quasi-experimental. The One-Group design shares all the threats to validity of the three immediately preceding designs and is more vulnerable than any of them to the following rival hypotheses:

1. Instability: Measures often fluctuate comparable amounts even in the absence of specifiable causes.
2. Long-term trends: Had the same measure been made regularly, prior time periods might have shown a comparable amount of change following the same trend.
3. Seasonal changes.
4. Effects of measurement: Test–retest effects of comparable magnitude may occur when a new measure is introduced for the first time. Such effects are regularly found for psychological tests. They may be expected for any new social indicator for which there is widespread participation in creating the data or the results of which are widely publicized. A change in measurement staff (interviewers or test administrators) or in the interviewer's knowledge of expected posttest changes can have similar effects.
5. Differential dropout: In some settings (e.g., where measures are anonymous), pretest–posttest differences may be produced by the systematic dropping out from the program of certain kinds of persons.
6. Other intervening change agents: Even more than in the three preceding designs, all other events in addition to the treatment that have occurred between pretest and posttest are available as alternative explanations of the effect.

Despite all these weaknesses, such data are probably worth collecting. Sometimes the total pattern of these data in combination with other data (including nonquantified expert judgments) will be convincing in showing that an effect either has or has not occurred. In any quasi-experiment, expert judgment and familiarity with the situation buttress the interpretation of findings. In a specific situation, such knowledge may render even this weak design interpretable.

## THE POSTTEST-ONLY COMPARISON GROUP DESIGN

In this design, there is an experimental group and a comparison group, but each has been measured only on a posttest; there is no pretest. If one were to look only at the 1957 data, Figure 4.15, one would have such a design. It can be conceived of as the Pretest–Posttest Comparison Group design lacking the pretest. Many of the rival hypotheses just listed for the One-Group Before-and-After design are relevant here: (1) instability; (2) long-term trends, interpreted as maturational trends; (5) differential dropout; (6) other intervening events in the sense of change agents specific to one of the groups; and, in addition, (7) selection differences, that is, preexisting differences between the two groups which have gone unmeasured and can usually provide more plausible explanations of the outcome than the hypothesis of a treatment effect. With this design, one enters the field of correlational analysis, including the efforts to derive causal interpretations from correlational data. Correlational studies lie beyond the scope of this book which has as its focus *experiments* in the sense of prospectively designed novel interventions. However, even here, there may be convincing bodies of data which somehow render implausible the many threats to validity which the design leaves uncontrolled.

Fleiss and Tanur (1972), after stressing the misleading effects of ordinary statistical adjustments, in agreement with the emphases of this chapter, suggest a mode of analysis which might well have made the 1967 survey of Figure 4.18, interpretable even had the 1963 data been missing. Figure 4.19 presents these data in the Fleiss and

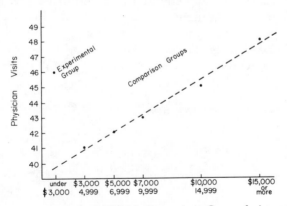

**Figure 4.19**  Posttest–Only (Multiple) Comparison Group design relevant to the effects of Medicaid. (1967 data from Figure 4.18.)

Tanur form. Because of the inequality of intervals, there is ambiguity about how the data should be plotted. Mean incomes for each of the six groups would probably be a better base for plotting. But any reasonable alteration in this or any form of curve assumed would leave the "under $3000" group far from the extrapolated value. In interpreting Figure 4.19 as evidence of the effect of Medicaid, one is assuming that the relationship between income and medical contact shown by Groups A, B, C, D, and E would also have held for Group F had Medicaid not been available to it. If one is willing to make this extrapolation, Fleiss and Tanur suggest an appropriate test of significance. One is, of course, assuming that no prior welfare effort had already produced this effect previous to Medicaid. The data of Figure 4.18 are thus much clearer.

## Remarks

There are many other quasi-experimental designs which could be useful in one situation or another. Campbell and Stanley (1963) list another half dozen or so. We believe that the seven we have discussed include those most useful and those most used for evaluating new programs. We believe they also serve to illustrate the problems of equivocal inference which characterize all such designs. They should be used only where randomization cannot be employed. Of course, many of the illustrations (actual and hypothetical) used in this chapter are ones in which randomization would have been impossible. In such situations, quasi-experimental evaluation of the type here discussed represents the most hardheaded evaluation available and again, for all of its equivocality, a considerable advance over most current practice.

# V

# Measurement in Experiments

In order to measure the effects of a social program, the experimenter must obtain systematic, reliable, and valid information about the features of the program, as well as the characteristics and behavior of participants in it. There are numerous methods of doing so, each coupled with some determinable level of credibility. In this chapter, we examine reliability, validity, and other desirable properties of a measurement system for experiments. The first three sections of the chapter are organized around three basic elements of the experimental paradigm: response variables, especially characteristics and behavior of program participants; properties of the treatment program; and initial conditions of the situation in which the experiment occurs. These sections generally emphasize quality of measurement and ways of solving measurement problems that occur in social experiments. In the fourth and final section of the chapter, we discuss the use of social and archival indicators in conjunction with experimental tests of social programs.

## Response Variables

Response or outcome variables here refer to the characteristics of participants in the program which, it is supposed, will be affected by the social program. To make credible comparisons among the experimental groups and to estimate program effects reliably, uniform and valid measurement of response variables in each group is essential. In the following remarks, we first describe some useful strategies for identifying the variables and their linkage to program goals. The principal methods of measurement and the problem of selecting good measures are discussed next. Since selection of methods of measurement must be made with some recognition of the quality of data needed, we then discuss indicators of quality and strategies for assuring integrity of measurement in experiments.

## PROGRAM GOALS, MEASURABLE OUTCOMES, AND RESPONSE VARIABLES

A recent General Accounting Office (1972) report lists some 28 Congressional bills and acts passed during 1967–1972 which mention the need for evaluation of particular social programs. Only half of these specify exactly which attributes of the program's target group are relevant to program goals; none contain any explicit requirement for measuring more than one response variable. The level of generality demonstrated by the statutes may be desirable in developing program legislation, because it permits imaginative and flexible strategies for achieving objectives. But the nonspecific character of current statutes does point up the fact that an experimenter cannot expect program goals and response variables to be well-defined in the program mandate. Frequently the process of identifying the variables that appear to reflect program goals, and of specifying valid ways to measure them are fundamental problems in experimentation and the first steps in the measurement process. The process requires close cooperation among the various parties (experiment manager, treatment delivery team, etc.) with interests in the experiment. Managerial strategies for achieving such cooperation are discussed in Chapter VI, but a brief sketch of the process is justified here.

Linking program goals to measurable characteristics and behavior of program participants can perhaps best be accomplished on an interaudience basis. That is, the various audiences for the experimental results (including critics or opponents of the program) should take part in specifying the connection between program goals and measurable outcomes. Where program goals are quite simple and readily endorsed by the various audiences of the experiment, the linkage process is easy and audiences may quickly settle on a single item. A manpower training program, for example, might be assessed entirely in terms of posttreatment employment rate of program participants. The response measure—employment rate—is simple and directly linked to program goals. Focusing attention on a single type of outcome, however, is usually inappropriate for large-scale social programs. Few programs are ever dedicated to a single and simple objective; few can be fairly judged with respect to a single criterion. So, additional response measures that reflect in different ways the various effects of the program may be justified.

Accordingly, a second step in the response variable specification process may require an enumeration of the multiple characteristics of the target group that the program is expected to affect (including negative side effects), and the methods by which these characteristics are supposed to be measured. For example, the Meyer and Borgatta (1959) appraisals of a mental rehabilitation program involved constructing a list of behaviors that were associated with the first (of several) diffuse program goals, patient "recovery." The specific behaviors included in their listing were: absence of institutional recommitment, patients' relative independence of the rehabilitation agency, patients' effectiveness in social relations, patients' economic independence, reality of patient orientations, patients' general well-being. The list demonstrates the notion that no single response variable (e.g., institutional recommitment) is likely to be a completely valid indicator of the goal or concept it is supposed to reflect (i.e., recovery). And it also recognizes different audience interests, including the possibility of negative program effects. Although recommitment rate may be low, for example, the patient's marginal social life, his dependence on public assistance, or his dependence on constant contact with program staff after his release should have implications for judgments about the effectiveness of the program. Despite the coarse character of this sort of listing, the list is a useful vehicle for obtaining some agreement from program supporters, opponents, and the other groups on what variables should be measured and analyzed; and it is a convenient device for communicating the goals of the program to the lay public.

Further specification of the list's contents will be necessary to the extent that a behavior (such as "reality orientation") is complex. Usually this requires additional discussion and consultation among interested parties which results in a more fine-grained list of response variables and methods of measuring them. Reality of orientation might, for example, be measured by several standardized psychological inventories, as well as by novel measures, for which actual test or questionnaire items must be made explicit (Krathwohl and Payne, 1971). This level of specification will normally be of little use in communicating measurement activities to the public, but it is frequently essential for program planning and evaluation; ill-specified response measures virtually guarantee equivocal judgments about the effectiveness of social programs, even in a controlled and randomized experiment.

As the number of response variables increases and measurement methods are specified more adequately, some structure for consolidating and reporting the information usually becomes necessary. The most effective one appears to be tabular presentation in which program goals are laid out, classes of response variable are linked to goals, and specific measures of each outcome are presented. Goals may then be ordered according to their priority or relevance to policy, for example, to simplify reporting and to facilitate evaluating the experiment itself.

*Complementary Measures.* Measurement of response to an experimental treatment will normally be focused on the group being serviced by the program. But other variables, especially those factors in the social–economic environment that might influence the success of the program, may also require measurement. Consider, for example, a program for training parolees in carpentry. Posttraining skills in carpentry and the acquisition of a carpentry job would normally be used as important response variables in an experimental comparison of such programs. A complementary social measure might simply be the number of carpentry jobs available within a 100-mile radius of the target population, or the attitudes and openness of local carpentry unions toward the graduates of such programs. Obviously these variables are relevant to the program operation as well as to its success or failure, particularly if one of the criteria for a declaration of program success is a high rate of job placement.

Such complementary variables as these are exogenous factors which affect outcomes independently of the treatment. There are, however, other kinds of complementary variables, which should be measured in a social experiment, namely those that are affected by the treatment, even if only indirectly. Hence, the housing allowance experiments (Buchanan and Heinberg, 1972) provide for measuring characteristics of the housing market in the cities where the experiment is carried out, for there may be variations in the availability or price of apartments in specific areas, for example, that are attributable to the treatment (i.e., to the housing allowance). Of course, there may be interactions, since changes in the housing market would probably affect decisions made by the individuals receiving the allowance.

Other classes of complementary measures can be developed, and it appears that such development is taking place widely in the social sciences. Both the Provo experiment and the Silverlake experiment

(Empey and Lubeck, 1971; Empey and Erickson, 1972) demonstrate a strong interest in indicating the ways in which the experimental delinquency programs are reacted to by external systems, that is, by local schools, neighborhoods, police, and probation departments. Reactions here may be treated as simple contextual characteristics in the experiment (insofar as they are not influenced by the delinquency program), they may be treated as response variables (insofar as they change with installation of the program), or as a treatment variable (insofar as they affect both installation of program and response). As in the case of identifying good measures of response characteristics in the target sample, the specification of important variables in the local social system will be an iterative and multiparticipant activity. Although it is not always essential that such complementary variables be measured (they are not strictly necessary for comparing treatment and control groups), the resultant information may help program developers to understand how and why a program appears to be successful, and the data may suggest strategies for program improvement.

Further specification of response variables important in the experiment must recognize the methods of measurement available to us and the ways in which the quality of measurement can be assessed. We proceed to these topics next.

## METHODS OF MEASUREMENT

The methods of measurement typically used in experiments are often rather narrow in scope, sometimes necessarily so for reasons of reliability and validity of measurement, sometimes unnecessarily so, for lack of adequate planning in the development of measurement techniques. The reader is probably familiar with many such techniques—tests, rating systems, interviews, inventories, etc.—and we provide only a brief description of each of these in the following remarks. The use of off-the-shelf methods of assessment and the development of specialized measures are also discussed in this section. Specific details on appraising quality of methods and resultant data are given in the next section of this chapter.

Tests of cognitive ability, of special skills, and similar measures can sometimes be tied directly to the goals of social programs, and they are often readily adapted to measurement of outcome variables in experimentation. Standardized, commercially available tests have been used in manpower training programs, compensatory education, and other programs with good results. Weikert (1972), for example, has used standardized tests effectively in conjunction with rating

schemes and other measures to document the intellectual development of children reliably in experimental tests of education programs.
With some investment of resources, they can be adapted to various
language groups or to specially handicapped target groups, and they
can often be coupled with specialized communication vehicles such as
interviews and computer-assisted instruction or video-assisted transmission devices.

Rating schemes are as common in experiments as they are in survey
research, especially in areas where observations by trained professionals
are the best available data, such as in mental and physical rehabilitation programs. A majority of the experiments listed in the **Appendix**
involve the use of rating schemes. They typically focus on attitude and
behavior change, on performance in specialized tasks, and on changes
in complex intangible characteristics of program participants. Self-
ratings by program participants, ratings of participants by their peers,
by their superiors, family, acquaintances, and program staff have also
been used, for example, by Krause, Breedlove, and Boniface (1971) in
experimental assessments of treatments for alcoholics and their wives.

In-depth descriptions of the state of the art in developing rating
**schemes in commercial, clinical, educational, and other applications**
are readily available (e.g., Cronbach, 1970; Guion, 1965; Scott, 1968;
Summer, 1970). Listings and descriptions of off-the-shelf rating schemes
for hundreds of social attitudes or behaviors are available in book
form (e.g., Buros, 1959; Robinson and Shaver, 1969; Robinson,
**Athanasiou**, and Head, 1969) and in data bank form (e.g., Pinneau,
Selin, and Chun, 1972).

Perhaps the most widely used technique for collecting data is the
personal interview—usually face-to-face in the home or at the workplace of the program participant being studied. While the interview
is most appropriately used to get personalized answers to questions
about complicated topics—questions that may be difficult to ask in a
**perfectly standardized way**—still the topical coverage of interviews
can be quite broad, ranging from simple demographic information to
complex mental and emotional states. A great deal of attention has been
paid to interviewing and the design of interviews, especially for eliciting opinions and beliefs. Practical advice on resolving problems in
development and application of the interview method has been
furnished by Hyman, Cobb, Feldman, Hart, and Stember (1954) and
Kahn and Cannell (1957), and in many professional handbooks in the
social and behavioral sciences (e.g., Matarazzo, 1965).

Mailed questionnaries or inventories are often used to elicit
factual information from program participants following their exit from

the program. Diary methods of eliciting information (e.g., recording and reporting household expenditures) are less common in experiments, but experimental tests of the methods (e.g., by Sudman and Ferber, 1971) suggest that they are a promising vehicle for accumulating fine-grained data on fairly simple behavior such as spending practices.

*Off-the-Shelf Instruments.* Off-the-shelf measures of response variables are those instruments which are available from commercial or academic test development organizations (listed in Holman and Doctor, 1972). Standardized tests of cognitive development; personality and social behavior inventories; and rating schemes for psychological, social, and economic attributes have certain advantages over a specially developed instrument when the variables they measure appropriately index program goals. At their *best*, the off-the-shelf measures will be well-standardized in their physical and procedural requirements, they will be well-documented with respect to the constructs or concepts they are supposed to reflect, and there will be empirical evidence for their reliability (see the section entitled "Quality of Measurement" later in this chapter, and Chapter VI). Test developers can often supply information on the use of their measures in various social settings, which suggests how valid and reliable will be the data derived from the measures. If the measures are standardized with respect to procedures and interpretation, their use will facilitate later attempts to replicate the experiment in other settings. And perhaps more importantly, standardization will generally decrease managerial problems and eliminate unnecessary local variation in the measurement process itself.

It may turn out, however, that available off-the-shelf instrumentation has no relevance to social program goals or to outcomes important to the experimenter. Available measures may be invalid in the sense that the information they elicit, however precise and dependable, does not adequately index the behavior that is supposed to be affected by the program. And even if the measure is appropriate and its use well-standardized, the measure may not work well with the participants in the program. They may be unable to furnish information if the instrument is intellectually too demanding for example; or they may be bored or frustrated by the measurement procedure. The upshot is that it will be difficult, if not impossible, to obtain meaningful data about program recipients or their behavior. Some technically excellent measures are simply impractical for some respondents.

The measurement of response variables is itself a legitimate subject for empirical investigation. In some cases, research on measurement is necessary *prior* to large-scale application in an experiment; development of the experimental program and of measures of response might be conducted in parallel. For a simple variable (such as "returning for trial" in the Manhatten Bail Bond experiment) prior work on developing a mechanism for measuring outcomes may be minimal. But in evaluating unique and more complex programs such as *Sesame Street* (Bogatz and Ball, 1971) the identification and development of valid measures of cognitive functioning, attitudes toward learning, and other characteristics was critical for standard, readily available measures were not always suitable.

Small pilot studies prior to formal experimentation or during the planning of the social program are desirable, and sometimes essential, for any reasonable appraisal of the utility of a given method of measuring the attributes of interest. Not only can tests, interview protocols, and the like be evaluated in preprogram experiment efforts, but quality control mechanisms to be used during the experiment can also be identified and tested beforehand. Lacking the opportunity for intensive preexperiment investigation of methods, quality control checks and research on measurement during the experiment will normally be useful for obtaining a reasonable description of the adequacy of the methods chosen.

*Relations among Response Variables.* The experimental evaluation of a simple ameliorative program will often require only one or two response variables, each measured in several ways. For the more complex programs, multiple characteristics of the target group, each potentially measurable in a variety of ways, may be of interest. Consolidating and interpreting the results of multiple measurements can be difficult however. In order to facilitate interpretation, one would like to identify redundant measures in the total set of variables, to understand relations among measures, and to assay their relative validity. Factor analysis, a statistical technique for summarizing information about relations among variables, can be a useful vehicle for doing so. If preexperimental studies are possible (base-line surveys, needs assessments, etc.), one can judge, for example, if two or three measures of some characteristic can serve as efficient substitutes for a dozen or so measures from the analysis. More generally, the technique can be used to gauge the relative effectiveness of alternative methods of measurement in actually measuring factors underlying the characteristics of interest in the target group; this type of information may be crucial for recently developed measures on novel characteristics, where what is being measured is not especially clear. Ultimately, factor analysis yields so-called factor scores which can be regarded as more clearly interpretable and consistent measures of the attributes under study than are the original measurements. The scores can be estimated for each participant in the experiment and used in analysis of variance. For example, the Sinisterra, McKay, and McKay studies of children's cognitive development capitalize on factor analysis to simplify interpretation of data on numerous measures of development, and use factor scores rather than raw scores in subsequent analyses to facilitate detection of an education program's effects.

Factor analysis is a complex topic, but a good technical description of relevant techniques is given by Mulaik (1973); applications-oriented treatments are given by Gorsuch (1974) and others. Goldberger and Duncan's (1973) volume covers analytical relations between factor analysis and structural equation approaches to assessment of quasi-experimental data.

## INDICATORS OF QUALITY OF MEASUREMENT

The important conventional concepts for describing the quality of measurement are reliability, validity, and completeness. These concepts identify desirable properties of all the measures used in experiments—measures of initial conditions and treatment processes as well as of the response variables. A detailed discussion of these concepts follows.

*Reliability of Measurement.* Conceptions of *reliability* usually involve the assumption that any observation (an achievement test score, a personality profile, etc.) contains both a systematic and a random component. The systematic portion of the score represents the stability or consistency in an individual's state of mind or condition while the random element represents unpredictable, random variation in measurement. This random instability may be attributable to a wide variety of external conditions under which the observation was made (e.g., noise and other distractions) as well as to fluctuations in mood or alertness of the subject of observation and to variation in the physical vehicle or mode of observation.

Information on the reliability of observations is often reported in the form of a product–moment correlation coefficient, based on data elicited in various ways from the same sample. Test–retest reliability, an index of short-term stability in observations, involves repeated observations on the same group within a short time interval. Since practice effects may artificially inflate a reliability estimate computed in this way, a researcher may prefer to observe the group twice using two different but parallel forms of measurement (e.g., two parallel forms of an achievement test). To obtain an estimate of reliability that eliminates temporal variation, a "split-half" reliability may be computed; the correlation statistic is based on data from two halves of the same test or inventory. (For more precise definitions of reliability see, e.g., Lord and Novick, 1968; Stanley, 1971.)

Depending on the particular measure, one or more of these indicators of reliability or others may be chosen to help understand how much the observations are affected by random variation. Such behavioral measures as an individual's achievement score, his attitudes, or his physical mobility will always be a useful but imperfect indicator of the attribute of interest. Accordingly, reliability data are essential for assuring credibility of measured experimental outcomes. Reputable test publishers can supply reliability statistics for their products, and good practice in measurement demands that evidence be obtained by the experimenter for the methods of measurement used in his particular situation.

By ignoring reliability considerations, the experimenter exposes himself to several hazards. In the first place, unreliability reduces one's power to detect differences among the various treatments, even with a good experimental design. Without sufficient evidence for the reliability of measures, the experimenter will be unable to tell if the program's impact appears to be small merely because the measures are not reliable or because the program effects were actually quite weak. And it will be difficult for him to make good judgments about the credibility of his estimates of the size of the program effect. When unreliable measures are unavoidable, there may sometimes be available techniques for ameliorating these problems, but they cannot be totally dissipated by postmeasurement statistical manipulation (see Campbell and Erlebacher, 1970; Cleary, Linn, and Walster, 1970; Cochran, 1968; Lord, 1960).

*Validity of Measurement.* Several types of validity in measurement are important for the design and implementation of experiments; they range from simple to complex, depending on the character of the response being measured. The simplest conception—criterion validity—concerns the extent to which observations stemming from a particular method of measurement are consonant with a generally accepted, and presumably more accurate, standard. One might check the program recipients' reports of taxable income, for example, against Internal Revenue Service records to appraise the validity of the former. Sometimes the validity of each individual report cannot be checked, but an average or aggregate validation procedure is possible. Thus, comparing electoral district votes with reports by carefully chosen samples of individuals shows that personal report of vote is not a valid measure. People tend to report an excess of votes for the winning candidates. In some cases, the criterion might be some future observable event. For example, alternative screening or selection procedures for college placement or employment can be validated by subsequent performance of the screened personnel in college or on the job.

Where the concept of a single, fixed, and universally accepted criterion for appraising validity of measurement is meaningless, as in opinion and personality inventories or in some psychological and educational tests, alternative conceptions of validity need to be recognized. "Content validity" and/or "construct validity" often become the main focuses of interest. Content validity concerns the extent to which a test or inventory elicits a reasonable sample of the totality of behaviors (or other attributes) which characterize the outcome variable of interest. In a manpower training program, for example, welding proficiency can be gauged by identifying all types of welds commonly required in industrial work, then requiring the trainee to demonstrate his skill in welding a representative sample of types. Ideally, one supports a claim of content validity by obtaining evidence that expert judges working independently are able to develop outcome measures that yield equivalent results, based on a broad initial description of the content area of interest. Normally, however, content validity must be established by obtaining the agreement of interested parties to the experiment (e.g., the action agency staff, program sponsors, etc.; see earlier discussion). If statistical indices show high agreement among judges and consistent results on the parallel forms of tests, this is evidence for content validity. Content validity should not be confused with what is usually called "face validity"—namely, the apparently obvious (on the face of it) relevance of some measure to the actual performance it purports to measure. For example, a form board test of manual dexterity might appear to be a valid measure of ability to learn typing. In fact, it is not. Face validity may nonetheless be important just because it appears to be valid to the subjects of measurement. Methods of measurement which, to the subjects, do not appear to measure what they purport to measure have little face validity; some face validity may be helpful in order to avoid subjects' negative reactions or confusion about the measurement process.

Construct validity, perhaps the most complex conception of validity, refers to the question, What attribute are we actually measuring? As such, construct validity addresses itself to the meaningfulness of the attribute under investigation, the extent to which methods actually reflect it, and the validity of interpretation of observations. The significance of this concept lies in its emphasis on linking such conceptually vague outcomes as "well-being" or "mental health" systematically to alternative methods of measuring and interpreting the construct. Two kinds of evidence for construct validity appear to be important. The results of a particular measurement process must correlate well with the results of other different methods of measuring essentially the same attribute. And the measurement process must distinguish systematically between the attribute of interest and other attributes (Campbell and Fiske, 1959). A particular measure of "creativity," for example, should correlate well with other measures of the same trait, and should not correlate particularly well with measures of other traits which are alleged to be independent of creativity (e.g., arithmetic ability). More generally, the process of appraising construct validity is an intellective one in which critics of a particular method of measuring some trait offer hypotheses about contaminating influences on its measurement. The researcher must be prepared to argue on the basis of empirical evidence or on a priori grounds against the plausibility of the hypotheses. For example, researchers in the National Educational Assessment program believed it necessary to do a small study to check the contention that school children with mid-Atlantic diction did better on standardized oral reading tests than Southern children because of the irrelevant influence of diction on the measurement process.

*Completeness of Measurements.* Completeness of the measurement process refers here to the character and frequency of missing data. No measurement process is perfect and there will inevitably be some missing observations, lost records, incomplete tests, skipped questions in interviews, or unidentified questionnaires. Omissions also occur because persons cannot be found at home, interrupt their interviews for urgent reasons, are ill, or simply refuse to cooperate. Some missing data is an inevitable condition—what matters is how large the omissions are and how they are distributed. In large experiments, a low level of randomly absent data will not interfere greatly with statistical analysis and interpretation. But high rates of missing data and, especially, differences between control and treatment groups in the character of missing data, decrease one's power to detect program effects and may undermine the credibility of analysis. Assuring completeness of data is principally a management rather than a scientific problem. Strategies for minimizing missing data due to attrition during the experiment are given in Chapter VI and some strategies for analysis are given in Chapter III.

*Using Quality Indicators in Evaluating Design.* Often, the evaluation design specialist has numerical estimates of reliability and validity of response measures prior to the program evaluation. The information may stem from pilot studies, from published reports on quality of the methods of measurement to be used, or from other sources. Furthermore, such information can be put to good account in designing an evaluation that permits detection of even small program effects. Specific techniques for incorporating data about quality of response into the design of an experiment make use of the following rationale.

Power of an experimental evaluation refers to the probability of detecting a program effect when in fact the program is effective. For response measures which are near perfect, power is a function of the sizes of the sample used in the experiment, the true mean differences among treatment conditions, and variance within treatment groups (see Chapter III). Experimental design specialists commonly specify a desirable power level (a probability near 1.00), assume plausible values for effect and variance, then compute (or make use of statistical tables for) the sample sizes required to detect an effect under those assumptions in the field experiment. When available, information about reliability and validity of response can be introduced to this computation so as to deduce the sample size (or test length, or other precision-inducing strategies) required for a given level of power. For example, with perfect measurement, a sample of 16 individuals per group is necessary in a two-group experiment if the design specialist wishes to be virtually certain (power level of 99%) of detecting a mean standardized group difference of 2. With fallible measures (test-retest reliability equal to .80, say), samples with 20 members per group are required for the same power level. See Cohen (1969) for the basic theory and statistical tables relevant to power analysis in experiments, and Cleary, Linn, and Walster (1970) for extensions of the theory to accomodate fallible measures.

*Summary: Reliability and Validity.* The best possible evidence for credibility of a particular measurement process in experiments is empirical data which show that with a treatment *known* to be effective, the measure reflects or indicates an effect. One does not often have the opportunity to investigate fully the sensitivity of all possible measures prior to an experiment, so indicators of reliability, validity, and completeness are often used a priori to support the contention that the measure meets basic requirements of sensitivity. Small empirical studies done prior to or during the main experiment can be used to support the contention more directly, and this strategy has been well established in some areas of experimentation.

## ASSURING QUALITY OF MEASUREMENT

Strategies for assuring the reliability and validity of measurement in an experiment are, in principle, no different from those normally used in surveys and other data collection activities. However, because program effects may be weak and sample sizes small in the experiment, the need for highly reliable observations can be more crucial; the experimenter is often interested in detection of small effects. Special kinds of threats to validity of measurement also occur in experiments and these may justify development of special quality control mechanisms.

*Reliability.*   If an experimenter can use standardized (off-the-shelf) measures that report satisfactory levels of reliability for samples of people and circumstances of administration that are comparable to those planned for the experiment, then he may be spared the task of testing his measurement methods for suitability, or of developing new measures. Such ideal circumstances occur rarely in social experimentation, however, and some development and testing is usually required.

It is prudent to investigate the reliability of even standardized measures for the population on which they are to be used and under the circumstances in which they are to be administered, in order to be sure that their level of difficulty or complexity is not so great, nor external distractions so powerful as to reduce reliability. Of course, the manager of the experiment must take steps to train administrators of tests and supervise coding or recording of responses to assure that measurement is carried out in the standardized manner prescribed.

When measures must be constructed *de novo*, considerable time and expertise will be needed to detect and eliminate ambiguities in instructions, in the meaning of questions or test items, in test format, and in scoring or coding. Time must be allowed for trying out new measures on appropriate population samples, developing internal and external checks on reliability, and eliminating sources of random variation in responses. Competent discussions of good practice in building educational, social, and psychological measures are given by Cronbach (1970) and Thorndike (1971).

For more personalized kinds of measurement—interviewing, subjective rating schemes, and the like—other methods of assuring reliability may be desirable. Careful development, standardization, and pilot testing of the methods are justified, but in addition, considerable

training may be required for the interviewer or rater. Critical deter-
minants of reliability (and of validity) in these cases usually include the
raters' (or interviewers') workload and level of expertise as well as the
clarity of questions or rating scales they are asked to use.

*Validity.* Collecting preexperiment evidence on the criterion, content, or construct validity of an outcome measure is a necessary but
insufficient condition for assuring validity during the experimental
evaluation. Certain kinds of threats to the validity of observations can
and do occur during a field experiment and if unrecognized they can
undermine the credibility of the experimental results. The remarks that
follow concern these threats and are generally applicable to measurement of treatment and of initial condition of participants in the social
program as well.

The most obvious, if not always the most likely, source of bias in outcome measurement is the individuals primarily responsible for the
measurement process. If the results of the experiment have (real or
imagined) implications for them, if they have a vested interest in the
decisions based on the experimental evidence, then their observations,
ratings, recollection of factual information, and so on may be critically
influenced by that interest. Observer bias is also a problem in any situation where strong traditions and beliefs may undermine the validity of
subjective rating schemes. So-called "blind" measurement is useful
for minimizing, if not eliminating this sort of bias on the part of raters,
interviewers, or coders. That is, the rater is not informed as to whether
the subject is a member of the treatment or the control group. This
ignorance helps to ensure that he will be unable to bias his observations,
consciously or otherwise, in a particular direction. Blind measurement
has often been used in experimental studies of medical treatment and
rehabilitative programs. Measurement by standardized achievement or
psychological tests is frequently *de facto* blind at least insofar as individuals responsible for coding and scoring cannot readily deviate from
standardized scoring techniques. Checks on the unbiasedness of
measurement can be developed in a variety of ways. Cross-checks of
interviewer reports and records from archival data systems will often
be sufficient for checking validity of factual information. For appraising
both factual and subjective reports, one might ask interviewers to guess
the group to which their interviewees belong. The extent to which
guesses are accurate beyond the chance level can be assessed with
simple statistical tests, thus providing indirect evidence about whether
measurements were actually blind or not (Beatty, 1972).

It may not always be possible or desirable to use blind measurement.
There are alternative strategies that allow the experimenter to estimate

the extent of bias (e.g., deliberately choosing observers with different biases), although they do not prevent biases with the same surety that characterizes blind measurement (e.g., Plutchick, Platman, and Fieve, 1969).

Bias in outcome observations may also be introduced, of course, by the participants of the social program. Their responses to interviewers, questionnaires, and so forth may be biased deliberately if participants feel that they have a sufficient justification for doing so. Or responses may be distorted unconsciously. Merely being measured or participating in an experiment can introduce some systematic irrelevancy into participants' reports. Deliberate distortion of reports of verifiable data can often be detected by independent spot checks and perhaps largely, if not completely, eliminated by publicizing the checking procedure. Systematic appraisals of criterion validity, and other commonly used quality control mechanisms are also helpful. In some cases, offering rewards for accurate and complete reporting will provide substantial increases in criterion validity of reports (e.g., Sudman and Ferber, 1971 have demonstrated the advantages of using gifts to assure completeness and accuracy of certain kinds of reporting). At times, distortion of response may be attributable to the subject's negative reaction to a specific aspect of a question, e.g. a woman may find questions about use of contraceptive devices objectionable in an experimental test of a family planning program. In addition to careful selection and training of interviewers, and the intensive pretesting of questions, one may use specialized methods developed in part to reduce embarrassment of the respondent in such situations. These methods include the use of alphabetic and numerical aliases by research participants, the systematic inoculation of response with random error (whose parameters are known), and other novel approaches. Most such methods have not been field tested exhaustively and some result in less precise estimates of treatment effects. However, they do appear to have some promise for eliciting valid information about potentially stigmatizing attributes of the research subject (see Greenberg, Abul-Ela, Simon, and Horvitz, 1969; Boruch, 1972a for technical approaches to some of these issues).

Unintentional distortion of responses to experimental treatment is usually more subtle and complex than that involving deliberate distortion. Such "unconscious" biasing occurs most frequently in subjective reports of behavior or internal state (feelings, motives, attitudes) which range along a continuum of "social desirability." That is, participants in a program are likely to report that they benefited from it—i.e., they consider themselves to be happier, more confident, or better adjusted as a result of it; or they tend to believe they have experienced other "socially desirable" outcomes toward which the program was directed. The likelihood of such testimonials is perhaps greatest for subjective reports, but objectively observable behavior can also be artifactually changed by the conditions of experimental treatment. Perhaps the most familiar of the unconscious phenomena are the so-called Hawthorne effects ("guinea pig" or "klieg light" effects), which take their name from observations made on worker productivity under varying environmental and social conditions. In one study of the effects of illumination of the workplace, it was noticed that when more light was provided, productivity increased; but it also increased when illumination was *reduced below* its original level (Roethlisberger and Dickson, 1939). This observation suggested that there may be behavioral effects that are irrelevant to the fundamental influence of the treatment and arise from the subject's knowing that he is a member of a specially treated experimental group. Usually the knowledge permits, perhaps fosters, his behaving in a way which he thinks is consonant with experimental objectives. Insofar as they introduce systematic biases into experimental observations, Hawthorne effects jeopardize the internal validity of the experiment. The phenomena can lead to specious differences between control and treatment groups—differences that are irrelevant to the main effect of treatment.

In some cases, Hawthorne effects can be minimized in the experimental group by refraining from informing them that they are indeed receiving an experimental treatment, as long as the subjects' rights are not violated in doing so. In quasi-experiments on job enrichment, for example, American Telephone and Telegraph (Ford, 1969) researchers informed none of the clerks, operators, or craftsmen holding jobs that were to be changed that the change was being evaluated experimentally. The experimental program itself appears to have been indistinguishable from the background of commonly occurring job changes, and participants in the program could detect few if any cues to the overall purpose and structure of the experiment.

In other cases, however, it may be impossible to keep the total experimental sample unaware of their membership in the experimental group, for ethical or legal reasons, or because physical conditions of the experiment require that they receive information about its nature and purpose (see Chapter VIII). Several strategies may then be useful for identifying and coping with the risk of Hawthorne effects: identifying outcomes or outcome measures that are least likely to be influenced by awareness of being experimented upon; structuring treatments to reduce the likelihood of the Hawthorne effects; and conducting side experiments to estimate effects. In the Negative Income Tax experiments, for example, researchers considered Hawthorne effects to be a minimally important influence on some outcomes; they argued, based on their own and others' experience, that mere participation in an income experiment would not affect outcomes such as fertility control and familial ties. It has been suggested that Hawthorne effects are likely to be minimal in educational experimentation, perhaps because school-children are accustomed to the frequent moderate changes in curriculum and classroom operations that teachers introduce (Cook, 1967). More generally, one might expect slighter Hawthorne effects in a somewhat turbulent environment than in one which is customarily stable. Where experience suggests that mere participation in an experiment will produce a Hawthorne effect, experimenters should maintain a low profile, avoiding publicity or actions that heighten participants' awareness of the experiment. To adequately estimate, and perhaps compensate for, major Hawthorne effects, side experiments are useful. One may, for example, delay furnishing complete information about the experiment to randomly selected members of experimental and control groups, to permit estimation of the size of Hawthorne effects on the remaining knowledgeable participants. Of course, if minimal treatments or place-bos are used, members of control conditions will be equally susceptible to Hawthorne effects that operate in the experimental group; presumably, if the fundamental treatment is strong enough, it will lead to persistent differences between the control and treatment groups, despite the systematic influence of Hawthorne effects on each. Where possible, minimal treatment conditions that the researcher expects to be ineffective can be used to serve as base-line data on the character and magnitude of subjects' reactions to merely participating in an experimental program.

The process of measurement itself may produce real changes in the property or attribute of interest, irrespective of Hawthorne effects. For example, Kershaw (1971) points out that participants in the Negative Income Tax experiment took an increased interest in their own financial affairs and in the nature of income subsidies, as the experiment progressed. That interest may have influenced outcome measures independent of any real effect of the income subsidy. On the other hand, routinized measurement is so common in some situations that the experimental measures may be expected to exert little influence at all. For example, Welch and Walberg (1970) conducted controlled side-experiments to determine whether administering an educational test *prior* to the experimental treatment made the subjects more aware of treatment and more responsive to it. They found that pretesting did not have a large sensitizing effect. But in these cases as in many other evaluations, the magnitude of effects induced by novel measurement processes may be quite difficult to anticipate, so side studies are well-justified.

One general strategy for minimizing measurement-induced changes is to develop measures which minimize or eliminate the program recipients' awareness of the measurement process. Experiments involving measurement of play behavior in children, or classroom behavior of students, often employ one-way mirrors to reduce the subject's awareness of being observed. In the field, the keeping of regular records (of labor turnover, for example, in tests of industrial innovations) is so acceptably routine as to make it unlikely that it will cause changes in subjects' behavior. Unless measurement is known to induce no real change or unless there is some way of completely eliminating this influence or estimating its effects (through side studies, for example) then it is advisable to assure that the effect is identical for control and experimental groups. Without evidence that measurement procedures are identical in their effects for all groups, there is some danger that empirical differences between the experimental and control groups will be erroneously attributed to treatment, rather than to the measurement process.

Participants in an intervention program will not always be familiar with the testing schemes or other methods used to elicit outcome information. This lack of familiarity and of practiced reaction to initially novel measures can invalidate response measures in several ways. First, random error may pervade subjects' responses to a test or an interview, decreasing the experimenter's ability to discriminate among subjects' behavior or to detect change. Second, responses may be biased systematically in the direction of nonresponse or in the direction of a socially desirable response if the respondent is suspicious of the measurement process. The combination of error and systematic bias can obscure initial differences between groups and may preclude detection of any treatment effect, regardless of the true final differences among experimental and control groups. Insofar as judges or raters are unpracticed, they may be inconsistent or erratic in the criteria used in making their judgments. Again, the best advice is that procedures that are novel should be used only when those responsible for measurement have had the opportunity to practice in their use and achieve a reasonable level of expertize, and when those being measured have become comfortable with the procedure. Stagewise introduction of various measures may also help to ameliorate the sense of being overwhelmed that may affect subjects who are suddenly confronted with the totality of measurement requirements.

*Side Studies for Assuring Quality.* The emphasis on small side studies as a device for assessing validity and reliability in reporting and for discovering the most effective method of alternative methods of measurement is a recurrent theme of this chapter. We believe that the information derived from side studies can be quite useful to improve the design of an experimental evaluation and to improve the analysis of experimental and quasi-experimental data. Moreover, if the side studies are themselves experimental in character, they can provide information that is relevant to both current and future program evaluations. That well-designed side experiments are feasible and useful in this context has been ably demonstrated (see Cronbach, Gleser, Nanda, and Rajaratnam, 1972, and references therein). Furthermore, side studies can be built readily into existing social indicator systems and program development efforts; the experience of the U.S. Census Bureau and of other public and private social research organizations is invaluable in this regard (Section VII of the Appendix).

## Measurement of Treatment Conditions

In this section, we consider the process of identifying, describing, and measuring experimental and control treatments, that is, the sets of conditions confronting each group in the experiment. At the simplest level, the process takes the form of documenting the fact that the experimental group has been subjected to conditions different from those encountered by control groups. Without valid identification of treatment conditions, of course, no valid comparisons among groups can be made and no estimation of program effects is possible. Perhaps more importantly, subtle treatment effects may go undetected, efforts to utilize or to replicate the program at other sites may be critically undermined, and understanding the reasons for success or failure of the program may be hampered unnecessarily.

The following remarks are organized around four functional classes of measurement at this stage of experimentation: simple accounting, intensive description of complex treatments, measurement of control conditions, and finally, measurement for treatment revision. Within each category, we discuss the justification, contents, and methods of measurement with special attention to the practical utility of the data obtained.

## SIMPLE ACCOUNTING

In conventional experimental designs, "treatments" are usually considered to be a fixed component of the experiment. That is, a treatment is regarded as a homogeneous and static entity, rather than as a dynamically changing process. This general perspective often has considerable justification. Administration of a vaccine by injection in the Salk trials, income subsidy payments in the Negative Income Tax experiment, and the relaxation of bail requirements in the Manhattan Bail Bond experiment serve as examples of clear-cut static treatments which are defined by readily measured physical behavior and material properties of the treatment process. Under the assumption of fixed treatment conditions such as these, the statistical models of the experimental situation are simple, and the subsequent statistical analysis is tractable and well specified.

This analytic conception of treatment implies that, as the specification of treatment program is refined progressively by sponsors, program designers, and program staff, a minimally sufficient description and clues to the identification of a fixed treatment process must evolve (see Chapter VI for managerial strategies that facilitate the evolution process). Translating a possibly vague program mandate into operational treatment-related terms, then, normally results in a listing such as the following:

1. Identification of the treatment source, including people responsible for treatment, locations at which treatment is offered, administrative mechanism of treatment delivery
2. Temporal character of treatment, including time, duration, and frequency of delivery
3. Transfer of physical material, e.g., drug dosage, welfare payment, etc.
4. Special behaviors of staff or subjects which help to define treatment

Often the main elements of the treatment can be viewed as a single, complex but readily identified activity, and a single indicator of the activity may be sufficient for a judgment that the treatment has, in fact, been administered to the experimental unit. Simply asking subjects whether they received treatment will under many conditions be a reasonable way to obtain information about treatment administration. More direct (and reliable) methods involve the experimenter's observing treatment administration. More typically, reliance is placed on the program's routine accounting records. Receipts and staff records serve as treatment indicators in the Negative Income Tax experiment, for example; admission and attendance records and the like have served the same function in many other experiments in which simple treatments were administered.

In some cases, the accounting system may be suspect; individuals responsible for its maintenance may be poorly trained, inept, or simply too bored to make accurate observations. Where records can be systematically biased, then multiple sources of reporting, or periodic validity and reliability appraisals may help to minimize or eliminate distortion. So, for example, a periodic audit of records from a systematic sample of individuals in the experimental Negative Income Tax group may assure that estimates of bias in the reporting of either staff or subjects were available for both managerial and analytic purposes. Well-publicized, periodic audits may help to reduce the likelihood of fraud in experiments that involve notable material benefits, or complex systems of benefits for members of the treatment groups. Naturally, the occurrence of audits does serve as a kind of treatment itself, at least in welfare experiments, since systematic audits are not always a strong quality control element in welfare systems that operate in the field.

### INTENSIVE DESCRIPTION OF TREATMENT CONDITIONS

A simple accounting will normally be sufficient for estimating program effects when the treatment program can be readily identified as a clear, uniform activity or event. Frequently, however, the program is characterized by ill-defined or very heterogenous activities which are difficult to document or measure. Identifying what the treatment program is may be difficult, if not impossible in some complex ongoing programs (Weiss, 1972). Integration of handicapped children into regular classrooms of the Texas school system, for example, involves a complex treatment (integration) which is unspecified as to ratio of handicapped to unhandicapped children required, timing (abrupt versus gradual), method (with and without preparation of staff and students), etc. A program of this sort usually justifies a more intensive measurement process.

If the experimental treatment changes often and dramatically, and if the changes are not introduced in accordance with a .sequential experimental design, then simple accounting measures of treatment may be inappropriate. A relatively stable treatment is usually necessary for fair experimental appraisal (unless the cumulative effect of an unstable treatment is important). In experimental therapeutic programs, for example, some therapists were observed to be shifting subtly to less demanding or more comfortable regimens than those specified in the design, justifying the use of more intensive measurement methods to determine just what treatment had been delivered (Krause, 1972).

The methods available for intensive characterization of treatment are conceptually similar to those described earlier for the measurement of response variables, but technically different. Some approaches that appear to be especially useful are discussed next, namely, real-time monitoring and retrospective reporting schemes.

*Real-Time Monitoring.* On-the-spot, periodic measurement of the character of treatment is possible and desirable in many experiments. At its most intensive, the method of measurement may take the form of task analyses commonly used in industrial and human engineering research. The actual measurement process might then involve time and motion studies, in-depth inventories of program staff activities, videotaping of treatment administration, and other similarly concentrated approaches. Intensive investigations of this kind would normally be well-justified in evaluations where the treatment itself undergoes change over time or where there is little prior documentation on the structure of the treatment (e.g., where there is little information on the exact activities and duties of program staff). In-depth task analyses will usually be limited by time and budget restrictions, however, and in some cases by resistance from program staff; and task analyses may be a rather expensive way to document the character of treatment if that character is likely to stabilize or if the structure of treatment is likely to become more clear at a later stage of program operations.

Less intensive but informative real-time monitoring is possible where treatment programs have stabilized sufficiently to permit the use of more economical measurement schemes. Questionnaires that elicit firsthand accounts of treatment delivery and observable characteristics of the treatment can be completed by program staff, subjects, and members of other interested communities. The research staff may physically monitor activities involved in the treatment program, using inventories, mechanical recording devices, and human observers to verify observations. The participant–observer strategies used in sociological inquiries may be particularly helpful in establishing the less obvious attributes of the treatment system, for example, detecting subtle lapses in delivery and acceptance of treatment, personal and institutional sources of resistance to the treatment, and so forth.

Empey and Lubeck (1971), for example, have used a "social systems" questionnaire to obtain treatment-related information from the subjects involved in an experimental appraisal of a community delinquency program. Administration of the questionnaire to both treatment and control groups helped to assure that elements of the treatment (e.g., counseling) were actually delivered and to monitor behavior of members of the control group. A "critical incidents" approach was also used to furnish information on the extent to which special features of the prescribed treatment were understood and employed by staff. In similar efforts, Meyer, Borgatta, and Jones (1965) developed their Casework Interview Checklist and Caplan (1968) his Blood, Sweat, and Tears Scale for real-time monitoring of the experimental counseling process in working with problem adolescents.

Intensive measurement of attributes of treatment takes considerable time and staff effort, and requires adequate planning. Changes in treatment standards or in the elements of treatment may require redesigning the method for documentation of treatment characteristics. On the other hand, intensive measurement can also foster more attention to prescribed treatment elements by program staff, and so serve as a quality control mechanism for the treatment. This may be especially true where outside research staff, rather than action program staff, are responsible for monitoring activities. The need for measuring attributes of treatment in the experiment may also suggest the need for similar monitoring activities if and when the experimental program is actually implemented on a large scale. At the very least, the need to monitor treatment activities at all can and should influence the decision on large-scale adoption of a program, since the monitoring activities will influence the operating costs of the program.

*Retrospective Reporting.* Retrospective reports from program staff, from subjects of research, and from program administrators are a less desirable source of information than contemporary reporting. The information *must* be suspect since it is influenced by memory lapses and later experience of the informants, phenomena which can undermine the accuracy and precision of reporting (e.g., Meyer and Borgatta (1959) found notable misreporting in the posttreatment reports of former mental patients). With some evidence for the integrity of such reports (e.g., small side studies of reporting validity), questionnaire data, anecdotal reports, and other methods of collecting data retrospectively *may* be useful. And aside from being an imperfect indicator of the delivery of treatment, such reports can sometimes be helpful in understanding the reasons for the success or failure of a program. Weikert (1972), for example, has elicited treatment-related information from teachers who were involved in experimental tests of his compensatory education programs. Their retrospective and open-end reports provide a richly textured description of teachers' varied reactions to the prescribed program, the variations in teachers' classroom interpretations of program requirements, the subtle problems associated with teacher collaboration in classroom efforts, and variation in the nature and frequency of teachers' objections to classroom interruptions which come about because of the researchers' need to observe students' behavior.

To appraise the character of the treatment retrospectively in large samples, the experimenter might employ standardized special-purpose questionnaires. In experimental evaluations of casework with wives of alcoholics, for example, Krause *et al* (1971) administered such questionnaires to caseworkers in order to assess caseworkers' attitudes toward alcoholism; standardized questionnaires on the therapists' attitude toward the treatment program were also used. Similarly, Goodwin (1972) elicited data from program staff on their attitudes toward the Work Incentive Program participants whom they served. Both sorts of information provide clues to the way in which the treatment was delivered as a consequence, or correlate of, the staff members' attitudes.

Again, preliminary research on the credibility of retrospective reporting is important, especially in complex treatment programs. Without prior investigation, the major experimental test of the program may be needlessly jeopardized by data whose validity is low.

*Remarks on Intensive Measurement.* The depth of description required in either real-time monitoring or retrospective reporting varies, of course, from experiment to experiment and depends on the character of the treatment as well as on the audience for the information. For the experimenter, substantial information on specific dimensions of the experiment can make more penetrating analysis possible and may be of help in detecting weak treatment effects; intensive specification may be required to decide whether a subject was actually treated completely. For the manager, the more intensive measurement may be a helpful, if burdensome, way of demonstrating that he has in fact been doing what he is supposed to be doing, and doing it well. For the program overseers and sponsors, a condensation of such data will enhance understanding of the program and improve judgments about its conduct.

The hazards of emphasizing intensive measures are of two kinds. First, there is always the possibility of "information overkill," a hazard in measurement of response variables and initial conditions as well. Unless the data are informative—in the sense of permitting unambiguous tests of program effects, of describing the extent to which replication or utilization is possible, and of describing the essential character of treatment for reporting purposes—the information probably should not be collected. Furthermore, an exorbitant demand for information can lead to perfunctory and careless filling in of forms, the purpose of which is not understood or not considered important. The second kind of danger stems from the limits of the data. The methods for empirical documentation focus on how closely the actual treatment matches the formal prescription for treatment, but do not address the question of how program elements might be changed to increase the likelihood of large program effects. That question is dealt with in the next sections, which consider measures of control conditions and measures for program revision.

MEASUREMENT OF CONTROL CONDITIONS

Because the control conditions in an experiment are a form of complex treatment, they can and should be viewed as a legitimate subject for measurement, just as elements of the experimental treatment are. Statistical tests of program effectiveness will, in the last analysis, be made *relative* to the control conditions; without good specification of what those conditions are, neither the experimenter nor the program manager can attach much substantive meaning to program effects.

Usually, though not always, it is necessary to collect data about individuals in the control group and about the character of control conditions prior to the design of the experiment. In many experiments there is some prior "survey of need" for the program, and the base-line data stemming from such a survey may serve as a coarse description of the program's target group and of the social conditions (i.e., the control conditions) in which control group members must function. Where such base-line data are inadequate, further specification of control conditions may be obtained as part of the process of documenting the character of the experimental program. The depth and character of the information requested depend on the experimenter's purposes in measuring control conditions, namely, interpretation and hypothesis generation; replication; and anticipation of interference effects in program implementation.

*Interpretation and Hypothesis Generation.*    At a minimum, some physical indicator of the control condition is essential for experimental analysis; nonparticipation in the experimental program is, of course, one such indicator but it may be a rather simplistic one. At a slightly more complex level, it may be necessary to document the kinds of institutional contexts in which control group members operate in order to delineate needs for the new treatment program or to identity processes or institutions that might be replaced or supplemented by the new program. Similarly, documenting characteristics of members of the control group will usually be of some help in assuring that they differ in no important respects from program participants; and the data may be useful in characterizing the influence of differential attrition on the experimental data (Chapter III).

A more intensive measurement regimen involves collecting data on gross similarities among subsets of control group conditions. For example, in experimental tests of morning broadcasts of *Sesame Street*, the natural treatments received by control group members might include other children's television programs and adult talk shows, as well as "treatments" that have nothing to do with television; e.g., eating breakfast, sleeping, or playing. Interviews, on-site observation, questionnaires, and/or diary methods would help to specify the range of these alternatives within the control condition. Where the alternative conditions are especially complex, in-depth description of small subsamples of individuals within a condition will often be an efficient substitute for complete documentation on every condition that prevails in the control group.

Given some basic information on various (naturally occurring) conditions within the experimental control condition, the experimenter will be in a position to do postexperimental appraisals which facilitate interpretation of experimental results and lead to plausible if equivocal explanations for the process underlying the behavior of control group members. As a consequence of the appraisal, the researcher might then be able to conduct later experiments to test hypotheses or explanations so generated. For example, following a formal comparison of treated and control groups, one might focus attention on major natural variations within the control group in order to identify those particular variations or conditions which could exert a strong influence on important response variables. In the *Sesame Street* example, one could identify children in the control group who watch adult talk shows rather than, say, cartoons or other programs commonly viewed by other control group members. Such children may acquire a wider range of vocabulary than those who view other programs, including *Sesame Street*. Although this information is equivocal (the child who chooses or is told to watch adult shows may be brighter to begin with), it does lay the groundwork for later experimental tests of a hypothesis, for example, that adult talk shows are about as effective as *Sesame Street* for particular kinds of learning.

*Replication.*   A second reason for measurement of control conditions lies in the need for data to predict the likelihood of successfully replicating the experimental program on a large scale. The particular sample from which control and experimental group members are drawn may be adequate for a fair test of the program, but it may be idiosyncratic in that other potential target populations are not represented in the ongoing experiment. If the conditions which prevail in the groups being studied in the experiment differ markedly from conditions which prevail in other populations, then it is reasonable to believe that additional testing of the program is required before it is offered to new groups. At the very least, the program designer may be able to make informed guesses about the desirability of additional experimental tests of the program, based on a review of data concerning control conditions. Ford (1969), for example, has used a similar rationale to plan the sequential testing of an innovative managerial strategy across divisional lines in a major corporation.

*Interference.*   The final sense in which systematic measurement and description of control conditions may be useful concerns the extent to which they interfere with the imposition of treatment. That is, some control conditions may affect the delivery, imposition, and reception of treatment, and their documentation may be crucial to the conduct and analysis of the experiment. Suppose, for example, that one wished to experimentally test a manpower training program in a ghetto area of a large city. Some experience suggests that the illegal or quasi-legal street economy—numbers running, sale of stolen goods, pimping, and so on—can be a major source of income for youths in the 16–24 year age bracket in certain ghetto areas. Young men in this age range would normally constitute a major target group for a manpower training program, and the illegal "treatment" programs which make up the control conditions can have a strong effect on the manpower training treatment. At the very least, these conditions may produce a severely restricted group of volunteers for training. (Why enter a training program that has unknown benefits after having invested considerable time and energy in a home-grown activity that fits in well with local institutional conditions?) Whether participation in the program is compulsory (to eliminate selection problems) or restricted to an admittedly narrow volunteer-only sample, the existence of illegal alternative treatment conditions can have several important effects.

If normal social conditions constitute a desirable alternative to the experimental treatment, some potential participants will resist or reject the program being introduced. Similarly, because the new program may damage local social structure or interrupt routinized social processes, this may hamper the experimental treatment or depress the program's effects (Suchman, 1967). Similar effects have been observed in quasi-experiments and demonstration projects concerned with family planning and health related programs (Katz, Levin, and Hamilton, 1972; Smith, 1965). If a treatment is ineffective because it encounters tough competition from the natural social environment, it is, nonetheless, ineffective.

No formal architecture has been developed for structuring the kinds of information that might be obtained regarding interference-related conditions in the control groups. No standardized instrumentation or interview protocols appear to be available, aside from attitude measures developed in specialized cases (e.g., Goodwin, 1972). This should not prevent the development of appropriate reporting systems that can capitalize on the experiences of program staff and of participants. Part of the information that can be acquired and handled well can be based on systematized observation and valid indicators of conditions that might interfere with treatment. Much of the information may, however, be unhandleable. "The unhandleable part—in peoples' minds, rough notes, and conversations—which is often of greater importance, still escapes all the tools of information pursuit except human memory [Tukey, 1962]."

## MEASUREMENT FOR TREATMENT REVISION

In its most simple form, the experiment is a blind test mechanism which can provide unbiased evidence for the contention that a program is effective. If the experimental designer adheres *strictly* to the infomation requirements of the simple experiment, then he will be able to estimate the program effects; but he may be unable to provide substantive recommendations for program improvement at the conclusion of the experiment. Several factors in real-world tests of social programs argue against this narrow conception of the experimenter's role.

First, sequential experiments can be (and have been) designed to test well-specified components, or refinements of components, of a particular treatment program. This planned test–revision–test cycle implies that even if the experimental designer is not directly responsible for recommending internal program changes, he will have partial responsibility for specifying when changes are necessary and what the *general* nature of changes will be; he becomes a part of the reporting system for program revision. The experimenter's efforts to measure treatments will have a bearing on managerial actions in other ways as well. If he finds that treatments are not in fact being delivered according to the plan, then the implications for managerial practice may be quite obvious. Where indicators of outcome are directly linked in theory and practice to measures of treatment, there are other implications for action by manager or program developer. Suppose, for example, that an experimental test of a compensatory program for general education reveals that reading ability is unaffected by the program but that math ability is improved. If the measures of treatment are training time or training mode, then the program designer or manager may be able to develop hypotheses about ways to improve the reading program from this information. The hypotheses might then be tested in a subsequent experiment. Where outcome measures are not closely tied to treatments (e.g., as in the case of recidivism and duration of postprison counseling), the measures of treatment may not be particularly helpful in determining the specific character of recommendations for program revision.

Where the experimental designer has generalized responsibility for program development, he may be required to develop treatment-related measures which will be directly relevant to program revision. The chief problem here of course is that specifying which measures of treatment can be informative in improving treatment (rather than in simply determining whether there are effects) is not an easy task. In some cases, the more intensive measurement schemes might include questionnaires or interviews with program staff and participants to elicit information on their perception of useless features of the treatment, weaknesses in the process of treatment delivery, aberrations in delivery, and so forth. In addition to their use in identifying the need for some program change and their possible use as pointers to substantive program change, the data might also be used to gauge the overall appeal of the program and to improve program packaging. Similarly, formal outcome or criterion measures repeated periodically during treatment can help to anticipate problems and suggest treatments in the ways discussed earlier in the section on outcomes. As in many developmental efforts, participant–observer methods, especially the use of program troubleshooters, can be coupled to experimental tests for detecting aspects of the treatment system that should be revised. The latter methods will, in the short run, frequently provide considerable benefits if only because turnaround time on receipt of information, and the time and effort needed to assimilate and act on the information, is usually short. In the longer run, both the information system for the formal experiment and the more flexible data collection strategies implied by participant–observation methods are likely to have the largest payoff when they operate jointly. There is a large body of literature dealing with the use of information (experimental and otherwise) for development of hypotheses and of alternative plans for revising an ameliorative program. The interested reader is referred especially to the literature on formative evaluation in education (e.g., by Bloom, Hastings, and Madaus, 1971; Scriven, 1967; and others), in communications (e.g., Palmer, 1973), in management theory (e.g., Cleland and King, 1968), in information systems (e.g., Sackman and Nie, 1970), in diagnostic and prognostic approaches to organizational change (e.g., Argyris, 1970), and to other systemic reports on survey types of information and its use in planning.

## Measurement of Initial Conditions

Measurement of initial conditions, or of inputs, refers here to the systematic description of certain characteristics of the target group, that is, the people or institutions to which goods, services, or other kinds of treatment must be provided in the experiment. This description, which must be obtained prior to delivery of treatment, is justified by screening requirements, assessment of the internal validity of experimental tests, and specialized uses of the data for judging program effectiveness. In what follows, we discuss the character of measurement of initial conditions and utilization of the resultant data.

Typically, some definition of the program's target group is given by the program mandate. And, because this definition is usually quite general, further specification occurs as the program is implemented. Systematic description of the demographic character of the group will normally be quite helpful in this specification process and in communicating the nature of the final target group to program sponsors, staff, and to the general public. Especially in the absence of a prior survey of needs for the program, the data on initial conditions may be the *only* vehicle for reliable identification of the target population.

Where criteria for selection of program participants are well specified prior to the experiments, the acquisition and maintenance of the data can, of course, serve as a quality control mechanism, assuring that members of the sample conform to the definition of the target population given by the program mandate. The methods of measurement applicable in this context are no different, in principle, from those used in description of response or treatment-related variables. Questionnaires, interviews, archival records, and tests have been used often and in a wide variety of field experiments to characterize the initial state of the experimental samples. Similarly, validity and reliability concepts are no less important here than they are in considering measurement at later stages of the experimentation. Checks on validity of reporting of initial status may be particularly critical in establishing the vulnerability of a program to corruption and in assuring that services do indeed reach the audience for which they are intended (see, for example, Orr, Hollister, and Lefcowitz [1971] and earlier remarks in this chapter on assuring reliability and validity of response).

The information acquired on members of the experimental groups prior to treatment also provides a basis for making some judgments about the validity of the experimental test. If, for example, control and treatment groups differ initially on a wide variety of demographic or other measures, the randomization process may be suspect (this is especially true in studies based on volunteer subjects). If these initial differences go unrecognized, the internal validity of the experiment— the assumption of equivalence of experimental groups—will be jeopardized. As a result, the experimenter would be unable to make a confident judgment about the extent to which any differences among groups following treatment are attributable to the treatment itself or merely to initial differences. Measurement of attributes of individuals entering the treatment program may also be helpful in generalizing experimental results. Such "commonsense" generalizations to target groups in other geographic areas, institutions, and so forth, are ordinarily a cheaper and quicker (though less reliable) strategy than empirical replication of the experimental test. The input data may, however, be quite helpful in examining the structural similarity between the samples used in the experimental test and other potential target groups, and may be helpful in anticipating problems of applying the tested program to other groups.

A third broad area of utilization of data on the initial condition of the experimental groups is analytic. Given background information on program participants, especially pretreatment data, one can improve the precision of the analysis of the experimental data so as to detect even small program effects. This use of prior data is described in Chapter III (especially the sections on covariance analysis and blocking). In some quasi-experimental designs, detection of even large effects of the program may be impossible without periodic measurement of the characteristics of the target group before their entry to the program (see Chapter IV).

# The Roles of Social Indicators
# and Archival Data Systems

Social indicators are statistical time series data that describe the condition of a group of individuals or a particular social unit. National crime statistics conform to this definition as do many other regularly collected Federal statistics. Although archival record systems serve primarily as a basis for making evaluative judgments about individuals, statistical summaries of the contents of records can also serve in effective description of the state of a social unit (Sackman and Nie, 1970). Motor vehicle registrations, reports of taxable income, and personnel records, for example, function not only as accounting mechanisms but, in aggregate form, as coarse demographic indicators as well.

Recent interest in social indicator and archival record systems has often been tied to development of government-sponsored social programs. Much of this interest is based on the premise that the information is sufficient not only for accounting purposes, but also for setting governmental priorities and for planning and evaluating social programs. Some students of such data have been more judicious however, especially with respect to their potential use in evaluation (Sheldon and Freeman, 1970). An indicator such as employment rate, for example, may be a useful economic indicator particularly when coupled with economic theory and political values. But in the context of assessing social intervention it may be difficult if not impossible to determine if an increase or decrease in the rate is due to installation of a new job-training program or to variations in local economy, population mobility, or other phenomena with which the program happened to coincide. With special quasi-experimental designs and stable, sensitive indicators, the inferential ambiguity may be reduced, but the data may still be insufficient for making unequivocal judgments about the effects of the program (see Chapter IV).

Social indicators need not be justified solely on the basis of their legitimate accounting functions or on the basis of their *potential* relevance to post hoc appraisals of social programs, however. The data can be quite useful in recognizing and clarifying problems prior to experimentation, in design of controlled experiments, and in the analysis of experimental results.

USE IN PROBLEM RECOGNITION

Consider, for example, the events preceding the Manhattan Bail Bond experiment as an illustration of the problem recognition function.

Social and archival indicators of socioeconomic characteristics of those arrested, time lapse between arrest and trial, frequency of posting bail, and other time series data revealed a phenomenon judged to violate both economic and civil equity values. That is, the poor were most likely to remain jailed prior to trial, depriving their families of a source of support and taxing the public for the cost of their maintenance. The data supported a contention that there was a problem and helped to characterize the problem well, but (prior to the experiment) provided little in the way of unequivocal support for proposed solutions.

USE IN EXPERIMENTAL DESIGN

Considering the design of controlled experiments, social indicators have been useful in specifying desirable sample size and sample character. Census Bureau data, for example, were used in selecting sites for the Negative Income Tax experiment. Similarly, national base rates for polio incidence coupled with local data on school-aged populations helped in designing an effective sampling scheme for experimental tests of the Salk vaccine in 1954 (Meier, 1972).

USE AS RESPONSE VARIABLE

If they are relevant to the goals of a given social program, social indicator variables and archival records can sometimes function as measures of outcomes in the experiment and can be used to improve the precision of analysis. For example, to appraise the comparative effectiveness of appeals to moral conscience, of threats of embarassment, and of threats of punitive action on certain types of income reporting for tax purposes, Schwartz and Orleans (1967) used income tax records as response measures. Techniques for eliminating problems of confidentiality of archival records without compromising research objectives have been worked out to facilitate this sort of utilization of existing records, and side studies can usually be done to obtain evidence for the credibility of records on file (see Chapter VIII of this volume and Boruch, 1972b). Where individual background information is available prior to beginning the treatment program, it can sometimes be used to improve the detection of small treatment effects, in the manner described in Chapter III.

USE AS TRACKING MECHANISMS

Some recent innovative applications of archival systems emphasize their use as tracking mechanisms in experiments. In appraisals of the effects of televised public service messages to encourage seat-belt use for example, motor vehicle records and license plates served as an economical device for identifying treatment and control group members (Robertson, Kelly, O'Neill, Wixom, Eiswirth, and Haldon, 1973). Here, the researcher's on-site observation of seat-belt use and auto license number in a particular sample of autos in traffic could be coupled to the region covered by the televised message through publicly available motor vehicle registration records. Region of telecast and households within region in this case were readily controlled by a multiple cable broadcasting system. (See Chapter IV and earlier remarks in this chapter for descriptions of other uses of archival data in assuring quality of data.)

In many experiments, using social indicators and archival records can be quite economical, and sometimes essential, for problem recognition, experimental design, and data analysis. In other cases, however, the benefits may not be quite so obvious. The social or archival data may be irrelevant to program goals and may be susceptible to random error and systematic biases. Nonetheless, with conscientious attention to and resolution of these problems, some indicators and archival records appear to be useful adjuncts or complements to experimentation. At the very least, capitalization on existing social indicators and record systems will expand the nature, quality, and magnitude of the pool of social data necessary for describing the social system in which experimental programs must operate.

# VI

## Execution and Management

The realization of the design and measurement features of an experiment is a complex function of the purposes of the experiment, the kinds of organizations involved in its sponsorship and execution, the specific topic and the treatment under study, and, of course, the particular social and institutional setting in which the experiment is conducted. It is difficult to provide prospective experimenters with any generalized guidance with regard to topics and settings, for the management problems differ considerably between, say, an experiment on the teaching of reading in elementary schools and one to assess the effects of personal counseling on the reduction of juvenile delinquency. Still other problems will be encountered in carrying out experiments like the Negative Income Tax, where a simple but obviously valuable treatment is involved. In the first example, negotiation of the design must involve the educational institution (including parental groups as well as teachers and school administration) and the advocates of the several teaching methods, for example, while the measurement of outcomes is (relatively) straightforward and simple. Almost the reverse was true of the delinquency prevention experiment, on the other hand, where the design problems turned mainly around the tactics of the treatment and there was a minimum amount of negotiation with local authority; but measuring outcomes, especially secondary effects, required a great expenditure of managerial effort. The Negative Income

Tax experiment required substantial negotiation with the community and considerable effort to preserve the integrity of the design, but actual delivery of the treatment was relatively straightforward. Such topic-specific and setting-specific considerations almost defy generalization, but some useful general remarks can be made with regard to other features of experiments.

The successful execution of a social experiment depends on solving many of the same problems that other "outdoor" field research encounters—carrying out the sampling design as precisely as possible; controlling the quality of data collected; establishing adequate data storage and retrieval procedures; carrying out the required analyses accurately; and adhering, in all these steps, to predetermined time schedules. (Most research projects fall behind schedule because of unforeseen complications of detail. Recognition of this fact, together with brisk management, may eventuate in setting reasonable time schedules that can be met.) In this chapter we shall assume that the general problems are recognized and give most attention to those problems which have special significance for experimental and quasi-experimental designs. Throughout, we emphasize the importance of coordinated efforts on the part of those responsible for delivering the treatment or administering the intervention program (called the "action team") and those responsible for executing the experimental design and measuring the variables under study (called the "research team"). Because the cooperation of all members of both these teams is required in order to keep the experimental design from being eroded, it is important that the pitfalls, safeguards, and necessary corrective changes be understood by all those involved. Otherwise, once in the field, because of unanticipated problems, the researcher will often be forced to take actions that he would usually not take. These actions, and the demands they make on others, have to be understood and appreciated if they are to be effective in maintaining the elementary integrity of the design. Thus, while this chapter is addressed to the problems of managing an experiment largely from a research point of view, it is important for program administrators and action practitioners, as well as researchers, to understand these concerns.

Briefly, the management of a social experiment is faced with five major tasks:

First, the management of the experiment must take responsibility for the complex negotiation required to make the experimental design a functioning reality. There is not only a large amount of detail to be developed in the course of realization but there are likely also to be differences of opinion and perspective, conflicting interests, and uncoordinated purposes on the part of the various parties to the experiment. The first task of management is to conduct a negotiation and clarification process that has the following aims: to develop a set of operational objectives and a set of measures related to those objectives on which parties to the experiment agree; to reconcile the value differences as much as possible and minimize the potential conflicts between action team and researchers; and to develop a harmoniously functioning staff that will be governed by high standards of quality in the execution of the experiment.

Second, the management has responsibility for the development of details of the research design, particularly in respect to measurement, the implementation of randomization, and the development of good working relationships with the community in which the experiment is being conducted. The managers must select or develop techniques that will be used for implementing the statistical features of the design (e.g., blocking and randomized assignment to treatment) as well as for assessing the effect of the treatment program on the target population. And these procedures must be appropriate to the social and political climate of the community where the experiment is being conducted, besides being made clear and acceptable to that community so that the collaboration of participants is made more likely.

Third, the managers of an experiment must maintain the integrity of the design while allowing enough flexibility in its details to accomodate the compromises that are inevitable in "open air" experimentation. Researchers are constantly faced with the necessity to keep a balance between practical and scientific necessities. By holding rigidly to an inflexible design and never allowing compromise, the experiment can be so overcontrolled as to severely limit its utility, that is, it can become so artificial as to have no external validity; yet if departures from design are unintentional, unnoticed, or undocumented, the analysis of the experiment will be confounded and the inferences shaky. A manager must also think in terms of maximizing the application of experimental information to the real-life problem—perhaps even if it means abandoning a true experiment and settling for some form of quasi-experiment. Of course it is desirable to avoid compromises in the design, but if compromises have to be made, the research team must be aware of them and must take compensating steps in order to minimize loss of inferential clarity and generalizability. In particular, the loss of subjects from an experiment during its course (attrition) is a special threat to the integrity of the design, and a later section is given over to this problem.

Fourth, the management must establish and constantly supervise procedures to ensure the quality of the data collected about all aspects of the experiment—their accuracy, completeness, and retrievability for analysis. This means that a series of checks, inspections, and reviews must be built into the data-collection process to make sure that correct information is being obtained from all of the respondent units at the right time; is being mechanically or electronically transcribed without error; and is being stored in such a way that an analyst who did not participate in collection or storage can, nonetheless, use the data without difficulty or error. No amount of statistical analysis, however clever and sophisticated, can overcome errors or omissions, carelessness, or misrepresentation at the level of raw data. It may seem obvious that quality control of data is essential; and some readers may wonder why this requirement is emphasized. Sadly, it is because quality control is too often ignored or slighted because it is tedious, may involve delicate nuances of suspicion and pedantry in personal relationships, and is intellectually unrewarding to most research workers. Questions of manpower selection, training, and career line are especially significant in regard to this aspect of social experimentation.

Fifth, the management must keep firmly in mind the need which the sponsor of the experiment has for a useful as well as a high quality assessment and interpretation of treatment effects. Both the design of the experiment and the plan for analysis of data should go beyond simply a narrow "boxscore" assessment of treatment effects. The report of the experiment should interpret those effects in relation to specific treatment features or operations: that is, not only to *what* happened, but also to *how* it happened. To be most useful, the report should discern which program components are most effective and which are least effective in producing outcomes; and, when and where appropriate, the differential effects of these program components upon the various groups and aggregates participating in the experiment. The report should be oriented toward the needs of policymakers and designers of social intervention programs. It should concentrate upon the practical and administrative significance of the results, rather than upon statistical or theoretical significance. The audience will be largely nonscientific, and to report in the jargon of the social science literature is not helpful. Furthermore, the particular analysis presented in the report should be chosen for its relation to policy and program decisions. Finally, the data collected should be made publicly available for reanalysis after being cleaned of personal identifying information about respondents and after a reasonable time interval during which the research team has had an exclusive opportunity to perform analyses of scientific interest for publication.

The reader may detect in these remarks an emphasis on the mundane, practical details of management, with an implication that these are sometimes ignored. The emphasis is deliberate and the reason for it is simply that the art and practice of managing large-scale field research is not well developed and is not easy to learn. Furthermore, the education of the majority of university-based social scientists has simply not exposed them to this range of practical problems. If anything, their education, and the reward structure of their profession, orients them more toward the elegant solution of theoretical problems than toward dogged coping with practical affairs.

Recruiting and maintaining a high quality research staff from the planning through the execution, evaluation, and write-up of the experiment is of great importance to the success of the total effort. Unfortunately it is extremely difficult to staff such a team. These manpower problems are generally recognized but the pressing need for good research managers and applied behavioral scientists continues, for a variety of reasons.

Social experimentation is "applied research" and it frequently does not carry with it the career rewards for social scientists that are associated with the more prestigious "basic" research. Many young, promising behavioral scientists, if given a choice, prefer to do research that builds theoretical or conceptual knowledge and are not interested in "service" research. Applied research has a low status in the eyes of some because it is directed to the interest of nonscientific consumers. Even lower status attaches to those situations in which the researcher has little influence in determining whom the knowledge shall serve or how it will be used. Thus service research rather than applied research may be the answer—applied research with relevance to basic scientific issues is perfectly acceptable as good science. An opportunity to incorporate some fundamental research into a social experimental design, so long as that does not impair the usefulness of the experiment, may attract better quality and more highly motivated scientific talent.

A second factor that affects research staff recruitment and continuity is that field operations in social experimentation are hard, demanding tasks that involve an element of the tedious and must be accomplished according to an external schedule rather than according to the internal clock of the basic researcher or theoretical thinker. Extensive documentation is required about all sampling, data recording, and storage procedures. Often, archival records must be searched, and that task can be tedious. The pretesting of instruments may come to seem endless, but it cannot be entrusted to untrained personnel. Interviewers or observers must be debriefed each day, and often their data must be corroborated. Sometimes there is friction between the action team and the research team; quite frequently there is a gap in values, interests, personal background, and purposes.

These difficulties are not insuperable, and some suggestions for managing them are found later in this chapter, where problems of research team building are considered. They are, however, well worth the attention of the experiment manager, and his sensitive appreciation of them will be repaid in results.

## Negotiating Design Objectives and Procedures

Putting an experiment into the field usually requires a considerable amount of discussion and negotiation among the parties who have an interest in the experiment, but who bring to it a rather varied, sometimes conflicting set of purposes, outlooks, talents, and assumptions. These differences stand in the way of implementing the experimental design and they must be reduced as much as possible by developing clear understandings and consensual agreement on objectives, procedures, and standards if the experiment is to succeed. This section is addressed to some of the most common sources of misunderstanding and obstacles to collaborative work, which must be overcome by thorough and often lengthy exploration of the issues.

It is useful to begin by examining the organizational roles involved and to view this first phase of experiment management as a problem of negotiating working relationships while at the same time trying to solve technical, scientific, and procedural problems. The two tasks are intertwined, but they may take rather special forms, depending on the relationships among the sponsor, the designer, and the action team (see Chapter VII for a fuller discussion of these roles). Indeed, the source which initiates the experiment may determine the power relationships among these roles and, accordingly, the severity of organizational problems. The point can be clarified by contrasting experiments undertaken for the purpose of evaluating ongoing (or independently conceived) action programs with experiments undertaken for the purpose of program development. In the latter case, the designer and the sponsor of the experiment are closely allied and the action team is a subsidiary portion of the enterprise, engaged for the specific purpose of executing the design and, presumably, with a minimum stake in the success of the treatment, but presumably with a considerable stake in the success of the experiment as a research and development venture.

In the case of experiments to evaluate ongoing programs, however, a quite different alignment of power, interest, and stakes is likely to obtain. Often the action team has designed the program independently of any research effort, sometimes even in ignorance that there was to be any research. The treatment program may accordingly not fit readily with a research design. The research may be perceived as intrusive and threatening; the action team may become defensive in the face of what they see as a proposed assessment of the merit of *their* program. Because this alignment of forces is not uncommon in social experimentation and because it presents the management with quite serious problems of negotiating an understanding between the action and the research teams that will permit a successful experiment, it is useful to examine the organizational problems in further detail. The next section takes up these problems which, we repeat, appear in their most difficult form when the experimental treatment has been conceived independently of the research design and when program evaluation rather than program development is the thrust of the experiment.

TEAM BUILDING

Nothing is more crucial for the successful management and execution of the social experiment than good cooperation between action and research teams. Under conditions where the treatment is tangible and concrete, that is, where the "action" involves little more than a simple transfer operation, no special problems may arise between those who administer the treatment and those who measure treatment effects. The income maintenance experiments are of this type. However, where the treatment is inseparable from the person administering it, as in counseling, teaching, or social work, then problems between researchers and action practitioners invariably arise; under these conditions cooperation is not likely to occur unless it is worked at. Single-site, tangible, unitreatment experiments, designed to attain a single objective, present the fewest problems; multiple-site, multiple or alternative version treatment programs, where treatment is dependent entirely upon practitioner skills, present the most difficult problems. For that reason, we shall be concerned mainly with the latter types of situations. But under either condition, anything done to persuade action agents to provide supporting rationale for changes will reduce conflict.

Researchers and action practitioners have very different perspectives. Their roles and functions are different, often incompatible, and, when extended across different sites over the duration of a social intervention program, such differences can lead to the collapse of the experiment. These differences can be a major source of friction between practitioners, administrators, and researchers. They are of several kinds.

*Objectivity versus Success.* The action agents usually enter into an enterprise with a presumption of success and some vague notion that the purpose of the research component is to document their success in a way that will make it known and understandable to a wider audience. It is sometimes expected that the researcher's function on the project will be that of an historian or journalist. All of this changes very quickly, however, once the quantitatively-minded researcher begins to scrutinize action practices, techniques, and skills that the action practitioner "knows" to work. It is a very rude awakening for the qualitatively-minded laissez-faire oriented action agent to submit his practices to the review and test of research procedures that seem unsympathetic or hostile. Research procedures often challenge the action agent's conviction (on the basis of his intuition and experience) that his skills will produce intended effects. It seems strange to the practitioner that the efficacy of his techniques are, perhaps for the first time, not accepted as self-evident. The researcher's scientific objectivity becomes viewed as inappropriate, somehow unfair, and threatening. The morale of the action team can be greatly affected by their understanding of the research inquiry. Yet, even if the threat is reduced, research may still be viewed as an undesirable and irrelevant burden.

Furthermore, not only is the action practitioner's ego involved in his competencies but his very career may be at stake (as well as refunding and continuation of the project). No action practitioner will want to hang around to the end if he senses that the research might show the treatment to be a failure. In consequence, it may be difficult to hold a team of committed action agents long enough to give the treatment variable a fair test if the research, that is, the internal logic of the experiment, is presented so as to be perceived as openly unsympathetic and potentially discrediting to action practitioner interests. Prior experience may also be a confounding influence. In her study of 10 major action–research programs, Weiss makes the following observation: "It is instructive to note that the one agency which dropped a goal-oriented quasi-experimental evaluation design (and substituted a qualitative analysis of program process) had had prior experience with evaluation. One of their earlier programs had been evaluated and found seriously wanting [Weiss, 1971]."

A number of things can be done to deal with this potentially high threat situation. Where possible, action performance should be distinguished from treatment effects. Managers and action practitioners should be evaluated not according to the success or failure of the treatment variable, but according to the extent to which they:

1. Construct administrative and environmental conditions that meet requirements made explicit in the design of the experiment
2. Construct administrative conditions and environments, and record-keeping systems that make evaluation possible
3. Make possible the best and most appropriate delivery for the specific treatment in question
4. Improve their level of functioning over time
5. Develop and maintain information systems (e.g., prepare procedures for collecting and documenting information relevant to performance)
6. Assist in quantitatively defining the action rationale
7. Give attention to record keeping
8. Assist in negotiating and maintaining the acceptability of the experiment to the participants
9. Give cooperation in locating respondents and in record keeping to hold down attrition and provide help in dealing with political and social barriers

If a series of programs is to be tested, the same squad of managers and change agents might be guaranteed that they will work on each sequentially for the next 5 years. If the experiment is a one-shot item in the context of an existing bureaucracy, some other sort of short-term job guarantee may be required.

If this distinction between the success of the action team as the treatment agent rather than as the treatment delivery system can be maintained, perhaps the very simplistic approach to "success of program" can be eliminated and the confusing paranoia associated with the action team performance and treatment variable effects reduced or even to a large extent eliminated.

Where the delivery agent and treatment agent are the same, as in professional counseling, arrangements can be made to guarantee continued employment for some specified period of time beyond the termination of the experiment—regardless of its outcome. A "fade-out" design which stages the imposition of a treatment effect may be useful to help minimize the perception of job risk, e.g.,

Time 1     Time 2     Time 3     Time 4

As time goes on, more people are randomly dropped from the experimental group and transferred to the controls as a special subgroup. Analysis takes into account differential lengths of exposure to the program. By gradually and planfully fading out the action team in this manner, the abrupt termination of a full team of persons with its attendant problems can be avoided.

The point to be emphasized to the action staff is the distinction between (1) embarking on a treatment activity which they might normally expect to continue and (2) doing an experiment to see if the treatment is worth doing and how widely to spread it; they are involved in the latter. If this is understood, the morale problems, the conflicts, the end-game effects, and the like can be brought within manageable limits.

*Value Differences: Science versus Practice Ethics.*    The researchers are disinterested observers committed to the dominant values of the scientific community. They are committed to running the action program as a true scientific experiment; in that context, they are not committed to providing "help" to all that need it but only to those in the experimental group.

Conversely, they are committed to see that the controls do not get "help." In a field study, such commitment to science may appear inhumane and incompatible with the practice ethics of the action team who are *service* oriented, not *science* oriented. Ideologically, action practitioners are committed to respond when they encounter someone who needs their services. To tell them that they are to serve only every fourth or tenth person in need; or that they are to treat only those on one side of the street and not on the other; to tell them *not* to help the controls even if sufficient treatment resources are available for allocation to nonexperimental eligibles—seem inhumane and contrary to their basic purpose in life. The internal logic of the experiment and the needs of the target population, as the action agent sees it, are incompatible.

To minimize this apparent insensitivity to need, perhaps those rejected by any one program should have an opportunity to fall into another program, or into minimal treatment groups. Multiple treatments may be more expensive, but they may make more sense in the long run; and if they do ameliorate action practitioners' abhorrence of "callous" behavior, they may be worthwhile.

This issue of overriding values goes beyond the apparent deprivation of the control group. Every action team learns new and presumably better treatment methods during the course of the experiment. But the experiment is best evaluated if no major action program changes are introduced in midstream. Prolonged submission to such restrictions on his freedom to do what is humane, in the interest of "science," is very difficult for the down-to-earth practitioner to endure. The problem becomes particularly difficult when (1) need for the treatment is acute and the treatment has great face validity, even though those benefits have not been really established; or (2) when the practitioners are unconvinced of the need for a control group because the treatment variable appears to produce an unmistakably powerful effect, i.e., the continuation of the experiment seems unnecessary.

Problems of cooperation that stem from the serious ethical issues raised by the presence of controls are difficult to deal with. There can be no doubt, however, that once designated controls are treated or if the treatment variable is allowed to change, valuable knowledge may be lost. But most problems in this area do not really reflect serious value differences. They arise because of a failure to communicate the importance of the experiment and the rationale for randomization and controls in experimental design. If the action staff understands these matters before they enter into the field, there is a greater chance for cooperation and compliance; if the action team is headed by a career experiment manager, the chances of this are even better.

Finally, if the experiment is one phase of a set of developmental program operations, then enough understanding of the treatment, the need to refine and test its effects, and so on can be built up so that the need for a critical experiment will be understood. If the experiment can be understood in the context of the larger issue, program development, then the need for the artificial impositions on the action team and on the sample group can be understood as part of a sequence of events that cannot any longer rely on the results of small-scale pilot testing; thus, the experiment will not appear unreasonable or unnecessary.

## TRANSLATING ACTION INTO WORDS

Closely related to the problems of team building are those connected with meshing the action and the research design through measurement. Translating the action procedures and intended effects into researchable terms is usually a lengthy and difficult process which can produce tension and frustration for both the action and the research staffs. Yet the goals, means, and intended effects must be defined with sufficient clarity to enable research to proceed. The problem touches on real differences, and, if it is not resolved with diplomacy, it can ruin action–research relations for the remainder of the experiment. Typically, the researcher accustomed to thinking in terms of single and well-defined independent and dependent variables finds himself committed to investigate ill-defined multiple-independent-multiple-dependent variables (broad-aim, nonspecific form of change-for-the-better package programs) experiments. In order to make some sense out of this situation, researchers may turn to the practitioners and place the responsibility upon them to articulate their goals, the means by which they intend to achieve these goals, and some agreement as to what will constitute success and what will constitute failure. Actually most social problems are so complex that no one could set down these operations, goals, and evaluation criteria into concise, easily researchable terms. But the researcher rarely seems to understand this and holds those associated with the action program responsible for the difficulty. In effect, it often appears that the researcher questions whether or not the planners and practitioners know what they are doing. Actually, more than semantics and different ways of looking at the world are involved. These translations are really a set of action–research *negotiations* involving the division of labor, the rules of the game, the grounds for evaluating performance, and the basis for determining the distribution of rewards. Practitioners feel intimidated and put down. Finally, after many hours, an explicit statement of final goals and a set of instrumental goals and practice operations may be put into words which satisfy the action team but not the sponsors, who may discover that the treatment or its goals in no way resemble what they had in mind.

It may be helpful in the negotiating process if the parties are aware of a tripartite distinction among *ultimate* program goals, *instrumental* goals, and *performance* goals.

*Ultimate* goals is used here to mean the final change objective the program is intended to produce. A reduction in the number of fatalities due to automobile accidents might, for example, be the ultimate goal of a highway safety program. Improvement in intellectual performance might be the ultimate objective of a compensatory education program. A program might have a number of independent ultimate objectives, for example, mental health programs might have for their final aim the reduction of admissions to mental hospitals, greater productivity or self-actualization on the part of those treated, greater community level understanding of mental illness, and so on. This class of objectives is, of course, the principal rationale for an experiment, but experimenters' attention should not be limited to ultimate goals.

*Instrumental* goals are the principal means through which the program intends to achieve its final or ultimate objective(s). Driver education, enforcement of traffic regulations, and so on might be instrumental goals, but not the ultimate objectives of a highway safety program. Building rapport, "reaching the unreached", and so on are examples of instrumental goals in counseling.

They are strategies for reaching ultimate goals. One might ask for what purpose "rapport" or "reaching" are wanted—what will they lead to? Thus, rapport-building and reaching those in need of some kind of help, while important to the attainment of some final goal, are means, not ends in themselves.

Instrumental goals in one project, however, may be the ultimate goals in another. For example, driver education may be the ultimate objective of a program designed to test the relative effectiveness of various teaching techniques; but in a highway safety program designed with the intent to reduce accidents, driver education may be only one of a number of possible instrumental means employed to accomplish the objective. The point to keep in mind here is that it is not always easy to distinguish between ultimate and instrumental objectives for a particular project; yet evaluation cannot proceed effectively unless that distinction is understood and the character of the various goals agreed to by the action and research arms of the project.

*Performance* goals include the details of the operational procedures involved in implementing the treatment program. They are the set of managerial and administrative criteria by which the day-to-day activities of the action team can be evaluated, independent of the program's final outcome. Performance goals, then, are the standard by which the action component can be evaluated as a delivery system charged with the mission to carry the treatment to the target groups or aggregates. Put bluntly, these criteria reflect how hard the team worked but little about what its efforts accomplished. With respect to a highway safety or counseling program, we would want to know if the designated persons in the target population received treatment; whether the treatment received matched the intended treatment, and, finally, we would like to know something about the cost effectiveness of the delivery strategy employed. When such performance data are available, there can be greater assurance that the treatment was tested; and, depending upon the required degree of change in relation to the amount of program resources necessary to produce that change, decision-makers can make judgments with respect to the practicality of the treatment in view of the action program experience.

It is hard to overemphasize the importance of learning precisely what concrete actions are being used to carry out the instrumental strategies that are believed to lead to the realization of ultimate objectives. An accurate, factual, firsthand account of what is actually being done under the program is important, especially where complex or diffuse treatments are being administered from a central headquarters. An experiment cannot safely assume that the operations planned (or even alleged to exist) by a headquarters action staff are in fact being carried out in the field. There may be a number of reasons for the discrepancy, including misperceptions or wishful thinking on the part of the staff, unrecognized conflict between agency conceptions and local conditions, unavailability of resources or personnel, or simply the inappropriateness or unrealism under field conditions of a plan that looks sensible from headquarters. Finally, it is abundantly clear from experience that adequate information about operations can almost never be obtained retrospectively. Observation by participant observers should be carried out while operations are proceeding.

From both a scientific and a managerial point of view, it is important to keep performance goals and criteria separate from instrumental and ultimate objectives. Scientifically speaking, the experiment is flawed if the treatment is not delivered according to specifications. Job counseling for adolescents, for example, may or may not be an effective instrument for reducing unemployment. But this cannot be found out if the counseling program is poorly carried out (e.g., too few sessions, poor counselor performance, absence or inadequacy of other resources) or if it does not reach employable adolescents in sufficient number (e.g., if the counselor waits passively in a school while the unemployed hang about on street corners). If the actual operations do not meet specifications, then the planned treatment is not being delivered, and both the action team and the sponsor of the experiment are entitled to know it, for it may explain why the experimental treatment failed.

From a managerial point of view, it is prudent to distinguish the effectiveness of the action team in implementing the treatment program from the effectiveness of treatment strategies for other reasons. For example, the treatment may be delivered correctly and fully but the expected (ultimate) effects not obtained. Under these circumstances, the action team should be absolved from blame for failure. This cannot be done unless the management of the experiment makes plans and takes steps to ensure that the operations of the treatment program are monitored and their adequacy assessed. It is vitally important to the fundamental purposes of the experimentation that an experiment be executed *as it was designed* (or deliberately and explicitly modified) rather than being covertly reshaped or changed in order to protect the action team. The action team should be rewarded for carrying out operations according to specifications and should not have to bear the burden of treatment failure if the treatment was in fact delivered.

An honest assessment of performance goals is an essential part of an experiment, with a somewhat different purpose and target than the measurement of ultimate goals. Performance assessment can not only help maintain the morale of the action team but it can uncover aspects of operational design that were unrealistic and suggest ways of reshaping operations.

By the same reasoning, one can appreciate the importance of trying to maintain an analytic distinction, at least, between instrumental and ultimate goals. The earlier example may carry the point home. Even if job counseling as a treatment is adequately delivered to an appropriate population, teenage unemployment may not be reduced because of some major economic disturbance occurring in the job market of the experiment. Many social programs are, in fact, "weak treatments" and marginally effective in relation to counteracting environmental forces. This is perhaps especially true of attempts to deal with urban problems through such social devices as job counseling, mental health clinics, street club workers, and so on, where the magnitude of the treatment input is so low that it could easily be washed out by uncontrollable (and often unexpected) events. Distinguishing between instrumental and ultimate objectives therefore is often a matter of deciding whether an instrumental strategy failed because it was inherently ineffective or whether it would have succeeded had not some swamping disaster intervened. This is basically a problem of the design rather than the management of an experiment; yet the designers may have failed to foresee and provide for a particular contingency, and it becomes the responsibility of as well as the opportunity for an alert program management to substitute new measures of instrumental goal achievement. For example, the job counseling program may be judged to be successful even if no employment was found (because a major factory closed), if the counseled group at least sought appropriate work.

*A Concrete Illustration.* The points we have tried to make in the foregoing analysis may be clarified by examining an actual instance of the process of translating actions into words. The following is an example of the negotiations required to develop a simple but explicit set of goals for a social action program.

The purpose of the research was to measure the effectiveness of a program designed to control and prevent delinquency. After some 30 hours of meetings between program administrators, action practitioners, and researchers over a 3-week period, the following interpretation of program objectives was agreed upon. Until then, there had been no way to know where to focus the research effort and no agreed upon set of objectives to which the action team could be held throughout the project. The researchers had merely had some vague idea of an action ideology without any sense of operational plans or specific and measurable objectives. But once these goals were agreed upon they served as an action–research contract: (1) the action team committed itself to accepting the degree to which they achieved these goals as a measure of program effectiveness and, in consequence, developed their action program and strategy around them; (2) the research team was able to start immediately to define these objectives further into quantifiable terms and to begin the development of measurement techniques. Throughout the course of the project there was full understanding of the basis for the final evaluation, and when the final data were made public there was no dispute with respect to whether or not the action team had been fairly evaluated. The following is the list of objectives:

1. To reduce the absolute amount of illegal and antisocial behavior in the experimental areas
2. To change the behavior of individuals and groups in the contacted part of the target population, where necessary, from the more seriously antisocial to the less seriously, and from the less seriously antisocial to the conventional, within the class and cultural norms of the local population
3. To help individuals and groups in the contacted part of the target population meet their emotional needs for association, friendship, and status by providing conventional, organized, and supervised activities for them, with a view to increasing their capacity for participation and autonomy
4. To increase the objective opportunities for youth in the external environment in the fields of education, employment, and cultural experiences
5. To help youth prepare themselves for conventional adult roles by providing guidance in the fields of education, work, family life, and citizenship through direct intervention in their life processes, especially at times of crisis
6. To relate the target population to local adults and institutions in positive ways so that communication channels between youth and adults might be developed through which a shared, conventional system of values might be transmitted
7. To develop in parents and local adults a concern for local problems affecting youth welfare, and to organize them with a view to having them assume responsibility for the solution of local problems
8. To create a positive change in attitude, in both youth and adults, about the possibility of local self-help efforts to improve the local community through active and cooperative intervention in community processes and thus to create a more positive attitude toward the local community itself

Goals 1 and 2 constituted what were referred to earlier in our discussion as ultimate program goals. Arrest rates and data on the type of offenses committed were to serve as the primary basis for evaluating how well the program succeeded in achieving these objectives. Goals 3–8 were instrumental goals. The expected changes in 1 and 2 were premised upon the belief that the instrumental goals were commonly related to delinquency. These instrumental goals were measured through survey techniques, and on-site documentation by action staff and nonparticipant observers from the research team.

Prior to the explication of these goals through discussion and negotation between the action and research components, the project was perceived by the action agent as a multiple-treatment, broad-aim project with no distinction between ultimate and instrumental goals. In fact, goals 3 through 8 were the preferred final goals of the action team because these were activities over which they believed they had control: They could organize the community groups to provide help to youth; they could meet emotional needs through counseling. By contrast, they were uneasy with delinquency reduction as a success measure, for several reasons: (1) They believed that delinquency was being taken too seriously by the program sponsors and by the police. Helping young people to remain in school, getting them into employment, and reducing alienation in the community were more important in their own right than delinquency. (2) They doubted the existence of a clear, positive relationship between delinquency and the instrumental goals. In short, the *purpose* of the experiment, the presumed relationship of goals 3 through 8 to the reduction of 1 and 2 and the action team's responsibilities in the context of the experiment, were all misunderstood. Once it was understood that their activities were to be evaluated by the accomplishment of tasks presumed necessary for the achievement of the instrumental goals, a major source of uneasiness disappeared.

The last sentence bears elaboration. Not only was the action team not held accountable for the success of the program in achieving goals 1 and 2, they were not to be held responsible for achieving goals 5 through 8. The *program* would be evaluated by the degree to which the ultimate and instrumental goals were achieved, but not the action team. The evaluation of the action team was to be based upon their performance in carrying out the tasks which were presumed related to the accomplishment of these goals, particularly the instrumental goals. For example, with respect to goal 4, action team performance was not to be evaluated by the degree to which employment opportunities for youth increased through education and cultural experience—a goal dependent to a large degree upon macroeconomic and other factors largely outside the control of the worker. The performance of the team was to be measured by how well they carried out the tasks prescribed as the means for increasing opportunities for youth, for example, their effectiveness in starting and managing tutorial programs and their contacting employers and informing them of the employment needs of youth in the experiment. Thus, the action team was charged with carrying out action practices that were presumed to be instrumentally related to the accomplishment of the program objectives; but the evaluation of their performance did not depend upon the consequences of their actions—only upon how well they carried out their tasks given the exigencies of the context(s) in which the experiment was to be implemented.

Thus, by the time a goal statement has been put into words and restated in measurable terms, it should be clear to the sponsors, action practitioners, and researchers just what it is that is being tested and, equally important, how evaluation of the program's usefulness differs from evaluation of the action team's performance.

## Implementing the Research Design

Once the goals of an experimental intervention program have been refined, it is necessary to find or develop appropriate behavioral statements and measures. One who has not tried to do this seldom realizes how difficult a job it is to be precise, realistic, sufficiently general, yet concrete. Almost everyone believes that he knows intuitively what highway safety, delinquency, or poverty mean, but very few, could offer a precise and generally agreed upon behavioral definition or measure of these variables. By "behavioral" we mean actions that are directly observable by outside observers. Either an action occurred or it did not occur; either a kind of behavior changed, or it did not change. There are, of course, many levels of "behavior," not all of which are directly observable or easily measured; but, as far as possible, treatments that are designed to modify behavior should be evaluated by objective behavioral measures. Changes in attitudes alone, or indices based on nonobtrusive "trace" data are valuable sources of supplementary data, but they are not as convincing as direct observations of the behavior in question.

Furthermore, an objective record of behavior is often more accurate than an individual's memory of that behavior. Where it is available, the objective evidence is to be preferred as a dependable record of the facts, although a skillful research worker may find it illuminating to compare actual behavior with what the individual recalls. A good illustration is found in a study by Menzel (1957) who interviewed physicians about their prescribing of certain drugs. He then checked the physicians' statements with prescription records in pharmacies in the neighborhoods where he practiced. Examination of these local pharmacy records revealed that physicians tended to overreport their use of up-to-date drugs, and further, this tendency to exaggerate was negatively correlated with a physician's standing among his peers. The personal reports by high-prestige physicians tended to coincide with their prescription records, whereas the lower-prestige physicians tended to distort the information given the interviewer, appearing more up-to-date in their use of drugs than was in fact so. Similar bias in survey data has been noted with respect to interviewer response to questions on contributions to community chest drives, voting frequency, and airplane trips (Kahn and Cannell, 1957). Studies of health behavior have found that in a sample with known hospitalizations, respondents in interviews underreported illnesses considered to be threatening or embarrassing such as malignancies or hemorrhoids, but reported accurately (nature of illness and length of stay in hospital) for illnesses that were not considered threatening or embarrassing. This tendency to "forget" was positively correlated with the amount of time lapse between hospitalization and the time of the interview. Further examples of selective forgetting, memorial distortion, and the tendency to present oneself in a favorable light can be found in studies of victimization by criminals, educational achievement, and financial transactions. All of these instances argue persuasively for trying to obtain objective or direct measures of behavior if possible, in order to maximize accuracy.

When direct measures are not feasible, then it is necessary to use nonbehavioral measures which most closely reflect the actual behaviors under study. For example, if the program being evaluated was designed to improve race relations, the objective behavioral outcome measure might be based upon changes in the number and type of interracial activities tabulated over time by observers. Attitudinal data are probably not the best indicators of changes in racial relations, but if supplemented by existing behavioral data, such as changes in number of arrests stemming from interracial conflicts, or nonobtrusive measures, such as grafitti, these data—to the extent that they "triangulate"—are very useful and might substitute as primary indices of change where observation of "real" behaviors is not feasible.

It is difficult and expensive to develop workable instruments and to validate behavioral or attitudinal measures. There is considerable advantage for the researcher, therefore, in using measures that have already been field-tested and validated. Not only will this save time—where such measures are applicable—but widely known measures simplify interpretation of finding, replication, and cross validation. At least three comprehensive collections of measures suitable for door-to-door use are available and worth examination before setting out to develop original measures. These are: (1) "Measures of Social Psychological Attitudes" (661 pages) by Robinson and Shaver (1969); (2) "Measures of Political Attitudes" (701 pages) by Robinson, Rusk, and Head, (1969); and (3) "Measures of Occupational Attitudes and Occupational Characteristics" (460 pages) by Robinson, Athanasiou, and Head (1969). The volumes contain complete lists of empirical instruments in these attitude areas, their actual items, scoring instructions for them, and comprehensive assessments of their strengths and weaknesses.

A number of techniques for measuring behavior in natural situations by means analogous to interviews can be found in Bickman and Hency (1972). This volume contains many examples of investigations in nonlaboratory contexts which illustrate techniques for validating survey information and also display research approaches to convergence validity and criterion data.

In social experimentation, as in other forms of applied social research, there is a complex trade-off among three desiderata: ease of measurement, conceptual appropriateness, and convincingness. Changes in Rorschach profiles over time are perhaps a conceptually appropriate measure of the impact of a mental health program, but are less convincing than changes in neurotic or psychotic behavior, which may be harder to measure. Admission rates to mental hospitals are easy to measure, but, since they may fluctuate in response to style of treatment or administrative practices, they are conceptually less appropriate and less convincing evidence of the program's effectiveness. Insofar as possible, the effort should be made to measure appropriate behavioral outcomes directly; for, to the extent that this requirement cannot be met, the research will need to use a wider variety of evidence to make the assessment convincing. All this simply emphasizes the necessity of operationalizing program objectives (of which more later in this chapter) as a means of deciding what will be counted as evidence of program effectiveness. In the absence of such operationalization, there is a risk that the choice of measuring instruments may be guided by their ease of application, familiarity to the research team, or rampant intuition.

Operationalization is also required for specifying the treatment. Some treatments are very much easier to operationalize than others.

Transfers of money are perhaps the simplest, as the Negative Income Tax experiment illustrates. Decisions had to be made about the amount of the transfer payments and the frequency of the disbursement but these were readily operationalized. On the other hand, where the treatment is inseparable from the person administering it, as in counseling, teaching, or social work; where the treatment is intangible; and where it may vary in intensity depending on the individual character of both the delivery unit and the unit being treated, then real difficulties arise in operationalizing. Variations in the skill of the action practitioner as well as in his judgmental adaptations of treatment to the individual treated can probably not be eliminated but only dampened, and provision will have to be made in the analysis to take note of such variation. The less tangible forms of treatments are always hard to operationalize and to standardize, but efforts should be made to do so.

Some treatments are designed to test the effectiveness of some *means* with high face validity to reduce or eliminate some clearly recognizable and pressing problems: for example, structural interventions like providing more police and better lighting to reduce street crime. Here the problems of identifying the defining *goals* are largely conceptual and semantic. On the other hand, in the case of exploratory programs or programs where means are generally considered meliorative but there is less certainty about ends (such as mental health, counseling or therapeutic programs) then the problem is to operationalize the latter. One may feel certain about the means, but must speculate about probable outcomes and then design the experiment to test for them. Where the experimental approach is used as part of a more general program development plan, sequential testing of prototypic treatments for effectiveness in producing specific effects leads to the accumulation of knowledge about both means and ends. Furthermore, additional knowledge about the delivery of the treatment will make it possible to set more specific and realistic performance goals for the action team.

IMPLEMENTING RANDOMIZATION

The basic statistical aspects of random assignment of units to experimental or control treatment were outlined and discussed in Chapter III. This section considers some practical details of procedures that experiment managers may wish to use.

It is worth beginning with a few remarks about the process of securing a list of eligible units, for ordinarily one would like to start with a total enumeration of the target population of the experiment. It is possible, and often necessary, to perform that enumeration through a house-to-house survey, although this is an expensive and time-consuming process. Alternatively the use of ready-made lists is sometimes possible, but they are to be regarded with suspicion as to their completeness. Telephone directories are biased lists because a substantial proportion of the population do not have telephones, and many with phones have unlisted numbers. Membership lists of community organizations are always biased no matter how comprehensive they claim to be; and official lists of taxpayers, licensed drivers, voters, and so on, define a special population, not a totality. The most complete listing of a geographically defined population is obtained by house-to-house enumeration by an interviewer. When institutionally defined populations are being studied (e.g., school children, inmates, or physicians), lists will probably have to be used, but the basis of their composition should be carefully scrutinized for omissions.

When the built-in bias of an existing list is either not great or not relevant to the criteria for selecting participants, considerable saving in cost can be achieved by using it instead of a house-to-house enumeration procedure. The latter is almost as expensive as a wave of interviews for collecting experimental data. Lists are most useful when a special segment of a population—corresponding to the experimenter's interest—has already been identified and enumerated for some other purpose.

*Timing of Randomization.* Deciding *when* to randomize assignment to treatment requires an appreciation not only of the design problems discussed in Chapter III (pp. 53ff.) but also of some quite practical management questions, especially relationships with the community in which the experiment is being conducted. The design of the experiment—its research methods and strategy—must be acceptable to prospective participants in order to ensure their cooperation and compliance with the ground rules of the experiment. The problem of explaining the design is particularly acute with respect to explaining randomization, especially when the treatment is valued and must be deliberately limited to the treated group while the cooperation of untreated control units is solicited to provide data. Resistance to randomization is further discussed later, in the context of maintaining good community relationships, but the matter has a distinct bearing on the timing of randomization.

It has been pointed out earlier (Chapter III) that the scientific problem is to maximize comparability between the experimental and control groups and to minimize attrition, especially from the control group. Ideally, the former requirement can best be met by deferring the point of randomization until a sample of eligible participants has been obtained who would all agree to take part whether they fell in the control or in the experimental group (i.e., no one would refuse treatment or refuse to cooperate even if it meant they were only to provide data). This would maximize comparability between treated and untreated units.

To revert to the example of the Negative Income Tax experimental design, such a procedure would have meant deferring randomized assignment until one had eliminated all persons who would refuse to accept the income supplement in the event that they did, through random assignment, fall into the experimental group as well as those who would refuse to cooperate by supplying information if by chance they fell into the control group. To implement such a procedure, it would be necessary to explain all of the experimental treatments and the control treatment to each prospective participant, as well as making clear the chance method by which assignment would be made—perhaps emphasizing its fairness by analogy with a lottery. One would select only those who agreed to participate in the experiment no matter what treatment the random lottery assigned them. This select group would then be randomly assigned to the several experimental and control treatments.

This extreme postponement of randomization is statistically sound, at least at the outset, and ethically satisfying, but it has the disadvantage that all participants are made aware of all treatment conditions. When a treatment has apparent value, those who fall into the control group may resent being deprived of a boon, as they see it. As a consequence, there may be differential drop out from the experiment, with controls refusing to live up to their agreement to cooperate with data collection requirements or seeking alternative treatments or opportunities to reapply to obtain treatment by other means. (There were apparently strong pressures on the part of control group units to obtain treatment in the initial polio vaccine trials, for example.) In either case, the initial equivalence of groups which was maximized by the postponement of randomization would be diminished by differential drop out. Accordingly, the extreme postponement of randomization is generally not the wisest course where randomization of *persons* or *families* is involved.

If ethical considerations counsel it, careful cultivation of community understanding of the experimental design is also advised for statistical reasons. To be sure, one can think of exceptions to this rule. Randomization from among well-informed volunteers seems particularly feasible where two alternative therapies are being compared, rather than one therapy versus no therapy. If used in the latter case, the dubious status of knowledge about the benefits of the therapy should be emphasized, and other ways of minimizing the perception of relative deprivation should be sought out. If one can guarantee to the controls that they will be given the experimental treatment, if they then want it, at the termination of the experiment, this should help. For some programs, it would be feasible to have the experimental and control groups reverse roles in a second phase of the experiment.

Where one is randomly assigning organized social units such as schools, one might well decide differently. Here one is usually dealing with so few units that loss of units after randomization is disastrous. Experimental treatments often involve much desired budgetary accruals, while control group status is only an administrative burden. It seems unfair to give the experimental boon to units that would have refused to be controls had the luck of the lottery gone against them and to exploit the more cooperative units who had no chance of receiving the boon. Awareness of the experimental design may still indirectly affect the behavior of control units but this bias is mitigated when the commitment to participate is made at an administrative level (e.g., by school superintendents or principals) but carried out by others (teachers and pupils).

Finally, there may be no randomization procedure that is effective in guarding against Hawthorne or other reactive effects and ensuring long-term cooperation as long as controls are given no treatment whatsoever. A suggestion for coping with this problem is made later in the chapter, in connection with maintaining good relationships with the community.

REAPPLICATION AND WAITING LIST
PROBLEMS IN RANDOMIZATION

The illustrations used so far have concerned one-time experiments set up separately from the regular ongoing activities of even those govenment agencies assigned to the same problems. But randomized experiments are also available under certain types of regular agency operation, and such uses have a very real contribution to make in evaluating ongoing programs. In such settings, new practical problems emerge, some of which will be discussed here.

The most typical situation where in this is possible is a social program in short supply, one in which there are more eligible clients than there is room for. The experimental treatment comparison in such studies will usually be the agency's program versus no treatment, or versus whatever alternative treatments the rejected applicants can find on their own. Such experiments have a great value in guiding the expansion or diminution of a given program, and in comparing programs, indirectly or directly.

To use randomization, the administrator must recruit a surplus of eligible applicants and be willing to treat these (or some portion of them) as essentially equal in eligibility. From among these, he randomly selects for treatment the number he has room for, rejecting the others but keeping records on them to follow up as a control group. (If he cannot treat any group or subgroup of applicants as equal in eligibility, but must give the few available spaces to those most eligible, the regression–discontinuity quasi-experimental design, discussed in Chapter IV, is available.) If the administrator controls two substitutable programs, random assignment to each of these may also be possible, providing a direct comparison of program effectiveness.

Since operating agencies rarely have precise data on degrees of eligibility among those who meet the basic requirements of eligibility, and since, when proper publicity is given to the program, there is usually a surplus of eligible applicants, this type of experiment could be widely used. Note that it provides the basis for a low-cost or postponed-cost study. The experiment would often be worth doing even if the only measures of effects came from records, where the expense of retrieval is small.

Right off, the operating agency meets new problems in the rejected applicants' right to reapply or in the creation of waiting lists. The rejected applicant for day-care space, for Job Corps training, or for a place in a special retirement home may wish to reapply for admission to the next session, or for any vacancy that may occur. Yet to allow such reapplication can produce systematic selection biases that undermine the integrity of the experiment. If this eventuality can be anticipated, then one can design a sequence of experiments in which the "reapplicants" can be offered treatment in a second, later phase and their outcome compared to a parallel group of subjects assigned to control treatment in the lottery for the second phase or session of the experiment. The justification for such a procedure arises both from considerations of equity and from society's need to know the effectiveness of the program.

Let us expose another problem. A person on a waiting list or having a reapplicant status is far from an ideal control comparison. Such persons may very well have suspended the self-help and search for alternatives that would have been present had the program not existed at all. They thus do not provide an appropriate base line against which to measure program effectiveness.

If reapplication is permitted but left up to individual initiative, then successful reapplicants will be a biased subsample of the original control group. When, for example a new facility is being opened and when subsequent vacancies are few in number compared to the original samples, one could consider the conservative analysis of treating successful reapplicants as though they were untreated controls, avoiding selection bias at the expense of underestimating the experimental–control difference. And under such conditions, the reapplication chances might be so obviously low that most controls would realistically seek out other alternatives, avoiding the waiting-list inanimation effect. But there are other ways to go about the task.

One could fill new openings in the program by randomly selecting persons from the entire control group. This would avoid the initiative-in-reapplying bias if all so invited accepted. If, however, some were so satisfied with their present status (retirement arrangements, day care, employment, or training) that they now refuse the opportunity they initially would have accepted, a bias analogous to the initiative-in-reapplying one arises, probably operating to eliminate the more able.

As a way to avoid this problem and that of waiting-list inanimation, it is suggested that the basic randomization create two nonexperimental groups. One group would be an explicit waiting-list group, told that they are given priority for program space, new openings, or the next session of the training program. The other group would be told that the luck of the randomization had failed to put them into either the treatment group or the waiting group, that their applications had been cancelled, that it would be useless to reapply, and that they should seek other solutions to their problems. This latter group would be the control group. The waiting-list group need not be analyzed at all.

The details of how to handle the waiting-list group would have to be negotiated in light of local conditions. Are they to be given priority over new applicants? Usually new applicants must be allowed for. Perhaps the waiting-list group should be pooled with the new applicants for new lottery drawings. For age-specific programs such as all three of our examples (day care, Job Corps, and retirement homes), waiting-list status probably should be limited to younger applicants and for a specific time period. (Older applicants who would otherwise have drawn waiting-list status should be kept separable from the regular control group in analysis.) Popular concepts of equity on a "first come, first served" basis might in some conditions give the waiting-list group total precedence over new applicants.

*Rate of Assignment in Randomization for Small-Batch or Trickle Processing.* Where a new facility is going to be opened on a specific date, or, periodically, a new class of trainees is to be started, one can use a single randomization process with fixed proportion of persons being assigned to treatment and control groups. If there are 100 spaces and 330 applicants, the first 100 random numbers chosen go into the treatment group, the next 50 random numbers, say, into the waiting group, and the remaining 180 into the control group. Each such batch constitutes a separate experiment.

But for many ongoing treatment programs, there are no such big-batch starting points. Instead, openings and applicants occur on a daily basis, beds or spaces cannot be left vacant for long, and waiting times for those accepted must be kept short. Under such conditions, admission decisions often must be made for each applicant as he appears or for small groups of applicants each week. Due to the vagaries of supply and demand, treatment–control proportions cannot be held fixed indefinitely, because waiting lists will become too long or unused vacancies will pile up.

If admissions decisions can be postponed to a weekly decision day, one might still fit the selection ratio to the vacancies each week. Pooling the admissions of several weeks into one composite would, however, create problems. These problems are best understood if one recognizes that each week is basically a separate experiment; the pooling of data is being superimposed to provide statistical stability and a summary estimate, where justified statistically. One should look for week-to-week or seasonal changes in the character of the applicants; but where analysis of the data separately for each week shows no such trend, pooling the data for all weeks is reasonable.

Where a decision must be made, applicant-by-applicant as application is made, a fixed randomized rate of admission must be used for a specific period of time. This rate should be chosen on the basis of expectations and prior experience with vacancy and applicant rates. Exact fitting of vacancies cannot be achieved. Instead, a randomization process should be used which, on the average, will produce the target rate. If the results of this process produce waiting lists that are too long or too many vacant slots, then the rate could be changed. All of those selected under one rate would be treated as one batch, with batches being combined as described earlier.

For small-batch and trickle processing it may be that the waiting-list and no-reapplication groups arrangement will not prove feasible. Indeed, in such situations it may be very hard to avoid giving everyone the right of reapplication. A strict first-come-first-served priority system may obtain. The specifics of the local situation will have to determine this. Methodological alertness to possible procedures and requirements should, however, increase the number of settings in which such experimental evaluations of programs in short supply can be executed.

SCOUTING THE SITE

Experimental designs, measures, and randomization procedures may be conceived in the quietude of a researcher's mind, but their implementation occurs in the hurly-burly of a real social setting—which can be known only through direct contact with field sites. If the first question that an experiment manager should ask is: What are the objectives of the experiment? certainly the second should be: Where will it be carried out? Once the manager has an explicit understanding of the hypothesis to be tested and an understanding of the treatment operations, he should visit the sites in order to gain some initial appreciation of how much scientific freedom he can expect to have in implementing the research design and what public resources he can draw on for assistance in preserving his design. The social experimenter cannot get by on technical ingenuity alone. Social experiments are political acts and their political significance is quickly grasped by community leaders and influentials. Managing these political consequences will present difficult and delicate problems. By scouting the site, the experiment manager can get information that will help him to plan strategies to handle such problems. By gaining the cooperation of important public agencies and community leaders early, the manager may be able to anticipate and even avert trouble in the community. Continued cooperation may be essential for the viability of the experiment, since the degree to which the manager has freedom and power to operate is in the hands of those who exercise political and social control at the local site level. Furthermore, such forces usually operate quite independently of the wishes or power of the sponsor of the experiment, regardless of his national prestige, excellent reputation, or high motives. Some community leaders demand a quid pro quo for the valuable information the experimenter is seeking—jobs for local people, a voice on the project's equivalent of a board of directors. Where this is the case, it is important to know it and to work out such matters prior to the introduction of the treatment rather than to discover it later and have to negotiate from a vulnerable midstream position the continuance of the experiment.

In addition to these political and institutional concerns, scouting can make the experimenter acquainted with local conditions that affect a multitude of research functions; sampling; communicating the purpose of the experiment in a comprehensible form; identifying indigenous persons who can act as local liaisons and "anchormen"; determining if there are related "treatments" already under way in the site; locating local resources such as interviewers and other staff, data processing facilities, and local records; determining transportation needs; finding office space; checking local ordinances (some municipalities prohibit or license interviewing); getting telephones installed. Firsthand observation of this kind is necessary to determine the peculiarities of a site that might affect its suitability but which may not be known from afar and, therefore, may not have entered into considerations regarding choice of site. More generally, it is essential to identify strata or sectors of the target population of the site and to determine focuses of receptivity or resistance to the experiment. Educational level, income occupational category, geographic location, ethnic composition, religion and, in particular, the local manifestation of these factors will have a bearing on organizational strategies for introducing the treatment and the data collection procedures.

The best reason for scouting a site—for spending several days or weeks in it before the decision to experiment there is irrevocably made—is a reason that cannot be made convincing to someone who has never done applied social research in field settings and does not need to be explained to anyone who has: You will always find something you did not expect.

COMMUNITY RELATIONS

Social experiments may take place in a variety of institutional settings, such as school systems, rehabilitation centers, military posts, courts of justice, and industrial establishments as well as in residential communities in the conventional sense. In this section, the term *community* is intended to apply to all such institutional sites for they all do include a social community with which an experimenter must deal. Most of the illustrations that follow are drawn from experience with (literal) residential communities where, experience suggests, some of the most difficult problems arise. The points to be made about them, however, apply to all sorts of communities.

The major point is that communities are not passive, unreactive collectivities just waiting for an experiment to take place. An experiment is a novel, perhaps unprecedented, event that will encounter interest, resistance, enthusiasm, or indifference—and probably all of these in various quarters. Experimenters must arouse enough interest in their project to obtain cooperation which, in turn, will lead to a desire on the part of community members to have some part in an activity that may have a considerable influence on their lives. In this fashion there arise pressures from the community to alter the character of the treatment(s) to influence the assignment of particular units of experimental treatment, to hire local people for jobs on the experiment staff, or even to block the execution of the experiment completely if community leaders view it as having deleterious effects. In social experimentation, therefore, the management must be attentive to the way the experiment is viewed by the community and must cultivate relationships with community members that facilitate execution of the design as planned. Gaining the collaboration of community leaders may not be difficult, requiring sometimes only a general explanation of the design and purposes as well as pointing out some of the advantages of the experiment to the community. Locating the informal leaders in a community may be a more difficult task, but effort spent in recruiting their sympathy will be well repaid.

Social experimentation differs from traditional forms of research in being a much more public undertaking. Because large sums of government money frequently are involved, the lay public and elected officials generally are aware of an experiment from the day field operations begin (if not before). Information about its purposes and progress frequently is demanded by quite different audiences than usually are interested in traditional research, for many more people are directly or indirectly stakeholders in the outcome of a social experiment. Furthermore, it is usually newsworthy.

Social experiments that involve action and research on a community-wide basis must be understood and approved by the community in a way that legitimates the project, permits access, and is ethical (e.g., through informed consent). Gaining approval and understanding depends upon the obtrusiveness of the treatment variable, the degree to which the participants share the goals of the sponsor, and the degree of cooperation needed for data collection. Very often there are no problems; in fact, the presence of researchers may be viewed as the cultural and social event of the year. On the other hand, an experiment can generate a great deal of social heat and the research may be seen as an incursion into private lives. Community acceptance is not easy to predict; a questionnaire that works in community A may cause a furor in community B. But, if the treatment variable can be introduced with a minimum of inconvenience and without provoking suspicion, and if data collection depends largely upon cooperation-free unobtrusive measures, then access and legitimation problems can be kept to a minimum. If, on the other hand, the program gets a lot of press and fanfare, if the treatment is perceived as involving a risk to the treatment group or if it appears that the experiment deprives the control of a valued resource, and if data collection is carried out frequently and requires the cooperation of inhospitable target and control populations, then gaining and maintaining community cooperation before, during, and after treatment may be very difficult. Some communities—Woodlawn (Chicago) and Somerville (Boston), two overstudied communities bordering on major universities—have come to equate social research with vivisection and, in consequence, have set up community committees to review, approve, and negotiate studies conducted in their areas.

All open community action programs encounter problems of establishing institutional and local liaisons and dealing with challenges by residents, intellectual dissidents, and others, but what sets the social experiment apart is the difficulty of explaining not only the action program, but the experimental design as well, especially, as noted earlier, explaining randomized assignment and justifying it in such a way as to ensure cooperation with the ground rules of the experiment. The analogy of a lottery is often helpful, and it may be useful, even necessary, to let community leaders inspect the randomization procedure to assure themselves of its fairness. Even if they are convinced the lottery is fair, community leaders may be reluctant to go along with an experimental plan that seems to them to bar some people (controls) arbitrarily from treatment for which they would otherwise qualify. Ethical considerations also enter, and the possible ethical advantages of explaining fully the control and experimental treatment procedures to all prospective participants must be balanced against the possible scientific drawbacks of differential attrition and Hawthorne or other reactive effects (see also Chapter VIII).

However, the fullest possible explanation of a classical experimental design, especially one that involves some perceived boon to experimentals and no (perceived) gain for controls, may not be the best way to obtain the long-term cooperation usually required in social experiments, where continued monitoring of behavior or repeated measurements and continuous tracking of respondents may extend over protracted periods of time. In situations where it seems strategically advisable or ethically unavoidable to make all potential participants aware of the control–experimental distinction, it may be wise also to consider modifying a classical design by abandoning the traditional untreated control group or by adding a control group that receives some minimal "treatment" that is plausible, equally desirable as (but different from) the real treatment of interest, and that can be expected to produce *some* reaction, thus simultaneously attempting to cope with several problems. Such a minimal level treatment ought to reduce attrition, blunt the sense of deprivation on the part of some participants, meet humanitarian and ethical requirements, and produce some reactive (e.g., Hawthorne) effect that can be usefully incorporated into the plan for analyzing the experiment. Equalizing experimenters' attention in this way would also help to achieve long-term cooperation on the part of controls as well as experimentals by blurring the distinction of "benefitted–not benefitted" in participants' eyes. An interesting example of a minimal treatment control design occurs in the nutrition and mental development experiment being conducted in Guatemala, in which the control treatment differs from the experimental only in respect to the composition of the dietary supplement provided to subjects; both controls and experimentals receive vitamins, medical care, and other benefits equally. This design appears to have gained most of the advantages cited earlier.

Building a cooperative relationship with a community and interlacing research requirements with the social realities of day-to-day life there can be facilitated by the establishment of a field office in the community and the hiring of indigenous staff to facilitate the implementation of the research plan. In any community people can be found with fingertip sensitivity as to what goes on in their community, who can be helpful to the management of the experiment. Their knowledge can be useful and their active collaboration can provide an important leverage in dealing with a wide range of operational difficulties, as well as reenforcing the legitimacy of the research. Such a person (or persons) should have a full-time position with real responsibilities to assist in the preparatory arrangements (enumeration, sample selection, determination of eligibility measures, pilot testing of measuring instruments, and preparation for analysis). A local agent can serve as anchor man for the entire field operation at the local level as data collection gets underway.

Even though the most crucial role played by this person would be during the period of actual data collection, the variety of important services he can provide prior to that time deserves special emphasis. He often knows best how to communicate and explain the purposes of the action–research program to the community. He can help to train interviewers who will work in his community; a great deal of experimentation involves interviewer-collected data and survey research methods. Interviewers (even if recruited from local residents) come to the field better prepared for the exigencies of field interviewing after role-play with other locally experienced persons. The anchor man can provide important help with the language and phrasing of interview items and can judge sensitivity of content. His knowledge of target areas can enable the sampling to overcome the drawbacks of outdated census information and thereby help to reduce sampling error. His knowledge of local conditions can also be valuable for feedback of research information to the community or to participants in the experiment.

Perhaps the most important service that an anchor man can provide is to locate and facilitate the cooperation of hard-to-find respondents, particularly in a lower-class neighborhood. Without such assistance, it is not unusual for trained interviewers to spend 2 to 3 hours or even 2 or 3 days of search time for each hour of interviewing. With the help of a geographically indigenous right-hand man, search time can be cut in half—with the anchor man, not the interviewer, spending his time searching. He knows how to find people in casual settings and how to ease the minds of respondents, many of whom may have heard from neighbors that a "strange man" (the interviewer) came around wanting to ask some questions. Moreover, even when persons cannot be located or refuse to be interviewed, it is often possible with the help of indigenous staff to determine the reasons for these noninterviews. Such information can be important in estimating biases in obtained data when the overall response rate is low. Finally, there is an important psychological advantage to having local residents on the research team. They perform a two-way interpretive function for the entire research operation. Interviewers, in particular, find a certain comfort in knowing that someone known to the community is always available to be of assistance.

Finally, in connection with relations with the community, it can be profitable to expose an experimental plan to the critical examination of individuals or groups who are peers of the experimental subjects, in order to get insight into possible unintended (side) effects. These can then be dealt with by introducing additional treatments modified to reduce the unintended effects if they are undesirable or by adding additional measures if the predicted side effects seem not harmful or even implausible. For many experimental topics, the community of interest will throw up spontaneous adversary "advisory groups," who can sometimes be consulted with double profit if the experimenters can reduce opposition at the same time that they learn, through explaining the purpose and the design of the experiment. Where natural "advisory" groups do not exist, it may be useful to create artificial ones (through role-playing or games) simply in order to bring critical acumen to bear on the design.

## Preserving the Integrity
## of the Design

The opportunities to compromise an experimental design in the field are almost endless and so are the incentives to do so. Nearly every facet of the design—from the randomization of the treated and control subjects to the coding and storage of data—could be realized more easily, cheaply, and quickly by slighting scientific requirements. Some temptations are especially seductive. It is usually more convenient to simplify the established random procedure for choosing a replacement when a chosen unit cannot be used; interviewers may avoid hard-to-reach sites or not make enough call-backs on the hard-to-find-at-home. Preventing subjects from dropping out of the experiment once it is underway or at least being aware of all the factors involved: the differing causes, effects, and implications of attrition are not the only important tasks of the experiment manager, but they certainly merit close attention.

### SOME PROBLEMS RELATING TO ATTRITION

*Minimizing Attrition.* It is vital to reduce as much as possible the number of participants who drop out of the experiment after it has begun. The reason is simply that most designs require the comparison of experimental and control groups at different points in time. If the initial randomization has been carried out correctly, and all relevant factors have been kept constant, then it would seem to follow that changes over time resulting in differences between the experimentals and controls are due to the impact of treatment. However, people move around, and by the time posttreatment measures are taken, a good many respondents on whom pre- and during-treatment data were taken may no longer be locatable for the final crucial measures. Attrition is related to randomization because the problem is not simply having enough respondents to fill cells for comparison purposes at the termination of the treatment; it also involves the *comparability* between the experimental and control groups over time. It is possible at the termination of an experiment to have large enough $N$'s, but to have lost randomization. Changes from Time 1 to Time 2 under such circumstances may be due to changes in group composition rather than to treatment, for attrition itself is never random; it always has a systematic component. Those who drop out of the experiment and those who stay usually differ on various dimensions of relevance; hence attrition undermines randomization and the appropriateness of statistical models. Furthermore, attrition is often differential across treatments, usually with greater losses from control than from experimental groups.

For projects extending one or more years, attrition rates as high as 20% are common, and a rate as high as 50% has been noted in one inner city study of unemployed youth. In the New Jersey Income Maintenance experiment, the attrition rates over 3 years range from 25% in the control condition to 6.5% in the high-payment treatment, with 15.6% attrition for all eight experimental groups combined. These rates allow the possibility for treatment group differences to arise purely on the basis of differential loss of participants. Where larger units such as schools have been randomized, and where no whole unit has dropped out, differential loss of cases within units can still produce pseudo-effects. For example, the experimental treatment might be so attractive that it motivates families to retain their residences in the experimental school districts, thus reducing classroom turnover in the experimental schools but not in the controls. Differential vigilance on the part of the research team in following up experimentals versus controls can have a similar effect.

Maximum investment should be made to keep such losses at a minimum. Strategies for achieving this are dealt with in a later section, but we preface that discussion with a general remark. The discussion of attrition here and the earlier discussion of nonresponse and refusals to cooperate make it clear that so-called "true" experiments move, in practice, toward quasi-experiments, in which pretreatment differences are to some extent confounded with treatments. Such a perspective might tempt one to throw up ones hands, give up the effort to randomize, and settle for the less controlled comparisons from the beginning. Such a conclusion is completely contrary to our recommendation. The meticulous attention to randomization has created a situation in which one becomes acutely aware of a few of the systematic selective forces that determine who gets exposed to what treatment. These same biases exist in at least equivalent degree in more natural, less well-controlled exposures to treatments. Furthermore, in place of the still very substantial role that randomization has played in determining treatments in a true experiment, in quasi-experiments there is substituted a host of very systematic processes and recruitment biases. Thus even though randomization in practice is never completely achieved and leaves sources of bias to which we should be alert relative to more casual quasi-experimental approaches, it has greatly reduced the overall magnitude of bias. Furthermore, it better enables us to identify the kinds of bias present—a point discussed more fully in the following.

*Attrition as an Outcome Measure.*   It first must be noted that what might be called changes or differentials in attrition may in itself be a valuable outcome measure. In many ameliorative programs, a major cause of attrition is residential and career instability: changes of address through failure to pay rent, failure to hold a job, exhaustion of credit at local grocery stores, and so on. Experimental treatments aimed at increasing the financial stability of the family or the employability of the wage earners may reduce such sources of mobility. In a day-care experiment, the assistance provided should increase family stability, for example, through increased opportunity of a parent to accept employment. For accurate interpretation it becomes important to ascertain the reasons for attrition and to distinguish those cases of simple refusal to submit to further measurement from those cases that have changed addresses. (Perhaps the outcome measure under discussion should be labeled change of address per se rather than attrition.) One should also avoid the differential in attrition that comes from greater vigor in following up experimental cases or the better follow-up contact with them.

While attrition rate can thus, under certain circumstances, be a valid and interpretable outcome measure, its effect on other outcome measures still operates as a source of bias.

*Attrition as a Function of Treatment.*   Attrition can be a function of treatment. If several treatments are tried simultaneously more people are likely to drop out from the groups getting the treatment perceived as less effective than from groups getting the treatment perceived as more effective. Thus, not enough of those getting the less effective forms of treatment may be located to test for differences at the termination of such an experiment. Similarly, if a single treatment variable is used but applied in differing amounts, attrition rates may vary with the degree of treatment. If income supplement is the treatment variable, it can safely be presumed that those getting the greater amounts of supplementary revenue will cooperate with the experiment longer than those getting lesser amounts. It might be wise under such conditions to give the lesser amounts of the treatment to a disproportionately larger number of subjects than those getting greater amounts, in order to ensure adequate numbers of the former for comparison at the termination of the experiment. If these changes can be monitored, then corrective statistical procedures can be instituted, for example, comparing early drop-outs and late-stayers and weighting covariables accordingly.

The most severe attrition problems of the true experiment pertain to the controls. Because the (untreated) controls receive less attention than the experimentals, contact with them may be more easily lost. Ordinarily this problem is handled by enrolling many more controls than experimentals. Since controls do not receive treatment, they are an inexpensive source of data, and an experimenter might be well advised to include in control groups all eligibles who are not randomly selected for experimental treatment. Note, however, as we mentioned earlier that a *large* control group does not protect the experiment against differential attrition.

*Countering Attrition.* Attrition may occur for reasons other than subjects' moving without leaving a forwarding address. Especially in the control group, refusals to be interviewed or tested repeatedly can occur in the course of an experiment because subjects become bored, suspicious, or fail to see any benefit to themselves from the procedure. Often they have good reason, but there are countermeasures an experimenter can take besides careful explanation of his purposes and appeals to subjects not to undermine the experiment by attrition. Kershaw (1971, p. 283 *et seq.*) offers some thoughtful suggestions for dealing with this problem and we recapitulate them here because they are sound and generally applicable. He suggests employing interviewers who are sensitive to respondents' attitudes and who can relate easily and comfortably to respondents. Enlisting the cooperation of community leaders who will endorse participation in the experiment and arming the interviewer with a list of such persons, of whom the prospective respondent can inquire, will help reduce attrition especially at the initial stages of the project (when refusals to participate produce bias in the sample). The problem sometimes lies directly at the experimenter's door, as when he uses an overly long interview or includes questions that are confusing, intrusive, or embarrassing. Finally, Kershaw concludes, "By far the most successful technique has been small, regular payments in cash . . . [p. 285]" not so large as to arouse suspicion and made at the end of the interview, not deferred till the end of the month or quarter.

The promise of cash payments to respondents for notifying the experiment when they change addresses has been tried but not always found useful in reducing the number of "lost" subjects. People forget such promises; but there will usually be some mobile and hard-to-trace participants who, if located, are willing to continue providing information. Some practical suggestions for tracing such persons are:

—The Post Office will provide address changes over a 5–year

period for a small fee.

—Inquiries can be made through utility companies (meter registrations), police, churches, schools, employers, the Division of Employment Security, and the Department of Public Assistance or equivalent agencies.

—Inquiries can be made of neighbors or of neighbors' children, asking them where their friends have gone.

—Asking others of the same name often turns up relatives who are willing to give the new address of the "missing" family.

—The records of local moving companies can be helpful.

—Inquiries of landlords and at stores and bars in the neighborhood is often effective.

—Finally, a well-informed member of the local community who knows what is going on can be helpful in tracing as he can be in other ways (see pp. 184–185) to the experiment.

Even though all of these steps are taken, there will inevitably be some persons lost to the experiment, and almost certainly the lost cases differ on the average from those remaining in the sample on a variety of attributes. If the rate of attrition is approximately equal in all groups, an experimenter can usually be confident that no comparative bias exists, and that the forces leading to attrition are of the same nature and of the same degree in all groups. In most cases this is probably so, but considerations of the specifics of the setting and of the experiment may indicate otherwise. For example, in the pretreatment losses in the New Jersey Income Maintenance experiment as discussed earlier, the control group losses were probably mainly due to low economic motivation to cooperate, while the experimental losses were in some part due to unwillingness to accept charity. While the rates actually ended up different, thus warning of a potential bias, the rates could have ended up the same and still have been due to these different causes, producing differential biases that could appear as differences due to treatment.

*Sources of Differential Attrition.*    As we cautioned earlier, it is essential to look for and to estimate the amount of bias attributable to differential attrition and to examine the dynamics of the attrition process so as to understand the probable *direction* of biasing upon experimental outcomes. The manager of the experiment should be attentive not only to techniques for minimizing attrition, but also to the forces that will inevitably produce it. He should be in a position to suggest hypotheses about the forces producing attrition and their effects.

Here are some illustrative hypotheses about attrition processes. In most inner city schools, it is probably the case that those who change addresses and schools most are from the homes least supportive of school achievement, inasmuch as unpaid rent and instability of family constellations are a major source of mobility. In such a setting if the experimental treatment reduces mobility, it might turn out that the subset of experimentals still in the same school at posttest would be less interested in formal academic achievement than the subset of the controls still in the same school. However, the subset of families that would defer moving for the sake of a program their children are receiving are almost certainly above average in support of their children's academic achievement, and this counters the other differential. Certainly, some of the movement out of the inner city school districts is a sign of upward mobility. If one has a program such as Ikeda, Yinger, and Laycock's (1970), focussed on the most able seventh graders in an inner city school, and finds much greater attrition in the control group, it becomes plausible to hypothesize that the control group is losing its most adequate families whose experimental group counterparts are staying in their old neighborhood just to keep their children in this special program. This biases the results in favor of making the treatment look more effective than it actually is. In Job Corps type programs which pay a salary to the trainees, much of the attrition is due to the more able trainees finding still better jobs. Such events in the control group are not regarded as attrition, and, if the dropouts are removed from the experimental group for analysis purposes, such attrition leads to underestimates of treatment effects. (Keeping the trainees from job hunting during the training period would produce a different bias as well as short-run deleterious effects.)

Some of the sources of differential attrition are less real and more nearly methodological artifacts, but, here again, theories about process are relevant. Three such can be mentioned: The experimental respondents are more motivated to cooperate with the follow-up measurement process because of gratitude for the treatment; the controls may fail to cooperate out of resentment or disinterest. Second, the addresses for use in initiating follow-up may be a year of more more up-to-date for those in the experimental group than for those in the control group because the treatment has also involved keeping in contact. Third, the experimenters may be much more interested in the subsequent fate of the experimentals than of the controls and may exercise much greater ingenuity and effort in following up experimentals than controls. The friendship patterns created by the experimental treatment may contribute to this differential traceableness.

It should be remembered that, for purposes of experimental inference, comparability is more important than completeness. It is more important to have similar attrition patterns in both experimental and control groups than to eliminate some of the experimental attrition at the expense of creating biasing attrition differentials. Thus, where the processes just described are probable, it is recommended that an independent agency to which the experimentals feel as little obligation as do the controls, rather than the treatment agency, collect the follow-up information (this may also reduce biases in response content).

## Data Collection

Accuracy and completeness of the primary data—the actual responses collected by interviewers, testers, or observers—are essential for a valid experiment. No amount of statistical manipulation or high-powered analysis can substitute for missing data or correct inaccuracy at the primary level. For this reason, the management must establish and maintain standards of quality through training (and perhaps periodic retraining) of interviewers; through careful supervision of interviewer performance, including revisits and validation checks, and through managerial procedures that keep track of data collection schedules and ensure that they are met.

For example, interviewers should know that 1 out of 10 interviews will routinely be checked for reliability—that someone from the research staff will pick a fixed number of interviews randomly from each interviewer's pile, go to that respondent and actually reinterview him and then compare the two interviews for interinterviewer reliability. Cheating is not at all uncommon on the part of interviewers who may duplicate (copy) earlier interviews or fabricate "interviews" out of whole cloth, either because they want to earn more money for less work or because they become bored and believe they know the respondent's answers (often true when they have seen the same respondent repeatedly in the course of an experiment). New interviewers more often cheat by making up entire interviews; more experienced ones by skipping questions. The complete interviews of individual interviewers should be kept separately and compared for unusual (idiosyncratic) response sets. Such response sets are particularly easy to detect on items such as the F scale where expected interrelationship among items cannot easily be faked. Reinterviewing for reliability and examination for individual response set is about the best combination of activities for checking on interviewers' honesty.

Interviewer honesty, as well as accuracy and sensitivity, can be greatly enhanced by adequate training. Major survey organizations have developed a substantial body of training materials and routines that teach both aspects of the interviewer's job: how to ask questions properly and how to develop rapport and understanding with respondents. Interviewing is not simply conversation. A well-trained interviewer knows how to introduce herself, secure the attention and cooperation of the respondent, explain clearly the purpose of the interview, set the respondent's uneasiness and curiosity to rest by answering questions, and get answers to a standard set of questions objectively, systematically, and reliably. That is, a well-trained interviewer does not allow her own beliefs, feelings, or knowledge to influence (even subtly) the content of the respondent's answers, while at the same time making sure the answers are clear and as complete as necessary. She works her way systematically through the questionnaire or schedule of items on which information is needed, proceding from item to item in an order that is predetermined and is the same for each respondent. She acts, insofar as possible, as a standardized measurement device in the sense that any well-trained interviewer would, ideally, obtain identical answers to the same questions from the same respondent.

Because personal interviewing is probably the most widely used as well as the most difficult variety of data collection in social experimentation, it serves well to exemplify the salient characteristics required of field staff: the capacity to gain entree and develop rapport with those from whom data is to be collected and the discipline to apply repeatedly and consistently an interrogatory procedure that has been carefully designed to elicit information in a standardized way. These same characteristics are equally important for all forms of data collection—administration of psychological or other tests, direct observation, and the use of indirect or unobtrusive measures.

All of these methods of collecting data involve learnable (and teachable) skills, and time and effort invested in a training (and supervision) program will be well repaid in the quality of data obtained. Initial training should include a full exploration of the overall purpose of the experiment as well as that of the particular test or interview the trainee will use. Supervised practice with the instrument, perhaps including role-playing exercises with the supervisor, is useful. Retraining and periodic checks on performance help to emphasize the importance of the primary collection job and, if carried out in the right way, can enhance interviewer morale as well as maintaining high standards of performance.

To be sure, some personal characteristics like intelligence, poise, and warmth facilitate the purposes of training, but no firm rules can be laid down for choosing field staff. It is often wise to recruit and train field staff locally so as to maximize similarity and rapport with the participants in the experiment, especially where there are distinct cultural, linguistic, or socioeconomic groups involved. There is a substantial amount of information available in the social science research literature about "interviewer effects," and managers of experiments should either be aware of it or consult experts who are. For example, a number of studies have shown that the race and social class of interviewers can affect the kinds of answers as well as the amount of information elicited from respondents of various races and social classes. In general, a conservative rule is to try to match interviewer and respondent characteristics in these respects. There is also reason to believe that an interviewer's *own* attitudes on a topic can subtly bias the respondent's replies—usually, but not always, toward consonance with the interviewer's opinion. This tendency can be mitigated by training, but it may be prudent to assess the interviewer's own attitudes before she goes out to interview. Such information may help, at least, to account for later observed biases in replies. Further information on interviewer effects can be found in texts on survey research and interviewing (Kahn and Cannell, 1957; Sudman, 1966, 1967).

Parallel problems may arise, in certain kinds of treatments, with members of the action team. In at least one therapeutic experiment we reviewed, questionnaires were administered to caseworkers in order to assess *their* attitudes toward alcoholism; and standardized questionnaires on the therapists' attitudes toward the treatment program were also used. This kind of information may reveal variations in the way the program was delivered as a consequence of staff members' attitudes.

Since personal interviewing is very costly (1973 prices averaged about $50 for a 1-hour interview where only local travel was involved) there have been numerous attempts to find satisfactory substitutes for it. Some studies (National Opinion Research Center, 1966) show that very high rates of cooperation are possible for self-administered questionnaires and telephone interviews *after initial rapport* has been established, usually by means of a personal interview. The rate of completion is close to that for personal interviewers, about 80%. Thus, it may be advantageous to adopt such a procedure for longitudinal data, especially in large experiments where participants are spread over a wide geographic area—there is about a 90% saving in the cost of obtaining the data when compared to the cost of face-to-face interviews by trained interviewers.

Furthermore, it should be mentioned that some kinds of respondents can be interviewed better by telephone and that there are certain kinds of data that are better obtained in this way. For example, the

National Opinion Research Center (Sudman, 1966) found that a (long-distance) phone call was the best and least costly means for interviewing physicians. Other researchers have successfully employed a combination of a questionnaire mailed out in advance followed after a suitable interval by a long-distance telephone call at an appointed time. This method gives the respondent opportunity to collect information and think about his answers and also avoids travel by interviewers. When participants are comfortable in dealing with written material and questions can be easily answered by checking boxes or giving simple facts, self-administered questionnaires can be sent through the mail, with follow-up phone calls or letters if they have not been returned within 2 weeks. A number of survey researchers have found that less personal contact methods result in more candid responses and less "social desirability" bias entering into the response. Hochstim (1967) found that mail surveys, rather than personal interviews, resulted in more valid data on items related to the respondents personal health. Topics that may have to be treated cautiously in a personal interview can often be dealt with more forthrightly through either of these interview methods. Finally, we should mention that when a personal contact is employed initially to establish rapport and when these alternative procedures follow the initial person-to-person interview closely in time, the return is greater.

If the questionnaire can be self-administered, costs can be reduced dramatically through the use of optical scanning scoring techniques. One page of an interview can be printed, scored, and tabulated for a few cents a page by computerized procedures. Moreover, such services are fast, often requiring only a 48-hour turn-around time. Thus, a 10-page interview can be scored, tabulated, and the data cross-tabulated within 2 days at about one-tenth to one-twentieth the cost of traditional methods—involving coding, check coding, card punching—and much more quickly. Experience with self-administered questionnaires prepared for computer-scoring has been almost completely confined to well-educated respondents accustomed to paper-and-pencil reports. High rates of return have been obtained, especially when telephone or mail reminders are used to follow up initial distribution.

DATA PROCESSING AND STORAGE

The organization and management of data from an experiment—especially one involving large numbers of respondents and multiple interviews or other records—demands a high level of technical skill as well as extensive planning and collaboration among computer experts, designers, and analysts. Huge amounts of data may be collected: the New Jersey Negative Income Tax experiment accumulated nearly 30 reels of magnetic tape representing the condensed contents of about 50 file cabinets of data. Such a storehouse is useful only if the data are accurate, the location and character of individual items is documented, and the data can be retrieved for analysis at reasonable cost. These requirements direct attention to the need for data editing and checking; the maintenance of a correct and up-to-date inventory of what is stored and where; current and useful identification of data so that sequential records can be matched for comparison and aggregation; and the design of a storage system that can both anticipate what items are most likely to be needed for analysis and be flexible (and economical) enough to allow unanticipated combinations of variables to be retrieved.

Errors and omissions are a persistent problem. The interviews, tests, observation schedules, or notes made by field staff need some working over before they are ready to be stored or used in statistical analysis. The raw data are ordinarily coded into machine-usable form but must be edited for completeness and accuracy before coding. The longer an interview or test, the greater the likelihood that some response item will be missed, either in the administration, the immediate recoding, or the later transcription from hand written record to card or tape. The same is true when many different sources of data must be assembled simultaneously or sequentially for the same individual (person, household, etc.). In the latter case, correct identification is essential so that individual records are not wrongly linked. Error-checking routines must extend to the identification of obviously wrong or suspect entries. For example, if a test score or a reply to an interviewer's question is quite out of line with expectations or with information collected earlier on the same respondent, one may suspect an interviewer error in recording or a clerical mistake in transcription. Sometimes items from a long questionnaire may be misplaced in the punch card or inadmissable entries may be punched; sometimes, in a longitudinal study with repeated measures over time, the data from two different respondents may be confused. Eliminating such errors requires careful editing of raw data instruments and checking of coded material by trained and responsible technicians.

After editing, data must be stored in an economical and accessible way. Most responses will be coded into categories that are more compactly represented on the tape than the original pure response could be. What information should be allowed to be lost through coding depends largely on plans for analysis, which should be thought through as far in advance as possible. The format of storage must also be carefully planned. Data storage on magnetic tapes must be retrieved in the order in which the data were stored on the tape. Because input and output devices operate comparatively slowly, if a whole reel of tape must be processed or if several reels must be run in order to retrieve two or three variables for an analysis, the computer is being used inefficiently (and very expensively). Variables most likely to be compared in analysis should be physically adjacent. Of course, it will turn out that many analyses will not have been anticipated, so that a system of storage that is flexible enough to permit economical reordering or retrieval of data is a desideratum. Finally, any storage system must be well documented or catalogued, so that future analysts, especially those who did not take part in designing the system, will know exactly what data are stored in the file and where. A tape unaccompanied by adequate documentation presents an exercise in cryptography.

This list of problems can be expanded to include the ever-changing hardware of computers and accessory devices, the rapidly expanding software technology, the preference of programmers for a particular machine language, and the unnerving discovery that magnetic tapes can be subject to physical decay in storage—thus losing all the information completely! The character of the various difficulties can be appreciated by people who have not tried to work with computer-based data systems, but the solution of these problems must rest on a management that is technically well-staffed, aware of the rigorous supervision required over data collection and storage, and capable of attaining collaborative forward planning from designers, technicians, and analysts.

MIDSTREAM MODIFICATIONS

Despite the emphasis of this section on maintaining the integrity of the experimental design, it must be recognized that circumstances unforeseen and uncontrollable may force modifications after the experimental treatment has begun. Despite the reluctance of experimenters to permit such changes, midstream modifications are admissible as long as they do not corrupt the design. When unforeseen events themselves threaten the integrity of the design, it is the responsibility of the experiment manager to take compensatory steps to minimize loss of inferential clarity and generalizability. For example, an experiment using street workers to reduce delinquent behavior was designed so that the experimental areas to which the workers were assigned were contiguous to matched control (no worker) areas for maximum homogeneity of neighborhood conditions. Experience began to show that some workers, who were convinced of the value of the treatment and dedicated to demonstrating its effectiveness, were quietly making arrangements with gang members to have "turf" arguments settled (and arrests made) in the contiguous control areas so that the experimental areas would show lower arrest records than controls. The experimenters adapted to this behavior by two changes in design. Instead of focusing on an area as a unit, they shifted to a "panel design" which examined changes in the delinquency behavior of a sample of individuals in the experimental area; and they relocated control areas to be geographically noncontiguous—in fact, distant and unknown (by location) to the street workers. In this example not only was the threat to integrity of design eliminated but, in fact, the power of the comparison was probably increased. A somewhat parallel example is drawn from an experiment to improve relations between black and white workers in industrial plants, through the use of change agents. Again, the original design provided for rather precise distinctions between experimental and control groups within each of several plants—for the purpose of maximizing homogeneity of social, economic, and regional context. When the change agents ignored the boundaries of their assignments and tried to change relationships all over the plant, the design was threatened. But, because several plants were involved, the change agents could be withdrawn from half of them and concentrated in the other half. The experiment became a comparison of treatment versus control factories, rather than several within-plant comparisons.

These examples make the point that an experimenter is constantly forced with balancing practical against scientific requirements and that an over-rigid adherence to early procedures and goals may lose the whole experiment. There are often practical, economic, political, or moral considerations that are unforeseen at the point of design, and a prudent experimenter will expect surprises.

It may be wise to formalize, in the design, the need to reorganize and respond to unexpected events. It has been argued (Kish, 1967) that survey designs ought to include a "surprise stratum," which is not interviewed unless some unexpected or significant event occurs that might affect the subjects being studied. In like fashion, one might construct "surprise groups" of eligible units that would receive no treatment or no attention beyond some initial base-line measurement unless some unexpected event or finding suggested the desirability of a shift in design. (In the delinquency prevention experiment exemplified earlier, the surprise groups were the noncontiguous control areas). The idea could well be applied to deliberate changes in treatment. If four treatments are being tested for relative effectiveness and early data indicate that some combination of these treatments might really be far more effective than any independent treatment, then a surprise group could be pressed into service to test the combination treatment or to test a new and relevant treatment that had not been discovered or available at the outset of the experiment.

Finally, maintaining the integrity of the design depends on the competence of the experiment manager. His day-to-day decisions on details, his assiduous attention to consistency of performance and adherence to specifications, together with a capacity to set and maintain high standards will make the difference between a good and a poor experiment.

The magnitude of the management job should not be underestimated, nor the talent and skill required to do it satisfactorily. A particular talent for the management of research is necessary; ordinary training in social research is not a guarantee of managerial capability. Yet the research manager must be able to understand the research design, the rationale of the sampling, and the overall purpose of the experiment, so that he can be alert to problems as they arise and correctly balance research needs against practical contingencies that arise in the field. It is perhaps more difficult to find such managerial talent than it is to obtain individuals with design and analysis skills (but every bit as important to have it), for graduate education in social science disciplines does not ordinarily train students in the needed skills. Furthermore, academic social scientists do not accord high status to those who have or want to acquire them. Experience in previous projects is good preparation, and an evinced interest in the management role is a good sign.

## Dissemination and Preparation for Utilization

A social experiment is unlike an academic scientific program that ordinarily culminates in a formal contribution to the research literature—a book or a journal article. The research management of a social experiment should be organized and prepared to deliver a series of reports on its conduct and progress, addressing, as the previous section implies, a variety of purposes and a multiplicity of target audiences.

Furthermore, these should not all be held off until the experiment has been completed. Interim reports are useful for at least three reasons: They mature thinking about program operations; they hasten and facilitate the final report; and they lay the basis for future feedback and for mid-stream modifications of treatment and design. Furthermore, they have several levels of audience, in particular, the sponsors, the action team, and the participant.

DISSEMINATION TO THE SPONSORS

It is best if the sponsor becomes aware of the program's effects through small doses of information over time rather than all at once at the end. Such information should be comprehensive and should focus on various aspects of the project so that some appreciation can develop of what might be successful as well as what might not be successful: A single, comprehensive measure or summative evaluation statement is not very instructive.

By providing information in this way, the sponsor has time to absorb the information and to consider what should be discussed informally with the action team. Valuable insights can be gained which will be helpful in accounting for the results. Also, the likelihood of public dispute over results is reduced by this procedure. As indicated earlier, it would not be unreasonable to incorporate the views of action staff members on the evaluation as part of the formal report.

Some comments should be made with respect to interim reports. An important thing about such reports is that they not be presented in a way that might seem threatening. The information must be put in usable form, interpreted so as to point out its implications for practice wth the evaluative connotation minimized. If it is presented as a "mid-semester grade," then there will be morale problems. Interim information should be focused to promote utilization of the knowledge gained for midstream changes as well as for its postexperiment implications. Interim reporting can help the sponsor develop an appreciation of the means–ends relation between instrumental and final objectives, that is, he can begin to evaluate the results in terms of the validity of the underlying action assumptions and the feasibility of implementing instrumental action practices under various conditions across different sites. Lastly, he is spared the sudden shock of negative feedback if the program, contrary to his expectations, proves ineffective.

Since many well-conducted experiments will expose the fact that the treatment failed undeniably, to produce the expected effects, the manager of an experiment should be prepared to deal constructively with this disappointment. It is important that an experimental outcome lead not to despair and the abandonment of effort, but instead to understanding why the treatment was ineffective and what might be done to improve effectiveness—in short, to replanning an effort to achieve basic objectives. This whole process will be facilitated if the manager emphasizes the positive findings of the experiment and creatively uses the results to suggest new strategies to the sponsor. The manager's objective in this phase should be to maximize constructive efforts at rethinking the problem and minimizing despair, while not distorting or denying the facts.

## DISSEMINATION TO THE ACTION TEAM

Earlier remarks on interim reports and on-the-spot feedback apply here as well. It should also be mentioned that it is unfortunate, but too often the case that the action team is the last to be informed of the program's final outcome; yet it is they who are, at the same time, most affected. Prior to any formal presentation of data, either to the sponsor or to the public, the results and their implications should be shared with the action team in order to iron out misunderstandings and resolve differences.

## DISSEMINATION TO THE RESPONDENTS–PARTICIPANTS

Those who have participated in the experiment should be provided with evaluative information, even if there exists the strong likelihood that they will use it for political purposes. This does not mean that every participant should receive a massive volume, full of tables and elaborate statistical analysis. What should be done is to report the highlights of the results in summary form to each respondent. It should, at the same time, be made clear to them that a more detailed analysis is available and how it may be obtained.

# VII

## Institutional and Political
## Factors In Social Experimentation

The mounting of an experiment is a political act. It indicates that the sponsor considers the issues it will address to be worthy of policy consideration. Its implementation in the field frequently affects local political alliances. Its results may favor one interest group over another or brand a particular program a success or a failure. Since experimentation is not a neutral, purely scientific activity, experiments should be undertaken only after considering their political impact and making a conscious determination that, on balance, the experiment seems feasible and likely to produce usable information that can be brought to bear upon social policy decisions.

The focus of this chapter is on the social institutional context of experimentation rather than on the internal organization and management of the experimental process. The chapter explores such questions as how to frame the experimental problem, where to place the institutional responsibility for social experimentation, and how to distribute or divide the various tasks of experimentation. Attention is directed to identifying and characterizing the principal agencies or institutions responsible for conceiving, initiating, conducting, and using the results of social experimentation, as well as the relationships among such agencies. The first section sets out a taxonomy of organizational roles in social experimentation, illustrates, and explains them. This provides the groundwork for a discussion of desirable institutional and organizational characteristics in a subsequent section. The next portion of the chapter is concerned with political aspects: site selection, the timing of data analysis and release of findings, the management of renanalysis and data storage. The chapter ends with some observations on the utilization of experimental results.

## *Organizational Roles in Social Experimentation*

The nature of an experiment depends largely on the nature of the organizations involved in it. Social science research institutes will propose different sorts of experiments from policy research offices. Agencies with particular substantive missions will define problems differently from those with other kinds of missions or from policy development groups outside mission agencies. Furthermore, the features of design that will be stressed may differ, depending on whether the research is conducted by a university-based group or by a private research firm, and the analytic emphasis may vary. Operating agencies will use experimental results in different ways from policy planning offices or research institutes. It is important, therefore, to examine the organizational roles in social experimentation, their interrelationships, and some of the consequences of different combinations of roles, and power in those roles, for the management of the experiment.

It is possible to distinguish at least six major roles in social experimentation, although the same organization may carry out more than one responsibility. The first role is that of the *initiator*, who determines research and/or policy needs and decides that an experiment will provide the necessary information. The second is the *sponsor*, the organization(s) that provides funds for the experiment and presumably guides it through its design, operational, and analytical phases. While the initiator and sponsor frequently are the same, they need not be, as would be the case of a local community (the initiator) seeking foundation or Federal agency support (the sponsor) for an experiment. In either case, the initiator–sponsor usually will turn to a third party, the *designer–researcher* for assistance in laying out the design measures and core analysis plans and in undertaking the bulk of the actual analysis. Next is the *treatment administrator*, or action team, which is responsible for carrying out the program or policy being tested. Essential to many experiments is a fifth actor, the *program developer*, the organization responsible for developing the treatments in sufficient detail for implementation in the field. In the most straightforward situation, the designer–researcher is responsible for the overall experimental design, including analysis; the program developer does what is necessary to realize the experimental strategy in the field, and the treatment administrator carries out the treatment operations.

The precise roles of these last three actors and the relationships among them will vary substantially according to the genesis of the experiment. If the treatment has been developed and the experiment is designed specifically to test it, the developer may play a substantial role in both the design and implementation stages; if the policy is conceptualized first and one or more treatments are subsequently devised to carry out that policy, the developer will play a quite different and more derivative role. Finally, there is the *audience–user*, a target that should be kept clearly in mind when the experiment is conceptualized, but which may change over the course of the experiment.

Potential audience–users range from the government bureau, which may utilize the information for planning, to the general public, which may be persuaded that certain consequences may follow from adoption of the policies or programs tested in the experiment. The audience may be local officials, who utilize the outcomes to choose among competing policies; research personnel, who add information from the experiment to their understanding of their field of specialization; or the Congress and the staffs of the White House and the Office of Management and Budget. Finally, the audience may be the experimenters themselves, who have added to their knowledge of research and evaluation methodology or who have learned to ask different sorts of questions about policy issues.

## EXAMPLES OF ORGANIZATIONAL ROLES IN SOCIAL EXPERIMENTATION

Social experiments have proceeded under a wide variety of oganizational arrangements. For example, the idea for the New Jersey Income Maintenance experiment first appeared in a local Community Action Agency's crude, preliminary proposal, which was slightly expanded by the Office of Research, Plans, Programs and Evaluation (RPP&E) in the Office of Economic Opportunity (OEO), which initiated the experiment. The research design was then elaborated by Mathematica, a Princeton-based research firm, and the Institute for Research on Poverty at the University of Wisconsin. As the program developed, it was expected that the University of Wisconsin and Mathematica would provide expertise in the design and analysis. Mathematica would mount the program of transfer payments while the sample screening and the survey research were to be carried on by a survey research firm. During a pilot operation in Trenton, it became clear that the survey firm did not have the necessary capabilities; consequently, Mathematica developed its own survey staff. The data editing and processing was done largely by Mathematica, while analyses were performed by both the Poverty Institute and Mathematica. Finally Mathematica had to develop an administrative structure through which negative tax recipients could be paid and accounts kept.

Thus, in this instance, the *sponsor* and *initiator* were OEO's Office of RPP&E. The *treatment administrator* and *program developer* was Mathematica. The *design* and *research* roles were jointly performed by Mathematica and the Poverty Institute, with continuous monitoring by OEO. The *users* of the results to date have been the Congress, several executive branch agencies and various university researchers.

A somewhat similar alignment of roles is found in an experiment to study the effects of protein–calorie nutrition on the mental development of children, which was begun in Guatemala in 1965. This project was *initiated* by a multidisciplinary group of pediatricians, psychologists, and other specialists who met in 1964 to review the conflicting data then available on the subject. The conference recommended to the National Institute of Child Health and Human Development (NICHD) that a prospective longitudinal study with controls was needed to answer basic questions. A group of pediatricians and biomedical scientists at the Instituto de Nutricion de Centro America y Panama (INCAP), with earlier experience in nutrition studies carried out in rural Guatemalan villages, was known to be interested in the problem and ready to make a research proposal. When the NICHD agreed to assume *sponsorship* its professional staff and an ad hoc group of scientific advisers envisioned an experimental design based on nutritional intervention in early childhood. They helped the INCAP staff, who had become *designer–researcher* under contract for a pilot study, to lay out the design and formulate the treatment plan in two experimental and two control villages. Almost 4 years were required to develop and validate measurements of physical and mental growth and to train staff. The *designer–researcher* hired, trained, and supervised the *treatment administrator*—the action team that made dietary supplement and medical care available to participants and also the measurement teams that performed the repeated mental testing of children in the villages. The *audience–user* role in this experiment is not well defined. The policy implications are obviously important to governmental bureaus (of any nation) concerned with the health, nutrition, and education of mothers and children, although the experiment itself stands at the preformulation stage of public policy. Furthermore, an important audience is the biomedical, educational, and psychological communities who are concerned with the scientific rather than the policy implications of the results.

In this example, then, there are only two organizations directly concerned: the *sponsor* and the *designer–researcher*, who was also the initiator and who managed *treatment administration* with the active collaboration of the sponsor.

Illustrative of a rather different constellation of organizational roles is the clutch of experiments for assessing the effectiveness of performance contracting methods for the teaching of reading and mathematics in elementary schools. The experiments were *initiated* and *sponsored* by the OEO, whose staff (Planning, Research and Evaluation) responded to reports that a performance contracting approach had been successful in some schools of the Southwest in improving classroom achievement of poor children. In such an approach, a contractor signs an agreement to improve students' performance in specified basic skills by a set amount and is paid according to his success in bringing students up to the prespecified levels. He is free to use whatever instructional techniques, equipment, or incentive systems he believes will work.

The OEO Experimental Research Division was largely responsible for the *design* of the experiment, although its research implementation in the field at 18 sites (school districts) was the responsibility of a management support contractor. This contractor followed OEO guidelines in choosing the sites and the commercial technology firms contracting to deliver the instructional treatments. Administration of tests of pupil performance, collection of the data, and data analysis were carried out independently by an external research contractor. The in-house staff of OEO carried out data analysis in parallel with this contractor. The *treatment administrators* were six firms, each of which had independently (and prior to the experiment) *developed* their own instructional *programs*, which represented a range of instructional approaches (i.e., differential emphasis on hardware, incentives, curriculum, or teacher training). The potential *audience–users* are school administrators and boards, educators, and performance contractors themselves.

In this example, the *initiator–sponsor* was OEO which also shared a considerable portion of the *designer–researcher* roles with two mutually independent organizations. The *program developers* were also *treatment administrators* and were unaffiliated with any of the organizations occupying the other roles.

# Functions, Characteristics, and
# Potential Actors for Organizational Roles

Experience suggests that there are some organizational characteristics that will be required in virtually any social experiment. This
section examines, in the light of available experience, some aspects of
the roles of the initiator and sponsor, designer–researcher, treatment
administrator, and program developer. Since the roles of initiator and
sponsor generally are performed by the same organization, they will
be considered together, as will the roles of treatment administrator
and program developer.

## INITIATOR–SPONSOR

*Functions.*    A social experiment begins with the information needs
of a policy planner and/or a researcher working on a social problem. The
proposal of a specific experiment is ordinarily preceded by a multi-
stage process of reviewing existing knowledge and assaying the significance of the problem. The initiator–sponsor should:

1. Identify the social problem(s) that is causing concern or moti-
   vating proposals for intervention. Are these problems sufficiently widespread and sufficiently debilitating to the society
   to merit the relatively high cost (in terms of both dollars and
   staff resources) generally required for experimentation? Is the
   problem now of interest to policymakers? More important, is it
   still likely to be of interest when the results become available?
2. Determine what is known about the proposed intervention.
   Exhaustive literature searches and "state of the art" studies
   may not be required before an experiment is undertaken, but
   the initiator–sponsor should have a comprehensive understanding of the intervention that will be tested, the circumstances (if any) under which it has already been tried, the
   effects it is likely to have on its subjects (including side or
   negative effects), and the policy implications of its success or
   failure.
3. Determine whether or not experimentation can increase understanding of the proposed intervention. An experiment is not
   always the only way to obtain estimates of program effects.
   Evaluation of existing programs can sometimes indicate the
   probable effects of a new program; theoretical models can be

constructed to estimate potential impact; survey research can offer insights. Will an experiment be the most cost-effective means of examining the proposed intervention? Does it offer the most viable means of influencing policy?

4. Determine the political feasibility of the experiment. Does it appear that interest groups will allow the experiment to be mounted? Is the experiment likely to jeopardize other programs through loss of political support by Congress or the funding decision-makers? If the experiment succeeds in demonstrating desirable program effects, is it likely that the program can be "sold" and mounted?

*Problem Identification.* The planning that preceded the mounting of the New Jersey Income Maintenance experiment illustrates the process of reviewing information needs and resources. Certainly the amount and distribution of povery in the United States in the 1960s meets the test of social importance and concern. Furthermore, there was a societal mandate. A provision of the Economic Opportunity Act required development of a 5-year plan to eliminate poverty. The objective was clear enough to policymakers although the means for its achievement were not. Most efforts to eliminate povery had focused on the development of human resources and on institutional change— manpower training, education activities, child care, community action. Responsible policy planners surveyed this range of programs and came to the conclusion that even if the programs were massively expanded, they could not be expected to eliminate poverty in the foreseeable future. Instead, they reached the tentative conclusion that a large-scale income transfer program was needed. Among the large number of questions that would undoubtedly be raised about such a program, however, the most critical was judged to be the potential impact of income transfers on work effort and labor supply.

Traditional forms of economic research could suggest some implications of a transfer system; indeed, researchers subsequently did derive several conflicting estimates using theoretical and existing data bases. But these analyses were based on a set of not totally persuasive assumptions concerning the work response of low-income individuals to nonwork income, and they utilized data collected for other purposes that had many deficiencies when confronted with the question at hand. No data were available on work responses associated with unconditional income transfers per se. Indeed, it become clear that the only way to get direct observations on this would be through trying out an income transfer program under controlled conditions.

Further, it was felt that a purely observational, theoretical, or simulation-based study would be much less persuasive than an experiment with "real" people and a "real" program. Therefore, the staff made the partially political choice of an experiment over traditional forms of research.

*Problem Definition.*    The way a problem is defined shapes what is done to solve it. That is, the definition of the problem suggests the targets and the methods of intervention, the change strategy, and the choice of a social action delivery system.

Problem definition is based upon assumptions about the causes of the problem and where they lie. Most explanations of social problems are either person-centered or situation-centered. For example, an explanation of unemployment may place the cause *within* the unemployed person: that he is untrained, poorly motivated, unskilled, unwilling to move to better opportunities, and so forth. Other explanations of unemployment place the cause in the *situation* in which the individual is caught up: union rules, racial discrimination, minimum wage rates, technological changes in the production process, a local taxation policy that discourages industrial expansion, a stagnant economy. Depending on which explanation is considered correct, the appropriate social intervention will, correspondingly, be individual-centered (e.g., training, counseling, etc.) or situation-centered (trying to open union membership, adjusting tax rates, changing welfare patterns, or offering public employment). Sometimes, indeed, the way in which a problem is defined not only determines what *is* done but restricts the possibility of doing anything else. A particular person-centered or situation-centered definition may preempt the scene and limit thinking so that alternative explanations are never considered or so that the possibility of joint causation from individual and situational sources is not entertained (Caplan and Nelson, 1973).

Because the definition of the problem shapes social experimentation in a very fundamental way, policymakers must be alert not simply to the limitations that a particular definition imposes, but of how they go about deciding upon a definition. A major consideration in this process is the source of professional or technical advice the policymaker obtains about a problem. Every profession and occupation tends to see the world from a special perspective. Psychologists, for example, are likely to prefer person-centered explanations of social problems whereas economists look for the reasons in the market, the tax structure, or some other feature of the situation. The probability of locating causation outside the area of one's own professional expertise is not great. Or, as Abraham Kaplan has expressed the point in the "Law of the Instrument," "It comes as no particular surprise to discover that a scientist formulates problems in a way which requires for their solution just those techniques in which he himself is especially skilled [1964, p. 31]."

This should not be taken as just a cynical remark. It would be idiotic to formulate a problem in a way that required for its solution a set of techniques or a body of knowledge that no one possessed. And it would be presumptuous, and probably misleading, to formulate a problem in terms that lay outside one's area of competence. The moral for policymakers, therefore, is simply to be aware of the professional biases of the oracles they consult and, ordinarily, since social problems are complex, to consult more than one bias. We shall take up a related point later in regard to interdisciplinary collaboration on the experimental research team. But the major thrust of the argument is that the choice of treatment to be used in the experiment will be influenced by the professional (as well as by the political, administrative, ideological, and, perhaps, personal) biases of those who make the decisions.

Having identified the problem, proposed a means of intervention, and satisfied himself that an experiment is the most efficient method to test that intervention, the initiator–sponsor must:

1. Specify the broad parameters of the experiment design
2. Lay out the tasks the researcher–designer is expected to perform
3. Determine, when necessary, that appropriate program development procedures be undertaken
4. Seek proposals for design and research or statements of organizational capabilities, and choose among the competitors
5. Develop a budget and funding guidelines
6. Monitor the activities of the designer–researcher, program developer, and, where necessary, the treatment administrator
7. Supervise the final analysis and disseminate the results

*Qualities Needed by the Initiator–Sponsor.* Perhaps the most striking aspect of this list of functions is the wide range of skills and knowledge that it implies. The skills needed will range from the conceptual and methodological knowledge necessary to specify the tasks of the designer–researcher, through an awareness of current and future policy issues, to the administrative and bureaucratic skills needed to manage a multimillion dollar project. Certainly, a capable and diverse staff is required, and there are organizational and locational considerations as well.

Clearly, one of the most important characteristics and capabilities the initiator and sponsor should have is the ability to weigh intelligently the possible questions that can be dealt with in an experiment. The determination of which questions are critical must come from some sort of policy–research planning process. There would seem to be three major sources of insight as to issues which merit experimentation. The first is the understanding gained through policy analysis or policy planning, which examines the attributes and consequences of new policies or programs or the modification of existing ones. Such analysis is often independent of empirical research, and it often seems to lead to insights and inspirations that may or may not be confrontable with the evidence on hand. A second source of ideas for experimentation would be researchers familiar with the gaps in knowledge and the shortcomings of existing data about a topic of social significance. Another source is administrative officers who may consider experiments to be a means of improving administrative practices and policies. The orientation of the sponsor–initiator depends greatly on where it is located, that is, on whether it is associated with a mission-oriented agency or a research-supporting agency, and on the professional–administrative mix of the organization's external constituency. The basic research programs of the National Science Foundation, for example, tend to be influenced more by the interests of academic and fundamental research workers than by policy planners, while the reverse is true of policy analysis offices associated with the Secretary's office of a mission-oriented agency such as Housing and Urban Development or Transportation. In between these extremes is the Program of Research Applied to National Needs (RANN) of the National Science Foundation and research units of governmental health agencies that are concerned with alcoholism, drug addiction, suicide, and other behavioral pathologies. These middle-range organizations exemplify an amalgamation of policy concern and research competence. There seems to be a trend, beginning in the mid–1960s toward the growth of staff organizations in major agencies that have responsibility for policy analysis, review, and planning in relation to the agency mission. In one or two instances, such organizations have been able to command funds for experimental research and to develop substantial programs. Their staffs are usually not researchers, although they may have been exposed to research training; but they are particularly sensitive to major policy issues that seem to have an enduring future and important unexplored dimensions. The growth of such staff organizations and their orientation probably reflects the need for, as well as the dearth of, policy-related social research, especially experimentation.

By and large, state and local government organizations that might initiate experiments are concentrated at the policy-planning end of the spectrum of agency interests. State and local jurisdictions have been traditionally unwilling and unable to allocate substantial resources to research of any sort, much less to research of an experimental nature. However, there is some indication of change in this posture in some of the larger states and cities, whose attempts to deal with social problems intuitively have failed. Planning offices in local communities, in school districts, and at the state level may be influenced to undertake more program-or policy-oriented social research (including some experiments), perhaps with the aid of revenue-sharing or direct subsidization from Federal sources, particularly for design and analysis activity.

Whatever the location of the initiator–sponsor there are a number of characteristics that experience suggests are essential to the successful carrying out of a social experiment.

1. Continuity: As noted, experimentation can be a lengthy and complex undertaking. The ability to analyze the results of the experiment depends critically upon an understanding of events that led up to and occurred during the experiment. As a consequence, it is important that the central staff of the initiator–sponsor as well as the principal investigators stay with the experiment from its beginning to its end.

2. The ability to define problems clearly and to predict whether an experiment can help solve them: This capability is essential to the issue of what questions an experiment will address, as discussed earlier. But a sharp research staff is essential if the experiment is also to be intelligently monitored. They should be capable of conducting research in a policy-oriented context themselves, and should occasionally demonstrate that capacity, both to set an example to outside organizations and to build the type of organizational image necessary to attract top flight personnel. To be credible in seeking others to do analyses or in monitoring their own grantees and contractors during the experiment, they must provide a model of analytical capability. If an experiment sponsor cannot himself define and investigate research issues, he can hardly ensure that others will do it properly for him. In-house research capability is also useful if the experiment design is to anticipate, and provide adequately for, the needs of those who will be analyzing its results. Without an understanding of sampling design, for example, the sponsor is at a loss to understand the costs and benefits of various treatment cell sizes or to suggest the appropriate allocation of subjects to treatments.

3. Ability to assess policy relevance: A degree of political "savvy"

is required if the initiator and sponsor are to assign priority among the different experiments that might be undertaken and among the questions a specific experiment might address. The staff of the sponsoring agency needs a keen understanding of current policy debate and an awareness of the factors on which legislators and other policymakers will actually base their decisions. The sponsor's staff must also be foresighted, since an experiment may be conceived in one presidential administration, operated in another, and analyzed under yet another. And, while the staff should not be short-sighted, it should also not be over-cautious. Cautious political "realism" in the mid-1960s would surely have ruled out a test of anything as radical (at that time) as an income maintenance program for the working poor.

4. Policy and program leverage: This final characteristic is one primarily of organizational location rather than an inherent capability of the staff, yet it is no less important than the characteristics listed so far. In essence, the initiator–sponsor organization needs to be situated in the best of all possible worlds. It needs adequate funding so it is not dependent on others to do its bidding. It needs a large staff that includes a variety of social scientists. It needs the active support of the agency or department head. And, finally, it needs access to and credibility with the audience it hopes to influence. While physical proximity is not very important, the initiator–sponsor must have good lines of communication to relevant policymakers—to agency and department heads, White House staff, and key Congressmen and committee staff members—if national policies are to be affected.

One additional point is worth noting. In any office whose primary mission is research, the perceived quality of the research and of the research staff that proposes it will determine which proposals are funded. Proposals for experiments will be compared with other, non-experimental research proposals that frequently would cost significantly less. In such an office an expenditure of as much as $500,000 or $1 million is unusual, and its staff is unlikely to be disposed favorably toward sponsoring such experiments. In an office that is concerned with program development or policy planning, however, the perspective is often different. Frequently a search for information on the consequences of adopting a policy will be viewed in the context of the ultimate program size. Operational social programs frequently cost $30 to $50 million or more a year. Expenditures of $3 to $5 million seem far more reasonable in this context, if they are the best means of obtaining information on the possible consequences of implementing such large-scale programs. The issues to which research will be devoted are usually more clearly defined when the decision on carrying out an experiment is made in terms of the best and most credible means of obtaining information. It comes as no surprise to find that major large-scale social experiments have been initiated or inspired by the interests of staffs who are closer to policy planning than to research sponsorship. It may be desirable, as well as inevitable, that policy-planning groups with research-funding capabilities will continue to be the principal initiators and sponsors of social experimentation.

DESIGNER–RESEARCHER

*Functions.*   The primary functions of the designer–researcher are:

1. To develop in detail the experimental research design, including specifying treatment variables in operational terms, determining measures of effect, specifying treatment and control groups, choosing sampling procedures, and scheduling data collection
2. To work out substantive and organizational details compatible with the experiment design for making the action and research phases operational, including negotiating with or establishing the treatment entity (treatment administrator), and negotiating with other parties that may be involved in the experiment (e.g., data-collecting organizations, local governments, and participants)
3. To develop information-gathering and processing procedures and coordinate them with the treatment operation
4. To develop means of monitoring the treatment over time to ensure that the action phase continues to meet experimental design requirements; or to describe deviations from the original design if deviations are allowed. (The ease of carrying out this task, of course, depends on the degree of complexity of the treatment. It is also fair to say that standard analytical techniques cannot utilize information resulting from this monitoring process. Instead, it serves primarily to alert the analyst to particular problems of interpretation.)
5. To analyze the experiment results and prepare a report for the sponsor. Because political pressures are perhaps at their height when it comes to the analysis and release of data, this issue is discussed at length in a later section of this chapter.

*Characteristics of the Designer–Researcher.*   The qualities that one ought to seek in a design–research organization are essentially the same as one would seek in any good research organization. They include:

1. Credibility: This characteristic is in part a subjective assessment rendered by members of the scientific community, augmented by expressions from the policymaking community who have had contact with social research organizations. It is an assessment not only of objective skills but also of the record of ingenuity in developing hypotheses, and care in treating data. It adds up to a belief that an institution is likely to produce high quality research. Conditions that foster the development of quality research potential include the ability of the organization to provide certain working conditions for its staff: (a) job security–tenure, with positions not tied to a specific project; (b) relative autonomy for the researcher to determine the way he goes about the assigned task, including scope of work and deadlines; (c) absence of a rigid hierarchy, particularly in terms of intellectual issues, so that more junior researchers have a fair amount of responsibility and autonomy, and (d) a strong emphasis on scholarly publications and peer review.

2. Integrity: It may seem trite to emphasize something so obviously a part of the normal scientific ethic, but in a complex undertaking like a social experiment, integrity is an extremely important quality for a design–research organization. Social experiments obey the well-known Murphy's law: If something can go wrong in an experiment, it will. Throughout the course of the experiment there will be deviation from the understandings that had been reached between the sponsor, the research organization, and the experimental subjects. In some instances, these will be the fault of the research team or the action team. But most often they will simply result from unforeseen circumstances or uncontrollable events occurring naturally in social life. Even when the fault does not lie with the research organization, however, there is perhaps a natural tendency to hide problems which seem to reflect unfavorably upon its competence. Such concealment must be avoided. Problems tend to accumulate and become compounded if they are not dealt with expeditiously, often leading to disastrous consequences for the experiment. The corollary of this requirement for integrity on the part of the research organization is the requirement for tolerance on the part of the sponsoring organization. The sponsor should recognize that things will go wrong. It must deal with the research organization in such a way as to encourage that organization not to hide its errors and its problems.

3. Staff continuity: The fact that experiments have a long life span makes it important to ensure that there is appropriate organizational memory. It is preferable, of course, that the principle investigators remain with the experiment over its entire life. They are the individuals who understand the original design and will be able to carry out the

analyses in line with that original intent. They will also presumably have a substantial understanding of the reasons for deviations from it. However, it is frequently difficult to retain people over periods of 5–7 years on any single project, especially when there is little opportunity for analysis between the start and finish of the experimental treatment. For this reason, it is unwise to allow an experiment to become totally dependent upon the knowledge and understanding of one person or a very few people. Extensive documentation of the activities should be required on a continuing basis so that others may assume major analytical and managerial responsibilities if the original investigators have to be replaced.

4. Flexibility: The design–research organization must have an incentive structure that rewards diverse skills and a management able to cope with a wide and ever-changing range of problems. A variety of special skills—for example, in statistical design, development of measures, training and supervision of field staff, and establishment and maintenance of data storage and processing systems—are required. Coming from diverse backgrounds, these specialists are accustomed to different working conditions and find different aspects of the experimental task rewarding. Managerial sensitivity is required to get the most out of each. Furthermore, the demands placed on the designer–researcher shift enormously as a social experiment proceeds through the design, treatment, and analysis phases. The organizational skills needed during each phase differ dramatically from one other. Finally, the emphasis of the experimental purpose may shift somewhat over time. Treatments may diverge from what was intended or the problems deemed most important to policymakers may change. The ability of the designer–researcher to adapt to these changes is extremely important.

A major responsibility of the designer–researcher is the development of staff and procedures for making measurements and collecting data about experimental conditions and participants' behavior. The importance of training and supervision of the data collection staff has already been discussed in terms of quality control (Chapter 5) and that discussion will not be repeated here. The function is critically important to the success of the experiment.

*Potential Researcher–Designers.*   Administrators of social experiments complain most about the lack of individuals and organizations capable of designing them, monitoring the work of the treatment administrator, and analyzing their results. This is not surprising since only a handful of such experiments have been conducted and there has been no opportunity to develop a pool of skilled labor. As more experiments are undertaken, more organizations specializing in experimentation will develop, and existing ones will enlarge their pool of talent.

The major candidates for the designer–researcher role range from purely academic departments of social science in universities to purely commercial research firms, both profit and nonprofit. There is so much variation in quality and capabilities within these categories that they do not provide a basis for specific consumer ratings. Rather, we offer some general observations about the kinds of capabilities that might be expected in each of the groups and some comments about the trade-offs the initiator–sponsor may have to consider.

Probably the best analytic talent lies within the university departments and university-based research organizations. These groups are inherently more likely to adhere to the high standards that are so important in maintaining the integrity of the project. It is also possible that there is greater continuity among individuals in university settings than among those in private organizations. However, university departments have serious drawbacks as potential designer–researchers in that they typically do not have the organizational and management talent or the structure necessary to mount a large field organization, to design an elaborate information retrieval system, or to manage a complex multidisciplinary research effort. Some university-based survey research organizations and some problem-centered research institutes may, on the other hand, have this management capability or be able to develop it quickly. But most university-connected organizations live in an academic environment that emphasizes publication for career progression. A researcher will have little opportunity to publish during the course of an experiment if he is heavily involved in its operation; a young faculty member can hardly afford to invest the 4–7 years required for an experiment if he cannot publish during that period. Unless this situation changes, perhaps through innovations in incentive structures and career patterns for university-based scientists, social experimentation will probably continue to be limited to a few exceptional individuals or organizations.

The last two decades have seen the growth of institutes and organizations that maintain loose ties to a university and private research organizations (profit or nonprofit) that are closely tied to policy concerns. These organizations typically have the advantage of being able to establish internal incentives that are consistent with the requirements of social experimentation. At the same time, they rely heavily on peer review procedures to maintain high research standards. Frequently they also have the managerial and organizational capabilities to carry out large-scale projects. They are not always able, however, to attract the very best scientists and as a consequence may not have the same level of analytic talent that could be assembled in a university setting.

Indeed, the ability of nonuniversity-based organizations to attract and retain high quality staff depends in large part on their financial stability, and it is, perhaps, financial stability that distinguishes the better from the poorer of these groups. Organizations without financial stability must constantly scramble for new grants and contracts, and this may affect their willingness to accept controversial projects that might stigmatize them as discoverers of unpopular research findings. Financially pressed organizations frequently must assign their best people to marketing and preparing proposals, leaving junior staff to conduct the actual project work. Rapid turnover in top project personnel is not unusual because of the pressure to seek out new business. On the other hand, their need to satisfy initiator–sponsors may lead such organizations to be much more responsive to the latter's needs than are the financially comfortable organizations. Thus, the initiator–sponsor may find himself forced to accept a trade-off between a responsive organization with high staff turnover and a less responsive organization offering staff continuity.

One key to the nature of a designer–researcher, as indicated from the preceding discussion, is the organization's need to compete for new grants and contracts. The federal government procurement process as currently structured certainly contributes to the financial instability of the private research organizations and exacerbates the initiator–sponsor's difficulties in selecting a designer–researcher.

There is currently no standard means in federal government procedure of selecting a designer–researcher. In some instances, agencies have simply gone to organizations in which they had confidence and asked them to prepare proposals for a grant. In other cases, designer–researchers were chosen through normal contract competitions. One agency has recently tried awarding several parallel contracts to promote effective competition (in effect, providing funds to several organizations to prepare detailed and specific project proposals); as well as awarding grants on the basis of statements of organizational capability, rather than elaborate project proposals. None of these solutions to the selection problem is totally satisfactory. The basic quandary springs from the great uncertainties that surround social experiments. Their designs must be modified as planning progresses, field problems require additional efforts or cause parts of an experiment to become less valuable, or analytical efforts turn out to be more complex than originally imagined. In short, experiments are plagued by all the problems of research generally—but they have larger cost consequences. Given these uncertainties plus the impossibility of research sponsors being able to lay out an experimental design in great detail until the analytic design work has been done, it is difficult to write a request for proposals (RFP) that is sufficiently specific to elicit proposals that are well enough worked out to form the basis of a contract. Moreover, contract competitions and negotiations are carried out under a set of rules that are designed to ensure fairness to all bidders as well as the procurement of the best research at a reasonable price, and it frequently appears that fairness gets a higher priority. Unfortunately, contracting regulations were developed largely for government procurement of materials for which tight specifications can be written. There are, furthermore, stringent limitations on discussions between potential contractors and the procuring office. There is a tendency to try to carry out a competition so that final decisions among the technically qualified competitors is made on the basis of price. Yet even when all the formalities are observed, it proves impossible and unreasonable to hold contractors to everything in their proposals and the elaborate judgments made on the basis of the competition seem somehow irrelevant to the final conduct of the research.

While a complete discussion of the problems of contracting for social experiments is beyond the scope of this volume, it is worth noting that some of the problems that are frequently observed—e.g., severe cost overrun, sloppy research, high costs, and poor utilization— are attributable to the contracting process itself, particularly when that process is tied to the governmental budget cycle. The rigidity of that cycle, coupled with the frequent use of 1 year appropriations, has resulted in the clustering of contract actions in the last quarter of a fiscal year. In order to survive and expand, research organizations must bid simultaneously on several RFP's, frequently proposing to deploy the same staff on each. If they win several contracts they must scurry to hire additional staff, with the risk of diluting quality and virtually guaranteeing that delivery will not measure up to the original proposal.

The episodic and hand-to-mouth existence of many small research organizations raises another serious problem. Carrying out a major research project is an organizational learning experience. The research organization may create field surveying capability, form a data analysis group, or upgrade a computer facility. Yet, if a new contract is not forthcoming at the end of the research project much of this capability may be dissipated (in fact, if not on paper). As a result, the next research program carried out by the organization will have to repeat the learning and development process all over again.

Outlining these problems does not imply advocating the abandonment of competition. Absence of competition can lead to favoritism toward a few select institutions; to failure to develop new institutional capabilities; or to ignoring existing capabilities. The important question is how the competition is carried out. Are the criteria for selection reasonable in light of the uncertainty of the task? For example, is the emphasis placed on people, their abilities and availability, rather than on what they propose to do? Are cost estimates viewed with the degree of skepticism appropriate to cost-based contracts? Continued trials of new means of selecting organizations to carry out social experimentation are needed.

TREATMENT ADMINISTRATOR AND PROGRAM DEVELOPER

These two roles are, in principle, closely related although the program development functions may be truncated in a particular experiment. There is, however, some role for a treatment administrator in every experiment. The role may vary in complexity from the rather mechanical disbursement of money payments or preparation of food supplements to the provision of educational, counseling, or therapeutic services. Whatever the level of complexity, the treatment administrator has the following functions:

*Functions of the Treatment Administrator.*

1. To deliver a specified good or service in conformity with the requirements of the experimental design, i.e., on schedule, in specified amounts, and as consistently as possible
2. To document the delivery process carefully, indicating as clearly as possible the extent of deviation and reasons therefore
3. To be alert for and report (for administrative use) unexpected conditions, unanticipated events (including unforeseen responses to treatment or factors affecting its delivery)

These functions require a combination of characteristics on the part of the action team administering treatment that is not easy to achieve and frequently requires careful and sensitive training. On the one hand, the people who deliver the treatment must be able to tolerate repetition of an activity, without boredom, over a long period of time and while sustaining a high standard of consistency and almost a compulsivity in record keeping. These characteristics must be balanced against the need for sensitivity and an alert understanding of the experimental purpose that is essential for the perception of unexpected conditions—especially when treatment delivery takes place in privacy, is geographically dispersed, or is otherwise hard to monitor. Finally, one may add the requirement that treatment administrative personnel must be able to exercise self-control in delivery, especially of personalized services—neither delivering more treatment than specified because they perceive a participant is deprived or deserving; nor less, because of opposite judgments.

*Characteristics of the Treatment Administrator.*    Because the skills required of treatment administrative personnel vary so much with the content of treatment, generalization about performance is difficult. Sometimes, rather highly trained individuals are needed—with higher degrees in an academic subject or certification in a profession. Experience suggests more conscientious performance can often be obtained from people with less prior education, who are given specialized training for the jobs they will have in the experiment. For a less well-trained person, the job may be a unique opportunity to enlarge his understanding and skills. To be sure, some treatments cannot or should not be administered by any but highly trained specialists; but over-educated persons in the somewhat repetitive jobs of treatment delivery can not only grow careless but can be injurious to morale.

It is rare to find an existing organization that is capable of delivering a specified treatment and prepared to provide appropriate personnel on short notice. Generally it is necessary to hire and train the treatment administrator for the particular experiment. Just whose responsibility this is depends upon the organizational role combinations in the particular experiment—a subject mentioned in Chapter VI and discussed in greater detail in a later section of this chapter. For the moment, however, let us assume that the management of treatment administration is in the hands of the program developer.

*Functions of the Program Developer.*    Of all the roles considered, that of program developer is least well developed or exemplified in the limited social experimentation so far undertaken. Perhaps that is because so few social problems have been attacked systematically in a sequential series of steps. Rather, social intervention programs often appear to spring full-blown from the brow of some political, academic, industrial, or financial Zeus. Even the process of relatively orderly and rational discussion that preceded experimental testing of the concept of a negative income tax was not truly program development. In fact, it became clear that even so simple a treatment as cash transfers involved decisions about such matters as accounting periods for earned income, frequency of income reporting and payments, and the status of unearned income in computing payments.

The functions of the program developer are:

1. To turn a general idea (a concept, a strategy, an attitude) into a set of specific components (materials, actions, settings) aimed at achieving the effects implied in the general idea under concrete circumstances
2. To realize the specific components in the form of usable materials, persons trained to perform the specified actions, and actual settings in which experimental tests of the program can occur
3. To revise any of the components in response to (experimental) evidence or replace them with others

*Characteristics of the Program Developer.*   Of all the organizational roles, program development probably requires the highest degree of imagination. It is an inventive act. Components of a program must be created—sometimes out of familiar materials, sometimes out of thin air. At the same time, it requires disciplined imagination which can adhere to a purpose—at least until it proves futile—and adapt or adjust to evidence.

The program developer needs a variety of talents. In the educational curriculum area, for example, where program development may have advanced furthest, it has been necessary to enlist subject matter specialists who understand the intellectual structure of the subject: classroom teachers familiar with pupil behavior; writers, artists, designers, and artisans who can prepare suitable materials; trainers of teachers; repairmen and maintenance personnel; as well as general troubleshooters. Corresponding skills are called for in other types of intervention. Program development is more than an intellectual task, for it is concerned with the actual production and installation of at least prototype interventions. Finally, after an effective model (or series) has come into being, the program developer may have the responsiblity for dissemination, marketing, or routine application. The program developer's responsibilities begin with the initial efforts to undertake an experiment but may extend well beyond its conclusion.

The program developer can have two quite distinct roles. First, the program developer may take a program idea that has been developed only in broad terms and devise a program package and operating structure to field test the idea. Second, the program developer may be the central figure in a program development cycle with the responsibility for developing alternate approaches in a social program area (e.g., early childhood education).

Few existing organizations have performed such developmental activities (especially the developmental cycle). It is our impression that most developers stop short of the kinds of efforts that seem necessary for the replication required in a program development cycle. The reasons for this are several. First, in many areas such as manpower training, health care delivery, community organization or housing development, the funding for and organizations to carry out such efforts either do not exist or are not at all well developed. Agencies responsible for funding such activities have not perceived them as being important (or, perhaps, feasible) and instead have funded numerous small demonstration projects. At the same time, organizations possessing the range of skills necessary to develop and routinize such activities do not exist and we are unsure how they should best be organized. It is our belief, however, that the program development role and the developmental cycle are critical factors in the introduction of social interventions, too often slighted in social experimentation and too often ignored by proponents of social innovations, who do not pay sufficient attention to the "debugging" of potentially effective treatments.

The program developer should generally not have a role in an experiment that is larger than the one he might play in policies or programs that are adopted as a result of the experiment. If he expects to provide technical assistance to all who adopt his program, for example, he should be involved in this fashion. But again, for the final experiment, the emphasis should be on creating conditions that as nearly as possible approximate ultimate field conditions.

The relationship between the program developer and the researcher–designer is problematic. The obvious self-interest of the developer could lead to biases in the experimental design and analysis, but program development requires sensitive and collaborative relationships with research. The question of this relationship, as well as relationship to the sponsor, is taken up in the next section.


RELATIONSHIPS AMONG ORGANIZATIONAL ROLES

The way in which the various roles are combined or separated among organizations has both managerial and political consequences for the conduct of the experiment and for its interpretation. Each combination involves some trade-off among such desiderata as: external validity, integrity of the design, relation of treatment to real policy options, and minimization of conflict and divisiveness.

When the initiator of the experiment is an "authority" or superordinate body, responsible for evaluating the claims of a program developer or for making budgetary or administrative decisions affecting the program, it is common for the initiator also to be the sponsor, but for the treatment administrator to be a separate organization from the designer–researcher. This separation is based on the theory that a greater degree of objectivity can thereby be achieved in the experimental evaluation. If the treatment administrator and designer–researcher roles were combined in a single organization, the reasoning goes, there would be undue risk of a self-serving result. Separation of the organizational interests of the treatment program from those of the research program and sponsor solves an external political problem. That view is probably correct in all but a small proportion or instances; but, as we pointed out earlier (Chapter VI), this organizational arrangement has some serious consequences for the management of the experiment. It forces the designer–researcher into a negotiating position with the treatment administrator, the "action team," which has ordinarily come into being prior to or independently of the decision to carry out an experiment and has its own interests to defend. The designer–researcher is seen as the creature of the initiator–sponsor who may wield the axe, and this is often a realistic perception. An organizational alignment of interests and power that appropriately solves a political problem external to the experiment may, at the same time, exacerbate internal, management difficulties.

Defensiveness on the part of the treatment administration may be inevitable in this way of combining roles, especially if the experiment constitutes a "summative" evaluation that will decide whether the intervention program is to be continued or to be cut off. On the other hand, if experimentation is being used in the course of a program development effort, the purpose of which is to improve a treatment or to decide among alternative ways of realizing a particular social policy, then the action team is more likely to be sympathetic to research and to be nondefensive, because the results of the experiments will be used to modify and improve their techniques.

If the roles of treatment administrator and designer–researcher are combined under the overall control of a program developer, not only is the problem of action team defensiveness minimized, but the utilization of research results to reshape social intervention programs is enhanced. Cooperative collaboration between treatment administration and research replaces rivalry. This structure solves many managerial problems, although it does not eliminate the possiblity of biased assessment of treatment effects should the program developer become attached to a particular treatment. Final, summative evaluation may still have to be carried out by an outside organization in order to restore objectivity. The outside organization may, however, tend to apply criteria which differ from those used by the program developer.

There is, then, a fundamental quandary of organization in social experimentation but no universally applicable strategy. The combination of roles that minimizes management difficulties and maximizes utilization of research results incurs the risk of losing objectivity and detachment. An organizational role combination that minimizes this hazard, risks interrole conflict and (often) painful, time-consuming negotiation. The distribution of these roles constitutes one of the major decisions for the sponsoring organization.


ORGANIZATIONAL ROLES AND RELATIVE POWER

The possibility of conflict between the various organizational roles in an experiment is great—at the beginning, in conception and design; in execution; and at the end, in the way results are utilized in program planning and policy formation. It can be magnified if the people who plan the action treatment are not the same as those charged with measurement and data analysis or if the two groups have different perspectives or conflicting purposes. For the same reasons, difficulties are likely to be encountered in utilization if the party or parties responsible for program planning or policy formulation are not the same as those who sponsored or initiated the experiment in the first place. An agency that did not ask for an experiment to be conducted on its programs and does not want to know the results can find many reasons for ignoring them, discounting them, or actively opposing them.

Ideally, all parties to the experiment should *want* it to occur; or at least should not actively oppose it. In real life this happy state of affairs cannot always be attained, but an experiment that begins in a conflict of views or claims is likely to wind up there, too. It is doubtful that social experimentation can be used punitively (as many "evaluations" of social action programs have been intended) and, at the same time, constructively. In fact, unless the alignment of power is very clearly on the side of the initiator–sponsor *and* the designer–researcher, the experiment is likely to end in disaster.

If the experiment is to be conducted in the context of some sociopolitical disagreement (the most common situation), the designer–researcher will need enough power aligned with his experimental purposes to protect the integrity of the design and to prevent the premature disclosure of results or a decision to cut off the project's funds. Such pressures are especially likely to arise from opponents who are totally outside both the experiment and the action program it is examining. Social activists and politicians whose purposes or perspectives differ from those of the experimental program, labor or management, and ethnic or religious groups who perceive their interests threatened by a possible outcome of the experiment, are all likely sources of opposition.

On the other hand, as we have observed in Chapter VI, an honest experiment can also be sabotaged from within—by convinced proponents of the action program being tested who have faith that their approach to the social problem is the best one. In such cases, the pressure that arises is not to stop the experiment but to warp it toward results that will sustain the claims of the action program.

It is worthwhile asking what *institutional* arrangements might be able to mitigate such pressures. Fundamentally, the problem is to separate the success of the experiment from the success of the action program. That is, the institutional arrangement should be such that the persons responsible for initiating, sponsoring, and designing and executing the research are rewarded for good experimentation rather than "good" programs. In terms of institutional arrangements, this conclusion strongly suggests that experimentation for program evaluation and planning shoud not be lodged in the hands of agencies responsible (or likely to become responsible) for a national program. In effect, this suggests that experiments should be done by an experimenting agency rather than by an action team.

Perhaps the point can be made by examining an analogy that is limited but instructive. For over a century, a large part of the biological and chemical research that has been a major factor in increasing the agricultural productivity of the United States was conducted in agricultural experiment stations at state colleges and universities, rather than at fertilizer manufacturers, feed producers, or implement manufacturers. Agricultural researchers occupied a distinctive institutional locus in this system of information dissemination and decision making about agricultural innovation. They were not subject themselves to market pressures to design successful and profitable products; what was demanded of them was accurate and dependable information, and this demand emanated from a very important segment of the community and one that could exercise a significant influence on the future of the agricultural experiment station itself (through the usual taxpayer devices). At the same time, the agricultural scientist could not simply retreat to his ivory tower of theory and abstraction, for he had to take into account such practical factors as the existing commercial materials and supplies, the habitual and customary practices of farmers, and the costs and benefits of trying to change either. It is reasonable to believe that this set of pressures helped to direct the efforts of agricultural research workers along the general lines mentioned earlier, namely, the conduct of objective, accurate, and utilizable experimentation. The analogy is far from perfect, and there are distinct differences between the problem of agricultural innovation in the early twentieth century and, say, educational innovation today. Nevertheless, the *structural* implications seem quite compelling. To the extent that an office can be divorced from concern with the provision of services, as, for example, was the OEO's Office of Planning, Research and Evaluation, it may be better able to accomplish the purposes of social experimentation in the same fashion that agricultural experiment stations have done.

## Political Aspects of Experimentation

Most of what has been said in the preceding sections applies generally to the conduct of social research, not exclusively to social experiments. Yet there are special political problems associated with social experimentation. The experimenter and his project cannot enjoy the luxury of anonymity while design problems are considered, participants chosen, the treatments delivered, and the analysis undertaken.

An experiment and its participants both benefit from, and are plagued by, the removal of the work from the shelter of academe. For example, the university researcher may feel his work is "dropped down a well," and that the publicity it deserves (and therefore the impact it should have on the research community) are seldom forthcoming. Experimenters seldom need to seek publicity; their problem is more one of ensuring that the publicity accurately reflects their intents and findings. Thus, while dissemination per se is facilitated by the public nature of an experiment, the experimenter must be prepared for certain problems.

This section deals with some of the problems created by the political nature of experimentation: problems of site selection, data analysis, dealing with the news media, and increasing the sophistication of audiences in interpreting experiment results. Finally, some suggestions are made about safeguarding experiment findings.

SITE SELECTION

Selecting a site for a social experiment requires balancing a complex combination of scientific, logistic, and political factors. The most important single question raised in connection with site selection is the generalizability of the experimental results: Can the results obtained be extended to other sites in which similar treatments might be applied? We remarked earlier (Chapter III) that it was more important to obtain a fair test of a treatment than to obtain a representative sample, in the statistical sense, of the personal characteristics and environmental attributes of the populations in areas that are intended ultimately to be served in the program. Nevertheless, a designer–researcher would want to avoid sites that were demonstrably out of the ordinary in respect to some putatively relevant characteristic of program participants. He would want the site to include at least some persons and some environmental conditions that resembled those toward which the intervention program was directed. They should then, at least, be illustrative of the range of variation in the program target. Geographical factors, whether cultural, economic, social, or vaguely "regional" seem to present particular complexity in this connection. Almost everyone would agree that New York and Los Angeles are different, but they would be hard pressed to say what effect the difference might have on response to a particular treatment. In the face of such mysteries, there is some tendency to try to minimize regional effects, say, by including diverse regional sites. In the case of a program that deals with individuals, this can mean that a national probability sample is chosen— if the delivery of the treatment is sufficiently simple. But the logistical impracticality of delivering the treatment to a national probability sample will usually preclude this.

The logistics of social experimentation, then, are a second significant factor. Early in the planning of the Negative Income Tax experiment, there was debate about whether or not to use a national probability sample of, say, 2500 individuals, so that the results obtained in the experiment could be readily generalized to the nation as a whole. This proposal also had appeal to those who were interested in obtaining good estimates of total operating program costs. The treatment administrators however, argued that it would be nearly impossible to administer an experiment with subjects scattered among many locations across the nation. It would also be nearly impossible to deal with the welfare laws that differed state by state in terms of experimental design, administration, and data analysis. The treatment administrator, therefore, urged selection of a relatively compact area that was not atypical of urban labor markets. New Jersey was finally chosen in part because of what appeared at the time to be a favorable situation with respect to welfare programs, in part because the state government seemed amenable and indeed supportive of the experiment, and in part because of the closeness of the site to the headquarters of those involved in field operations and analysis.

While all this seems reasonable, there is no question that the labor market in the area chosen is not representative of all urban labor markets. The population is not demonstrably "typical" of the population of the United States, and it is particularly "unrepresentative" of rural areas. Other income maintenance experiments with different types of populations may fill in the resulting gaps, and it is hoped that these several experiments will provide consistent as well as comparable evidence. The effects will have to be looked at very carefully because if they differ among sites, and if those differences cannot be easily explained in terms of local market structure or special characteristics of the experimental groups, the findings of the New Jersey experiment will be in doubt.

In the case of the Performance Contracting experiment, one site selection strategy would have been to choose a number of communities randomly, with the probability of their selection being in proportion to their representation in the total population or in the target population, i.e., disadvantaged youngsters. Because this would have required extensive negotiation with each community chosen, this alternative was not considered feasible. Rather, the designer chose sites illustrative of different geographic regions, rural–urban location, size, and minority pupil populations from among applicant communities, making special efforts to solicit applications from all types of areas. Willingness to cooperate, of course, implies some self-selection on the part of communities and gives rise to the possibility that an experiment conducted on communities that did not volunteer for it might have produced different results from one carried out on those that did volunteer.

While one may, in such situations, have to abandon randomization as a means of obtaining representativeness, one should not, of course, relinquish randomization for comparability. For programs such as performance contracting, eligible schools can be recruited to volunteer their participation, each agreeing to cooperate whether they end up as control or experimental schools. These schools can then be stratified, blocked, or even matched on relevant variables, and then be randomly assigned to treatments. While such randomization has not generally been done, we believe it is important and that it usually can be done if there is sufficient administrative commitment.

Situations can also be imagined in which the costs of an experiment or quasi-experiment are so great, or the chances of disrupting the participant population so great, that only one or two sites will volunteer. In these instances, the possibility that the site differs from non-volunteering sites is large, so researchers must give special attention to atypical local factors that may influence the outcome of the experiment. These examples are sufficient to indicate that the problem of site selection is one of balancing the need for representativeness and generalizability against the need for logistical feasibility and local willingness to cooperate. It is a major judgment "call" by the sponsor–initiator and the research team.

DATA ANALYSIS AND RELEASE

The problems of data analysis in a social experiment are also different in many ways from those in other forms of research.

For experiments involving simple pre–post measures, the major analysis will have to be accomplished after the completion of the full experimental treatment. In the case of experiments which produce sequential information, as, for example, in the case of the income maintenance experiments, analyses can begin at an earlier point in time. Experience suggests that while preliminary analysis can be valuable, it is not totally without its dangers.

On the positive side, preliminary analyses force the research team to think through and modify their analytic plans. It seems to be almost impossible to specify analysis activities in detail prior to actually beginning the analysis. Once the analytic effort begins, problems with data collection become clearer. It is frequently possible to modify data collection efforts, perhaps by improving the questionnaire structure, to deal with some of the problems that are raised in these early analytical activities. Preliminary analyses are also likely to give both the designer–researcher and the initiator–sponsor a more realistic feeling for the length of time that will be required for the final analysis (which will be undertaken after the experimental treatments are completed).

The danger of initiating analyses early is that the sponsor and/or others will naturally want to see the analysis results, but may be unable or unwilling to understand the limitations and caveats that should be placed on the data. Early analyses in experiments are likely to be based upon data that have not been fully edited and "cleaned," treatments that have not had a full opportunity to work and perhaps have not been fully implemented, and analytical plans which have not been fully completed.

Ideally, the research contractor should produce a final report, to be submitted to the sponsor. The results should then be given the same kinds of review and critique that any scholarly research should receive. Reanalysis of the data could be carried out by others than the principal investigator and counterinterpretations be prepared.

Many of the major social experiments have not proceeded so routinely. Instead, summaries of analyses have been released or leaked to the press. Early analyses have been published, court actions have been brought to force release of data, and, in general, events have conspired to pervert normal research reporting processes.

This should not be unexpected, in that a major experiment is undertaken because of its policy relevance. Thus, it is natural that there will be pressures for the earliest possible release of information so the policymaking may proceed. Indeed, the very presence of the experiment may create a tendency on the part of politicians or policymakers to delay making important decisions about the structure of a program or the design of a policy until the results of the experiment are available. This will be particularly true in very controversial program areas. As a consequence, as data become available within an experiment or as the time for a scheduled final report approaches, the pressures upon both the research team and the sponsor increase. If a policy issue has been or is being debated in Congress or in the executive branch, a researcher is very likely to want to extract information from his experiment that he considers relevant to those debates. If a policy is going to be decided before the experiment's completion, he reasons, the decision ought to be made with the best available evidence, even if that evidence is incomplete.

Again, the New Jersey experiment provides a good example of the kinds of problems that can arise. The OEO and the research staff at Mathematica and the Institute for Research on Poverty had observed the unfolding of the debate on the president's Family Assistance Plan. They were regularly asked whether anything from the experiment would be relevant to that debate. As a consequence, they jointly decided to examine some very early data from a portion of the sample for evidence of clear trends in work behavior. The data were rapidly extracted, analyzed in a descriptive fashion, and given to the president and cabinet, then released to the press and Congress.

There has been much debate over the propriety of this action. Critics of the release of the data have argued that the analyses were too descriptive and tentative, that the conclusions were too sweeping and broad, and that the presentation was too political. The OEO argued, on the other hand, that the data were the best available on the issue of labor force withdrawal, that the conclusions were crude but nonetheless supportable, and that public understanding of the issues surrounding welfare reform was heightened by the release of the information.

The Performance Contracting experiment provides another example of the pressures to release data. The initial plans for the experiment (which were unduly optimistic) called for the analysis and release of information by early fall, 1971. The problems of coding, editing, and retrieving data (as usual) turned out to be more difficult than anticipated and there was continued debate over the types of analyses that ought to be used. As a consequence, the date for making the information public continually slipped. When the initial results were made available to the OEO, they suggested that, on the whole, the performance contractors had done no better than the traditional school systems. Recognition of the implications of such findings, for the contractors in particular, led OEO to check and reanalyze the data to ensure that the results were not significantly changed even if the data were analysed differently. In the middle of the analysis, a teachers' organization filed a court suit to obtain the data from one site under the Freedom of Information Act. The teachers' organization had been bitterly opposed to the performance contracting project in that city. While OEO resisted releasing the information until it could be properly analyzed and put into proper context with data from other sites, there was continued pressure for the release. As a result, OEO promised to release the data by a specific date and rushed to complete its overall analysis by that time.

In the Performance Contracting experiment, there was a particular quandary from the scientific point of view. Virtually everyone concerned with the project would have preferred to take a good deal longer over the analysis of the data so as to attempt to tease further insights from them and to increase confidence in the general conclusions drawn from them. On the other hand, by the time the data were released, the control–experimental comparisons had been analyzed in at least four different ways, each of which confirmed the general conclusions. School districts were considering the possibility of entering into further performance contracts, and the data, if not released fairly quickly, would not be of any help to them in making their decisions. The OEO decided that, on balance, there was sufficient information and confidence in the results to merit their release in time to be utilized by local school districts.

The experiment sponsor will face pressures not only to release the findings early, but also to release findings that support the viewpoints of his own agency or department and/or those of special interest groups having a stake in the outcome. There may also be pressures not to publicize an experiment that is not considered scientifically rigorous and, to some extent, pressures to minimize interpretations that are inconsistent with the broad beliefs of the scientific community.

The opportunities for out-and-out falsification of data or for purposeful misanalysis of data are not large. There are simply too many participants and too many opportunities for others to obtain the data and analyses to permit an individual or group of individuals to purposely falsify information. The problem is more subtle. The sponsor, as the manager of the experiment, can choose which issues to treat and which issues to ignore. He can phrase the problem he wants to investigate in his own fashion. He chooses the analytical technique to be used. When a report is publicized, he will have a substantial role in highlighting what he thinks is important in the analysis and ignoring other aspects. This problem is not, of course, unique to social experimentation but rather pervades all research and analysis that is undertaken to support public policy and decision making. But, unfortunately in the public's (and frequently in the policymakers') eyes, the analysis and interpretation emerging from an expenditure of several million dollars will be examined differently, and be paid more credence, than the results of a $100,000 research endeavor. The problem is further heightened by the fact that sponsors of experiments very frequently use the press as a medium for the dissemination of results, and whether intentionally or not, this raises a substantial problem.

THE PRESS AND SOCIAL EXPERIMENTATION

As social experiments have proliferated and been publicized in the policymaking process, the interest of the press in experimentation has become greater. There is little one can say in general about these relationships. It is important to note, however, that to the extent that the intent of social experimentation is to influence policy, the experiments themselves and their results are clearly a proper subject for press concern, just like any other input to the policymaking process. Indeed, because the press provides a very important means of dissemination, it is to everyone's advantage for the press to be as informed and sophisticated about the experiment as possible.

There are problems however. The press must provide a relatively short and simplified story. The normal qualifications and caveats of the researchers regarding interpretation of the findings will usually not be reported. Examples can be given: Findings concerning performance contracting have been widely reported in the press as indicating that performance contracting did not work or was a failure. The actual OEO report is a good deal more circumspect in its conclusions, indicating rather that an experiment lasting just one year with six specific contractors using only existing technology had not produced results that were significatly different from those in the control schools. The income maintenance experiment provides another example. At the beginning of the experiment and again toward the middle, the press attempted to find individuals to interview about how they used the money they had received from the experimental treatment. In the minds of the reporters, this was a legitimate means of keeping the public informed about the experiment. The public had a right to know the results, they argued, and this was the most understandable way to present the facts. The OEO, Mathematica, and the other investigators supported this point of view early in the experiment; thus, several persons who had expressed their willingness to be, were so interviewed. Subsequently, however, it was decided that this constituted quite inappropriate publicity. A major intent of the experiment had been to change the way in which the welfare system was examined—to move from anecdotal evidence to systematic evidence collected from a carefully drawn sample of observations. The individual interviews, while no doubt of substantial interest to the public, could not convey the same kinds of information that were obtained from the statistical analysis of the total samples. As a consequence, both the OEO and the research staff subsequently refused to provide any kind of assistance to reporters and news broadcasters in locating and interviewing individuals.

POSSIBLE SAFEGUARDS AGAINST MISINTERPRETATION

There is no foolproof way in which to guarantee that experimental results will be adequately analyzed and not misinterpreted. But a number of precautions are available and should be considered by experiment sponsors.

The most important single step is to ensure that the analyses and data are available for examination and reanalysis by other interested scholars and researchers. Such availability has at least two major benefits. Obviously it permits the analysis of the data from alternative perspectives, with different types of questions than originally contemplated. But, in the context of this volume, the most important consequence of wide availability of the data is the incentive to the research staff to carry out analyses that are responsible and defensible. The knowledge that subsequent reanalyses may be done should promote integrity in the original analysis.

Making data available is not a trivial activity for the sponsor. It requires that data be in a form accessible to and understandable by the general research community and also be documented in a way that maximizes the likelihood of responsible use and interpretation. This is not an inexpensive task. Moreover, since it is time consuming, it is seldom undertaken, much less completed, until most of the original analysis has been done. As a consequence, the data are not available as quickly as they ideally should be.

Steps should be taken by agencies funding experiments to facilitate the use of data by researchers other than those connected with the experiment, specifically by providing for the establishment of storage and user facilities. Such a data center has been designed for the OEO-sponsored income maintenance studies. It is intended to make the data available for legitimate research purposes, especially the testing of novel hypotheses through secondary analyses. The repository is intended "to facilitate and encourage research . . . through . . . the provision of both consultative and computational services to potential users," in recognition of the difficulties an individual researcher who was not part of the original team faces in trying to exploit the richness of so large and complex a file. The repository will contain data from both urban and rural income maintenance experiments, stored in machine-readable form, resulting in a retrieval system that will incorporate certain special features and flexibilities of the file structure of the rural experiment while preserving the file structure of the urban experiment. Presumably it should be possible to accomodate data from other income maintenance experiments as they become available. The repository is designed to respond to requests for special extracts (in tape form) from the body of data; to carry out a limited number of statistical analyses on request; and to prepare a limited number of standard subject matter tapes (e.g., on migration, family composition and stability, occupation) that would presumably be of interest to a number of specialists in a variety of research fields. A consultation service is intended both to help researchers and to exercise some control over the release of data, so that, for example, respondent confidentiality is not violated.

While it highly desirable that both administrative and research files be made available, after the original analysis, for use by other investigators, decisions as to which files should be preserved are not as easy to make as may appear. As a minimum, one should preserve, in a form free of identifying information, the main bodies of data actually used in analysis by the original investigators. Data collected but never used or never coded may be of too little value to justify the substantial costs of preparation for use by others. Similarly, there may be large bodies of administrative data, much of which would be meaningless to outsiders without a great deal of interpretation and guidance. Judgments about how much of this data should be preserved must be made on a case-by-case basis in light of the resources available. Our inclination is to lean in the direction of preserving too much rather than too little. The budget of the experiment ought to make provision for the preparation of the archive.

Even releasing data simultaneously with the analysis is only a partial answer to problems we have raised. Frequently an experiment will have its major impact in the initial months after findings are released. Clearly, because of the time required to reanalyze the data responsibly, rebuttals to the conclusions of the initial analyses will not be available for 6 months to a year. Thus, there remains the problem that the sponsoring agency or the initial researchers alone will determine conclusions.

It has been suggested that the data be available simultaneously to more than one analyst initially so alternative interpretations can be offered. This would be feasible if experiments proceeded in the sequential fashion many envision, with data collection being completed and the files cleaned before the beginning of any analytical activity. In fact, analytical activities tend to lead to a reexamination of data and a constant iterative process of data and analysis refinement. Documentation is continuously changing during the course of this process and the practical problems of having two or more groups analyze the same data are virtually insurmountable. A partial solution to this problem has been found in the Income Maintenance experiments, where several investigators are carrying out basically independent analyses under the general direction of the principle investigator.

In general, sponsoring agencies are not very eager to support this kind of simultaneous analysis because they do not have the capacity to deal with the ambiguity that such analyses would inevitably raise. There is a possibility that such a process could result in strongly conflicting conclusions, reflecting the different perspectives of the analysts. This is almost too much for a sponsor to contemplate. If an experiment is intended to resolve some policy issue, it would be difficult indeed to report that nothing but more ambiguity has resulted.

It has also been proposed that some form of review body be set up to examine the quality of the analysis at the time it is made public or perhaps before. Many such bodies can be envisioned, ranging from those that are appointed by the research organization itself to ones appointed by the sponsoring agency, to bodies such as the General Accounting Office (GAO) that might be designated by Congress. Presumably such groups would examine the process by which the experiment was designed and carried out, so as to assess the quality of the analysis and perhaps point out pitfalls in data interpretation. Some formalization of this process is probably desirable in order to ensure that the results of social experiments are not misused in the formation of public policy.

The staff of the GAO has begun to perform such a function for the public and the Congress. They have been monitoring the major social experiments sponsored by the Federal government, auditing the procedures used to collect and process the data, examining the treatments applied to the experimental subjects, and subjecting the analyses that have been performed to critical review. In performing this function, the GAO has sometimes seemed to be following its traditional role as a kind of investigatory body, concerned with finding flaws in experimental procedures rather than asking whether the conclusions drawn are justified by the data and the analyses. Augmentation of the office's staff competence in social science methodology and statistics would probably improve its performance in the latter realm. Whatever the current limitations of the GAO, it is clear that the function its staff is trying to perform is essential to the field of social experimentation and that the Congress has every reason to want an independent body capable of reviewing the conclusions of the executive branch. The quality of the review and critique has to be equal to that of the original design, however, and the congressional agency should be prepared to discharge its responsibilities with high competence.

By way of concluding comment for this section, we emphasize two points. First, social experiments require research organizations of the highest quality, whose members will value their professional integrity and independence. Such individuals will not readily suppress data or analyses to satisfy the sponsoring agency, nor will they happily forego opportunities to extract the maximum amount of information from available data. This is as it should be. Yet, secondly, given the limitations of social science methodology, it seems wholly prudent for policymakers to encourage more than one analyst and more than one approach to a body of experimental data from which conclusions are to be drawn regarding public policy or social interventions. In fact, where crucial decisions are at stake it may even be wise to ask for replications of the experiment, and to scrutinize with special care experimental results that are inconsistent with conclusions reached by other methods and other investigators.

## Utilization

Finally, this chapter ends, as good experiments should end, with consideration of how the results of the experiment are to be used in program planning and policy formulation. Instead of the conventional remarks about clarity and simplicity in report writing, we should like to focus on the institutional features of utilization problems as they relate to a variety of experimental contexts. Several points are relevant.

First, the degree of decentralization of decision-making centers in the system is crucial to utilization. When decision making is *relatively* centralized, as in the case of Federal programs that are legislatively determined and executed by a single administrative agency, the results of experimentation are generally brought to bear through testimony in hearings, sometimes augmented by newspaper or magazine articles directed toward legislators and administrators, and by consultation with those who conducted the experiment as well as through the reading of their reports. Despite the apparent number of actors in this situation, the ones who are seriously involved can ordinarily be gathered together in a common meeting; they are linked by a chain of command (or at least of power); and the *range* of countervailing or discordant views is considerably less than in decentralized systems. In contrast, a system such as the public secondary and elementary educational system in this country is highly decentralized, and the power linkages between *any* experimenter and *all* the schools in the country is by definition weak or nonexistent. Utilization of results from an experiment must take quite a different form, and they closely resemble the problems of disseminating innovation in agriculture, for example, or in medicine. There are a large number of independent practitioners, they face various marketing conditions, and they have varying incentives to undertake innovation.

Second, the use of results of experiments for evaluation or planning can at times be quite direct and obvious. Following the Manhattan Bail Bond experiment, for example, the New York criminal court adopted a relaxed bail policy (the experimental treatment) for the kinds of offences considered in the experiment. Subsequently, judicial systems in at least three other cities used the results as evidence and guidance, changing their own bail requirements. Similarly, governmental agencies in other countries have adopted fertility control and education programs after experiments. Perhaps the most direct utilization has occurred in the case of experiments which appraise social science methods (rather than substance or theory) for achieving agency missions. For example, administrative changes followed soon after experimental investigations of different survey techniques and reporting methods conducted at the United States Census Bureau and other public and private information agencies. In these examples, incidentally, the relative costs and benefits of alternative programs could be estimated in a reasonably direct fashion and this probably facilitated active use of results.

Third, the institutional arrangements which provide insulation between experimenters and proponents of social action programs are beneficial in protecting the objectivity and integrity of the experiment; but they may also serve to insulate those who implement policy and design action programs from the results of experiments. Special efforts may be needed, at the conclusion of an experiment, to publicize its results among strategically chosen audiences, i.e., user systems. It may not be enough simply to publicize results (except in the case of negative ones, news of which is likely to travel fast and wide). Indeed it may be advisable to disseminate results actively, through informational meetings and seminars; by attention to the needs of potential user groups; by attempts to overcome obstacles to utilization, e.g., ignorance, resource constraints, bureaucratic regulations; and by providing incentives to utilization.

Fourth, in some cases, the process of direct utilization can be stimulated (and simultaneously evaluated) by a secondary sequence of experiments. Welch and Walberg (1970), for example, have fostered the dissemination and use of special high school curricula by building an incentive system for teachers (no-cost travel and consultation for user–trainees). The curriculum itself was tested in randomized field experiments and the utilization process involved experimental appraisal of the effects of the programmed dissemination. The effectiveness of different modes of encouraging the utilization of experimental research results was evaluated through field experiments; the modes included accessible data, consultants, and training workshops.

Fifth, while almost all experimental results are likely to need adaptation to the circumstances of a particular action practitioner or site, it is particularly likely in the case of distributed decision-makers and individual practitioners that the task of adaptation will be poorly done. Ordinarily an experimenter does not concern himself with the installation of a new program to whose design he has perhaps contributed only partly. If any "engineering" or adaptation for installation is undertaken, it is more likely to be done successfully in the context of centralized decision making and action responsibility. When, instead, a distributed system is involved, there are classically two modes of handling the problem. One is for the producer or marketer of a product (for example a new drug or a new computer) to supply personnel who help to choose the correct equipment for the problem at hand, advise on methods of its operation, train users, and make themselves available for further technical assistance. The second method, more favored by agencies in the public sector, appears to be to designate an "installation" role; hire and train a corps of persons to fill it; and provide the services as an adjunct to some other public sector venture—as in the example of the agricultural extension agent associated with an agricultural experiment station.

Sixth, one must be prepared for the possibility that the relationship between experimental results and possible subsequent action may not always be clear. At least one-quarter of the field experiments we have examined in preparing this volume are characterized by a good deal of ambiguity in the relation. It is quite difficult to tease out the extent to which political and economic values, competing experimental results, and other kinds of information are weighted into decisions, as against the results of some experiments.

The experiments that exhibit the most ambiguity in this regard are the ones that find no significant effect for the program under investigation. An experiment that indicates significant treatment effects does imply a clear decision; the implications of one that suggests that a current or new program is not particularly effective are not so clear. Usually, the null findings do not lead to the complete rejection or discontinuation of the program. In some cases, they have led to generation of new ideas; in other cases, only to a lowering of morale and an increased defensiveness on the part of action agency officers.

Inappropriate utilization of experimental results is rather difficult to define, much less detect. Judging from available data, premature usage and specious generalization are perhaps the most obvious hazards. The former has already been commented on. Specious generalization of experimental results is a more subtle phenomenon. Again, identifying instances in which experimental results are extended to irrelevant populations is difficult because little has done in the way of follow-up studies of social experiments. However, there have been experimental evaluations that demonstrated the researchers' awareness of the hazards and their ability to circumscribe the benefits of the experimental program in an effective way. Recent experiments by the personnel division of the American Telephone and Telegraph Company, for example, involve a strategy of repeated replication of experiments across organizational divisions, to assure the credibility and generalizability of the job enrichment program under scrutiny (Ford, 1969). The broad class of behavior modification experiments in the clinical areas (exemplified by Bandura, 1969) also depict a strong emphasis on sequential development of treatments and on sequential experimental testing of treatments in a variety of institutional environments.

Seventh, when experimental results show a null or a negative outcome—i.e., the proposed action program has no effect or undesirable effects—experimenters must be prepared to deal with the real-world consequences of such an outcome. Recall the remark near the beginning of this chapter that "mounting an experiment is a political act." The same is true of utilization of results. Almost any outcome of an experiment will contradict someone's opinions, and experience suggests that his attack will focus on the methodology of the study. Flaws in design or analyses are particularly meaty game because they are the property of experts. Disputes over methodology lie outside the comfortable competence of most policymakers and program managers, but they understandably become suspicious and reluctant to take decisions on the basis of evidence that is being coldly derided or hotly disputed by "experts."

Such disagreements can perhaps never be altogether avoided, as long as the experiment is concerned with important matters such as resources, careers, and emotional or ideological commitments. Nevertheless, we believe that the extent of disagreement and its damaging consequences for replanning can be mitigated if some effort is made *early in the development of the experiment* to anticipate the consequences of decisions based on a variety of outcomes of the experiment. These may be outlined during the design stages of the experiment, when participants, including those with vested interests in the program, agree on what constitutes evidence for labelling a program as "successful." Or, anticipatory strategy may evolve, as it often does, from the experiment itself, as experimental measurements reveal hostility, indifference, or naive enthusiasm among action agency workers, research subjects, and other participants. In any case all the experiments that we have examined suggest that experimental results are more likely to be used if clear and acceptable strategies are developed beforehand to facilitate the use of negative as well as positive findings.

Eighth, it is commonly believed that evidence from experiments is a weak weapon in combat with established and dedicated opposition. Yet experience suggests that experimental evidence may be just what is needed to overcome resistance from strong vested interest groups, e.g., the Manhattan Bail Bond experiment, where professional organizations of bail bondsmen actively opposed the selective relaxation of bail requirements.

Finally, while the foregoing observations center upon utilization of experimental results by individuals who are responsible for the maintenance of the program under examination, e.g., program managers, legislators, foundation officers, and the like, it should be noted that subjects (clients, recipients) of the program, can also use experiments. If, for example, a group of potential clients see some benefit in a program, they might use the experiment as evidence to justify the program's continuation. Or, there may be opportunity to use information from an experiment in class action suits against a publicly supported program that appears to be ineffective. Although survey data have been used as evidence in both legislative and judicial settings, the information resulting from field experiments has not frequently been so used. The continued use of the experimental method and the increasing sophistication of courts, legislatures, and the public may eventually result in a new type of utilization: one related as much to judicial decisions as to bureaucratic ones.

# VIII

## Human Values and Social Experimentation

This chapter covers two main topics—the ethical problems of experimentation and the problem of confidentiality of experimental data. There is a large and growing literature (scientific, philosophical, and legal) on the ethical problems of social research. Efforts to identify and resolve ethical issues in research on human subjects are evident in all of the social sciences. They include codes of ethics developed by professional organizations (e.g., the American Psychological Association, 1973), casebooks on ethical problems in experimentation with human beings (e.g., Katz, Capron, and Glass, 1972), essays on the character of ethical issues in applied social research (e.g., Kelman, 1968), and finally, research on, and articulation of, alternative strategies for resolving particular kinds of ethical problems in biomedical research (e.g., Shaw and Chalmers, 1970; Nejelski and Lerman, 1970; Zeisel, 1970; Barber, Lally, Makarushka, and Sullivan, 1973).

It would be quite impossible to summarize or evaluate all of this literature here. The present discussion must, therefore, take as its guiding principle the special characteristics and problems of experiments designed to evaluate social programs and the relation of such experiments to the areas of research ethics and confidentiality.

245

*Ethical Problems*

THE ETHICAL STATUS OF THE PROPOSED PROGRAM

It is difficult to separate the ethical problems of a proposed social program from the ethical problems of an experimental evaluation of this program, if only because the evaluation involves a controlled trial of the program itself. Nevertheless, it is worthwhile for the researcher to ask at the outset whether the proposed program involves ethical problems such as possible harmful side effects, "withdrawal effects" at the end of the program, or unwarranted intrusion into the lives of program participants.

Most social programs are designed to help some client population and the question of whether they may instead be harmful to this population or to others will not normally arise. However, expensive and well-intentioned programs sometimes do turn out to have a net adverse effect. For example, a large public housing project (Pruitt-Igoe in St. Louis) has recently been largely abandoned because it proved to have been designed in a way that encouraged a high crime rate and other forms of social disorganization. The project is now being rebuilt with half the buildings demolished and the rest reduced in size and remodelled.

This example involves unanticipated side effects of a program, and in many cases it is not clear that such effects can be avoided by any amount of prior introspection. Somewhat easier to anticipate is the question of "manipulation" of participants in the program. Does the proposed program involve benefits only at an excessive cost in the external direction of the lives and behavior of participants? For example, one might want to reject a proposed program of recreational activities for teen-agers if the content of the activities were rigidly prescribed by national guidelines that left no room to reflect the preferences of the local community or the program participants. Recent British criticism of the television program *Sesame Street* involved this issue of an unacceptable degree of "manipulation."

The problems just considered are likely to be somewhat less severe or more easily anticipated in a program subjected to experimental tests than in an operating program that is introduced by administrative action or by law, without prior experimentation. This is true first because the launching of experiments, more than in the case of nonexperimental programs, usually involves a careful and dispassionate consideration of alternatives. It is true also because experiments tend to begin on a smaller scale and involve the explicit measurement of outcomes. They therefore may permit detection of unforeseen adverse effects before substantial damage has been done. On the other hand, there may be less opportunity for community participation in an experiment than in an operating program, and this could reduce the ability to anticipate problems.

We suggest that before policymakers and researchers undertake an experimental program they should satisfy themselves that the program will, with high probability, provide benefits that will outweigh any foreseeable adverse side effects or any loss of initiative or freedom of program participants. Clearly this asks for a subjective judgment that will be made differently by different social scientists and policymakers. What seems an important benefit to one may seem trivial to another. What one experimenter sees as a real threat to freedom may be seen by his colleagues as fanciful or ephemeral. The best advice we can offer for resolving such differences is that it is best to discuss them openly and systematically.

The most promising procedure so far devised for the consideration of the ethical problems of research or of new operating programs involving human beings is the peer-group review, where the term *peer* refers primarily but not exclusively to the scientific peers of the researchers. This procedure is already well established at most universities and other large institutions doing research under government grants and contracts, because it is required by the United States Department of Health, Education, and Welfare and may soon be required by other granting and contracting agencies.

Peer-group review requires that the institution have a review committee made up of people (preferably from its own staff if the institution is large enough) whose maturity, experience, and expertise will command respect, and who have varying backgrounds. The committee must initially approve all projects involving potential risks to human subjects and must continue to monitor those projects that in its judgment involve actual risks. The range of problems that must be considered by such a committee are not confined to those included in this section; they include most of those touched on in this chapter.

We do not consider peer-group review to be in any way *absolute* protection against unethical experimentation. Not only do committees make mistakes but there are no objective standards by which to judge conclusively when mistakes have been made. Nevertheless, peer-group review is a *substantial* protection against the poor judgment or over-zealousness of the individual researcher or project team, and it is one that we strongly recommend where it is not already required.

The protection offered by peer-group review is likely to be weak in small or new research organizations, including those organized for profit. In such cases the desire to promote or maintain the goals of the organization or to ensure its survival may bias judgments about ethical problems. In cases involving research organizations whose scientific integrity is not yet well established and recognized, we recommend that the sponsoring agency require that some or all of the members of the review committee be chosen from outside the organization performing the research. Procedures for choosing such members should be prescribed by the sponsoring agency.

When "open-air" experiments are to be carried out in a community, we also recommend that members of the community be involved in the prior review of possible ethical problems, either through membership on the review committee or through a separate procedure; that is, the review should involve the peers of the subjects as well as the peers of the researchers. If there is a single well-recognized organization that can speak for the community, its leaders should be consulted. If not, the researchers can consult a variety of community leaders, including clergymen and elected officals, such as councilmen or aldermen.

We recognize that any such review process may mean that some valuable scientific experiments will not be conducted or may have to be moved to alternative sites. This is a risk that must be faced.

DAMAGING TREATMENTS

The problem of damaging experimental treatments arises most frequently in the context of biomedical research, in which subjects may be subjected to pain or physical deprivation, given potent drugs or deliberately infected with living organisms. Somewhat similar problems arise in psychological experiments that could cause subjects to feel severe humiliation, embarrassment, or loss of self-esteem.

Analogous problems seem much less likely to arise in the experimental evaluation of social programs. The treatment in these experiments usually involves the provision of some presumably valuable good or service (housing, money, training, or counseling, for example). Ordinarily the worst outcome that could be expected is that the treatment is useless (those who receive counseling or training do no better than those who do not).

However, we have learned of one case in which it became clear during the course of a social experiment that the treatment was damaging. A program designed to reduce juvenile delinquency was in fact resulting in more delinquency in experimental areas than existed in untreated control areas—an outcome that could not have been anticipated at the outset. The solution was to drop the experimental program before the end of the planned experimental period.

This example says as much, or more, about the dangers of *not* experimenting as it says about the dangers of experimentation. There are two alternatives to an experimental evaluation. One is never to try the program at all; the other is to introduce it as a nonexperimental operating program, to be evaluated in some other way. Suppose that this delinquency prevention program had been introduced in all areas of the city. Any subsequent rise in delinquency might then have been attributed to external causes, and it might have taken much longer to discover that the program was in fact counter productive.

Although it is seldom likely that experimental social reforms will prove damaging to the subjects, there may be incidental features of the experiment other than the main treatment that could be considered damaging. For example, generalized preemployment training that improves the speech and dress of lower-class girls may increase their employability but might also alienate them from their families or friends. In a large Income Maintenance experiment, some members of the research staff proposed to take blood samples from the experimental subjects. The proposal was rejected by the whole staff as a needless intrusion into the privacy of the subjects, one that they might properly resent. However, if the proposed procedure had been more closely related to the main purpose of the experiment (for example, if the experiment had been concerned with adequacy of nutrition) the collection of blood samples from informed and consenting subjects might have been entirely justified. The question of informed consent is further discussed later in this chapter.

## THE FAILURE TO PROVIDE BENEFITS
## TO UNTREATED GROUPS

Many social programs are, or are perceived to be, highly beneficial to those that participate in them. However, the experimental evaluation of such a program involves a random allocation of this benefit between a treatment group and an untreated control group. This allocation may be viewed as arbitrary or unfair by those who believe that the benefit should be allocated on some other basis, such as merit or need.

We should like to make several comments about this problem. First, the problem is less acute the less clearly it is known in advance that the proposed program is beneficial. If it were known for certain that the program was beneficial, there might be no need to experiment at all. (The exceptions are cases where an experiment is designed to choose between alternative benficial programs or where the treatment is clearly beneficial to the subjects but involves unknown costs that they do not bear.) The more doubt there is about the efficacy of the program or about its superiority over existing alternatives, the less severe the moral dilemma, if any, created by the scientific need for random assignment.

Similarly, the severity of any ethical problem is reduced if measures of merit or need are inaccurate. If different observers cannot agree on who is needy or deserving, the moral case for random assignment is stronger.

There are some experiments where neither of these considerations is persuasive, such as the Income Maintenance experiments. Here the nature of the treatment, the transfer of substantial sums of money, ensures that both subjects and experimenters will perceive a substantial advantage in being in the treatment group rather than in the control group. Measures of preexperiment income and family size furnish a clear, if not entirely accurate, scaling of need. In such a case, the scarcity of resources furnishes a moral case for randomization. The experimenters clearly lack the resources to help all poor people; randomization may therefore be as fair a way as any of selecting a small group to receive benefits.

The clearest case we have encountered posing an ethical problem because benefits are not given to the control group is the nutrition experiment being conducted by the Institute of Nutrition of Central America and Panama (INCAP). The purpose of this experiment is to determine whether feeding protein supplements to pregnant women and small children will improve the mental development of children. The experiment involves two experimental and two control villages; in the control villages pregnant women and small children receive a vitamin-enriched soft drink with no protein value.

The issue arises here because the treatment (protein supplement) is known to have beneficial effects on physical development, whatever its effects on mental development may be. It can be argued that it is immoral to fail to provide the protein supplement in those villages where the added cost of doing so would be very small, once the feeding stations and research staffs have been established. But to do so would, of course, nullify the whole experiment. It would be impossible to procure information about the effects of protein supplement on *mental* development. It can also be argued that the people of the control villages are no more deprived than those of hundreds of other Central American villages not involved in the experiment and that the sponsors of the program clearly do not have enough resources to introduce mass protein-feeding programs in all of the villages where deficiencies exist. Furthermore, unless the experiment is performed and yields positive results, the only basis for making a protein supplement feeding program the vehicle of choice for improving *mental* development is faith. In this experiment the "social benefits" that follow from bringing together mothers and children in the community, from psychological testing, and from vitamin supplementation of the soft drink accrue to control villages as much as to the experimental villages. Nevertheless, some moral uneasiness remains. We are not all of the same view on these issues, and we commend them to the reader for his careful consideration.

Where the necessity for admitting the neediest or the best-qualified to an experimental program is compelling, we recommend the use of specially designed experiments that meet research objectives in a partial way without violating ethical sensibilities. For example, suppose that people are being selected for admission to an experimental training program on the basis of test scores. One can develop a threshold experiment in which it is decided that those with scores of 100 or above *must* be admitted on merit while those with scores of 90 below will not be able to benefit from the program. Should there be more applicants with scores between 90 and 100 than can be accommodated, instead of using an intermediate cutting score such as 95, we would propose the random assignment of those with scores between 90 and 100 to an experimental and a control group, so that a true experimental test of the program is still possible (Zeisel, 1970; also Chapter IV this volume). It should be clear, however, that the decision to admit all those with scores of 100 or above has reduced the power of the experiment and the ability to generalize from it. It is possible to tell whether or not the experimental program helped those within the threshold range of test scores but not possible to tell as clearly how much it helped those with scores of 100 or above, since no such people were selected as controls. Nor is it possible to tell if the program could have helped those with scores below 90, since they were excluded from both groups.

In some cases it may be possible to design true experiments in which there are no controls, but there are two or more treatments. The question then becomes not, Does the treatment work? but, Which treatment works best? In situations for which a variety of competing treatments have been proposed, this solution has obvious appeal. However, it also has a serious difficulty. If two treatments are tested and produce similar outcomes, one may not be able to distinguish between the hypotheses that they are equally effective and that they are equally ineffective. This difficulty can often be overcome by adequate pretest and post-test measures for both groups.

## THE PROBLEMS OF TEMPORARY BOONS

All experiments with which we are familiar have been conducted for a limited period of time. It would be theoretically possible to fund an experiment in which the treated group was given the treatment for as long as they wanted it or as long as their need persisted. In most cases such an experiment would actually give a better measure than a short experiment of the effects of a proposed permanent social reform. The barrier to doing things in this way has been its very substantial additional cost over giving a boon for a limited period. More consideration should be given to duration of treatment as an experimental variable than has typically been given in social experiments. At the limit, this could include giving some random subset of subjects a permanent or lifetime program of benefit, without rights of descendants and heirs. However, the benefits of such a procedure are primarily scientific rather than ethical.

It is sometimes felt that it is unethical to make people better off temporarily and then return them to their original condition. The experimenter is accused of "playing God" and of leaving subjects feeling themselves to be worse off than if they had never participated in the experiment in the first place.

The merit of this contention depends in part on the nature of the experimental treatment. Where the treatment involves training, counseling, or physical rehabilitation of some sort, it is presumed, or at least hoped, that it will leave the subject permanently better off because of his enhanced skills or capacities, so that the end of the program does not involve the withdrawal of the boon. Even where the treatment consists of cash grants, as in the Income Maintenance experiments, some subjects may be permanently better off. Some may use their grants to finance training or to purchase durable goods that will last beyond the end of the experiment. The subject indeed has the option of saving and investing all of his grant and consuming only the income on this investment, though in reality this is quite unlikely. He is more likely to have used his payments to reduce debts, and in this way to come out of the experiment in a better financial position than when he entered.

Where the subject is clearly informed (as we believe he should be) of the limited duration of the treatment, the judgment as to whether participation will make him better off in the long run is probably best left to him. If he feels that it does not, he can refuse to participate.

Some subjects may later come to regret their decision to participate, but one cannot hope to provide complete protection against regret.

As a temporary experiment draws to a close, the researchers should make sure that subjects are aware of its approaching end and should offer them assistance, if possible, in making any needed transition. The nature and feasibility of such assistance would of course vary widely, depending on the nature of the experimental treatment.

It should be clear that, moral considerations aside, the scientific power of the temporary experiment (its ability to predict correctly the effects of a permanent program) can often be increased by misleading the subjects. If subjects were informed (or rather misinformed) at the outset that the treatment would continue indefinitely or as long as it was needed, their behavior would more closely simulate that of people affected by a permanent social reform having the same characteristics as the experimental treatment. We reject such deception as inconsistent with the doctrine of informed consent to be discussed later in this chapter.

In some cases, a temporary experiment may bring changes into the lives of people other than the subjects, for example, the teachers, social workers, or other members of teams administering the treatment. Their work may become more interesting during an experiment, and they may feel let down when it is over. The organizations in charge of experiments should consider the possibility of such effects and ways of alleviating them. One device that is sometimes appropriate is to involve the action team in the preparation or review of reports of the experiment.

INFORMED CONSENT AND DECEPTION

There is now wide acceptance of the doctrine that experiments on human subjects should be performed only with the informed consent of the subjects. There is perhaps equally wide disagreement about what this doctrine should mean in particular cases.

The problem arises most clearly in biomedical experiments in which subjects are exposed to risks of pain, injury, or disease. The prevailing view is that the subject should be given a realistic appraisal of such risks and that there should be a chance of benefit great enough to outweigh substantially the risks involved.

There are few precise analogues to this situation in social experiments. Training, counseling, cash grants, and the similar treatments involved in typical social experiments do not usually pose hazards against which subjects must be warned, other than the risk that a subject will have wasted his time if treatment is ineffective. However, in some cases the experimental treatment will be distinctly less effective than the routine alternate or control treatment and the subject will be worse off for having participated in it. In the original plans for experiments on health insurance (not actually implemented), participants were to have been given payments to induce them to take experimental forms of insurance coverage, some of which would not have protected them as fully against particular risks as the insurance they originally held. In particular cases, the subject might have been worse off even though the payments exceeded the actuarial value of the coverage that was to be discontinued. This is an instance in which fairness requires that the subject understand fully the risks involved in entering the experiment.

One would not expect a subject to agree to participate in training or counseling without being told something about the nature of the program he was being asked to enter. The question of how detailed such information must be depends on how such information would influence the effectiveness of the treatment, and on the age and educational level of the subject. In enrolling subjects, one should generally be prepared to furnish detailed information if it is requested, but it may be unwise to try to provide details to those who have stated that they are not interested in them. Subjects who develop doubts during the course of an experiment should be given an opportunity to request further information as the treatment proceeds.

A related question arises as to whether the controls should be told that they are controls. Presumably the controls are being observed or interviewed, but not otherwise treated. They could be left with the impression that they were involved in survey research rather than in an experiment. If they are specifically told that they are controls, it becomes obvious to them that they are not being given a possibly beneficial treatment that is being received by others in similar circumstances. We do not see any general obligation to inform controls that they are controls, particularly if they are being compensated in some way for their cooperation. In those cases when for some reason it is advisable to tell controls that they are controls, it would seem best to inform all members of the subject population about the nature of the experiment and about the chances of falling into the experimental group, before the assignment of subjects to experimental and control groups is made.

In some experiments it is highly important that the subject not know whether he is in the treatment or the control group. This is the reason for the use of placebos in medical experiments, where the placebo is an inert or innocuous substance or procedure made to look, taste, or feel exactly like the drug or procedure being tested. The need for the placebo arises because a patient's mere belief that he is receiving an efficacious treatment can temporarily produce an improvement in his condition. An additional measure of protection against error is afforded in the "double blind" experiment, in which neither the researcher nor the subject knows during the experiment which subjects are receiving the treatment and which the placebo. Such experiments are common in medical research and often expose the extent to which a placebo treatment is as effective in relieving a patient's distress as is an experimental treatment (Katz, Capron, and Glass, 1972).

We all know that there are analogues in social experiments to the effects of placebos. These are often called "Hawthorne effects," after the Hawthorne Works of Western Electric Company in Chicago, where it was found that the mere observation and measurement of groups of workers in productivity experiments improved their performance, even when objective working conditions were made less favorable by, for example, reducing the intensity of lighting. Not only is the social analogue to the *effects* of placebos common, but there is an analogue in social experiments to the placebo itself. This is the minimal alternative treatment of a control group. One example is the Preschool Education experiment (Palmer, 1973), in which a treatment group of 2-and 3-year-olds was given individual teaching using a new curriculum being tested, while one control group was given the same number of teaching sessions in which the teacher merely reacted to the child's initiatives. In this particular case, the minimal treatment proved to be as effective as the experimental treatment.

The control value of minimal treatment is of course destroyed if the subject knows that the treatment is considered minimal, that is, that the researchers believe the minimal treatment to be relatively ineffective. He cannot then serve as a control for psychological pseudo-effects of the treatment. If the deception involved in the use of minimal treatments is viewed as unethical by some researchers (a view that we do not share), the best course would be to tell the whole subject population that only some will receive the stronger treatment, before the experimental and control subjects are chosen.

# Confidentiality and Disclosure of Identity

## THE NATURE OF THE PROBLEM

The questions of privacy and confidentiality are closely related. Issues of privacy are involved in the process of observation or data gathering when a researcher intrudes on the physical isolation or private activities or beliefs of a research subject or group. More generally, privacy could be violated by asking respondents to divulge views or facts that they do not care to share with others. Where such issues are raised in experiments, they can be dealt with by obtaining the informed consent of subjects in advance and by preserving the right of individual subjects to withdraw from experiments while they are in progress, or to refuse to answer particular questions.

The problem of confidentiality arises when there is a request during the course of research or afterward that information about a particular subject or respondent be divulged in a way that permits him to be identified. In the course of experiments and other studies in the social sciences, researchers often acquire information that could be embarrassing or incriminating to subjects or respondents if disclosed. For example, it might become known that respondents failed to pay taxes, gave or accepted bribes, or engaged in homosexual activities. Such ordinary statistical information as annual income can become evidence of failure to pay income taxes, if it can be collated with the respondent's tax returns.

Although the most dramatic danger to respondents is that of criminal prosecution, this is by no means the only one. Others range from loss of employment to social ostracism or loss of face with friends and neighbors, if embarassing material is disclosed.

It is of course routine for a researcher to promise subjects and respondents that information collected during a study will be kept confidential to the best of the researcher's ability, and that the identity of respondents will not be made public. Researchers have a strict moral and professional obligation to keep this promise. However, there are circumstances in which the researcher may find it difficult, or even impossible, to keep his promises. One of the most important of these is when the data in his possession are subpoenaed by a legislative committee or by judicial authorities.

In recent years there have been several cases in which government authorities have attempted to secure confidential data from social science researchers, and at least one in which they have succeeded in doing so (Walsh, 1969). Two of the attempts concerned an Income Maintenance experiment from which confidential information was sought by a powerful member of a United States Senate committee and by a county grand jury. Experimental evaluations may be more vulnerable than other kinds of social science research to attempts to breach confidentiality. Their large scale often attracts the attention of legislative bodies and prosecutors, and political controversy over the programs being evaluated can also induce attempts to obtain confidential data that might seem to discredit the results of the experiment.

THE CONFLICT OF RIGHTS

The issue of confidentiality is a difficult one because it involves conflicts among several sets of rights and obligations claimed or asserted by different parties. We shall try to identify these rights and some of the areas of conflict.

First there is the right of the subject to confidentiality and the obligation of the researcher to protect it. Second, there is the right of society to the kind of knowledge that can be obtained through social science research and used to develop better social programs. If research subjects and respondents become sufficiently concerned about breaches of confidentiality, much of such research might become impossible and the knowledge that could be gained from it would be lost. These two sets of rights have led researchers to resist requests for confidential information.

On the other hand, there is the responsibility of the police, the prosecutors, and the courts to detect and punish crime, and the right of society to be protected from it. One can imagine circumstances in which a social scientist might agree that this set of rights was paramount— for example, if in the course of research a social scientist had discovered the identity of the Boston strangler before he had been caught. In general, however, subjects or respondents in social science research ought not, merely because they are respondents, to be at greater risk of having petty crimes detected than the population at large. If participation in surveys or experiments brings real risk of identification and exposure, it is unlikely that there will be participation of representative samples of the population, and society will therefore be deprived of useful information.

Finally, there is the right of the public to have access to information resulting from the expenditure of public funds or the funds of private, tax-exempt institutions. This right must be given special weight when the purpose of the research is to help resolve important questions of public policy.

In the process of keeping the public informed, newspapers, television broadcasters, and other news media may attempt to obtain interviews with respondents or subjects in social research or experiments. Journalists usually want "human interest stories" rather than mere statistics, and the release of some personal information may only whet their appetites for more. It is tempting for researchers or their sponsoring agencies to be as cooperative as possible with the news media, since cooperation can result in coverage that gives the experiment wide, and perhaps favorable, publicity. In our judgment, this temptation must be resisted at all costs. Under no circumstances should researchers disclose the names and addresses of their respondents to the news media, even when they are threatened with unfavorable publicity or editorial censure for refusal to cooperate. Journalists should have some sympathy with this position, for it is similar to their own position regarding the confidentiality of news sources—the view that disclosure of identity of informants would have a "chilling effect" on the flow of information to the press.

There may be classes of cases where the public "right to know" includes the right to know about named individuals, organizations, or products. For example, if research on a product sold to consumers demonstrates that the product is worthless or dangerous, it is reasonable to conclude that consumers should be told the identity of the product. This argument for disclosure of identity is far less powerful when the individual involved is a private citizen drawn into a social scientist's sample by some random sampling process. We quite agree that in this case the public has the right to know the results of the research, including general statistical information about the composition of the sample. At the conclusion of the research, data from which individual identification has been removed should be available to other researchers for secondary analysis. However, none of this involves anyone outside the original research team knowing the identity of the individual subjects. Where the identity of respondents could be inferred from particular constellations of responses, data should be made available only through a mediating institution (a data repository) that will take proper precautions to prevent identification by such means.

TECHNIQUES FOR PROTECTING PRIVACY

In this section we consider briefly two types of solutions to the problems of protecting respondent privacy. The first, for want of a better term, is called "mechanical solutions," the second, "legal protection."

*Mechanical Solutions.*  The main burden of the argument is that the mechanical solutions offer more protection for the postexperiment storage of information than they do for research activities during the experiment itself, and that, indeed, for many experiments they are a less desirable class of solutions than legal protection.

There are a variety of mechanical strategies for assuring confidentiability of data during the experiment; their appropriateness depends mainly on the structure of the experimental program and of the experimental design. At the simplest level, good practice requires good physical security for records containing identification and information on personal attributes of individuals. More elaborate systems for safeguarding data may depend on administrative or technical tactics employed during the information collection process. For example, one might encourage participants in a methadone treatment experiment to use aliases, to assure that the questionnaires they complete and return to the researchers are characterized by some degree of anonymity without jeopordizing the continuity of research records. If interviews regarding sensitive behavior are necessary in the research, one might employ one of the recently developed statistical methods for assuring confidentiality. These methods involve eliciting information in a way that allows the experimenter to estimate proportions (and other statistics) of interviewees in a particular sample who have a potentially stigmatizing characteristic, but they preclude the ability to link an identified individual with a particular item of information (Greenberg, 1970).

More elaborate variations on these mechanical devices have been developed and used in collecting sensitive information from respondents in social surveys and small experiments. But they will not always be appropriate for use during experimental assessments of large social programs. The need to make periodic checks on the validity and reliability of the data collected during the experiment, the critical requirement for continuous linkage among sets of data collected on the same individuals over an extended time period, and other factors argue against the use of aliases or similar devices for ensuring confidentiality. The statistical methods usually require much larger sample sizes in the survey or experiment in which they are employed in order to detect program effects at a reasonable level of confidence. And the statistical methods do require additional testing to ensure the credibility of results. In either case, the special procedures necessary to implement some of the novel methods of eliciting information can increase the cost of the research and complicate technical and managerial efforts to elicit, collect, and consolidate information in the experiment.

To summarize, it appears to us that, during the course of an experiment lasting several years, researchers must have data in accessible and verifiable form. Moreover, it is during this period, rather than after it, that the threat to the confidentiality of data is likely to be most severe. It is our impression that mechanical protection of experimental data will frequently be impractical during the very period when the risks of disclosure of identity are the greatest.

*Legal Protection.* In this section we consider two kinds of legal protection of the confidentiality of research data. The first is protection against subpoena, often known as testimonial privilege. The second is legal penalities for unauthorized disclosure.

There are several situations in which a person in possession of information is legally protected from having to divulge it, even in a court proceeding. The most important and general of these privileges are those of a husband or wife to refuse to testify against his or her spouse, the right of a priest not to testify against a penitent, and the right of a lawyer not to testify against his client. The right of a journalist not to divulge his news sources has been claimed as an extension of the freedom of the press, but has not usually been respected by the courts.

At the present time, no general protection exists for respondents or subjects in social science research. A few states protect the relationship of psychologists and their patients, but this relates to clinical rather than social psychologists. The United States Bureau of the Census is *obligated* by law to protect the confidentiality of its data. The Secretary of Health, Education, and Welfare is *authorized* to give such protection to data on drug abuse gathered in research pursuant to the Drug Prevention and Control Act of 1970 and the Alcholism Rehabilitation Act of 1970, and to extend this protection to data gathered by contractors and grantees. (The distinction between obligation and authorization is of some importance.) There is also a statutory basis for protection of data gathered under the Social Security Act, and the Department of Health, Education, and Welfare has tried to extend this to contractors by provisions in its contracts.

Beyond this, social scientists have no firm legal protection to offer their respondents or subjects, even when the researchers are government employees, contractors, or grantees. They can claim, and in a few cases have claimed, a testimonial privilege between researcher and subject, but this claim must be based on constitutional rights or common law rather than on statute law, and there is no assurance that it will be respected. A social scientist who refuses to honor a court order to disclose confidential data supplied to him by the subjects of research could be punished for contempt. We know of no case in which such punishment has been carried out, but the possibility is not remote.

We recommend strongly that the data collected by social scientists in survey research and in experimental studies be protected by law against disclosure. We recognize that this recommendation creates problems that deserve careful study. Lawyers are easily defined through their admission to the bar; social scientists are less strictly defined. Nevertheless, some legal definition should be possible, in terms of the training, degrees, and publications of the principal investigators or of the accreditation of the sponsoring institution.

Where there is doubt, we would err in the direction of breadth. For example, it is sometimes suggested that protection be given only to studies conducted or funded by the United States government. Presumably, such studies in some sense most clearly serve the public interest, and thus have values that can counterweigh such opposing values as detecting and punishing crime. But it is also true that some areas important to science and policy may not be studied by government because they are politically sensitive. Moreover, in some areas, especially those involving unpopular beliefs, government sponsorship of a study could be a disadvantage.

Legislation creating a researcher–subject privilege should extend to the data themselves rather than merely covering the person who gathers them. Social science researchers are unlike lawyers, priests, or psychiatrists, whose confidential information is often in their heads or in personal private files. Members of these professions have high status and prestige, which has helped to win testimonial privilege for their professions. Social science data usually come to rest in large organizations, no member of whose staff, however humble his position, should be required to divulge them.

We are sometimes told that creating a researcher–subject privilege by legislation is a hopeless task because it will require 51 laws, 1 Federal and 1 for each state. We reject this as a counsel of despair. Full coverage might take a long while, but one must begin somewhere, and some protection is better than none.

Full legal protection of confidentiality should include legal penalties for a member of a social science research staff who discloses the identity of subjects. This provision would parallel the existing Census law. It seems a logical obligation to place on research staffs as a counterpart to the testimonial privilege.

In recommending legislation to prevent the disclosure of data gathered in studies by qualified social scientists, we are in part urging protection of our own professional interests, and in part the protection of the people who are the subjects of our studies. But the real benefits go far beyond this. They are the possibility of more rational and effective social and economic policies than we have had in the past, based on the experimental evaluation of new social programs.

## Ensuring Confidentiality and Data Access

Experimental data are expensive to collect; they should not be discarded after the original analysis. Furthermore, alternative analyses of such data and interpretation of results can have a vital bearing on important questions of social policy. Finally, the data can often be reanalyzed to illuminate fundamental scientific as well as practical questions. For all these reasons, it is desirable that both administrative and research files be made maximally available after the original analysis, for use by other investigators and for other purposes, insofar as this does not jeopardize confidentiality of records maintained on particular individuals. The importance of critical reanalyses must not violate the promises given to the respondent regarding confidentiality, nor increase his risk of blackmail, invidious gossip, or other damage that might come from identifying his person with the information provided. At the same time, data should not be withheld until past the time when their reanalysis might affect public policy through reinterpretation of results. In this respect the OEO has pursued an admirable policy of the prompt release of research data for reanalysis (exemplified by OEO Headstart and performance contracting data, and promised for the Negative Income Tax experiment).

This section addresses two common types of outside use of files: intrasystem analysis and intersystem linkage and analysis. It assumes the existence of confidential data files, with individual identifiers attached, incorporating data resulting from an experiment or archival or institutional records that can be used for statistical analysis.

INTRASYSTEM ANALYSIS BY OUTSIDERS

In what follows, five procedures are briefly considered for assuring outside researchers' access to data without compromising confidentiality requirements: deletion of identifiers; crude report categories for, and restriction of, public variables; microaggregation; error inoculation; and in-file capacity to run outsiders' statistical analysis. (For detailed description of strategies and their vulnerability, see Boruch, 1972a, 1972b).

*Deletion of Identifiers.* In releasing data for reanalysis, a basic strategy for assuring confidentiality is deleting the names, social security numbers, and street addresses from the data released on individuals. In some settings this may provide sufficient protection, provided that release does not increase the chances of the respondent's loss of privacy nor increase the risks of breach of confidentiality. In deciding whether it will, two features seem crucial: the number of the items of information in the record on each person and the availability of some of the same items of information on other public lists with names attached. For example, deletion of identifiers might be sufficient for release of anonymous records on a 1% sample of the 1970 Census or Social Security Administration files, because of the extremely scattered nature of the sample and the absence of parallel lists. However, even here, for a low-frequency, but visibly listed profession such as M.D.s, if census tract, age, and speciality are given, individual identification could frequently be made and the other information on the record could be identified with the person, thus making it possible for a corrupt user to infringe upon the doctor's privacy (Hansen, 1971).

Where the research population is compact, and where some of the variables are conveniently recorded with names on public or semipublic lists, the deletion of identifiers is still less adequate. Thus, for a study conducted within a single school, just the date and state of birth can be sufficient for indirect disclosure of identification of an "anonymous" student record.

*Crude Report Categories and Public Variables.* For those data in the confidential file which are also readily available elsewhere with names attached (*common*, usually *public*, *variables*), very crude report categories should be used in the data released: e.g., county rather than census-tract, year of birth rather than date, profession but not speciality within profession, and so on. For variables unique to the research project (*unique variables*) which therefore do not exist on other lists with names attached, this precaution is not necessary. Thus for a multi-item attitude test, individual item responses and exact total scores can be made available without jeopardizing confidentiality. (Such data probably *should* be made available because of their relevance to the estimation of error for use in generating alternate statistical analyses of the same data, an issue of ever increasing concern.)

With a large number of gross categories on common variables, such as geographic area, level of education, and age, combinations emerge in which only one or two persons occur, and discovery of individual identity becomes possible. To reduce the likelihood of such indirect disclosure, there should be a restriction on the minimum cell sizes of the full combination of public variables. For example, the rule might be adopted that there should be no combination of public variables yielding a frequency of less than five persons (see Hoffman and Miller, 1970; Hansen, 1971, for discussion of such rules). Before criteria of restriction are chosen, their utility in hindering indirect disclosure should be tested, using actual data and actual public variables.

*Microaggregation.* The idea of microaggregation is to construct average (synthetic) persons from data on individuals and to release the data on these, rather than on individuals. Thus instead of releasing data on the 1200 participants, of the Negative Income Tax experiment, one might group them into 240 sets of 5 each, and release average data on every variable for each set. The outside user could then do all of his secondary analyses on these 240 synthetic persons.

Feige and Watts (1970) and their colleagues have done such analyses on Federal Reserve data on banks and have been able to compare microaggregate analyses with individual data analyses. Their conclusion is clear that such microaggregation is much more useful than no release at all. It does result in a loss of efficiency, but does not necessarily bias estimates of important parameters. For most conceivable groupings of variables, anonymity and confidentiality are preserved at the individual level.

For reasons of efficiency, Feige and Watts recommend flexible microaggregation, choosing the bases so that later statistical analyses will yield accurate and reasonably precise results. This requires that the agency maintaining the archival data file also maintain some statistical analysis capacity. If this is done, the capacity may be very nearly as much as would be required for doing the customer's analyses for him internally, releasing only the statistical indices, as described in the following.

*Error Inoculation.*    There are methods for collecting and storing information about private, sensitive, or incriminating characteristics of individuals that depend on deliberately inoculating error into individual records while leaving the aggregate data unchanged. Two general approaches are involved: adding random error whose distribution and parameters are specified beforehand, and random score substitution.

The former approach is suitable for continuous variables such as age, years of education, purchase cost of house, etc. The analyst generates a set of "error terms" with mean of zero and a small variance, and simply assigns an error term at random to each individual response. Thus, individual responses are *guaranteed* to be randomly inaccurate.

A similar result is obtained from random score substitution, which is suitable for dichotomous variables or category systems that cannot be connected into continuous variables. But, instead of adding a random error term to the stored data, the analyst uses a random method to decide whether an incorrect designation should be attached to an individual name and, if so, which of several incorrect designations it is to be. The random method can be designed to inoculate a specified rate of error into individual entries while leaving the original overall distribution of categorical designations undistorted. (Details of technique can be found in Boruch, 1972a.)

Under an error inoculation scheme, the individual's privacy cannot be fully protected since damage from gossip and the threat of blackmail may be based upon randomly produced misinformation as well as upon valid information. Therefore, the nature of the procedure has to be made clear and public so that all parties understand the guaranteed incorrectness of individual records. In addition, identifiers should of course be eliminated. Public variables should almost certainly be error-inoculated, with enough error so that all individual records contain some imperfection on at least one of the public variables. That is, a file interrogator who has complete lists on all the public variables should not be able to make exact matches. Perhaps under these conditions, unique variables, even those with sensitive or incriminating information, could be spared error inoculation.

The process of error inoculation decreases the likelihood of disclosure of identifiable information, but has undesirable side effects. Like the microaggregation technique, it generally increases the overall variance by a predictable amount and attenuates statistical indices of relationships (e.g., correlation coefficients, regression coefficients, slopes, and test statistics) a predictable and correctable amount, for those relationships where the ordinary linear statistical model holds. While error inoculation methods decrease efficiency of estimation, one can still obtain unbiased estimates of important parameters for the data by using the known properties of the inoculated error. The methods used are an expedient safeguard that still permits valuable reanalyses to be done.

*Capacity to Run Statistical Analyses for Outsiders.*   One of the desirable features of a useful set of Federal data archives would be that each archival agency have a statistical analysis capacity that could be made available, at cost, to qualified research workers and under suitable safeguards. Furthermore, social policy and Federal programs would benefit if nongovernmental archives with large relevant record sets had a similar capacity to allow their files to be used as adjunctive data in social experiments. For example, the records of Blue Cross–Blue Shield and other carriers of medical, automobile, or life insurance could all be made accessible for this purpose, perhaps merely assuring that each has a statistician and a computer programmer capable of responding to legitimate and appropriate research requests for the purchase of statistical analyses.

Where summary statistics on continuous data (e.g., correlations) are the output, no problems are met. Where the user requests data on specific cells specified by public variables, there should be no output provided where the public variable cell size is less than five. Where an outside user is able to request repeated separate analyses, he might be able to decode data on a single person by using his public variable knowledge to move that person from one cell to another in two subsequent analyses, keeping the other people intact, learning that one person's data by a sequential, 20-questions stratagem. This may be so unlikely in some cases as not to be worth worrying about. On the other hand, if indirect disclosure of this sort is a hazard, the precaution of deleting one or more persons at random from each cell (deleting a different person for each reanalysis) or adding a random number (whose distributional properties are known) will depress the likelihood of such disclosure.

INTERSYSTEM LINKAGE AND ANALYSIS OF CONFIDENTIAL DATA

The second major category of archival data files involves estimation of statistical relations among variables contained in two independent and confidential data files. In accordance with the general perspective of the present report, this must be achieved without increasing the number of file personnel or users who have access to confidential information about persons unless a satisfactory, higher level of confidentiality protects the merged data. That is, if File A is being related to File B, the custodians of File A must not gain access to the confidential information of File B, and vice versa. Neither file must expand its amount of confidential information unless appropriate protection can be furnished. File linkage must be accomplished without merging an individual's identifiable record from one file with his identifiable record from the second.

At the same time, linkage among data sets can be an extremely valuable tool in research. For example, Fischer (1972) reports on the use of income tax data in conjunction with research data for appraising the effectiveness of manpower training programs. While such data are not perfect or complete for the evaluation of such a training program, they are highly relevant, as would also be claims for unemployment compensation, welfare requests, and so forth. Archival records can be used economically in the design and implementation of experiments and in the analysis of results (see Chapters IV and V of this volume). And the utility of the data increases when a number of independent files can be linked without compromising confidentiality of the data.

The requirements for achieving such linkage are more complicated than for reanalysis of a single file. But linkage can and has been accomplished with adequate safe-guards of confidentiality (Schwartz and

Orleans, 1967; Fischer, 1972; Heller, 1972; Steinberg and Pritzker, 1969; Bauman, David, and Miller, 1970). Even though such use requires special restrictions, its potential value justifies making these procedures routinely available. In what follows, three procedures are discussed: direct linkage with statistical safeguards, link file brokerage; and mutually insulated file linkage; more detailed 1972 treatment of these and other general strategies are given in Boruch (1972b).

*Direct Linkage with Statistical Safeguards.*   Microaggregation can be extended beyond analysis of a single agency's data file to assure confidentiality of records in linked files. For example, one might use an aggregation basis such as census tract or neighborhood to link Internal Revenue Service data with data stemming from experimental research on the same sample of tracts or neighborhoods (assuming treatments had been applied to the whole area specified). Similarly, one might link two files on the basis of individual records in which each file is inoculated with error whose distributional properties are known. In many cases these strategies may be unacceptable due to legal restrictions on the original file, loss of efficiency, or the need to link highly accurate data on individuals. Link file brokerage or insulated data bank strategies may then be appropriate, and such statistical safeguards can easily be coupled to these.

*Link File Brokerage.*   A number of researchers have proposed that a responsible broker, located perhaps in another country, maintain a code linkage among sets of files. Each archival agency would prepare a list of names, or other clear individual identifiers, and file-specific code numbers that would be turned over to the linkage broker. Using the individual identifiers, the broker would prepare a list lacking the individual identifiers, but linking the two file-specific codes; the broker would then destroy its own copy of clear identifiers. Subsequently, the files maintained by each agency would provide data sets identified only by file-specific codes. The broker could then merge such decks from the two files and turn the merged deck over to either of the files, with both file-specific codes deleted.

This suggestion comes out of a well-justified policy of keeping the data of a research project separated, insofar as possible, from the names and addresses of the respondents during data analysis. It also assumes that deletion of identifiers provides adequate protection of confidentiality. For the standards being recommended in this report, this is not sufficient, insofar as one can use various deductive strategies and publicly available information on the same sample to penetrate individual privacy.

Furthermore, personal identifiers can be recombined with the total merged data set by either of the agencies maintaining the original files. Each agency could easily covertly maintain its original data with personal identifiers. The replication of its original data on the new composite deck would provide a basis for exact matching, making the reinstatement of personal identifiers on the merged deck a simple process and thus giving File B access to the confidential information of File A, and vice versa.

For the goal of preventing disclosure and misuse and of restricting identifiable data to the files for which permission has been given, this system seems vulnerable without additional safeguards, such as the other methods described here.

*Mutually Insulated File Linkage.* This phrase is used here to cover a group of similar devices for linking files without merging, while preserving confidentiality. The essential notions involved have no doubt been hit upon independently on many occasions, particularly in statistical research with government records. Of published discussions, probably the first and certainly the most cited is by Schwartz and Orleans (1967) in a study linking public opinion survey responses to income tax returns. But it is clear from Steinberg and Pritzker (1969) and Heller (1972) that similar processes are regarded as feasible practice rather than just an innovation in a number of government agencies.

A concrete illustration seems the easiest way to explain the model. The hypothetical setting is to relate the Negative Income Tax experimental assignment of persons to the Social Security Administration's records on earnings subject to FICA deductions, each year for a 4-year period (covering 3 years during the experiment and 1 year after). It is assumed that both files are to be kept confidential from each other.

The Negative Income Tax experiment staff would prepare numerous short lists of persons homogeneous on some variables of importance to them. Each of these lists would be given a unique, meaningless, randomly chosen list designation. For example, the list itself could consist solely of person identifiers useful in the Social Security Administration's retrieval operation, such as name, social security number, and address. The Social Security Administration would delete one or more persons at random from each group, locate the data on all variables of interest for the remainder, compute for each variable a mean, variance, and frequency for the persons on the list for whom FICA deductions were on record, and send these summary statistics back to the Negative Income Tax staff, identified with their unique list designators. The Negative Income Tax staff would then reassemble these cell-by-cell data into their meaningful dimensional order and compute summary statistics.

While the Social Administration staff would get individual identifiers, they would get no interpretable data about these individuals. In return, they would send back no information about individuals, but instead, summary statistics about a group, which the Negative Income Tax staff would decode as a data cell in a statistical grid. The returned data is microaggregated, but by an aggregation scheme unrevealed to and undecodable by the Social Security Administration.

The mutually insulated data bank strategy can be varied in structure and coupled with microaggregation, error inoculation (or random deletion), and other mechanisms to further reduce the likelihood of improper disclosures of identifiable records.

CONCLUSIONS

The need for ensuring confidentiality of certain archival records is evident. But it is quite possible to adhere to confidentiality requirements without seriously undermining the researcher's ability to reanalyze data based on such records, or to link records from different sources for purposes of statistical analysis. A number of strategies for doing so have been developed and applied. The strategies described in this section are useful and, at their best, help considerably to expand the pool of data available for design, development, and assessment of social programs, without jeopardizing individual privacy.

# Epilogue

The national capacity for conducting social experiments is, at present, severely limited. Major departments and agencies of the Federal government charged with trying to meet perceived social deficits may seek to devise programs and policies based on social experimentation; but they find there is a shortage of capable people and well-managed institutions that can wisely use the resources available for experimentation. Furthermore, agencies seem frequently to be unsure of the purpose their research is intended to fulfill—whether it is to increase the pool of knowledge about human behavior and society, to develop program models, to clarify policy options, to test the claims of advocates of a program, to change existing institutions, or to advocate solutions to social problems. The agency is often unclear whether the audience for the work is other researchers, administrative officers in policy-making positions, the Congress, state or local governmental officials, or some vaguely defined "public at large." Partly as a result of the uncertainty, experiments are proposed but never carried out or begun but not finished. Information is generated and is irrelevant to decisions. Issues of prime importance to human welfare are not investigated. Hopes for change are raised, then dashed. Attention wanders to new topics.

What should be done to improve the situation? On the basis of the present limited experience in using social research, especially experimentation, to solve social problems, we believe that the nation must develop the capacity to carry on this kind of work as well as a longer time horizon with respect to programs of social intervention.

## Time Perspective

Taking up the latter point first, it is well to recall that the development of hardware and physical technologies such as satellites, rotary automobile engines, television receivers, jet aircraft, and nuclear power plants typically require between 8 and 18 years of persistent, concentrated effort. Often several development teams are working simultaneously on design variations. Extensive testing of prototypes "delays" decision on a final design further. After one has been chosen, problems of production, marketing, installation, and servicing must be faced.

In the case of social "software" technology, quite different time perspectives and expectations obtain. Approaches to solutions of social problems are sketched in broad terms, tried out almost impulsively, and abandoned on the basis of casual experience or political expediency. Rarely is there solid evidence about the efficacy of the principal components of treatment in a program at its inception. Few systematic efforts have been made to develop programs in a patient and thoughtful way. Seldom are sources of failure identified in such a way that programs can be redesigned. For example, it is not clear why a significant proportion of the disadvantaged population has not responded to compensatory education. We do not know whether it is because the techniques are poor, because teachers are inappropriately trained, because disadvantaged students frequently attend classes with other disadvantaged students, because they frequently come from homes where there is no support for education, because programs are not given enough resources, because they are started too early or too late in a child's life, because classes are too large, because teaching materials are culturally biased, or because tests in use do not measure children's capabilities adequately. It is likely that all of these factors are part of the explanation, and sorting out their relative importance is difficult and takes a lot of time.

To many people, any "delay" for the purpose of systematic study or experimentation with alternative forms of programs is intolerable. The problems of the disadvantaged, like many social problems, cry out for immediate solutions. The issues are volatile and controversial. The solutions are bound to embody value judgments that properly make them subject to political decisions. But politicians generally have short time horizons. They want to do something quickly. They do not want to wait 7 years to see if something can be developed; and they are quick to turn away from a policy that seems to be faltering, well before all the evidence is in. While this impatience and instability is understandable, it is also debilitating to the society. It has led to so many false starts, unfinished tasks, and failures that many people have lost faith in the capacity of governmental institutions to deal with social problems; it has also discredited social research, in some quarters, because social programs are widely thought to have been based on systematic research. In fact, they are not. (If they were, most ameliorative programs of the sixties would not yet be operating—and some might be quite different in character.) Comparatively little money has been invested in systematic program development, evaluation, and redesign in an experimental mode.

## Institutional Capacity

Yet, even if more funds and more patience had been available for experimental research and development of social interventions, we believe it could not have been wisely spent because of the limited national capabilities in this area. To some extent this is a hen and egg problem; the demand for institutions and agencies capable of carrying out field experiments has not been great; and this is so partly because potential sponsors of social experiments have not been aware of, or able to count on, the existence of such institutions.

We believe that the time is opportune to create or enhance the capability of institutions to carry out social experiments. These institutions must have the ability to attract staff of high professional and managerial qualifications and to retain such staff over substantial periods of time. Because the experiments are in support of public policy formulation, these institutions must be able to bring such considerations to bear on the conception, design, and execution of social experiments. They must have the capability to deal with all levels of the community in matters that frequently entail considerable ethical and political controversy. With all of these other qualifications, such institutions must also possess a rare degree of integrity.

While we have not formally surveyed the field, our strong impression is that institutions possessing these skills are scarce. Indeed, we are doubtful that any possess all such skills in depth. There are an increasing number of institutions with professional staff who are capable of carrying out research on policy issues; but these existing organizations possess little or no capability to design experiments and manage a flexible field organization. At the same time, we are not persuaded that there are many organizations possessing the types of field research and treatment administration skills noted earlier in this volume.

The committee that prepared this volume considered three alternative approaches to support the development of the needed institutional capacity:

(A) To create one or two applied social science organizations of the type recommended by the Special Commission on the Social Sciences of the National Science Foundation (NSF 1969), which would concentrate on the problems of social experimentation through the provision of substantial sustained institutional support. This would probably mean developing a field management, design, and measurement capability as well as the substantive competence appropriate to specific experiments. Such institutions might also participate in nonexperimental research and policy analysis, but if they are to carry out high-quality social experiments they must develop survey or other data collection capacity and appropriate field staffs.

(B) To create a major public corporation charged with developing field capabilities to be utilized by Federal agencies, or grantees of Federal agencies, in carrying out social experiments and program evaluations. It might be advantageous to task this corporation with one or more large-scale national surveys that would provide the motivation for maintaining a core of technical and field staff.

(C) To provide smaller amounts of support, in the form of grants, to a larger number of promising research institutions (or consortia of institutions) to enhance existing capabilities. Between 6 and 10 grants ranging in size from $250,000 to $500,000 a year might be required to provide start-up resources while the institution was building staff and engaging in small-scale experiments and methodological research. These grants should run for at least 5 years and should be conditional upon a genuine expansion of experimental capability. The institutions chosen would compete for experimental projects without additional favored treatment. Appropriate candidates for such sustaining support would include institutions that had been engaged in experimentation and wanted to preserve existing teams of personnel.

We recommend the third alternative, the provision of relatively small institutional grants to a number of institutions. Among our reasons are the following:

1. We feel there are a number of existing institutions lacking capabilities in one or two critical areas that could become competent performers of social experiments with the addition of a small number of people possessing specialized competence.

2. We believe it highly desirable to preserve and promote competition among potential experimenters to a greater extent than proposals (A) and (B) would do.
3. The potential geographic dispersion of capability might help to bring these talents to bear on the important opportunities we believe exist at the state and local levels.
4. There is less risk of making a poor or wrong choice of institution than would be the case in proposals (A) and (B).
5. The cost of proposal (C) seems reasonable in terms of the national social science research budget, and the dispersion among a number of institutions seems politically more feasible.

To some extent our failure to endorse strongly the other suggestions is the obverse of the reasons for supporting proposal (C). If institutes of applied social science are created, we would hope to see one or more focusing on experimentation; but we are reluctant to pin all our hopes as a first priority on a single institution. Moreover, even if such an institution became a sparkling success, it would be unlikely to be able to meet the multiplicity of demands we can expect to develop. Who would choose which problems to study, which "clients" to work for, and what designs to use? All these problems become more difficult if there are only one or two institutions available—particularly where there is a substantial base of institutional support within that institution.

Proposal (B) we feel merits serious consideration. Such a corporation, formed under legislative mandate from Congress, could provide better protection against improper disclosure to both researcher and respondent than is currently the case. It could also carry out studies that the Census Bureau is currently unable or unwilling to perform. From the point of view of the Federal agencies, the ability to negotiate with another government agency to carry out fieldwork simplifies the contracting process significantly. This simplification is, of course, bought at the price of reduced competition among sources of fieldwork services.

There are some trade-offs that must be considered in deciding what strategy to follow, especially that between the continuity of an experimenting organization and its responsiveness to the experiment sponsor's needs. An organization with an assured financial base and solid expectations of continuity can attract and hold a higher quality of professional and technical personnel, as well as accumulate experience and proficiency. The same feature, however, is likely to make it less responsive to the sponsor's needs than a hungrier, less stable institution. At this stage of the art of social experimentation, it is our view, that continuity is a preferred attribute.

We recommend that if proposal (C) is followed, the recipient institutions should be chosen on the basis of recent or current performance in social research together with evidenced interest in and potential for policy-oriented experimentation. Current staff competence and estimated capacity to attract addition high quality personnel—at a growth rate of, say, five persons per year—should play an important part in the judgment. Our recommendation is not intended as a remedial program for disadvantaged research institutions, but for enlarging the scope of institutional capacity for methodologically sound, policy-relevant work. Methodological research (e.g., on measurement error and on quasi-experimental designs and analyses) should be an important component of an experiment-conducting organization's program.

Whatever the pattern of development or the specific institutions chosen for support, we recommend further that experiment-conducting institutions should:

1.  Place the results of an experiment in a suitable repository where confidentiality of records can be maintained and where access is facilitated by a service support group, so that statistical data can be reanalyzed by other qualified researchers (without compromising confidentiality or violating personal privacy).

    Experimental data should be made available for reanalysis as soon as possible after completion of the study and public release of reports. (At least one Federal agency has used 60 days as a standard. Shorter or longer lags may be warranted by the magnitude and character of the data.)

2.  Have the right to publish the results of analysis of all data obtained in social experiments, as long as personal privacy of participants and confidentiality of records are preserved.

3.  Receive multiyear funding in order to avoid the wasteful practices that are regularly associated with 1-year-at-a-time funding: hastily prepared research designs and treatments, undesirably short treatment periods, curtailed planning perspectives, inadequate analyses, and possibly premature reports of progress.

4.  Devise and adapt appropriate methods of accounting for the cost of experimentation and develop techniques for evaluating benefits of experiments, such as human resource accounting. Experimenting agencies should publish or make available such data in order to advance cost–benefit analysis.

5. Engage in longitudinal follow-up studies of the direct and indirect results of experiments, including the replication of experiments, the adoption of treatment programs in new sites, and other uses of findings.

Substantial improvement in the national capacity to deal inventively and constructively with central issues of social policy will, we believe, come about throught the adoption of these recommendations.

# APPENDIX


*Illustrative Controlled Experiments
for Planning and Evaluating
Social Programs*

This appendix lists references to and abstracts of illustrative, *randomized* experiments for appraising the effects of social programs.[1] Each abstract is based solely on published sources, and includes information on the objectives of the experiment, the design of the program and of the experimental study, the response variables measured in the experiment, and the results of the research. Most of the citations listed here refer to at least one test in a series of experimental assessments necessary for the development of a particular program. A wide variety of social programs have been tested experimentally; for convenience in presentation, they have been grouped into the following categories.

    I. Experiments in Delinquency and Criminal Reform
    II. Experimental Tests of Law-Related Programs and Procedures
    III. Experimental Tests of Rehabilitative Programs in Mental Health
    IV. Experimental Assessment of Special Educational Programs
    V. Sociomedical and Fertility Control Experiments
    VI. Appraisals of the Effectiveness of Communication Methods
    VII. Experimental Tests of Methods for Data Collection, Transmission, Retrieval
    VIII. Experiments in Research Utilization
    IX. Economic Experiments

The contents of the appendix serve as empirical evidence for the contention that randomized experimental tests are feasible in a wide variety of program settings. The list is intended to be *illustrative* rather than exhaustive or representative of the population of such studies. No attempt has been made to synthesize the substantive results of experiments in a particular area; we rely on state of the art work, such as Gage's *Handbook of Research on Teaching*, to consolidate and interpret substantive results of experiments, quasi-experiments, and other evaluations, for example, in education.

---

[1]These abstracts were compiled by Robert F. Boruch with the assistance of Stephen Davis.

# I. Experiments in Delinquency and Criminal Reform

Abstract of: The community treatment project: History and prospects, by M.O. Warren. In S. A. Yefsky (ed.), *Law enforcement, science, and technology.* Washington, D.C.: Thompson, 1967.

and: *The status of current research in the California Youth Authority* (Annual Report). Sacramento, California: Department of Youth Authority, 1972.

*Objectives:* The series of experimental tests were conducted to develop community-based delinquency programs and to assess their effectiveness relative to traditional institutional efforts to reform juvenile offenders.

*Description of Program:* Phases I and II (1961–1969) of the Community Treatment Project (CTP) involved developing and testing a large-scale system for differential treatment of youthful offenders: Offenders were assigned to treatment strategies on the basis of clinical subtype (e.g., aggressive, conformist), and treatment personnel were assigned on the basis of their ability to implement a particular treatment strategy. Phase III (1969–1974) involved systematically broadening the target group and the use of two program strategies: direct release of offenders to differential community treatment and intensive institutionalization with treatment followed by community treatment.

*Study Design:* For Phases I and II, a randomized experiment was mounted to test the effectiveness of CTP relative to regular institutional correctional programs. Systematic attempts were made to identify the importance of matching treatment and treatment agents to offenders, and the importance of intensive versus extensive intervention and of the level of ability of personnel in treating offenders. Phase III involved a randomized experimental test of a refined treatment program aimed at a broader target group.

*Response Variables:* The major criterion variables included recidivism and honorable versus poor discharge.

*Results:* The CTP was considerably more successful than regular institutional programs in reducing recidivism and in inducing honorable discharge from the program. Degree of success varied with offender subtype. The major factors in determining effects appear to be differential and intensive treatment. Data from Phases I and II suggest that the program has a failure (reconviction) rate of only 38% by comparison to regular institutional rates of 61%.

Abstract of: *Rational innovation: An account of changes in the program of the National Training School for Boys from 1961 to 1964.* Washington, D.C.: Federal Bureau of Prisons, 1964.

*Objectives:* The study was designed to test the effects of intensive, nonpunitive counseling and of specialized recreational and incentive programs on the behavior of boys in a correctional institution.

*Description of Program:* The program was implemented and tested during 1961–1964 at the National Training School for Boys, a United States Bureau of Prisons correctional facility. The treatment progam itself consisted of intensive individual counseling for boys, reduced workloads for counselers, intensive group counseling, specialized recreational programs, and finally, the introduction of incentive plans whereby special awards were given to boys demonstrating marked improvements in their in-school behavior. The intervention program was confined to one cottage of the multicottage facility.

*Study Design:* Boys were randomly assigned to both the demonstration and control cottages. Besides the control cottage with randomly selected occupants, all other cottages at the institution served as a secondary control group.

*Response Variables:* Data on boys' in-school conduct, attitudes, self-concepts, and morale, and observations on boys' social relationships and institutional adjustment were used as dependent variables.

*Results:* Boys in the experimental group were released sooner from the school; there were no significant differences among the project groups in overall recidivism rates. The experimental releases stayed out of trouble longer than controls, and the reincarcerated experiments were recommitted for less serious offenses than the controls. By comparison to control group members, the boys in the experimental group demonstrated better social behavior, better academic and skill level achievement, and positive changes in attitude and conduct. As a result of this study, the entire school adopted this treatment program at the end of the 2 years.

Abstract of: *Final report: Federal offenders rehabilitation program,* by P. B. Bell, M. Matthews, and W. S. Fulton. Olympia, Washington: Coordinating Council for Occupational Education and Division of Vocational Rehabilitation, 1969.

*Objectives:* The Federal Offenders Rehabilitation Program was designed to appraise the effectiveness of providing intensive vocational rehabilitation services to releases and men on probation from three federal correction institutions.

*Description of Program:* Funded by the Vocational Rehabilitation Administration (now the Social Rehabilitation Service), this program was conducted during 1965–1969 by the United States Probation Service, the United States Bureau of Prisons, the United States Board of Parole, and seven state vocational rehabilitation agencies. The treatment program involved intensive rehabilitation, including supportive medical treatment, counseling and guidance, vocational training and provision of tools, family maintenance, and an overall emphasis on planned vocational rehabilitation. Control cases received the usual vocational rehabilitation services consisting of normal counseling, guidance, and placement services.

*Study Design:* The 2654 eligible clients in the selected areas (eight major cities) were labeled according to probability of success outside prison: Within each category they were then randomly allocated to either the experimental group (623) or one of two control groups.

*Response Variables:* Employment and recidivism were the two primary indices of performance of the subjects in both groups.

*Results:* The effect of treatment in terms of either recidivism or employment depended in a complex way on city and on character and degree of treatment within city as well as on characteristics in treatment and control groups. But few differences were substantial. The treatment appeared to have had a direct impact on the justice system within each city (positive *and* negative) and consequently on recidivism, rather than a direct impact on behavior of the release and consequently on recidivism. For example, in many cities, participation in the program appears to have made it more likely that criminal or civil violations would be detected (increasing recidivism for the treatment group), while in other cases participation appeared to make revocation of parole less likely (depressing recidivism rate). Differences in employment rate were small and, again, varied.

Abstract of:   Surgical and social rehabilitation of adult offenders, by R. L. Kurtzberg, H. Safar, and N. Cavior. *Proceedings, 76th American Psychological Association Convention,* Washington, D.C.: APA, 1968.

*Objectives:* "The Surgical and Social Rehabilitation of Adult Offenders Project was a 3-year experimental investigation of the rehabilitative effects of plastic surgery."

*Description of Program:* Supported by the Social and Rehabilitation Service, United States Department of Health, Education and Welfare, this project was conducted in the New York jail system. The subjects were disadvantaged New York residents with disfigurements such as knife scars, lop-ears, needle marks, and tattoos. Treatment groups were Surgery and Services, Surgery only, Services only, and No Treatment. The plastic surgery was performed on the inmates after their release from prison. The social and vocational services consisted mainly of referrals, with some direct counseling.

*Study Design:* After screening, disfigured inmates who had volunteered for the program were assigned *randomly* to treatment groups. Follow-up data were collected 1 year after surgery or release.

*Response Variables:* The program was evaluated on the basis of recidivism rates and releasees' vocational success and psychological adjustment.

*Results:* The subjects were divided up on the basis of heroin addiction. Non-addicts who underwent surgery (with and without services) showed 36% less recidivism; those who received services only showed 33% more recidivism than controls. The latter subjects also showed poorer psychological adjustment after 1 year. Addict subjects who received surgery only showed 8% less recidivism (not significantly different) than those not receiving surgery; addicts who received services only had 31% less recidivism; those who received both surgery and services had 29% less recidivism; and finally, addicts who received social and vocational services appear to have benefited vocationally while becoming more psychologically dependent. Surgery was more beneficial when performed on facially disfigured subjects than on bodily disfigured subjects.

Abstract of: *The Silverlake experiment,* by L. T. Empey and S. G. Lubeck. Chicago, Illinois: Aldine, 1972.

*Objectives:* This study had as its first objective the determination" . . . of the capacity of a particular theory of delinquent behavior and to suggest measures for intervention." Its other principal objectives were to learn about the operational problems of theory-based intervention efforts and to study the problems of the field experiment as a knowledge-generating device.

*Description of Program:* This program involved an experimental treatment with low throughput, higher than usual staff–boy ratios, and intensive guidance and group meeting systems. The treatment itself was operated partly on an outpatient clinic analogue, with boys attending local outside schools, but returning to residency afterward. The control subjects were assigned to Boys Republic, an existing, privately funded institution for delinquents. The experimental group treatment was implemented in the community by the Youth Studies Center of the University of Southern California.

*Study Design:* The 3-year experiment plus 1 year of follow up involved 121 control and 140 experimental subjects; all subjects were randomly assigned.

*Response Variables:* Recidivism rates, seriousness of offenses, questionnaire and interview data, runaway attempts, failures (boys terminated during program), and critical incidents were documented and used as measures of outcome.

*Results:* Recidivism rate did not differ substantially across treatment and control groups. The control condition appeared to be even more effective than the new program in reducing recidivism among graduates who completed the programs, but the recidivist group, those who had participated in the control program, were more likely to be repeat offenders.

Abstract of: *Girls at Vocational High,* by H. J. Meyer, E. F. Borgatta, and W. C. Jones. New York: Russell Sage Foundation, 1965.

*Objectives:* The general objective of this research was to " . . . study the effectiveness of social work for interrupting potentially deviant careers . . . " of adolescent females from a vocational high school. In addition, the study attempted to get to potential problems early by referral from the high school, rather than from the Youth Board.

*Description of Program:* Begun in 1955 and running 3 years, this study was conducted under the auspices of the Youth Consultation Services of New York and in cooperation with the New York City Youth Board and the New York Department of Education. Treatments for this experiment included individual and/or group therapy, increased caseworker contacts (although this varied from subject to subject), and maintaining some contact with each subject throughout. The treatment was not the same in the first year as in subsequent years, as the first involved pilot testing and feasibility study of proposed treatments.

*Study Design:* The records of four entering cohorts of girls at Vocational High were screened and potential problem cases identified from each cohort. Of the problem case group, 189 girls were randomly assigned to the experimental group and 192 to the control group.

*Response Variables:* Limited appraisals by school guidance personnel and information concerning in-school and out-of-school performance were collected for use in assessing effects of the program. Clinical measures were collected on students' attitudes toward life and toward themselves, on incidence and nature of their problems, on their plans for the future, and on other variables.

*Results:* There were very slight, but consistent, differences on most outcome measures, favoring experimental treatment. The experimental treatment did not appear to have a significant effect on school completion; girls who earned better grades were helped to stay in school by the program. There was a tendency for less truancy in the experimental group. There were no effects on attitude response, but more favorable personality measure scores were found for the experimental group.

Abstract of:   *The Provo experiment: Evaluating community control of delinquency,*
    by L. T. Empey and M. L. Erickson. Lexington, Massachusetts: Lexington Books, 1972.
    and:   The Provo experiment: Research and findings, by L. T. Empey. In H. Gold and F. R. Scarpitti (eds.), *Combatting social problems: Techniques of intervention.* New York: Holt, Rinehart, and Winston, 1967.

*Objectives:* This study had as its goal appraisal of the theoretical and practical features of a rehabilitation program for delinquents, set up as an alternative to normal incarceration methods for juveniles with serious offenses.

*Description of Program:* This 6-year program was designed to rehabilitate repeat offenders (male, aged 14–18) in the Provo (Utah) community rather than in reformatory correction centers. The program was structured around requirements that participants act in accordance with desirable social norms and hold legitimate jobs in the community. Pressures to do so were exerted by participants' peers within the program and by authorities within and outside the program. The peer groups were the central source of pressure, a vehicle for resolving participants' personal problems, and a channel for communication of group information (e.g., that failures are sent to a state correctional institution—it is the only alternative to succeeding in the program). A second phase of the program was developed to ensure employment and rehabilitative assistance for releasees.

*Study Design:* The original research design required that offenders on probation be randomly assigned to control or to experimental probation with treatment conditions, and that offenders who were sentenced to incarceration be randomly assigned to incarceration or to the treatment program. However, because of the low proportion sentenced to incarceration, the design was altered so that all incarcerated boys were accepted into the experimental program; a comparison group was selected from the population of boys sentenced to Utah institutions, to serve sa the control for the experimental treatment group.

*Response Variables:* Dependent measures included attrition rates from the program, treatment of offenders, supervision time of offenders, arrest frequencies, number and seriousness of the posttreatment offenses, and costs of the new program as well as of the normal program.

*Results:* Both the experimental and control probation groups appeared to help reduce delinquency. The same was true, although less so, for the incarceration experimental group. Institutional incarceration appeared to increase delinquency in relation to delinquency rates for program participants. Both experimental probation and experimental treatment groups were superior to their respective control groups.

Abstract of:    *The Chicago Youth Development Project*, by H. W. Mattick and N. S. Caplan. Ann Arbor, Michigan: Institute for Social Research, 1964.

and:    Treatment intervention and reciprocal interaction effects, by N. Caplan. *Journal of Social Issues*, 1968, 24, 63–88.

and:    The nature, variety, and patterning of street-club work, by N. S. Caplan, D. J. Deshaies, G. D. Suttles, and H. W. Mattick. In M. W. Klein and B. Meyerhoff (eds.), *Juvenile gangs in context: Theory, research, and action.* Englewood Cliffs, New Jersey: Prentice-Hall, 1967.

*Objectives:* The Chicago Youth Development Project was designed initially as an action program for preventing and controlling juvenile delinquency in two inner city areas of Chicago. The research portion of the project was intended to evaluate the success or failure of the action program as well as to analyze various action techniques.

*Description of Program:* Funded by the Ford Foundation, this 6-year program began in 1961, with the research portion conducted by the Institute for Social Research, and the action portion undertaken by the Chicago Boys Club. The treatment consisted of: street-club work with young people and community organization work with local adults and community leaders. Control areas did not receive this two-fold treatment.

*Study Design:* Two experimental areas were selected because of a need for a program of this type, because they contained a Chicago Boys Club unit, and because of the possibilities of collecting demographic and statistical data. Two control areas were originally selected for their natural unification and similarity to the experimental areas. However, after the 1960 census they were found to be inadequate matches, and, accordingly, three spatially dispersed census tracts were selected on the basis of a high degree of equivalence to the various experimental area census tracts to serve as comparison conditions for each experimental area. Pretreatment data and posttreatment data were used in evaluating the program, and participants in the study were monitored over a

5-year period. This study then employed an internal panel design within two experimental areas with natural contiguous control areas, and within matched noncontiguous areas.

*Response Variables:* Youth employment, school attendance, community supervision over offenders, contact with youths known to the police, arrests, and convictions were all dependent measures of interest.

*Results:* In spite of many organizational (political–institutional) problems in implementation, the Chicago Youth Development Project was successful in achieving instrumental goals: contacting and maintaining contacts with adolescents, obtaining community cooperation, and so forth. Adolescents appear to have been helped by guidance and counseling, but the program had no marked effect on the rates of youth employment, school dropouts, arrests, or conviction of arrested youths.

Abstract of: *An experiment in the prevention of delinquency: The Cambridge–Somerville Youth Study,* by E. Powers and H. Witmer. New York: Columbia University Press, 1951.

*Objectives:* This program was undertaken to test the hypothesis that "delinquency can be prevented by establishing a sustained friendly relationship with boys in trouble."

*Description of Program:* The original treatment plan consisted of having counselors seek out boys considered predelinquent, gain their friendship, and sustain the contact for 10 years. Once friendship was established, the counselor was to invite the boy home at times, fight for the boy's rights, be a moral "source of inspiration" throughout, be willing to discuss the boy's problems, and attempt to meet each of the boys' needs. Thus, the actual treatment was widely diversified and varied from counselor to counselor. The control group did not receive sustained friendship, or as much help from social workers.

*Study Design:* From public and parochial schools in Cambridge and Somerville, Massachusetts, boys were chosen and then placed into 325 similar pairs. Subgroupings of from 2 to 25 such pairs were then chosen for homogeneity. Allocation to treatment or control group was random, first individually, and then by subgroups. Each boy was finally matched to counselors based on the counselors' preferences and prejudices.

*Response Variables:* Clinically ascertained social adjustment before and after treatment, frequency and seriousness of delinquent acts, case analyses by professional social workers, grades in school, boys' and counselors' assessments of whether or not the program was helpful, boys' terminal behavior, and batteries of psychological tests were all used as indicators of the program's success.

*Results:* World War II interrupted the project, removing both boys and counselors from the program before its planned termination. For the final 254 cases in each group, none of the response measures indicated any marked differences between groups.

Abstract of:   *Parolees, problems, aspirations, and attributes,* by J. J. Berman. Ph. D. Dissertation, Northwestern University, Psychology Department, 1972. and:   *The volunteer in parole program.* by J. J. Berman, Manuscript, University of Nebraska, 1973.

*Objectives:* This study was designed to appraise the effectiveness of the Volunteer in Parole Program, a program developed to provide nonlegal assistance regarding employment, personal finances, and other advice to parolees of Illinois correctional institutions. The assistance was furnished by young volunteer lawyers, members of the Illinois Bar Association.

*Description of Program:* Financed by Woodrow Wilson Foundation, Russell Sage Foundation, and the National Science Foundation, this study involved collection of evidence on effectiveness of the program in improving parolees' social and economic status and adjustment. Treatment consisted of a lawyer spending at least 1 day a month with his parolee in order to help him resolve problems of obtaining and maintaining a job, getting professional and community services where required, and other practical social adjustment goals.

*Study Design:* A randomization procedure was used to allocate nominated parolees to treatment or control groups; both pretest and posttest data were collected.

*Response Variables:* Dependent measures of major interest included reincarceration rate, employment rate, attitudes of the parolees toward the judicial system and police, attitudes toward society, feelings of well-being, needs for assistance seeking, and effective usage of the lawyer–parolee relationship.

*Results:* The special program did not appear to have affected parolees' rearrest rates, employment status, attitudes toward the courts, or perception of themselves. There was some evidence for the program's inducing more positive attitudes regarding society's concern for the parolees and positive changes in realism of parolees' job expectations.

Abstract of:   *Interim report: Vera supportive employment programs,* Research Department, New York: Vera Institute, 1973 (Mimeo).

*Objectives:* The experimental program, supportive employment for former narcotics addicts, was created to ameliorate their problems of low skill level, job discrimination, and employment barriers on leaving prison, and to facilitate their rehabilitation. The experiment was designed to test the effects of the program and to identify program elements that appear to have the most influence.

*Description of Program:* The supportive employment programs were specially designed to facilitate rehabilitation of the ex-addict and to ease his transition from prison to normal employment situations. The jobs to which ex-addicts are assigned are mainly service-oriented; employment is subsidized by public and private funds. The jobs include, for example, employment in newspaper recycling groups, rodent control projects, Off-Track Betting offices, and others.

Candidates are screened prior to entry to the program and while on the job must meet established performance standards under supervised conditions.

*Study Design:* Ex-addicts judged to be acceptable program participants were randomly assigned after screening to treatment and control groups (the latter being normal postprison support). About 300 men are expected to be allocated to each group for the 1972–1973 tests.

*Response Variables:* The outcome variables fall into four major classes: work performance (e.g., number of full days worked), drug abstinence, criminal activity (e.g., crimes committed or arrests), personal relations (e.g., with family and fellow employees).

*Results:* This evaluation was initiated in June 1972; because longer-term follow up is necessary for adequate appraisal of program effects, no firm conclusions can be drawn from the data currently available. *Preliminary* results suggest that the experimental group fares better in maintaining its jobs and in completion of drug programs.

# II.  Experimental Tests of
Law-Related Programs and Procedures

Abstract of:    The Manhattan Bail Project: Its impact in criminology and the
criminal law process, by B. Botein. *Texas Law Review*, 1965, 43, 319–31.
and:   The Manhattan Bail Project: An interim report on the use of pretrial parole, by C. E. Ares, A. Rankin and H. Sturz. *New York University
Law Review*, 1963, 38, 67–95.
and:   Experiments in the criminal justice system, by H. Sturz. *Legal
Aid Briefcase*, 1967 (February), 1–5.

*Objectives:* The Vera Institute (New York) initiated the Manhattan Bail Project
to furnish criminal court judges with evidence regarding the contention that
many persons could be successfully released prior to trial and without bail if
verified information concerning defendants' backgrounds were available to
the court at the time of bail determination.

*Description of Program:* The target group included individuals accused of felonies,
misdemeaners, and certain other crimes; individuals charged with homicide
and other serious crimes were excluded from the experiments. New York
University law students and Vera staff reviewed defendants' records of employment, family, residences, references, current charges, previous records, etc. in
order to make judgements about whether a pretrial release without bail should
be recommended to the court. Recommendations were made to the judge in the
experimental group only.

*Study Design:* The total group of recommendees was split randomly into control and experimental groups.

*Response Variables:* Paroles (pretrial release) granted, case dispositions, sent-
ences, and default rate were all dependent variables in the experiment.

291

*Results:* Judges in the first year granted parole to 59% of the recommended defendants, compared to only 16% in the control group; recommendations based on information then served to increase the rate of release without bail. Sixty percent of the recommended group was either acquitted or had their cases dismissed, compared to 23% of the control group. During 1961–1964, less than 1% of the experimental group failed to show up in court for trial, suggesting that the relaxation of the bail requirement did not result in unacceptable default rates. Following this experiment, the New York Probation Department extended this program to criminal courts in all five boroughs of the city. Also, similar projects were launched in Des Moines, Washington, D.C, and St. Louis, according to Botein. Many of the experimental treatment features were incorporated into the 1966 Bail Reform Act.

Abstract of:    *In defense of youth: A study of the role of counsel in American juvenile courts,* by V. Stapleton and L. E. Teitelbaum. New York: Russell Sage, 1972.

and:    *Counsel in juvenile courts: An experimental study,* by N. Lefstein and V. Stapleton. Unpublished manuscript, National Council of Juvenile Court Judges, Chicago, Illinois, July, 1967.

*Objectives:* The 3-year study was undertaken to determine the effects of encouraging defendents in juvenile court to engage legal counsel. The impetus for the study was a 1967 Supreme Court ruling which declared that despite traditional juvenile court emphasis on nonadverse, paternalistic treatment of juveniles, the youthful defendent does indeed have a legal right to counsel and to participate in an adversary process.

*Description of Program:* Under the auspices of the National Council of Juvenile Court Justices, lawyers in the experiment were introduced into juvenile court in advocacy roles. Experimental subjects were strongly urged, personally and otherwise, to engage legal counsel. Control subjects were advised fully of their rights to counsel, but received no extraordinary encouragement to be represented in court by a lawyer.

*Study Design:* Candidates for control and treatment groups were selected randomly by an intermediary group. With attrition from the assigned experimental group and with control subjects seeking other legal counsel, some marked differences between control and experimental groups were evident prior to trial in one of two cities involved in the research.

*Response Variables:* The major variable measured in this study was case disposition.

*Results:* Because the courts in the two sample cities differed considerably in their operations, the impact of the treatment differed between cities. The introduction of legal counsel in one had a substantial effect. Experimental group cases were dismissed more frequently, more cases were continued under court supervision without a formal declaration of delinquency, and fewer individuals were committed to institutions, relative to the control (no lawyer) condition. In the second city, differences between disposition of treatment and control group cases were generally small and in some cases, negative.

Abstract of:   *The pretrial conference and effective justice,* by M. Rosenberg. New York: Columbia University Press, 1964.

*Objectives:* Columbia University's Project for Effective Justice was planned in 1959 to test the effects of pretrial conferences on court efficiency, fairness of court processes, and case dispositions.

*Description of Program:* With the aid of the Supreme Court of New Jersey, this experiment was conducted in New Jersey Civil Courts and with personal injury (liability) cases during 1960–1963. Pretrial conferences involved a meeting of lawyers and their clients prior to a formal trial; at the conference they were to discuss and specify the nature of the court action, facts pertaining to the case, claims admissions, limitations in numbers of expert witnesses, etc. One group (C) was invited to forego a pretrial conference; and Group A was the control group with mandatory pretrial conferences.

*Study Design:* The original design called for random allocation of 1500 cases to a control group and 1500 to a treatment group. However, due to legal and ethical constraints, the individuals in the no-pretrial conference group were given the option of requesting a pretrial conference. The A group contained 1495 cases, B had 758, and C had 701.

*Response Variables:* The dependent experimental variables included improvement of the quality of the conduct of the trials, including clearness and conciseness of the advancement of legal theories by lawyers. Whether available evidence was introduced without confusion was an area of interest; use of the judge's time was another. Also, average money recovered by plaintiffs was a dependent measure. Applications for retrials and appeals that were granted were indirect measures of erroneous trial judgments.

*Results:* The findings were mixed and complex, but among them were the following: With pretrial conferences, the quality of the trial was increased; lawyers were better prepared; opposed theories of the cases were more clearly presented; gaps and repetition in the evidence were eliminated; and tactical surprise was curbed. The efficiency of the court was reduced by requiring pretrial conferences rather than leaving it up to the lawyers' discretion. In the A group the average amount of money recovered was noticeably higher than in the B plus C cases. The data on subsequent appeals suggested that cases in Group A were more prone to appeal, but if appealed they were less prone to reversal. In retrials, A cases only had 9% granted as against 19% in the B plus C cases. Finally, it was found that compulsory pretrials did not markedly increase the frequency of settlements before trial.

Abstract of:   *Police recruit training: Stress vs nonstress,* by H. H. Earle. Springfield, Illinois: Charles C. Thomas, 1973.

*Objectives:* This 3-year study was designed to test the contention that policemen trained under high-stress conditions perform on their jobs at a higher level of proficiency and are more satisfied with their work than policemen trained under nonstress conditions.

*Description of Program:* The treatment groups were high-stress and low-stress training programs in the Los Angeles County Sheriff's Department Police

Academy. The courses for both randomly assigned halves of the class of police recruits were the same. For the stress half, a strict military environment was established. The nonstress conditions, in contrast, involved a "college-campus atmosphere."

*Study Design:* The academy took candidates at the start of the 16-week course and divided them into matched pairs. One member of each pair was then randomly allocated to the stressful conditions, the other to the nonstress conditions. The experiment was replicated, using 74 recruits from the first experimental class and 100 in a subsequent class.

*Response Variables:* Supervisors and trainees in both groups completed work quality and proficiency questionnaires and rating inventories; after training, data on complaints and commendations on both groups were obtained to assess performance during the recruits' first 2 years in the field. These surveys gave both objective and subjective data.

*Results:* The nonstress group had more job knowledge, were better marksmen, were more adaptable, were more responsible, got along better with other officers and superiors, and felt the public placed a higher value on their work. "They even wore their uniforms better." Similar results were obtained with two sequential experimental tests. Partly as a consequence of the experimental tests, the training program in the Los Angeles Sheriff's Department has been altered.

Abstract of:    A controlled experiment for the use of court probation for drunk arrests, by K. G. Ditman, G. G. Crawford, E. W. Forgy, H. Moskowitz, and C. MacAndrew. *American Journal of Psychiatry*, 1967, **124**, 160–163.

*Objectives:* In order to ascertain whether "the use of probation with suspended sentence would be an effective way both of getting the chronic drunk offender into treatment and of decreasing the likelihood of his being arrested," this study was initiated. Three types of treatment were compared for their relative effectiveness.

*Description of Program:* Conducted at the Municipal Court of the city of San Diego, this study compared three treatment processes: (1) no treatment–1 year of probation; (2) alcoholic clinic; and (3) Alcoholic Anonymous–attendance at five meetings within 30 days required or the subject considered a treatment failure. The total sample consisted of 301 "chronic drunk offenders" defined as having "had two drunk arrests in the previous 3 months or three drunk arrests in the previous year." These subjects were all fined $25 and given a 30-day sentence, suspended for 1-year probation.

*Study Design:* Each offender was randomly assigned to one of the treatment conditions by the judge. Follow-up data were collected for 1 year.

*Response Variables:* Recidivism rate was the major variable of interest.

*Results:* There were no significant differences in number of rearrests among treatment groups, although there was a slight trend for the no-treatment group to have fewer rearrests. Possible explanations for the absence of differences were suggested by the authors: (1) the threat of 30 days in jail was strong enough treatment that the other treatments were not able to add to it; (2) there may not have been enough treatment sessions in either the Alcoholics Anonymous group or the alcoholic clinic group to help; and (3) the court referral conditions may have induced anxiety, driving the subjects to drink.

# III. Experimental Tests of Rehabilitative Programs in Mental Health

Abstract of: *Social psychology in treating mental illness: An experimental approach,* edited by G. W. Fairweather. New York: Wiley, 1964.

*Objectives:* The research was initiated to develop, study, and test a new rehabilitative program for chronically hospitalized mental patients. The specific aims were to compare the new program with a more traditional approach and to research the nature and structure of the new program in a field setting.

*Description of Program:* The new program was developed around the establishment of autonomous, continuing, patient-led task groups in the hospital setting. The groups, a kind of rough social analogy to groups normally formed in the outside community, were composed of a small number of matched patients and were maintained by the patients to facilitate recovery and the transition to community life.

*Study Design:* The experiment was conducted in two (nearly identical) wards of a mental hospital, one run under a traditional regime of ordered patient activities, the other under the new regime. Grade levels of personnel were equal in each ward and midway through the experiment, the staff of one ward switched to the other to equate for any unrecognized staff differences between wards. Patients, matched on age, diagnosis, and length of previous hospitalization, were formed into groups of four and then randomly assigned to one of the two treatment conditions. To fulfill a hospital requirement that no beds remain empty, patients admitted after the initial randomization were assigned randomly but without matching as replacements for releases.

*Response Variables:* Follow-up questionnaires were used to elicit information on postrelease employment and community adjustment, including rehospitalization. Indices of group activity, attitudes toward mental illness, and perceptions of the treatment program were obtained on each patient prior to release. *Results:* Follow-up studies of patients revealed that employment rate and level of social involvement and adjustment were considerably higher for the participants in the new program. The average duration of hospitalization was significantly (a month) less for this group than the 5-month average for the traditional program participants. A small average difference in time until rehospitalization was observed, favoring the experimental treatment group.

Abstract of: *Dann Services Program: Report and plans,* by D. N. Daniels, *et al.*
   Research Report, National Institute of Mental Health Grant No. 02332, January 1968.
   and: *Cost-effectiveness of mental health: An evaluation of an experimental rehabilitation program,* by P. D. Fox. Dissertation, Graduate School of Business, Stanford University, 1968.

*Objectives:* The reports describe an evaluation of the Dann Services Program, an experimental mental health system conducted at the Veterans Administration Hospital in Palo Alto, California, and by the Department of Psychiatry of the Stanford School of Medicine. The program was designed to rehabilitate chronic mental patients and began in 1965.

*Description of Program:* The treatment program consisted of diversified rehabilitation in psychiatric wards. Patients were employed in industrial jobs, and the employment service was run mainly by patients. Patient task groups were given major responsibility for making decisions within the hospital ward. Control group patients still received active and intensive care, but were not involved in employment or decision-making activities.

*Study Design:* Early in the experiment, patients were assigned to ward (condition) on the basis of bed availability; after March 1966, a randomization procedure was used to assign patients to experimental and control wards. This resulted in four experimental groups: a nonrandom and a random control ward, and a nonrandom and a random experimental ward. After comparing random and nonrandom groups on multiple measures, it was decided that they were similar enough to be combined without confounding the results of the evaluation.

*Response Variables:* Requirements for rehospitalization, employment history, and patient attitudes were all used to evaluate the program.
*Results:* The experimental treatment was more effective in reducing the need for rehospitalization (control ward patients spent 38% more time in the hospital after initial discharge). However, roughly two-thirds of all patients required rehospitalization within 18 months. Experimental patients had significantly better employment histories. In contrast to these results, "control ward patients reported less tension and depression" than experimental patients. This is not surprising "in light of the amount of confrontation and scrutinization of behavior that occurs in the experimental program."

Abstract of:   Schizophrenics in the Community: an experimental study in the prevention of hospitalization, by B. Pasemanick, F. R. Scarpetti, and S. Dinitz with J. Abini, and M. Lefton. New York: Appleton-Century-Crofts, 1967.

Objectives: The study was designed to assess the feasibility and the effectiveness of home care treatment for schizophrenics. The home care, one of a number of possible elements in larger-scale (planned) community health centers, was regarded as a potentially effective substitute for long-term hospitalization.

Description of Program: Home care consisted of regular visits by public health nurses, visits by staff psychiatrists as needed (mainly for diagnostic purposes), and drug medication. Drug treatment was maintained to alleviate acute symtoms and to ameliorate patient difficulties in holding jobs and maintaining relations with family. The main point of the home care effort was to prevent the alienation of patients from society and their families that frequently characterizes long-term hospitalization and to facilitate rehabilitation. Specialized methods were used to introduce the program to the community and to circumvent institutional blocks to the program.

Study Design: Subjects were randomly chosen and assigned to treatment (home care) and control (hospitalization) groups from schizophrenics who had just been admitted to a state mental hospital. Ninety-eight people were eventually assigned to the experimental group and 54 people were assigned to the control condition.

Response Variables: The physical outcome variables included day of hospitalization, days until rehospitalization, and similar indicators. Assessment of functional behavior of patients was accomplished through a battery of four psychological tests, two types of psychiatric evaluations, and ratings of patient functioning by nursing and psychiatric staff.

Results: On the average, control group patients required rehospitalization after release more frequently than the experimental group members did. The program was successful in maintaining at-home treatment and in preventing long-term hospitalization of home care patients. Patient improvement on the psychological measures did not differ across experimental and control groups.

Abstract of:   An experiment in mental patient rehabilitation, by H. J. Meyer and E. F. Borgatta. New York: Russell Sage Foundation, 1959.

Objectives: The original purpose of this study was to determine the effectiveness of Altro Health and Rehabilitation Services methods of rehabilitating individuals hospitalized for psychiatric disorders.

Description of Program: This program was begun and conducted by Altro Health and Rehabilitation Services (New York). Treatment consisted of patients coming to the Altro workshop, where they were expected to remain for about a year; patients worked in a factory environment, but with work pressures adjusted to their health and needs. This treatment was designed to ease the patients' transition from hospitalization to normal community living.

Study Design: Individuals were randomly assigned to Altro versus control (non-Altro) conditions, but subsequent screening of the experimental group by program staff, patients' rejection of the offer to participate in Altro, and other factors reduced the size of the experimental group and introduced systematic differences between the Altro and comparison groups. Normal attrition from the Altro group further reduced the group's size.

*Response Variables:* The dependent variables were duration of patient participation in the program, psychiatric diagnoses, and patients' adjustment, attitudes, and behavior, as measured by psychological tests and other observation methods. Follow-up measures included need for recommitment, continued agency contact or extended psychiatric treatment, extent of patient's social relations, economic independence, and reality of the patient's general orientation to life.

*Results:* The experimental group was more aware of and favorable toward the Altro program. The data suggested that participation in Altro might have reduced somewhat the likelihood of rehospitalization. Other measures also showed a slight but positive effect of the treatment. These inferences were treated as questionable by the researchers, however, because of the small sample size and the extreme attrition (only about one-third of the assigned experimental subjects actually entered the program).

Abstract of:   *Casework with wives of alcoholics,* edited by P. C. Cohen and M. S. Krause. New York: Family Service Association of America, 1971.

*Objectives:* The project's purpose was "to explore, develop, and test a treatment regime which would be effective in (1) holding in treatment the wives of male alcoholics, (2) promoting treatment of the alcoholic husband, and (3) retarding or reversing disintegration of the family."

*Description of Program:* This 4-year research project was undertaken by the staff of the Family Service of the Cincinnati Area, and was funded by the National Institute of Mental Health. Phase I of the project consisted of developing techniques, training staff, and collecting a sufficient number of cases for the project. The treatment in Phase II consisted of: helping the wife understand and accept the concept that alcoholism is a chronic disease; helping her examine how her behavior could influence her husband's drinking; providing her with support as she faced her own stresses; giving her aid from community resources; when possible, taking on the husband as a project client; and giving treatment to some children in the project families. The overt control group received traditional treatment, but without the viewpoint that alcholism is a chronic disease and that the wife's behavior could contribute to the problem.

*Study Design:* Four groups of cases were formed for comparison by allocating cases randomly to groups. The four groups formed were experimental, overt control (aware that they were a control group), ostensible overflow (non-aware control), and pretreatment.

*Response Variables:* Research interviews were conducted at the close of a case to ascertain the incidence of premature termination, the alcoholic husband's progress, changes in family roles, wife's changes in attitude and personality, and improvement in family functioning and adjustment.

*Results:* Two of the project's goals were achieved: It successfully developed and described a method for engaging and holding in treatment the wives of alcoholics; it successfully developed and described a method for promoting the alcoholic husband's treatment and treatability. But it may or may not have successfully reversed or retarded the disintegration of the family. There was less drinking by alcoholic men in the experimental group, as reported at case termination, but this effect disappeared several months after the treatment ended.

Abstract of:    *Behavior modification of the mentally retarded,* edited by T. Thompson and J. Grabowski. New York: Oxford University Press, 1972.

*Objectives:* The goals of the program were to eliminate maladaptive behavior and establish or strengthen self-helping behavior. For many residents the goal was to provide "the opportunity to engage in activities which would serve as reinforcers and to increase the range . . . of behavior leading to them."

*Description of Program:* Behavior modification treatment methods were developed and tested at Faribault State School and Hospital in South Dakota. The research consisted of a series of quasi-experiments in each of which a token reward system was introduced to produce favorable behavior on the part of the residents of the hospital. One side-study was a randomized experiment; it tested chlorpromazine treatment against behavior modification methods and included a placebo control group.

*Study Design:* The major portion of the program had a quasi-experimental orientation, with most attention directed at behavior changes before and after various behavior modification techniques were introduced. Comparisons were made over time and against nonparticipating residents. The chlorpromazine study utilized a randomized crossover design and was a double blind true experiment, with continuous measures of behavior during and after the periods of treatment.

*Response Variables:* Observable behavior, including self-feeding, less assaultive behavior, verbal interaction, following instructions, and bathing were the dependent variables.

*Results:* Token reward and behavior modification systems led to consistent gains in a variety of self-care behaviors. In the experiment, there were no major differences in behavior between the chlorpromazine and placebo groups; drug treatment appeared to neither help nor hinder the rehabilitative program.

# IV. Experimental Assessment of Special Educational Programs[1]

Abstract of:   *An evaluation of the Self-Directed Search: A guide to educational and vocational planning*, by T. B. Zener and L. Schnuelle. Report No. 124. Project No. 61610-05-02, Grant No. OEG-2-7-061610-0207, Center for Social Organization of Schools, Johns Hopkins University, February 1972.

*Objectives:* The *Self-Directed Search* (SDS), a self-administered vocational guidance inventory was evaluated in this study to determine its effectiveness in helping high school students consider a broad selection of occupations and choose more appropriate occupations for themselves.

*Description of Program:* The SDS consists of an assessment booklet and an occupational classification booklet. By going through a checklist of preferred activities, competencies, occupational preferences, and self-ratings, the student can obtain a personality profile. Then, on the basis of that profile, he can obtain a list of occupations corresponding to his interests. In the non-self-administered version of SDS, the experimenter scored, summarized, and interpreted all of the information for the student.

*Study Design:* Over 1000 students in three grade levels at five schools were randomly assigned to three treatment groups: the regular SDS; the SDS scored by the experimenter; and regular, school-based vocational experiences. The Student Vocational Interest Questionnaire was administered to all subjects to collect pretreatment and posttreatment information about students.

*Response Variables:* While both SDS groups considered more occupations than members of the control group did, the regular version SDS led students to

---

[1] See Earle's *Police Recruit Training* in Section II also.

consider more appropriate ones (based on interests and abilities). Both SDS versions also increased satisfaction and certainty about vocational choices. The self-directed SDS students also understood the workings of the SDS better than the non-self-directed students. Finally, the students rated both SDS versions as moderately positive or favorable.

Abstract of:   Minimal intervention at age two and three, and subsequent intellective changes, by F. H. Palmer. In R. Parker (Ed.), *Preschool in action: Conceptualizations in Preschool Curricula Conference.* New York: Allyn and Bacon, 1972.

*Objectives:* This experiment attempted to test the presumptions that very early (preschool) learning of simple universal concepts fosters better subsequent learning of more complex concepts, and that sustained intellectual growth for the preschool child is associated with positive affect.

*Description of Program:* The program began in 1965, at the Harlem Research Center in New York. The formal treatment included a special curriculum which emphasized preschool, sequential, simple to complex concept learning. A dummy curriculum (no treatment) was developed to roughly duplicate the amount of personal contact with students, allowing appraisal of Hawthorne effects. Instructors were rotated to eliminate systematic skill effects.

*Study Design:* Black children in the Harlem area were identified, selected, and allocated randomly to treatment (120), dummy treatment (120), and control group (70).

*Response Variables:* Covariates in analysis were age and socioeconomic status. Outcome variables included concept knowledge in different circumstances, a specially constructed concept formation index, and some intelligence measures (e.g., Stanford–Binet).

*Results:* Positive and persistent changes in concept formation and learning occurred up to 2 years after treatment for the special curriculum group, but there were few significant differences between the treatment and dummy groups; only between controls and experiments were there major differences. Better learning of concept formation seems to obtain when intensified teaching is given at age 3 rather than 2, and training at either age is better than nothing. Attrition rates were 30% for controls and 20% for experimentals.

Abstract of:   *Middle Start: Supportive interventions for higher education among students of disadvantaged backgrounds,* by J. Yinger, K. Ikeda, and F. Laycock. Final Report. Project No. 5-0703, Grant No. OE6-10-255, Psychology Department, Oberlin College (Oberlin, Ohio), November 24, 1970 (ms).

*Objectives:* Middle Start was designed and implemented as a program for enhancing academic, cultural, and other abilities of disadvantaged junior high school students.

*Description of Program:*   The program was run by Oberlin College's administrative staff and faculty, and by local school administrators. Student selection at the five schools was based on school teachers' and administrators' recommendations of students having some initiative; data on effects of the program were reported for the first three summers' students, 1964–1966. Treatments consisted of 6-week summer sessions characterized by high teacher–pupil ratios, a broad but intensive period of educational, artistic, and recreational experience, substantial counseling and other adult support; and post-summer activities.

*Study Design:* Students were matched and then within the resultant 195 pairs randomly allocated to treatment or control groups. An additional, nonequivalent control group was also utilized to assess influence by experimental students on controls.

*Response Variables:* Staying in school, attaining good grades, selection for special academic schools, and entering college were all dependent measures.

*Results:* In general, the experimental group demonstrated a significantly higher academic achievement rating than the control group, even when the quality of the matching process was considered. "With pre-program advantages taken into account, 43% of the experimental children gained, 36% held their own, and 21% lost, relative to their partners." The total program costs were less than $2,000 per student, over a 5-year period. Three ingredients were found to be necessary for success in this type of program (1) a different, new, exciting, and challenging experience; (2) sponsors to help the students become aware of life's possibilities; and (3) supportive persons, particularly parents, to facilitate the program's effectiveness.

Abstract of:    *A national experiment in curriculum evaluation,* by W. W. Welch and H. J. Walberg. *American Educational Research Journal,* 1972, **9,** 373–384. and:    *A review of the research and evaluation program of Harvard Project Physics,* by W. W. Welch. ERIC Center for Science and Mathematics. Ohio State University, Columbus, 1971.

*Objectives:* The study was designed to evaluate the effects of Project Physics on students' interest and the improvement of their laboratory, mathematical, and other physics-related skills.

*Description of Program:* Professionally affiliated high school teachers were invited to participate in the evaluation of the system. Teachers in the experimental group attended a 6-week briefing session, took a series of tests, taught the project course during the 1967–1968 academic year, and administered pretests, midtests, and posttests to their students. The teachers in the control group attended a 2-day briefing session and administered the same tests to their students; they continued to teach their *regular* physics courses.

*Study Design:* Teachers were chosen randomly for invitation to the project. Of the acceptors, 46 were randomly allocated to the experimental group and 26 to the control group. Due to attrition, the experimental group finished with 34 teachers and the controls with 19.

*Response Variables:* Cognitive skills tests, course grades, affective inventories, course satisfaction, Learning Environment Inventory, a course reaction questionnaire, Semantic Differential Test, and a physics perception test were included in the measurement system.

*Results:* Project students scored as well as controls on cognitive measures, perceived their course as "more diverse and egalitarian and less difficult . . . , and saw physics as more historical, philosophical, and humanitarian and less mathematical." Finally, the course had special appeal to the middle-range IQ group, 112–119, which has increasingly tended to elect not to take physics in high school in the last decade.

Abstract of:   *Relationship of curriculum, teaching, and learning in preschool education*, by D. P. Weikart. In J. C. Stanley (ed.), *Preschool programs for the disadvantaged*. Baltimore, Maryland: Johns Hopkins University Press, 1972. and: *A comparative study of three preschool curricula*, by D. P. Weikart. In J. Frost (ed.), *Disadvantaged child*, (Second Edition), New York: Houghton, Mifflin, 1970.

*Objectives:* The objectives of the study included determining whether preschool makes a difference in later performance in school, and which type of preschool curriculum is best.

*Description of Program:* The Ypsilanti Preschool Curriculum Demonstration Project was a 3-year program consisting of a cognitively oriented open framework preschool, a task-oriented language training preschool, and a traditional nursery school. Two teachers were assigned to each model, having stated a preference for that type of program. The school programs consisted of daily class, and a home teaching session every other week.

*Study Design:* Functionally retarded 3-and 4-year-old children were stratified according to sex and race, and randomly assigned to one of the three treatment groups. Both pretest and posttest data were collected.

*Response Variables:* Stanford–Binet IQ test scores; classroom observations; observations in free play settings; ratings of children by teachers and independent examiners; and evaluations by outside critics were obtained.

*Results:* All three programs led to student improvement. There were no differences between groups at either the pretest or posttest. Children seemed to profit from any curriculum based on a wide range of experiences. However, a falling off in the effectiveness of the traditional method by the third year indicated that intense planning and supervision by the staff are necessary for the program to be effective.

Abstract of:   The Early Training Project for Disadvantaged Children: A report after five years, by R. A. Klaus and S. W. Gray. *Monographs of the Society for Research in Child Development*, **33** (4), Chicago, Illinois: University of Chicago Press, 1968.

*Objectives:* The Early Training Project attempted to develop an intervention package consisting of those variables which seemed most likely to be influential in later school performance, in order to offset the progressive retardation of disadvantaged children.

*Description of Program:* Researchers at the George Peabody College for Teachers introduced this 5-year program in a town in the upper South, in 1962. The first treatment group attended a 10-week preschool during 3 summers, and had 3 years of weekly meetings with a home visitor during that part of the year when the preschool was not in session. The second group had 2 summers of special preschool plus 2 years of meetings with the home visitor.

The preschools were designed to affect the children's achievement motivation, persistence, delay of gratification, interest in schoollike activities, and identification with achieving role models, in addition to perceptual development, concept formation, and language development.

*Study Design:* On the basis of a city census of all children born in 1958, a small sample of children were selected on the basis of their poverty level and disadvantaged backgrounds. The treatment groups were formed using random allocation.

*Response Variables:* A program of testing was conducted from the time just before the first summer of intervention to the June following the second year of public schooling. The Stanford–Binet test, the Wechsler Intelligence Scale for Children, the Peabody Picture Vocabulary Test, and the Illinois Test of Psycholinguistic Abilities, were all used as dependent measures. In addition, the Metropolitan and the Gates Reading Readiness Tests, the Metropolitan Achievement Test, Primary Battery, and the Stanford Achievement Test were used.

*Results:* There were no group differences at the beginning of the study. After treatment, however, on intelligence measures the experimental children were superior to the controls. This is true for full scale, verbal, and performance scores, and for seven subtests. On the tests of language and reading readiness the experimentals were again superior. In general, gains were obtained in the experimental groups at a significant level for 4 years. The gains were modest, however, in spite of the relative intensity of the program.

Abstract of:   *Project Breakthrough: A responsive environment field experiment with preschool children from public assistance families,* by W. W. Hudson and D. L. Daniel. Cook County Department of Public Aid, Cook County, Illinois, 1969.

*Objectives:* "The primary objective of Project Breakthrough was to raise the skill level of preschool children in public aid families in the area of reading and language development."

*Description of Program:* The treatment consisted of a special educational program for the children, and/or intensive social work services for their families. The educational program involved intensive use of the Edison Responsive Environment Talking Typewriters (ERE) (computerized learning machines). For 8 months, Group I received intensive social work services and ERE training; Group II received intensive social work services only; Group III received regular social work services and ERE training; and Group IV received regular social work services only.

*Study Design:* Once qualified families agreed to take part, the children were matched by IQ scores into pairs, the members of which were randomly allocated to Group I or II. Once these two groups were filled (34 in each group), the same matching techniques were used to assign regular casework children to Groups III and IV.

*Response Variables:* The Stanford–Binet Intelligence Scale, the Peabody Picture Vocabular Test, the Metropolitan Readiness Test, the Vineland Social Maturity

Scale, the Stanford Achievement Test, and the Family Functioning Instrument were all used.

*Results:* Project Breakthrough training significantly increased children's intelligence ratings and reading readiness levels, but not their social maturity or family functioning capacity. Intensive social work services were found to markedly increase Peabody Picture Vocabulary Test scores, and reading readiness, but not IQ scores. It also significantly increased the social maturity of the children and their families' functioning capacities.

Abstract of:   *The second year of Sesame Street: A continuing evaluation.* Volumes 1 and 2, by G. A. Bogatz and S. Ball. Princeton, New Jersey: Educational Testing Service, 1971.

and:   *Sesame Street revisited: A case study in evaluation research,* by T. D. Cook with H. Appleton, R. Conner, A. Shaffer, G. Tamkin, and S. J. Weber. New York: Russell Sage (in preparation).

*Objectives:* The studies attempted to evaluate the effectiveness of the television program *Sesame Street* in benefitting, both intellectually and culturally, all preschoolers, but especially disadvantaged children.

*Description of Program:* Staff of the Educational Testing Service designed the initial study and carried out the original data analysis and evaluation. Secondary data analysis and evaluation were performed by T. D. Cook and others. The major treatment was directed at children and their parents and consisted of intensive encouragement to watch *Sesame Street.* Target subjects in 1970 were selected from Boston, Durham, Phoenix, and rural areas in California, Philadelphia, Los Angeles, and Winston–Salem; the target sample consisted mainly of middle class and disadvantaged youngsters.

*Study Design:* Children were randomly allocated to treatment or control groups, with a 2:1 treatment:control ratio in 1970, and a 1:1 ratio in 1971. Because of the program's popularity, the randomized character of control and treatment groups could not be sustained, however.

*Response Variables:* Changes in cognitive functioning were measured by a battery of achievement tests during the first year of the study. In the second year, in addition to cognitive measures, cultural tests were also included. Data on parental aspirations for their children were also collected.

*Results:* Encouragement increased viewing time at all sites except Philadelphia and Boston (unencouraged subjects in those sites viewed as much as encouraged subjects at other sites); learning increased with increased encouragement. Skills which received the most attention in the program itself were generally learned best according to ETS. Learning occurred with and without adult supervision. Younger viewers appeared to benefit more than older viewers. Disadvantaged youngsters who watched the program a great deal achieved at about the same levels as middle-class youngsters who watched very little. A second year evaluation has been conducted to verify these results with additional new groups of youngsters.

Abstract of:   *Prelude to school: An evaluation of an inner-city preschool program,* by I. Kraft, J. Fuschillo, and E. Herzog. Children's Bureau, Social and Rehabilitation Service, United States Department of Health, Education and Welfare, 1972.

*Objectives:* The purpose of the Howard University Preschool Project was to find out "whether and to what extent a standard nursery school that includes work with parents can enhance the later school achievement of children who live in a slum area."

*Description of Program:* The treatment group attended preschool for 7 hours a day, over two 10-month school years. In addition, the parents of the children in this group attended group meetings at which the children and the school were discussed and made individual school visits to see the preschool in operation and determine how the students were doing. Control group children did not attend preschool, although their families were visited at home by the research workers, and were encouraged to see themselves as involved in a "university-centered study of some significance."

*Study Design:* By canvassing preselected census tracts in Washinton, D.C., 200 families containing 3-year-olds were identified. The two most populous tracts were then randomly allocated to treatment or control designations. From the treatment tract, families were randomly selected to be invited to participate. Likewise, comparison families were randomly selected for invitation from the other tract (plus some from an additional tract to fill out the group). Pretreatment and posttreatment observations were obtained.

*Response Variables:* "Basic achievement-related skills as language usage, perceptual discrimination, concept formation," etc. were all measured by standardized tests.

*Results:* All of the treatment children except two gained in IQ (Stanford–Binet) over the 2 years of preschool. On other measures, the treatment group also significantly gained, but at the end of 2 years they "were still over a year below their age norm in associative language ability and grammar." The comparison children also significantly increased in IQ, but their average gain was much smaller than the gain in the treatment group.

Abstract of:   *A training, demonstration and research program for the remediation of learning disorders in culturally disadvantaged youth* (Seymour Feshbach, Project Director). Final Report (in 2 parts). Fernald School, Department of Psychology, University of California, Los Angeles, 1970.

*Objectives:* This project had two major objectives: (1) allowing professionals in education to work with culturally disadvantaged children and (2) evaluating the effects of this intensive compensatory education effort.

*Description of Program:* The Fernald School treatment group received schooling which was different from regulation education in three ways: (1) each student's needs determined his curriculum and each received individualized instruction, (2) the student–teacher ratio was 4:1, and (3) the school atmosphere was more persuasive and the curriculum very wide in scope (art, photography, black history, etc.). The School Enrichment Program group received a transplanted Fernald School type of instruction in schools in disadvantaged areas. Finally, the control group received no unusual treatment. All students who participated were either in elementary school or in junior high school and participated during their summer vacations and during the academic year.

*Study Design:* The disadvantaged youngsters were grouped in matched triplets. A member of each triplet was then randomly allocated to one of the three groups. A special comparison group of advantaged youngsters was selected from the regular Fernald School students, based on matching with the disadvantaged children with respect to learning disabilities and IQ's, and assigned to Fernald School. Pretest and posttest data were collected.

*Response Variables:* A wide variety of measures were used to measure changes in cognitive skills, attitudes, intelligence, interests, etc. These included the California Achievement Test, Vocational Checklist (boys' form), Witkin Rod and Frame Test, Wechsler Intelligence Scale for Children, Attitude Survey, and the Ethnic Attitudes Instrument.

*Results:* The major experimental finding was the increase in achievement observed in the disadvantaged children attending the Fernald School and the failure of the enrichment program to exert an influence significantly greater than that provided by the control experience. Each academic year, both Fernald School groups made increases in grade-placement scores of slightly more than 1 year, and both groups were significantly better than the enrichment or control groups. On all attitude scores there were no significant changes. The summer session groups showed no marked achievement change scores or atitude changes.

# V.  Sociomedical and Fertility Control Experiments[1]

Abstract of: *Stimulation of intellectual and social competence in Colombian preschool children affected by multiple deprivations of depressed urban environments*, Progress Report #1, by L. Sinisterra, H. McKay, and A. McKay, and Progress Report #2, by H. McKay, A. McKay, and L. Sinisterra. University Center for Child Development, Human Ecology Research Station, Universidad del Valle, Cali, Colombia, (November 1971 and September 1973).

*Objectives:* The study was designed to evaluate the effectiveness of a large-scale program for stimulating intellectual and social competence in disadvantaged Colombian children.

*Description of Program:* Conducted under the auspices of the Universidad del Valle, this research project was funded primarily by the Ford Foundation.

Once chosen as sufficiently disadvantaged to qualify for the experiment, the children were assigned to the medical, nutritional, and educational treatment (Group I); just medical and nutritional treatment (Group VI-A), or control groups; in addition to these, a group of nondeprived (middle-class) children formed Group V, a quasi-experimental comparison. The treatment for Group I consisted of preschool (30 hours per week), food at school and at home, and medical attention daily. Group VI-A received weekly medical attention and packaged food at home. The controls received medical attention only if a social worker happened to note it was needed when visiting.

*Study Design:* Three-year old children were grouped by neighborhood and ran-

[1]See the Kurtzberg, Safer, and Cavior study in Section I also.

domly assigned to treatment conditions. Each year a "lottery" was planned to determine the participants in the treatment groups for that year. Pretests and posttests were used.

*Response Variables:* Medical–nutritional measures, daily food intake, medical records, cognitive measures, family and economic measures, and data on health and sanitary conditions were collected annually.

*Results:* This experiment is currently in progress and there has been no final data analysis. Preliminary analysis shows that the preschool plus nutrition treatment group progressed on cognitive measures to the extent of covering 80% of the discrepancy between untreated controls and the middle-class comparison group. Nutrition alone had no effect on cognitive test results but did affect health measures.

Abstract of:   *Family planning in Taiwan: An experiment in social change,* by R. Freedman, J. Y. Takeshita, *et al.* Princeton, New Jersey: Princeton University Press, 1969.

*Objectives:* The experiment was designed to test an intensive field program for family planning and to test the acceptability of IUDs.

*Description of Program:* The design of the program involved four treatments directed to 36,000 married couples in Taichung with wives 20–39 years old. The four treatments were: (1) Everything—husband and wife (Ehw): personal visits to both husband and wife, information mailed, and neighborhood meetings; (2) Everything—wife only (Ew): everything but the personal visit to the husbands; (3) Mailings: no personal visits, unless requested, or meetings, instead a series of mailed information; (4) Nothing: no effort made to reach the couples directly.

*Study Design:* Treatments were allocated by *lin,* a neighborhood unit containing about 20 households. Each lin was located in one of three density sectors, which differed only in the proportion of lins getting the Ehw or Ew treatments; lins were randomly allocated to treatment. Both pretreatment surveys and posttreatment surveys were carried out.

*Response Variables:* Acceptance and use of contraceptives were primary dependent variables.

*Results:* During the program, 5454 couples accepted family guidance planning. Nearly 80% chose the IUD, less than 2% the oral pills, and about 19% traditional methods (mostly condoms). The lowest level of IUD usage occurred among the couples personally visited, presumably because fieldworkers explained various methods, whereas word of mouth diffusion of information concentrated on the IUD. The home-visit treatments yielded the best results, but husband visits did not add much. The mail campaign was not especially effective.

Abstract of:   An experiment in the rehabilitation of nursing home patients, by H. R. Kelman. *Public Health Reports* (Public Health Service, United States Department of Health, Education, and Welfare) 1962, **77,** 356–366.

*Objectives:* This study attempted to answer two questions: (1) "Would a large-scale rehabilitation program offered to physically disabled patients in nursing homes significantly alter this population's level of self-care?" and (2) "Could subgroups who would differ significantly in their response to rehabilitation treatment be identified?"

*Description of Program:* Two treatment and two control groups were used in the study. The Nursing Home Treatment (Group B) subjects were treated by mobile rehabilitation teams with individualized therapeutic programs for each patient. Maintenance programs were instituted once the patients had maximally benefited from therapy. The Hospital Treatment (Group C) subjects were transferred for treatment to hospital rehabilitation centers. After completion of active treatment, the patients were returned to the nursing homes for maintenance services. Control Group A was equivalent to treatment groups B and C in selection, but received only the usual care and services. Control group D was not equivalent, but also received only the usual nursing home care. All treatments continued for 1 year.

*Study Design:* The experimental design for Groups A, B, and C utilized matched samples of randomly allocated subjects selected from 11 nursing homes. Group D was selected from 4 additional nursing homes to serve as a comparison group for estimating possible effects of contact with special treatment patients. Pretreatment and posttreatment data were collected on the 100 members of each group.

*Response Variables:* Self-care data (patients' locomotion, dressing, feeding, etc.) incidence of hospitalization during treatment, and ratings of psychological and physical states of the patient during the year of treatment were outcome variables.

*Results:* Comparison of pretreatment and posttreatment data suggested that neither hospital nor nursing home rehabilitation altered the patients' self-care abilities significantly. Comparison of all treated patients with all controls likewise showed no substantial differences. Necessary hospitalization of many patients during the 1 year of treatment undermined programmatic efforts to encourage increased self-care. There were notable differences between hospital rehabilitation and nursing home treatment, as reflected by extent of activities of patients within each group (the hospitalized group performed at high levels). Subgroups which were most likely to improve with rehabilitation included younger men and individuals who were more emotionally stable and interested in rehabilitation.

Abstract of: *The family and population control: A Puerto Rican experiment in social change,* by R. Hill, J. M. Stycos, and K. W. Back. Chapel Hill, North Carolina: University of North Carolina Press, 1959.

*Objectives:* This study was launched to ascertain how the high fertility rate in Puerto Rico could be decreased by family planning programs.

*Description of Program:* The experimental phase consisted of testing the effectiveness of two methods of communication, pamphlets versus group meetings, and of three types of program content: "(1) values favorable to family planning and information about birth control; (2) family organization, mainly communication between husbands and wives; (3) a combination of the two topics."

Preprogram interviews were given to identify and classify the experimental families. Then, 2 months after the educational programs, interviews were also conducted. No special educational programs were initiated in the comparison groups.

*Study Design:* Twenty-three rural communities were canvassed and then randomly allocated to treatments. In each village, families of each of four types were matched according to values, family organization, and knowledge about birth control. The four types of families were: ready for contraception use, uninformed about birth control, inefficient users of contraception, and opposed to contraception.

*Response Variables:* Reported change in contraception practices, changes in familial communications, and changes in attitudes toward contraceptive practices were observed.

*Results:* Pamphlets were found to be more effective in promoting the starting of contraceptive usage although the meetings led to more continuous use, measured a year later. The values information program was most effective in maintaining use among those starting contraception and least effective in maintaining use among families already using contraception.

Abstract of:    Korea—The relationship between the IUD retention and check-up visits, by S. Bang. *Studies in Family Planning,* **2** (5), May 1971.

*Objectives:* This study was conducted to explore different ways of raising IUD retention rates. The hypothesis was that "the sooner the revisit, the better the retention rate since special counseling would reassure the acceptor."

*Description of Program:* The Korean National Family Planning Program, under the auspices of Yonsei University, conducted this experiment in 1967. At the time the IUD's were provided to acceptors in the Koyand County health centers, the acceptors were told to return to the clinic for a checkup after 1 week, after 2 weeks or after 1 month.

*Study Design:* Acceptors were randomly assigned to treatment groups: checkup after 1 or 2 weeks, or after 1 month.

*Response Variables.* Retention of the IUDs was the sole dependent variable.

*Results:* Exactly opposite to what was predicted, it was found that the 1-week group had the lowest retention rate and the highest IUD removal rate; the 1-month group had the highest retention rate and the lowest removal rate. Apparently, encouraging a visit to the clinic during the early period of stress (first week) offers more opportunity for removal, which more than offsets the advantage of extra counseling.

Abstract of:    Family planning experiments: A review of designs, by W. P. Mauldin and J. A. Ross. In the *Proceedings of the Social Statistics Section of the American Statistical Association,* 1966.

This article discusses a number of field experiments designed to assess large family planning programs.

*India–Harvard–Ludhiana Study:* This 4-year study involved 16,000 people in an experimental test of the effect of advice regarding contraception. The treatment consisted of information about foam tablets. Sixteen villages were randomly assigned to treatment groups. Tests were made relative to a working control population (to isolate the effects of the contraceptive advice and materials), and a blank control population (no project workers collecting individual information). Observations included births, deaths, and natural increases in the population. The impact of the program on fertility was minimal.

*Singur Study:* This study was an outgrowth of the Harvard–Ludhiana study and was designed "to offer several simple methods of family planning, using local field workers, and to provide more systematic information about family planning. Eight experimental villages and 15 control villages were randomly chosen for the study. Treatment consisted of small group meetings, involvement of community leaders, and visual aid education of the experimental group concerning a wife variety of birth control devices." Periodic surveys enabled the researchers to improve the educational aspects of the program. Fertility rates fell more rapidly in the experimental than in the control areas.

*Koyang Experiment:* In order to raise the level of contraceptive use in Korea, 14 villages became the target of two birth control programs. Seven villages were assigned to the treatment condition and seven to the control condition. The treatment consisted of a more intensive local program while the controls received the national program treatment. In spreading favorable attitudes on family planning, raising levels of use of birth control devices, and reducing pregnancy rates, both programs succeeded, with the local, intensive program being more effective.

# VI. Appraisals of the Effectiveness of Communication Methods[1]

Abstract of: *Experiments on mass communication,* by C. I. Hovland, A. A. Lumsdaine, and F. D. Sheffield. Princeton, New Jersey: Princeton University Press, 1949.

*Objectives:* These studies attempted to measure "changes in knowledge, opinion, or behavior produced by a film or other communication devices."

*Description of Program:* During World War II the Experimental Section of the Research Branch in the War Department's Information and Education Division conducted a series of studies on the effects of three types of films: orientation films, training films, and films designed to satisfy general interests. Orientation films were shown to new recruits "to acquaint members of the Army with factual information as to the causes, the events leading up to our entry into the war, and the principles for which we are fighting." The experimental groups saw the films while the control groups did not. Audience evaluations of films were also determined by several substudies employing experimental designs. Effectiveness of alternative presentations (movies versus film strips, presenting both sides or one side only of a controversial topic, etc.) was tested by a series of randomized experiments. The effects of audience participation were also studied.

*Study Design:* Most of the experiments involved random allocation of units of men to experimental or control groups. Pretests and posttests were utilized in some, posttests only in others. Several posttests were utilized to determine long-term effects, in several studies.

[1]See also the Welch–Walberg experiment in Section IV and the contents of Section VII.

*Response Variables:* Changes in knowledge of factual material; changes in interpretations, opinions, and "morale"; evaluation and acceptance of the films; and changes in overt behavior were all dependent measures.

*Results:* The films had definite effects on the men's knowledge of facts, and to a lesser extent on opinions specifically covered in the films. More favorable opinions toward the war and its background were not produced. It was found that the more men liked a film, the more they were affected by it, but that men who thought the films were propagandistic were somewhat less affected. The more intelligent the viewers, the more they learned from the films; the more motivated the audience, the more they learned; and participation led to greater learning. Opinion change was found to be related to intellectual ability and initial opinions in a complex way. Giving both sides of an argument appeared to cause more opinion change.

Abstract of:   *Getting out the vote,* by H. F. Gosnell. Chicago, Illinois: University of Chicago Press, 1927.

*Objectives:* This study attempted to determine the extent to which some of the factors causing voting behavior could be controlled in a given election.

*Description of Program:* A large-scale mail campaign was instituted by Gosnell to stimulate voter registration in the experimental group prior to the presidential election of 1924. The first mail out treatment to all adult residents in the sample included Polish, Czech, Italian, and English versions of documents containing factual information on registration dates; the second notice was an informative printed cartoon; the third was a personal notice. Interviews with the subjects provided background data.

*Study Design:* Allocation to experimental and control groups was random, by area of residence within precinct. Checks on demographic features of both groups yielded no pretreatment differences.

*Response Variables:* Records of voter registration were furnished by poll books and poll watchers. Actual voting behavior was also a dependent measure.

*Results:* About 9% more registration per treatment was evident in the treatment groups. This varied from 3 to 23.3%, however, depending on ethnic group, race, and educational training. In actual registered votes cast, the experimental group also showed 9% improvement over the control group. This also varied according to ethnic group, race, and education level.

Abstract of:   *A controlled study of the effect of television messages on safety belt use,* by L. S. Robertson, A. B. Kelley, B. O'Neill, C. W. Wixom, R. S. Eiswirth, and W. Haldon. (Washington, D.C.: Insurance Institute for Highway Safety), *Public Health,* 1973, in press.
and:   Safety belt ads have no effect, by the Insurance Institute for Highway Safety. *Status Report,* **7**, (11), June 12, 1972.

*Objectives:* This experiment was designed to appraise the effectiveness of different types of TV advertisements encouraging seat belt usage.

*Description of Program:* Under the auspices of the Insurance Institute for Highway Safety, which acts in part as a research arm for the insurance industry, different messages were broadcast over two different cables of a dual TV cable system. The messages were shown for 9 consecutive months.

*Study Design:* The experiment used a near random assignment of people to treatment groups (TV cables) and random selection of subjects of observation. Observations of drivers' seat belt wearing behavior were made before, during, and after the treatment. Treatment–driver linkage was determined by matching license plate information to cable coverage of households. The study was double blind in that the TV viewers did not know they were being studied and the observers did not know the purpose of the study or in what group the persons being observed belonged.

*Response Variables:* On-site observation of seat belt usage was the sole dependent measure in this study.

*Results:* Television messages appeared to have had no effect on drivers' behavior.

Abstract of:   *Television and aggression,* by S. Feshbach and R. D. Singer. San Francisco, California: Jossey-Bass, 1971.

*Objectives:* This study was designed to assess the effects of television violence on viewers.

*Description of Program:* With the cooperation of a number of private schools and boys' homes, the television viewing of preadolescent and adolescent boys was systematically controlled for a 6-week period. The experimental group viewed predominantly aggressive shows, while the control group viewed nonaggressive programs. The boys watched a minimum of 6 hours of television per week.

*Study Design:* In seven private intitutions, 395 boys were randomly assigned to conditions, in most cases individually, but in some cases by clusters. Aggressive behavior was measured during the 6-week period, and both groups were then compared.

*Response Variables:* Input and output measures included Bendig's overt hostility scale, the lie scale of MMPI, Saltz and Epstein's conflict scale, and Black's neuroticism scale (based on the MMPI). Behavioral rating scales were also used daily by teachers; peer ratings were completed by subjects.

*Results:* The results indicate overall that exposure to aggressive content on television does not produce an increment in aggressive behavior. In fact, in the boys' homes, "Boys exposed to aggressive TV content manifested significantly less behavioral aggression toward peers and authority." It was also found that the controls reported less fantasy aggression.

# VII. Experimental Tests of Methods for Data Collection, Transmission, and Retrieval

Experimental designs are often used by public and private agencies to determine the most effective method of eliciting and transmitting data from a large number of people or institutions. One might, for example, wish to gauge the effect of using second-class mail rather than first-class mail in producing a higher response rate, for a census using mailed questionnaires. These efforts are too numerous and too diverse to be listed here with any adequacy. But some illustrative experiments are summarized below to give the reader some feel for the role which experimental testing can play in the development of methods for improving information collection, transmission, and retrieval.

Experiments in a wide variety have been conducted to determine the best methods of assuring sampling validity and of assuring completeness in response. Once the sample is specified, individuals who are contacted in, say, a mail survey may not respond for a variety of reasons. In order to foster high response rates, one can design randomized experiments in which the mode of initial contact is varied. Randomly selected groups of college students, for example, have been sent certified letters, special delivery letters, and first class mail, to discover which strategy produced the highest response rate. Astin and Panos (1970) found that special delivery mail yielded highest response rate and lowest average cost; auto-typed versus mimeo letters were also tried, with auto-typing resulting in best response rate. Other studies with the same objective have varied the process of eliciting information in other ways and with other populations. Hochstim (1967), for example, has conducted experiments in which he found that mail surveys (by the California Public Health Service) with repeated follow up via mail and telephone yield response rates and questionnaire completion rates which are comparable to all-telephone and all-interview surveys; costs for the mail and follow-ups were substantially lower than costs for other methods. Some interesting experiments in response rate research has involved the manipulation of orientation in cover letters and length of questionnaire. In large sample questionnaire experiments, Champion and Sear (1969) found that letters which appealed to the ego of the respondent (his opinion, his feeling, etc.) were significantly more effective for lower socioeconomic groups than were other approaches; the highest response rates for upper socioeconomic groups were obtained with form letters which stressed altruistic motives for responding (contribution to society, science, etc.).

A number of experimental studies have tried to appraise the veracity of responses as a function of mode of eliciting data; validity of response is examined generally by measuring correlations between respondents replies and administrative records on the same topic. The Hochstim (1967) studies mentioned earlier involved asking personal questions regarding cervical cytology; in validating women's responses that they had in fact discussed cytology with their husbands, Hochstim found that mail surveys, rather than personal interview or telephone, yielded the highest validities. Experimental studies of distortion in opinion and attitude surveys, where identified and anonymous reporting constitute the treatments, have also been conducted. This work has involved employee groups (Pearlin, 1961), military and community groups (see Roman, 1960, for a listing of these), and others.

Another sort of experiment involving accuracy of reporting and of measurement is the experimental analysis of testing procedures in governmental, industrial, or commercial laboratories. Mandel's (1959) work on this topic has stimulated a wide series of experiments to determine the relative accuracy and degree of agreement of interlaboratory testing.

Some of the most ambitious efforts to appraise the sources of random and systematic error in educational and psychological measurements involve randomized experiments designed specifically for that purpose. Research by Cronbach, Gleser, Nanda, and Rajaratnam (1972) has general implications for analyzing the components of variability in any social measurement, gauging the sensitivity of measures for optimizing costs of testing, and examining sources of fallibility in measures. Summaries of experimental tests of influences in laboratory research in the behavioral and social sciences have been compiled by Rosenthal and Rosnow (1969) and others.

Large-scale experiments for evaluating the best mode of data processing quality control have been conducted at the United States Census Bureau by Minton (1969) and others. Treatments are essentially methods of keypunching, transcription, and verification of data. Since inaccurate coding, open-ended responses, and keypunching error are defined by both process and skill of personnel, the manipulation of treatments is essential for development of good estimates of error rate and of acceptable limits of nonsampling error in statistical reporting. Similar experiments have been conducted to appraise quality in business censuses, in economic and geographic censuses, and in social survey systems.

Data retrieval experiments have frequently been conducted with textual rather than fully quantified information. For example, to test alternative indexing systems for retrieval of complex patent information, King (1963) has devised experiments for the United States Patent Office. Although the experiments have been small they appear to have been helpful in assessing indexing systems. Cornog (1963) has investigated the research subjects' influence on research results in patent experiments.

## Source Materials

Astin, A. W., and Panos, R. J. *The educational and vocational development of college students.* Washington, D.C.: American Council on Education, 1969 (Appendix D).

Champion, D. J., and Sear, A. M. Research Notes: Questionnaire response rate: A methodological analysis. *Social Forces,* 1969, **47,** 335–339.

Cornog, J. R. How people influence experimental results. *Proceedings of the American Statistical Association, Social Statistics Section,* Washington, D.C.: American Statistical Association, 1963, pp. 119–122.

Cronbach, L., Gleser, G., Nanda, H., and Rajaratnam, N. *The dependability of behavioral measurements.* New York: Wiley, 1972.

Hochstim, J. R. A critical comparison of three strategies of collecting data from households. *American Statistical Association Journal,* 1967, **62,** 976–989.

King, D. W. Designs of experiments in information retrieval. *Proceedings of the American Statistical Association: Social Statistics Section,* Washington, D.C: American Statistical Association, 1963, 103–118.

Mandel, J. and Lashof, J. W. The interlaboratory evaluation of testing methods. *ASTM Bulletin,* 1959, **239,** 53–61.

Minton, G. Inspection and correction error in data processing. *Journal of the American Statistical Association,* 1969, **64,** 1256–1275.

Pearlin, L. I. The appeals of anonymity in questionnaire response. *Public Opinion Quarterly,* 1961, **25,** 640–647.

Roman, N. A. Anonymity and attitude measurement. *Public Opinion Quarterly,* 1960, **24,** 675–679.

Rosenthal, R. and Rosnow, R. L. (Eds.) *Artifact in behavioral research.* New York: Academic Press, 1969.

# VIII.  Experiments in Research Utilization[1]

Abstract of:  *Utilization of applicable research and demonstration results,* by E. M. Glaser, H. S. Coffey, and others. Los Angeles, California: Human Interaction Research Institute, 1967.

*Objectives:* This study was undertaken to study the factors which facilitate the diffusion and use of information about innovations (specifically, the Tacoma Project) in the vocational rehabilitation field. It was also designed to identify the barriers which prevent agencies from developing their own or adopting others' innovations.

*Description of Program:* Two strategies were developed and applied experimentally. One strategy developed and applied three types of communication: a pamphlet was sent to the target institution; a conference was held; or an experienced spokesman was sent to advise and consult with target institutions. The second strategy consisted of more intensive consultation with the management staff of five vocational rehabilitation organizations.

*Study Design:* In both strategies, the target organizations were selected randomly for the control or experimental groups.

*Response Variables:* Interest in the Tacoma Project, knowledge of the project, and adoption of the project (in terms of features adopted) were all dependent measures.

*Results:* The pamphlet and conference communication techniques were effective both in communicating and in stimulating others to use the reported methods. The spokesman technique was not successful in either way. In the consultation strategy, agencies for which consultation was provided showed more improvement than agencies which were offered no consultation.

[1]See the Welch–Walberg experiment described in Section IV, also.

# IX.  Economic Experiments

Abstract of:   *Income maintenance: Interdisciplinary approaches to research*, by L. L.
Orr, R. G. Hollister, M. J. Lefcowitz, and K. Hester (eds.). Chicago, Illinois:
Markham, 1971.
and:   Adjusted and extended preliminary results from the urban graduate
work incentive experiments, by H. W. Watts. Institute for Research on
Poverty Research Report. Madison, Wisconsin: Institute for Research on
Poverty, 1970.
and:   Further preliminary results of the New Jersey graduated work incentive experiment, United States Office of Economic Opportunity, Washington, D.C.: O.E.O., (May) 1971.
and:   Graduated work incentives: An experiment in negative taxation,
by H. W. Watts. *American Economic Review*, 1969, **59**, 463–472.
and:   A negative income tax experimnt, by D. N. Kershaw. *Scientific American*, 1972, **227**, 19–25.

*Objectives:* The Income Maintenance experiments were initiated to appraise the
effects of simple income supplements on the socioeconomic behavior of the
working poor, and to test alternative income supplement plans.

*Description of Program:* Specialized income maintenance programs were initiated
in areas of New Jersey and Pennsylvania (urban), Iowa and North Carolina
(rural), Washington, Indiana, and Colorado. The target group for the urban
experiment was restricted to "male-headed families with a nonstudent male
head, 18–58 years of age, able to work, and with a normal family income
no more than 150% of the poverty line for each family size." There were eight
tax plans (treatments), with tax rates from 30 to 70% and guaranteed income
levels from 50 to 125% of the poverty line. To further the range of inference

of these findings, the rural experiment also included families with female heads or heads over 58 years of age. The sample was drawn from North Carolina and Iowa. Five program alternatives were set up, with 30, 50, and 70% tax rates, and 50, 75, or 100% of the poverty line guaranteed income levels. *Study Design:* In the urban experiment, once eligibility was determined, the families were randomly allocated to one of the eight negative income tax plans or to a control group. The eight treatment groups and one control group were contacted quarterly. All nine groups received a pretreatment interview and will receive a posttreatment interview.

In the rural experiment, families were selected randomly from chosen areas and, if eligible, were randomly allocated to control or treatment groups. All households were interviewed each quarter.

*Response Variables:* Outcomes of interest in the urban experiment include the extent to which income supplements serve as disincentives to employment and lead to differences in earning patterns of primary and secondary wage earners. Attention is also focused on labor migration, job changing and skill utilization, vocational improvement, savings patterns and spending behavior, and changes in familiar structure and growth rates. Effects on attitudes and economic behavior, as well as governmental costs, are the primary dependent measures of interest in the rural experiment.

*Results:* Preliminary analyses of the in-progress urban experiment suggest that the treatment (i.e., subsidy) had no effect on families; there did appear to be a tendency for families to actually increase, rather than decrease, their hourly earnings over those of the control groups. This slight increase prevailed despite indications that secondary workers (wives, etc.) worked fewer hours per family per year. So far, there has been no significant tendency for subsidized families to work fewer hours per family per year; people in the experimental group appear to take more time to look for better jobs, by comparison to control group members' job seeking efforts.

The rural experiment had not been completed at time of writing.

Abstract of:    *Housing allowance household experiment design. Part 1: Summary and overview,* by G. Buchanan and J. Heinberg. Washington, D.C.: The Urban Institute, 1972.

and: *Housing allowance experiment design. Part 2: Household response, program variations, and allotment to design space for the housing allowance experiment,* by J. Heinberg and R. Tinney. Washington, D.C.: The Urban Institute, 1972.

and: *Housing allowance household experiment design. Part 3: Response measures and scaling approaches,* by C. Thomas and T. Ling. Washington, D. C.: The Urban Institute, 1972.

and: *Housing allowance experiment design. Part 4: Sampling issues,* by G. Buchanan, T. Ling, and R. Tinney. Washington, D.C.: The Urban Institute, 1972.

and: *Housing allowance experiment design. Part 5: Analysis plan for the housing allowance household experiment,* by T. Ling, G. Buchanan, and L. Ozanne. Washington, D.C.: The Urban Institute, 1972.

*Objectives:* "Inducing households to purchase adequate housing rather than housing at a poverty threshold," is the objective of the program; the program evaluation is designed to determine which of several different income subsidy techniques best induces this objective.

*Description of Program:* An experimental design was developed for the United States Department of Housing and Urban Development as one part of an over-all Housing Assistance Research Program, by the Urban Institute. In all treatments, households will be subsidized for adequate housing costs, the money will be specially earmarked for housing, and counseling and information will be given to recipients to aid their selection of housing. Three treatment plans have been proposed: (1) the household will receive the difference between the housing cost estimate and some percentage of disposable income, given that they occupy housing that meets some minimum standards; (2) same as 1 except that instead of meeting minimum standards, the housing must meet minimum rent requirements; and (3) the households will be subsidized for a percentage of their rent. A null procedure may also be utilized, in which eligible households will not have their subsidies earmarked for housing costs.

*Study Design:* Site selection is to be based on a range of characteristics. In each site, about 300 households are recommended for random allocation to the control group, about 270 randomly to each of the three levels of price subsidy in each site, and 700 to each of the seven housing gap levels.

*Response Variables:* Administrative costs, dropout rates, household preferences, housing selection processes and market constraints encountered, unintended results, households' satisfaction with program, and overall effectiveness are dependent measures in the experiment.

*Results:* At time of writing the experiment had not yet been implemented.

Abstract of:    *A design for a health insurance experiment,* by J. P. Newhouse. Santa Monica, California: Rand, 1972.

*Objectives:* The study is designed to test the effects of alternative insurance plans and to obtain data useful in developing national policy regarding such plans.

*Description of Program:* A number of alternative plans are being developed. At this writing, the plans under consideration include: free insurance, free care through a health maintenance organization maintained through tax payments, deductible coinsurance and nondeductible coinsurance plans, and others. The target group includes individuals under 65 with family incomes less than $12,000.

*Study Design:* The assessments of alternative plans are randomized experiments in which families are randomly allocated to alternative plans and to control conditions.

*Response Variables:* Data which will be collected from families include demographic characteristics; earnings; measures of tendency to seek medical care, of quality of care received, and of satisfaction with alternative plans; measures of health status and local market response to plans; and other variables.

*Results:* The experiment had not yet been implemented at time of writing.

# References

American Psychological Association. *Standards for educational and psychological tests and manuals.* Washington, D.C.: American Psychological Association, 1966.

American Psychological Association. *Ethical principles in the conduct of research with human participants.* Washington, D.C.: American Psychological Association, 1973.

Argyris, C. *Intervention theory and method.* Reading, Massachusetts: Addison-Wesley, 1970.

Baldus, D. C. Welfare as a loan: The recovery of public assistance in the United States. *Stanford University Law Review,* 1973, **25,** 123–250.

Bandura, A. *Principles of behavior modification.* New York: Holt, 1969.

Barber, B., Lally, J. J., Makaruska, S. L., and Sullivan, D. *Research on human subjects.* New York: Russell Sage Foundation, 1973.

Bauman, R. A., David, M. H., and Miller, R. F. Working with complex data files: II. The Wisconsin assets and incomes studies archive. In R. L. Bisco (Ed.) *Data bases, computers, and the social sciences.* New York: Wiley, 1970.

Beatty, W. W. How blind is blind? A simple procedure for estimating observer naiveté. *Psychological Bulletin,* 1972, **78,** 70–71.

Becker, H. B., and Geer, B. Participant observation: The analysis of qualitative field data. In R. N. Adams and J. J. Preiss (Eds.) *Human organization research: Field relations and techniques.* Homewood, Illinois: Dorsey, 1960.

Bickman, L., and Hency, T. *Beyond the laboratory: Field research in social psychology.* New York: McGraw-Hill, 1972.

Bloom, B. S., Hastings, J. T., and Madaus, G. F. *Handbook on formative and summative evaluation of student learning.* New York: McGraw-Hill, 1971.

Bogatz, G. A., and Ball, S. *The second year of Sesame Street,* Vols. 1 and 2. Princeton, New Jersey: Educational Testing Service, 1971.

Boruch, R. F. Relations among statistical methods for assuring confidentiality of data. *Social Science Research,* 1972, **1,** 403–414. (a)

Boruch, R. F. Strategies for eliciting and merging confidential social research data. *Policy Sciences*, 1972, **3**, 275–297. (b)

Box, G. E. P., and Jenkins, G. M. *Time series analysis forecasting and control*. San Francisco, California: Holden-Day, 1970.

Box, G. E. P., and Tiao, G. C., A change in level of a nonstationary times series. *Biometrika*, 1965, **52**, 181–192.

Buchanan, G., and Heinberg, J. *Housing allowance household experiment design. Part I: Summary and overview*. Washington, D.C.: The Urban Institute, 1972.

Buros, O. K. (Ed.) *Seventh mental measurements yearbook*. Vols. 1 and 2. Highland Park, New Jersey: Gryphon, 1972.

Campbell, D. T. Reforms as experiments. *American Psychologist*, 1969, **24**, 409–429.

Campbell, D. T., and Erlebacher, A. How regression artifacts in quasi-experimental evaluations can mistakenly make compensatory education look harmful. In J. Hellmuth (Ed.) *Compensatory education: A national debate*, Vol. 3 of *Disadvantaged Child*. New York: Brunner-Mazel, 1970.

Campbell, D. T., and Fiske, D. W. Convergent and discriminant validation by the multitrait–multimethod matrix. *Psychological Bulletin*, 1959, **56**, 81–105.

Campbell, D. T., and Stanley, J. C. Experimental and quasi-experimental designs for research on teaching. In N. L. Gage (Ed.) *Handbook of research on teaching*. Chicago, Illinois: Rand McNally, 1963. (Reprinted as *Experimental and quasi-experimental design for research*. Chicago, Illinois: Rand McNally, 1966.)

Canosa, C. A., Salomon, J. B., and Klein, R. E. The Intervention Approach: The Guatemala Study. In M. S. Read, W. M. Moore, and M. M. Silverberg (Eds.) *Nutrition growth and development of North American Indian children*. Washington, D.C.: Government Printing Office, 1972. [DHEW Publication No. (NIH) 72–26.]

Caplan, N. Treatment intervention and reciprocal interaction effects. *Journal of Social Issues*, 1968, **1**, 63–88.

Caplan, N., and Nelson, S. D. On being useful: The nature and consequences of psychological research on social problems. *American Psychologist*, 1973, **28**, 199–211.

Cleary, T. A., Linn, R. L., and Walster, G. W. The effect of reliability and validity on power of statistical tests. In E. F. Borgatta and G. W. Bohrnstedt (Eds.) *Sociological methodology*. San Francisco, California: Jossey-Bass, 1970.

Cleland, D. I., and King, W. R. *Systems analysis and project management*. New York: McGraw-Hill, 1968.

Cochran, W. G. Some effects of measurement error on multiple correlation. *Journal of the American Statistical Association*, 1970, **65**, 22–35.

Cohen, J. *Statistical power analysis for the behavioral sciences*. New York: Academic Press, 1969.

Cook, D. L. The impact of the Hawthorne effect in experimental designs in educational research. Columbus, Ohio: Ohio State University, Psychology Department (U.S. Office of Education, Bureau of Research, Project No. 1757), June, 1967. Mimeo Research Report.

Cronbach, L. J. *Essentials of psychological testing*. New York: Harper, 1970.

Cronbach, L. J., Gleser, G. C., Nanda, N. and Rajaratnam, N. *The dependability of behavioral measurements: Theory of generalizability for scores and profiles*. New York: Wiley, 1972.

Empey, L. T., and Erickson, M. L. *The Provo experiment: Life and death of an innovation*. Lexington, Massachusetts: D. C. Heath, 1972.

Empey, L. T., and Lubeck, S. G. *The Silverlake experiment*. Chicago, Illinois: Aldine, 1971.

Feige, E. L., and Watts, H. W. Protection of privacy through microaggregation. In R. L. Biscoe (Ed.) *Data bases computers and the social science*. New York: Wiley, 1970.

Fienberg, S. E. Randomization and social affairs: The 1970 draft lottery. *Science*, 1971, **171**, 255–261.

Fischer, J. L. The uses of Internal Revenue Service data. In M. E. Borus (Ed.) *Evaluating the impact of manpower programs*. Lexington, Massachusetts: D. C. Heath, 1972.

Fleiss, J. L., and Tanur, J. M. The analysis of covariance in psychopathology. In M. Hammer, K. Salzinger, and S. Sutton (Eds.) *Psychopathology*. New York: Wiley, 1972.

Ford, R. N. *Motivation through the work itself*. New York: American Management, 1969.

Freedman, R., Takeshita, J., et al. *Familiy planning in Taiwan: An experiment in social change*. Princeton, New Jersey: Princeton Univ. Press, 1967.

General Accounting Office. Legislative references to evaluation 1967–1972. Mimeo. Report from the Comptroller General's Office. Washington, D.C.: U.S. General Accounting Office, 1972.

Glass, G. V., Tiao, G. C., and Maguire, T. O. The 1900 revision of German divorce laws: Analysis of data as a time-series quasi-experiment. *Law and Society Review*, 1971, **6**, 539–562.

Glass, G. V., Wilson, V. L., and Gottman, J. M. *Design and analysis of time series experiments*. Research Report, Laboratory of Educational Research, Univ. of Colorado, 1972.

Goldberger, A. S., Selection bias in evaluating treatment effects: Some formal illustrations. *Discussion Papers*, #123–72, April 1972, Madison, Wisconsin: Institute for Research on Poverty, Univ. of Wisconsin.

Goldberger, A. S., and Duncan, O. D. (Eds.) *Structural equation models in the social sciences*. New York: Seminar Press, 1973.

Goodwin, L. *Do the poor want to work? A social–psychological study of work orientation*. Washington, D.C.: The Brookings Institute, 1972.

Gorsuch, R. L. *Factor analysis*. Philadelphia, Pennsylvania: Saunders, 1974.

Greenberg, B. G., Abernathy, J. R., and Horvitz, D. G. A new survey technique and its application in the field of public health. *Milbank Memorial Fund Quarterly*, 1970, **68**, (4, Part 2), 39–55.

Guion, R. M. *Personnel testing*. New York: McGraw-Hill, 1965.

Hansen, M. H. The role and feasibility of a National Data Bank, based on matched records and alternatives. *Report of the President's Commission on Federal Statistics, Vol. 2*. Washington, D.C.: U.S. Government Printing Office, 1971.

Heller, R. N. The uses of social security administration data. In M. E. Borus (Ed.) *Evaluating the impact of manpower programs*. Lexington, Massachusetts: D. C. Heath, 1972.

Hochstim, A. R. A critical comparison of three strategies of collecting data from households. *Journal of the American Statistical Association*, 1967, **62**, 976–989.

Hoffman, L. J., and Miller, W. F. How to obtain a personal dossier from a statistical data bank. *Datamation*, May, 1970, 74–75.

Holman, M. G., and Doctor, R. *Educational and psychological testing: A study of the industry and its practices*. New York: Russell Sage Foundation, 1972.

Hyman, H. H., Cobb, W. J., Feldman, J. J., Hart, C. W., and Stember, C. H. *Interviewing in social research*. Chicago, Illinois: Univ. of Chicago Press, 1954.

Ikeda, K., Yinger, J. M., and Laycock, F. Reforms as experiments and experiments as reforms. Ohio Valley Sociological Society Meetings, Akron, May, 1970. Duplicated. 28 pp.

Kahn, R. L., and Cannell C. F. *The dynamics of interviewing: Theory, technique and uses*. New York: Wiley, 1957.

Kaplan, A. *The conduct of inquiry*. San Francisco, California: Chandler, 1967.

Katz, J., Capron, A. M., and Glass, E. S. *Experimentation with human beings*. New York: Russell Sage Foundation, 1972.

Katz, E., Levin, M. L., and Hamilton, H. Traditions of research on the diffusion of innovation. In G. Zaltman, P. Kotler, and I. Kaufman (Eds.) *Creating social change*. New York: Holt, 1972.

Kelman, H. C. *On human values and social research.* San Francisco, California: Jossey-Bass, 1968.

Kendall, M. C., and Smith, B. *Tables of random sampling numbers.* New York: Cambridge Univ. Press, 1954.

Kershaw, D. Administrative issues in income maintenance experimentation: Administering experiments. In L. L. Orr, R. G. Hollister, M. Lefcowitz, and K. Hester (Eds.) *Income maintenance: Interdisciplinary approaches to research.* Chicago, Illinois: Markham, 1971.

Kershaw, D. N., and Fair, J. (Eds.) Report on the New Jersey Negative Income Tax Experiment, Vol. III. Administrative Procedures and Findings. In preparation.

Kish, L. *Survey sampling.* New York: Wiley, 1967.

Krathwohl, D. R., and Payne, D. A. Defining and assessing educational outcomes. In R. L. Thorndike (Ed.) *Educational measurement.* Washington, D.C.: American Council on Education, 1971.

Krause, M. S., Breedlove, J. L., and Boniface, K. I. An evaluation of the results of treatment. In P. C. Cohen and M. S. Krause (Eds.) *Casework with wives of alcoholics.* New York: Family Service Association of America, 1971, pp. 121–146.

Krause, M. S. Experimental control as a sampling problem in counseling and therapy research. *Journal of Counseling Psychology,* 1972, **19,** 340–346.

Lohr, B. W. An historical view of the research on the factors related to the utilization of health services. Duplicated Research Report, National Center for Health Services Research and Development, Social and Economic Analysis Division, Rockville, Md., January, 1972, 84 pp. In press as a NCHSRD publication, U.S. Government Printing Office.

Lord, F. M. Large-scale covariance analysis when the control variable is fallible. *Journal of the American Statistical Association,* 1960, **55,** 307–321.

Lord, F. M. A paradox in the interpretation of group comparisons. *Psychological Bulletin,* 1967, **68,** 304–305.

Lord, F. M. Statistical adjustments when comparing pre-existing groups. *Psychological Bulletin,* 1969, **72,** 336–337.

Lord, F. M., and Novick, M. R. *Statistical theories of mental test scores.* Reading, Massachusetts: Addison–Wesley, 1968.

Matarazzo, J. D. The interview. In B. B. Wolman (Ed.) *Handbook of clinical psychology.* New York: McGraw-Hill, 1965.

Meier, P. The biggest public health experiment ever: The 1954 field trial of the Salk Poliomelitis vaccine, In J. M. Tanur, with F. Mosteller, W. B. Kruskal, R. F. Link, R. S. Pieters, and G. Rising (Eds.) *Statistics: A guide to the unknown.* San Francisco, California: Holden-Day, 1972.

Menzel, H. Public and private conformity under different conditions of acceptance in the group. *Journal of Abnormal and Social Psychology,* 1957, **55,** 398–402.

Meyer, H. J., and Borgatta, E. F. *An experiment in mental patient rehabilitation.* New York: Russell Sage Foundation, 1959.

Meyer, H. J., Borgatta, E. F., and Jones, W. C. *Girls at vocational high.* New York: Russell Sage Foundation, 1965.

Mulaik, S. *the foundations of factor analysis.* New York: McGraw-Hill, 1973.

Nejelski, P., and Lerman, N. M. A researcher–subject testimonial privilege. *Wisconsin Law Review,* 1971, 1085–1148.

Office of Economic Opportunity. An experiment in performance contracting: Summary of preliminary results. OEO Pamphlet #3400–5, February, 1972.

Orr, L. L., Hollister, R. G., Lefcowitz, M. J., with Hester, K. (Eds.) *Income Maintenance: Interdisciplinary approaches*. Chicago, Illinois: Markham, 1971.

Palmer, E. L. Formative research in the production of television for children. In *NSSE Yearbook on early childhood development*. 1973.

Pinneau, R., Selin, H., and Chun, K. T. *The repository of information on psychological measures: User's manual*. Ann Arbor, Michigan: Institute for Social Research, Univ. of Michigan, 1972 (Mimeo).

Plutchick, R., Platman, S. R., and Fieve, R. R. Three alternatives to the double blind. *Archives of General Psychiatry*. 1969, **20,** 429–432.

Porter, A. C. *The effects of using fallible variables in the analysis of covariance*. Ph. D. dissertation, Univ. of Wisconsin, June, 1967. (University Microfilms, Ann Arbor, Michigan, 1968.)

Rand Corporation. *A million random digits*. Santa Monica, California: Rand Corp. 1955.

Rivlin, A. M. *Systematic thinking for social action*. Washington, D. C.,: The Brookings Institution, 1971.

Robinson, J. P., Athanasiou, R., and Head, K. B. *Measures of occupational attitudes and occupational characteristics*. Ann Arbor, Michigan: Institute for Social Research, Survey Research Center, 1969.

Robinson, J. P., Rusk, J. G., and Head, K. B. *Measures of political attitudes*. Ann Arbor, Michigan: Institute for Social Research, Survey Research Center, 1969.

Robinson, J. P., and Shaver, P. R. *Measures of social psychological attitudes*. Ann Arbor, Michigan: Institute for Social Research, Survey Research Center, 1969.

Robertson, L. S. Kelly, A. B., O'Neill, B. O., Wixom, C. W., Eiswirth, R. S., and Haldon, W. *A controlled study of the effect of television messages on safety belt use*. Washington, D.C.: Insurance Institute for Highway Safety, 1973.

Roethlisberger, F. J., and Dickson, W. J. *Management and the worker*. Cambridge, Massachusetts: Harvard Univ. Press, 1939.

Rosenberg, M. *The pretrial conference and effective justice*. New York: Columbia Univ. Press, 1964.

Ross, H. L., Law, science, and accidents: The British Road Safety Act of 1967. *Journal of Legal Studies*, 1973 **2,** 1–78.

Ross, H. L., Campbell, D. T., and Glass, G. V. Determining the effects of a legal reform: The British breathalyser crackdown of 1967. *American Behavioral Scientist*, 1970, **13,** 493–509.

Ross, J. A. Cost analysis of the Taichung experiment. *Studies in Family Planning*. February, 1966, 6–15.

Sackman, H., and Nie, N. *The information utility and social choice*. Montvale, New Jersey: AFIPS Press, 1970.

Savage, L. J. *Foundations of statistics*. New York: Wiley, 1954.

Schwartz, R. D., and Orleans, S. On legal sanctions. *University of Chicago Law Review*, 1967, **34,** 282–300.

Scott, W. A. Attitude measurement. In G. Linzey and E. Aronson (Eds.) *Handbook of social psychology*. Vol. 2. Reading, Massachusetts: Addison-Wesley, 1968.

Scriven, M. The methodology of evaluation. *American Educational Research Association Monograph Series on Curriculum Evaluation*, 1967, **1,** 39–83.

Shaw, L. W., and Chalmers, T. C. Ethics in cooperative clinical trials. *Annals of the New York Academy of Sciences*. 1970, **169,** 487–495.

Sheldon, E. B., and Freeman, H. E. A note on social indicators: Promises and potential. *Policy Sciences*, 1970, **1,** 97–111.

Sinisterra, L., McKay, H., and McKay, A. Stimulation of intellectual and social competence in Colombian preschool children affected by multiple deprivations of depressed urban environments. Progress Report (mimeo.), University Center Valle, Cali, Colombia, November, 1971.

Smith, M. B. Motivation, communications research, and family planning. In M. C. Sheps, and J. C. Fidley (Eds.) *Public health and population change*. Pittsburgh, Pennsylvania: Univ. of Pittsburgh Press, 1965.

Stanley, J. C. Reliability. In R. L. Thorndike (Ed.) *Educational measurement*. Washington, D.C.: American Council on Education, 1971.

Stanley, J. C. (Ed.), *Preschool programs for the disadvantaged*. Baltimore, Maryland: Johns-Hopkins Press, 1972.

Stapleton, W. V., and Teitelbaum, L. E. *In defense of youth*. New York: Russell Sage Foundation, 1972.

Steinberg, J., and Pritzker, L. Some experiences with and reflections on data linkage in the United States. *Bulletin of the International Statistical Institute*, 1969, **42** (Book 2), 786–805.

Suchman, E. A. *Evaluation research*. New York: Russell Sage Foundation, 1967.

Sudman, S. Quantifying interviewer quality. *Public Opinion Quarterly*, 1966, **30,** 664–667.

Sudman, S. *Reducing the cost of surveys*. Chicago: Aldine, 1967.

Sudman, S., and Ferber, R. Experiments in obtaining consumer expenditures by diary methods. *Journal of the American Statistical Association*, 1971, **66,** 725–735.

Summer, G. F. *Attitude measurement*. Chicago, Illinois: Rand-McNally, 1970.

Sween, J. A. The experimental regression design: an inquiry into the feasibility of nonrandom treatment allocation. Ph. D. dissertation, Northwestern Univ., August 1971.

Thistlethwaite, D. L., and Campbell, D. T. Regression–discontinuity analysis: an alternative to the ex post facto experiment. *Journal of Educational Psychology*, 1960, **51,** 309–317.

Thorndike, R. L. Regression effects in the matched groups experiment. *Psychometrika*, 1942, **7,** 85–102.

Thorndike, R. L. (Ed.) *Educational measurement*. Washington, D.C.: American Council on Education, 1971.

Tukey, J. W. The citation index and the information problem. Mimeo Research Report: NSF Grant # G22108. Princeton, New Jersey: Statistical Techniques Research Group, Princeton Univ., 1962.

Walsh, J. Antipoverty R and D: Chicago debacle suggests pitfalls facing OEO. *Science*, 1969, **165,** 1243–1246.

Weikert, D. P. Relationship of curriculum, teaching, and learning in preschool education. In J. C. Stanley (Ed.) *Preschool programs for the disadvantaged*. Baltimore, Maryland: Johns Hopkins, 1972.

Weiss, C. H. *Evaluation research*. Englewood Cliffs, New Jersey: Prentice-Hall, 1972.

Welch, W. W., and Walberg, H. J. Pretest and sensitization effects in curriculum evaluation. *American Educational Research Journal*, 1970, **1,** 605–614.

Wilder, C. S. Physician visits, volume and interval since last visit, US 1969. Rockville, Maryland: National Center for Health Statistics, Series 10, No. 75, July 1972 (DHEW Pub. No. (HSM) 72–1064).

Zeisel, H. Reducing the hazards of human experiments through modification in research design. *Annals of the New York Academy of Sciences*. 1970, **169,** 475–486.

Zener, T. B., and Schnuelle, L. An evaluation of self-directed search. A guide to educational and vocational planning. Research Report #124, Center for Social Organization of Schools. Johns Hopkins University, 1972.

# Author Index

Numbers in italics refer to the pages in the Reference section on which the complete biographical entries are listed.

# Subject Index

335

5
B  6
C  7
D  8
E  9
F  0
G  1
H  2
I  3
J  4

WIDENER COLLEGE
WOLFGRAM
LIBRARY
CHESTER, PA.

WIDENER COLLEGE